SOUTH AMERICAN BIRDS

A Photographic Aid to Identification

JOHN S. DUNNING

Research Associate,
Academy of Natural Sciences of Philadelphia

Laboratory Associate
Cornell Laboratory of Ornithology

With the collaboration of
ROBERT S. RIDGELY, Ph.D.
Academy of Natural Sciences of Philadelphia

HARROWOOD BOOKS
NEWTOWN SQUARE • PENNSYLVANIA

Library of Congress Cataloging-in-Publication Data

Dunning, John Stewart, 1906-1987
South American Birds

Includes index.
1. Birds – South America – Identification I. Ridgely, Robert S., 1946- . II. Title.
QL689.AID86 1988 598.298 88-6299
ISBN 0-915180-25-1
ISBN 0-915180-26-X (pbk.)

Harrowood Books
3943 N. Providence Rd.
Newtown Square, PA 19073

PRINTED IN THE UNITED STATES OF AMERICA

10 9 8 7 6 5 4 3 2 1
(last number denotes the printing)

Dedicated to my wife,
Harriet W. Dunning

IN MEMORIAM

On December 31st, 1987, after a spirited fight, John Dunning succumbed to cancer at the age of 81.

When I heard the news from his wife, Harriet, I was upset that John would not see his finished book. Despite his illness, he worked painstakingly with Harriet to complete the project and the first color proofs had been sent to him only days before his passing.

Looking at John's photographs, I think of the many years he dedicated to his work in Central and South America and reflect on this true conservationist who cared so deeply for the world around him. Not only did John give his time and money to fight for preservation of natural habitats but his daily life bore witness to his belief that we are caretakers of this beautiful planet and should not squander its resources. I know that waste was anathema to him ... occasionally, I would receive notes written on the back of photocopies of an old manuscript, enclosed in an envelope that had originally been sent to him by The Nature Conservancy appealing for funds. Material for this book went back and forth in the same cartons many times!

John was an honest man, devoid of airs and affectations, given to Good Work. He gave much to us and will be missed, but not forgotten. Although he dedicated this book to his dear wife, it will remain as a testament to his skill, diligence and caring.

Paul N. Harris
Publisher

CONTENTS

Introduction vi

Learning to Identify South American Birds vii

Chart of a Bird and Sample Account xiii

Abbreviations xiv

Black Birds xv

Order of Groups xvi

Species Accounts 1

Methods and Equipment 315

Index 319

Introduction

BY JOHN S. DUNNING

This book describes all the birds likely to be seen in interior South America including the fresh water lakes. Dr. Robert S. Ridgely, collaborator on this work, has helped greatly by doing the maps, identifying similar species and suggesting clearer name changes.

The birds are photographed where they live by capturing them in mist nets, putting them in a portable enclosure, then trying to get them to pose with natural foliage. This method is described in detail on page 315. After photographing, the birds are, of course, released in their own territory to pursue their normal lives.

The photos are organized in groups roughly following the family order in A GUIDE TO THE BIRDS OF SOUTH AMERICA (BSA) by Rodolphe Meyer de Schauensee with some generally accepted changes in the years since BSA was published. Within each group the species are generally listed by size with an effort to keep all birds of one genus and same general size together.

This work is based on the only detailed guide in existence, at this time, of all the South American birds – BSA. Several excellent guides covering parts of the continent are available and an extensive guide for the whole area by Ridgely and Tudor is in press but not yet finished.

In order to present over 2700 species in a field-usable book, the descriptions have been kept very short (see sample account on page xiii). Abbreviations are frequently employed according to the list on page xiv. Also on page xiv is an attempt to define descriptive terms to designate a definite, narrow meaning. Following the English name, in **CAPITALS**, is a series of abbreviations giving the habitat where the bird is usually seen – first in the height above ground, then a hyphen and the type of habitat. The next line gives the scientific name in lowercase letters, followed by the approximate size in centimeters. The size used is the normal perching length from bill tip to normal tail end. This is shorter than the length of a museum skin used in some books. Extended tail feathers are noted separately to avoid a false impression of bird size. Lengths are in centimeters only, with a conversion scale on the inside front cover.

Points clear from the photo or in the general information at the top of the page are often not included in the descriptions. All descriptions are of the male unless noted. If the female is not mentioned, she is similar to the male though often duller. Special features of a family or genus noted at top of page apply to all members unless noted. If the bird you are looking at does not appear within the area on the map beside the name, it can probably be disregarded as a possibility.

In the twenty-five years spent photographing birds for this book, I am indebted to far too many people to list here. Special help has been given by Dean Amadon, Marco Andrada, Camilo Arroyo, Ernesto Barriga, Bill Belton, Janice Blanck, Alexander Brash, Tom Butler, Ney Carnevelli, Robin Clarke, Gary Clements, Carmen Crichton, Art Dreiner, Elizabeth (Bea) Dunning, Gene Eisenmann, Chick Falconi, Mark Fisher, Diego Gallegas, Tina Garzon, Mary Lou Goodwin, Paul Greenfield, Max Gunther, Paul Harris, Chris Hrdina, Bud Lanyon, Carlos Lehmann, Horace Loftin, Tom Lovejoy, Noel Kempff Marcado, David Oren, Manuel Parada, Ted Parker, Roger Pasquier, Sewall Pettingill, Billy Phelps, Hank Reichert, Jon Ribot, Horacio Robriquez, Augusto Ruschi, Tom Schulenberg, Joop Schulz, Helmut Sick, Flavio Silva, Ram Singh, Kjell von Sneidern, Gustavo del Solar, Nina Steffee, Betsy Thomas, Edward W. Thomas, Alex Wetmore, Dora Weyer, Richard White and Scott Whitehill. My wife, Harriet, has been an essential part of this whole project which could not have succeeded without her.

Learning to Identify South American Birds

Almost everyone is a beginner when it comes to identifying birds in South America. With a little experience, we can turn quickly to the correct plate in a field guide to consider the fine points of identification – color of the crown, one wingbar or two, etc. Initially, however, we face the difficult and often frustrating challenge of finding the correct color plate with a few similar species, before our mental image fades. Not knowing what kind of bird it was, we search from the first color plate to the last, usually several times. In North America, the beginner must patiently consider a few hundred possibilities. In South America, we face several thousand possibilities, with many unfamiliar names, such as jacamar, tapaculo, or euphonia. Even the more familiar names of some South American birds can be misleading. The variety of lifestyles adopted by flycatchers here, for example, can be thoroughly confusing.

To help you get started identifying South American birds, we provide an introduction to them. On page xiv, for example, is a summary of all-black birds one might see. We refer you also to page xv, which lists the order of the groups of photographs. Some of these groups are familiar North American birds, namely ducks and coots, as well as hawks, pigeons, parrots, owls, kingfishers, woodpeckers, hummingbirds, swallows, jays, robins, and mockingbirds. Most thrushes, wrens and warblers resemble their North American counterparts. They need no further introduction. Most of the unusual large landbirds and large waterbirds also can be easily identified by studying the plates.

The next five pages introduce many of the basic kinds, or families, of the more unfamiliar birds you will encounter. To familiarize yourself with these, we suggest you ignore the details of color patterns, for the moment, concentrating instead on the general appearance of the bird – its shape, posture, and behavior – and whether or not it is brightly colored. We suggest also that you compare the descriptions and associated line drawings with the appropriate photographs to develop a mental image of each group. Then, with only a little practice in the field, you should be able to turn quickly to the correct part of the book for the next phase of the identification process.

We would like to express our gratitude to · Frank B. Gill, Mark B. Robbins, Douglas Wechsler, and Dawn Coughlan of the Academy of Natural Sciences of Philadelphia for the contribution of this "Learning to Identify South American Birds" section to the book. – Ed.

NIGHTJARS AND POTOOS (p.58)

Look like North American whip-poor-wills and nighthawks, except potoos, which sit with upright posture cryptically resembling a dead snag; eyes shine in headlights at night.

CUCKOOS (p.54)

Some resemble North American species including anis (black), others are large birds with long tails, as depicted here.

TROGONS (p.94)

Brightly-colored, iridescent green back with red or yellow belly; sit upright; motionless for long periods; stocky with long square-tipped tails; bills short and broad.

MOTMOTS (p.94)

Large, inconspicuous birds with long racket-tipped tails that swing sideways; sit quietly with erect posture; long, heavy bills.

TOUCANS AND ARAÇARIS (p.106)

Huge bills render large toucans unmistakable. Aracaris and toucanets are smaller but have the same distinctive shape and proportions.

JACAMARS (p.98)

Quiet medium-sized perching birds with long, narrow tails and very long, thin, straight bills; usually iridescent green above; solitary or in pairs; make short sallies to catch flying insects.

JACAMAR

PUFFBIRDS (p.100)

Chunky, medium-sized, forest birds with large heads, thick bills and short tails; solitary and sluggish; upright posture; group includes aberrant swallow-wing and nunbirds.

BARBET

BARBETS (p.104)

Large-headed, large-billed, stout, often brightly-colored birds of mid-level forest strata and canopy; horizontal posture; move in pairs with mixed species flocks.

PICULETS (p.116)

Tiny woodpeckers, nuthatch-like; tail inconspicuous.

WOODCREEPERS (p.119)

Brownish birds that hitch up trunks like woodpeckers; have long, stiff, rufous tails; bills range from short and peg-like to long and curved.

FOLIAGE-GLEANER  SPINETAIL  CANASTERO  CINCLODES XENOPS

FURNARIIDS (p.124)

Sombre-colored birds, including miners, spinetails, ovenbirds, thornbirds and foliage-gleaners; range in size and shape from thrush- or wren-like birds, to nuthatch-like *Xenops;* mostly brown, often with white or buff spotting or streaking; vary greatly in habitats and behavior.

ANTSHRIKE ANTSHRIKE

ANTSHRIKES (p.147)

Sparrow- to robin-sized birds with heavy, hooked bills and chunky bodies, usually in thickets or undergrowth; horizontal profile; tails often quiver when the birds call; some raise crests when excited.

ANTPITTA ANTTHRUSH

ANTPITTAS, ANTTHRUSHES (p.150)

Shy and inconspicuous, chunky, ground-dwelling robin-sized birds; long legs, big eyes, and either no obvious tails (antpittas), or short, cocked tails (antthrushes); antpittas hop, antthrushes strut like little rails.

ANTWREN ANTBIRD

ANTBIRDS, ANTWRENS (p.158)

Larger antbirds stay low in understory, and may have colored bare skin around eye; small, active, wren-like antwrens maintain horizontal profile and feed by probing into clusters of dead leaves or other vegetation; usually in pairs; often with army ant swarms or mixed species flocks.

TAPACULOS (p.175)

Secretive ground-dwelling birds of forest understory and thickets; small species are mouse-like and dark gray; large rail-like species are big-footed and often boldly-patterned.

COTINGA

COTINGAS (p.177)

Lethargic, chunky birds that maintain vertical profile while perched quietly in forest; often gaudy colors; most have short bills which enhance rounded-head appearance; some species crow-sized, others robin-sized; tityras are black-and-white birds of forest edge.

♂ TITYRA

MANAKINS (p.186)

♀ MANAKIN

Small, plump, and short-tailed; males brightly-colored, many species display in groups; females and young males mostly olive, and resemble tiny flycatchers; rapid, whirring flight.

♂ MANAKIN

ELAENIA

TYRANNULET

GROUND-TYRANT

TODY-FLYCATCHER

FLYCATCHERS (p.195)

Most do not perch upright as do North American species; vary from kinglet to jay-sized; ground species of open country are long-legged and resemble small thrushes; large species often are bright yellow below and perch conspicuously like kingbirds; numerous small olive-colored species (such as tyrannulets), which behave much like warblers.

FLATBILL

KISKADEE

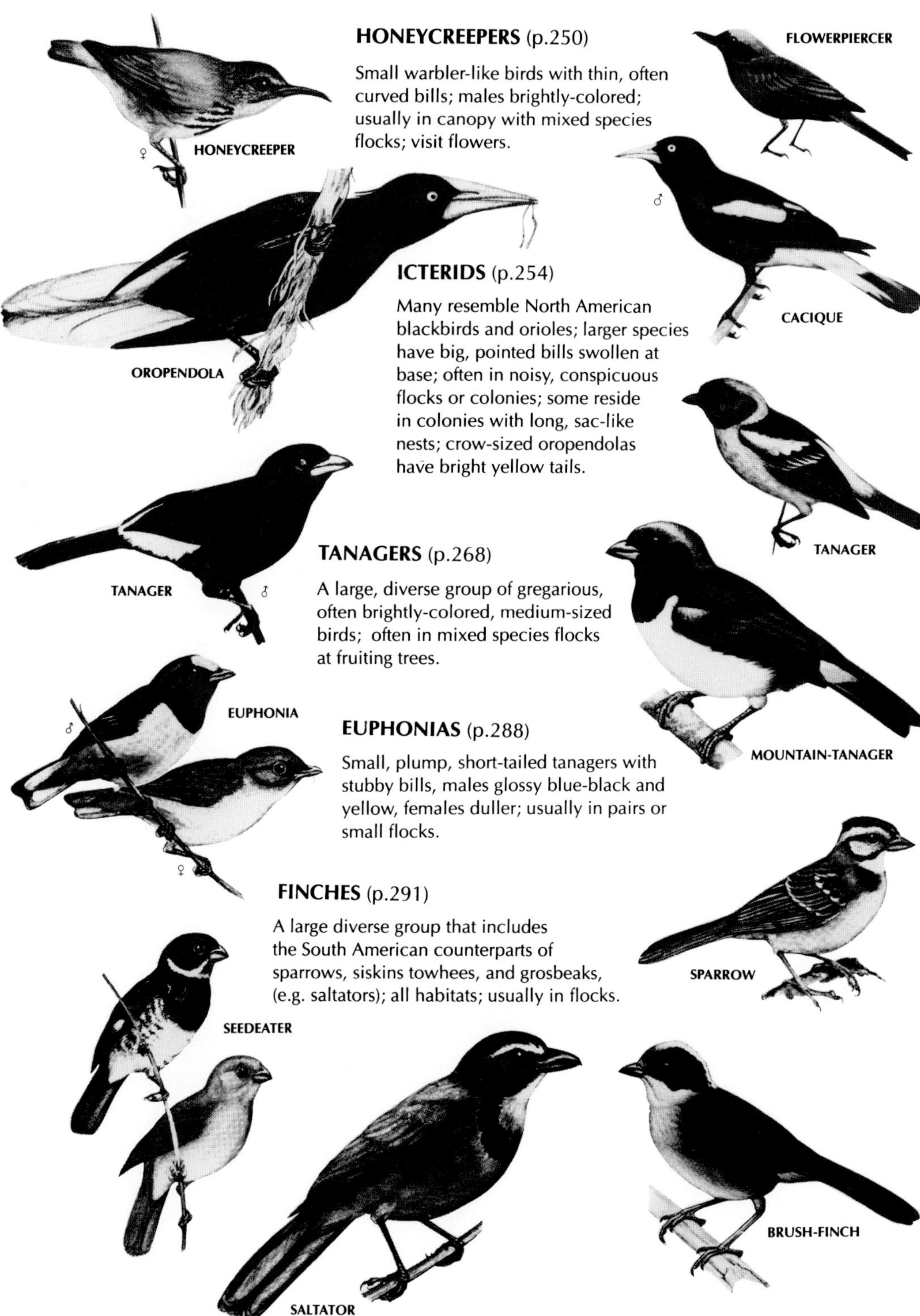

HONEYCREEPERS (p.250)

Small warbler-like birds with thin, often curved bills; males brightly-colored; usually in canopy with mixed species flocks; visit flowers.

ICTERIDS (p.254)

Many resemble North American blackbirds and orioles; larger species have big, pointed bills swollen at base; often in noisy, conspicuous flocks or colonies; some reside in colonies with long, sac-like nests; crow-sized oropendolas have bright yellow tails.

TANAGERS (p.268)

A large, diverse group of gregarious, often brightly-colored, medium-sized birds; often in mixed species flocks at fruiting trees.

EUPHONIAS (p.288)

Small, plump, short-tailed tanagers with stubby bills, males glossy blue-black and yellow, females duller; usually in pairs or small flocks.

FINCHES (p.291)

A large diverse group that includes the South American counterparts of sparrows, siskins towhees, and grosbeaks, (e.g. saltators); all habitats; usually in flocks.

Sample Account

Note: Words in italics indicate special distinguishing marks.
Female like male except as noted.
An asterisk after the scientific name denotes a migrant.

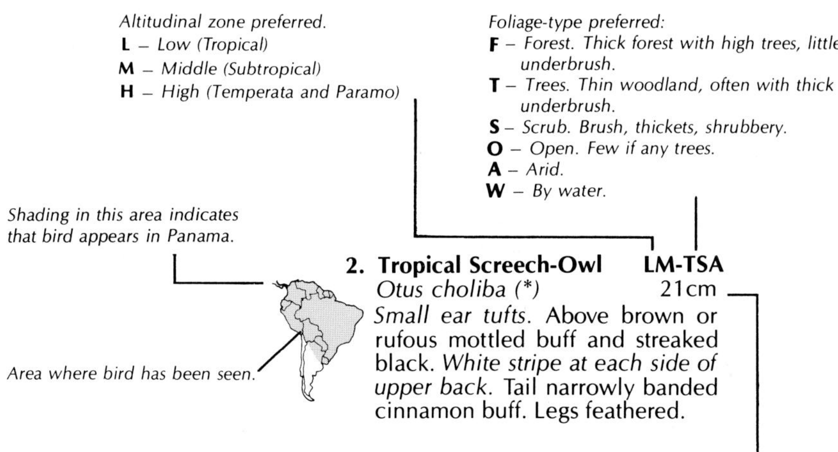

Chart of a Bird

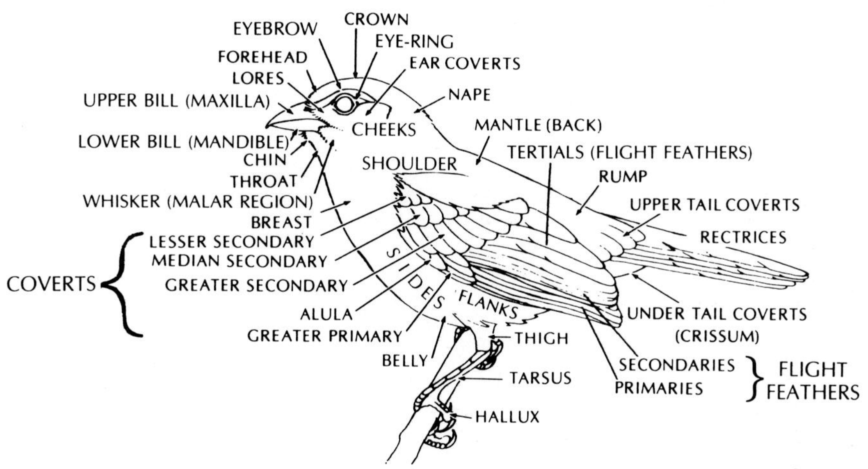

Abbreviations & Definitions

/ – narrow range along coast.
* – after scientific name = migrant from another continent (not breeding in SA).
A – arid, desert.
Above – mantle, rump and back (not head, wings or tail).
Band – stripe across wing or body. Not visible on closed wing.
Bar – stripe across wing or body. Not visible on closed wing.
Below – breast, belly and crissum or below described throat or breast.
Bob – move tail up and down.
Brow – eyebrow, not forehead.
Buff – very light brownish yellow.
Cap – whole top of head to below eye.
Chestnut – dark reddish brown.
Cf. – compare (to confusingly similar bird possible in same range).
Cinnamon – light yellowish brown with reddish tinge.
Crissum – undertail coverts.
Crown – center of top of head. (When raised it is a crest).
Curved – bill curved downward. If curved up, it is so marked.
Dewlap – skin hanging from throat.
Dorsal – in middle of back.
e – east.
Eye stripe – line through eye or behind eye.
F - forest – thick forest with tall trees, little underbrush.
H – Highlands (Temperate and Puna Zones) over approx. 2500 meters.
Hood – head, nape, neck and throat.
Imm – immature - a young bird approaching plumage of an adult.
Juv – juvenile - a young bird not near plumage of an adult.
Knob – swelling on bill.
Lores – area between eye and bill.
L – lowlands (Tropical Zone) up to approx. 1500 meters.
M – middle altitude (Subtropical Zone) approx. 1500-2500 meters.
Malar (or malar stripe) – stripe below eye from base of bill across cheek.
Mantle – upper back.
Migrant – does not breed in South America.
Nape – back of head and upper neck.
nb – non-breeding plumage.
n – north.
O – open country, grassland.
Ochraceous – brownish yellow.
Orbital – area around eye.
Rufous – reddish brown.
Rump - lower back.
s – south
S – scrub, brush, thickets, shrubbery, few or no trees.
Speculum – wing-spot.
Streaks – stripes parallel to length of bird.
T – trees, thin woodland, often with thick underbrush.
Tawny – light reddish brown.
Underparts – throat, breast, belly and crissum (not wings or tail).
Upperparts – crown, nape, mantle, back and rump (not wings or tail).
Vent – area between belly and crissum.
Vermiculated – marked with fine, wavy lines.
Wattle – skin hanging from chin or neck.
w – west.
W – by water, marshes, swamps, river banks.
Wag – move tail side to side.
Whisker – vertical line beside throat, often call moustache.
Wing-band – band on primaries, usually not visible when wing is closed.
Wing-bar – bar (often two) on wing coverts, visible when wing closed.

Black Birds

BIRDS IN WHICH MALES OF SOME RACES APPEAR ALL BLACK IN FIELD

(except bill, eyes and legs).

SIZE	NAME	PAGE
LARGE		
78	Black Curassow	1
71	Crestless Curassow	2
65	Wattled Guan	3
66	Sharp-tailed Ibis	13
53	Green Ibis	13
43	Bare-faced Ibis	13
55	Black Vulture	29
58	Great Black Hawk	31
47	Zone-tailed Hawk	32
43	Common Black Hawk	31
38	Short-tailed Hawk	32
33	White-rumped Hawk	33
43	Black Caracara	36
43	Amazonian Umbrellabird	177
43	Long-wattled Umbrellabird	177
35	Slender-billed Kite	29
MID-SIZE		
41	Greater Ani	54
33	Smooth-billed Ani	54
31	Groove-billed Ani	54
26	Solitary Eagle	31
26	Red-rumped Cacique	256
25	Austral Cacique	256
25	Solitary Cacique	257
25	Scarlet-rumped Cacique	256
23	Yellow-billed Cacique	257
18	Ecuadorian Cacique	257
36	Great-tailed Grackle	256
25	Golden-tufted Grackle	256
22	Carib Grackle	256
19	Velvet-fronted Grackle	256
33	Giant Cowbird	255
20	Shiny Cowbird	261
17	Screaming Cowbird	261
30	Great Thrush	234
20	Pale-eyed Thrush	237
20	Scarlet-throated Tanager	268
21	Streseman's Bristlefront	175
18	Slaty Bristlefront	175
18	Black-throated Grosbeak	292
17	Slate-colored Grosbeak	292
15	Blue-black Grosbeak	293
18	Epaulet Oriole	259
17	White-backed Fire-eye	158
20	Unicolored Blackbird	257
25	Austral Blackbird	257
22	Bolivian Blackbird	257
22	Forbe's Blackbird	257
22	Chopi Blackbird	257
21	Scrub Blackbird	258
16	Chestnut-capped Blackbird	258
SMALL		
17	Southern Martin	63
17	Purple Martin	63
17	Glossy Antshrike	148
16	Castelnau's Antshrike (f. only)	149
14	Black Antshrike	149
15	Wren-like Rushbird	136
16	White-lined Tanager	277
16	Ruby-crowned Tanager	277
15	Red-shouldered Tanager	277
17	Immaculate Antbird	157
15	Sooty Antbird	157
14	Blackish Antbird	160
12	Most Tapaculos	175-177
18	Crested Black-Tyrant	206
17	Velvety Black-Tyrant	206
15	Blue-billed Tyrant	207
14	Riverside Tyrant	206
12	Amazonian Black-Tyrant	209
13	Capped Conebill	250
13	Glossy Flower-piercer	251
12	White-sided Flower-piercer	252
12	Black Flower-piercer	251
13	Black Manakin	187
12	Jet Manakin	188
15	Great-billed Seed-finch	303
13	Large-billed Seed-finch	303
12	Lesser Seed-finch	305
10	Sooty Grassquit	313
9	Blue-black Grassquit	312

(All sizes are measured in centimeters)

Order of Groups

Page

1. LARGE LAND BIRDS
4. MID-SIZE LAND BIRDS
9. LARGE WATER-EDGE BIRDS
14. MID-SIZE WATER-EDGE BIRDS
19. SMALL WATER-EDGE BIRDS
21. OPEN WATER BIRDS
28. VULTURES and KITES
30. EAGLES and HAWKS
35. CARACARAS and FALCONS
38. PIGEONS and DOVES
42. PARROTS with NARROW or POINTED TAIL
49. PARROTS with SQUARE TAIL
54. CUCKOOS
56. OWLS
58. NIGHTJARS and SIMILARS
62. SWIFTS, MARTINS, SWALLOWS
66. HERMIT HUMMINGBIRDS and SIMILARS
69. LOWLAND HUMMERS with LONG BILL
70. LOWLAND HUMMERS with MID- LENGTH BILL
77. LOWLAND HUMMERS with SHORT BILL
79. HIGHLAND HUMMERS with LONG BILL
83. HIGHLAND HUMMERS with MID- LENGTH BILL
88. HIGHLAND HUMMERS with SHORT BILL
94. TROGONS and MOTMOTS
96. KINGFISHERS and JACAMARS
100. PUFFBIRDS and BARBETS
106. TOUCANS and ARACARIS
110. LARGE WOODPECKERS
113. MID-SIZE WOODPECKERS
114. SMALL WOODPECKERS
116. PICULETS
119. WOODCREEPERS with HEAD STREAKED
122. WOODCREEPERS with HEAD NOT STREAKED
124. FURNARIIDS with ELONGATED TAIL
126. FURNARIIDS on GROUND

Page

132. FURNARIIDS in LOW VEGETATION
137. FURNARIIDS in TREES
141. FURNARIIDS-SPINETAILS, Crown all rufous
143. FURNARIIDS-SPINETAILS, Crown half rufous
144. FURNARIIDS-SPINETAILS, Crown with no rufous
147. ANTSHRIKES
153. ANTPITTA-LIKE ANTBIRDS
158. LARGE ANTBIRDS
161. MID-SIZE ANTBIRDS
166. SMALL ANTBIRDS
174. GNATEATERS
175. TAPACULOS
177. COTINGAS
186. MANAKINS
192. SMALL PLAIN MANAKINS (by leg color)
195. FLYCATCHERS on GROUND or ROCK
198. LARGE FLYCATCHERS
207. MID-SIZE FLYCATCHERS
218. SMALL FLYCATCHERS with WING- BARS
227. SMALL FLYCATCHERS with NO WING- BARS
233. JAYS
234. THRUSHES
239. MOCKINGBIRDS
240. WRENS
245. MISCELLANEOUS
247. VIREOS
250. HONEYCREEPERS
254. ICTERIDS
262. MIGRANT WARBLERS
264. RESIDENT WARBLERS
268. LARGE TANAGERS
276. MID-SIZE TANAGERS
286. SMALL TANAGERS
288. EUPHONIAS, Crown nearly or all yellow
289. " Crown about half yellow
290. " Crown with no yellow
291. LARGE FINCHES
299. MID-SIZE FINCHES
306. SMALL FINCHES

Rhea: Ostrich-like.
Pterocnemia
Crax: No dewlap.
Pauxi: Large knob on forehead.
Mitu: Thin bill red, arched.

1. GREATER RHEA L-O
Rhea americana 120

Mostly grayish, crown and patch at base of neck black. Underparts white. Flightless.

2. LESSER RHEA LMH-O
Pterocnemia pennata 95

Very like 1-1 but lacks black on crown and neck. Flightless.

3. BLACK CURASSOW L-F
Crax alector 78

Black. Belly and crissum white Bill red or yellow at base. No knob or wattle. Legs gray.

4. GREAT CURASSOW L-F
Crax rubra 83

Like 1-3 but large knob yellow. F: Chestnut, more or less barred. No knob or wattle.

5. YELLOW-KNOBBED CURASSOW L-F
Crax daubentoni 82

Like 1-3 but knob and wattle bright yellow. F: Bill black. No knobs. Breast barred white. Belly crissum and tail tip white.

6. WATTLED CURASSOW L-F
Crax globulosa 80

Like 1-3 but large knob and wattle red. F: Belly rufous. No knob or wattle.

7. BLUE-BILLED CURASSOW L-F
Crax alberti 80

Like 1-3 but large wattle blue. F: Belly chestnut. Tail tipped white.

8. RED-BILLED CURASSOW L-F
Crax blumenbachii 79

Like 1-3 but small knob and wattle red. F: Belly chestnut.

9. BARE-FACED CURASSOW L-F
Crax fasciolata 78

female

Like 1-3 with base of bill yellow and tail tipped white. F: Above barred. Crest whitish. Below buff.

10. HELMETED CURASSOW L-F
Pauxi pauxi 86

Black. Large horn bluish. Bill and legs red. Belly and tail tip white.

11. RAZOR-BILLED CURASSOW L-F
Mitu mitu 77

Bill red, narrow, ridge greatly elevated. Belly chestnut. Tail tipped white.

12. SALVIN'S CURASSOW L-F
Mitu salvini 72

Like 1-11 but bill less elevated and belly white.

Mitu: Thin bill red, arched.
Nothocrax: Head and neck red.
Penelope: Red dewlap.

13. CRESTLESS CURASSOW L-F
Mitu tomentosa 71

Like 1-11 but bill little elevated and tail tipped buff

14. NOCTURNAL CURASSOW L-F
Nothocrax urumutu 58

Mostly rufous. Skin above eye yellow. Tail tipped white. Legs gray.

15. CRESTED GUAN L-F
Penelope purpurascens 83

Very like 2-17 but crown brown. Rump and belly chestnut. Legs red.

16. SPIX'S GUAN L-F
Penelope jacquacu 75

Like 2-17 but dewlap larger and legs reddish.

17. DUSKY-LEGGED GUAN LM-F
Penelope obscura 75

Crown blackish Above, neck and breast dark brown, feathers edged white. Below dark brown or rufous brown. Legs dark gray.

18. RED-FACED GUAN MH-F
Penelope dabbenei 70

Like 2-17 but face red and legs pink.

19. CHESTNUT-BELLIED GUAN L-F
Penelope ochrogaster 65

Like 2-17 but crown reddish-brown and much more rufous below.

20. WHITE-BROWED GUAN L-F
Penelope jacucaca 65

Crown brown. Conspicuous eye-brow white. Below and wing covert feathers edged white.

21. WHITE-CRESTED GUAN L-F
Penelope pileata 65

Crown white. Back glossy green streaked white. Underparts deep chestnut.

22. RUSTY-MARGINED GUAN L-F
Penelope superciliaris 63

Crown brown, narrow eyebrow whitish. Wing covert feathers edged chestnut.

23. BAUDO GUAN LM-F
Penelope ortoni 60

All drab brown. Neck and breast feathers conspicuously edged whitish. Feet and legs light reddish.

24. MARAIL GUAN L-F
Penelope marail 60

Like 2-17 but above dark green. More crested.

25. ANDEAN GUAN MH-F
Penelope montagnii 57

Like 2-17 but dewlap small and browner above.

Penelope: Red dewlap.
Aburria
Pipile: Large white patch on wing.
Chamaepetes: Large facial skin blue.
Ortalis: Red skin on throat, no dewlap.

26. WHITE-WINGED GUAN **L-F**
Penelope albipennis 56

Brownish olive. Crest grayish white. Primaries white. Prominent malar stripe black.

27. BAND-TAILED GUAN **M-F**
Penelope argyrotis 56

Mostly bronzy olive with conspicuous silvery white streaking on face and neck. Feathers of back and under-parts edged white. Tail tipped rufous or buff.

28. WATTLED GUAN **M-F**
Aburria aburri 65

Black. Base of bill bright blue. Long round yellow wattle hang ging from throat. Legs yellow.

29. BLUE-THROATED PIPING-GUAN **L-F**
Pipile (Aburria) pipile 56

Black. Crown, nape and large patch on wings white. Dewlap blue.

30. RED-THROATED PIPING-GUAN **L-F**
Pipile cujubi 56

Very like 3-29 but face black and dewlap mostly red.

31. BLACK-FRONTED PIPING-GUAN **L-F**
Pipile jacutinga 56

Very like 3-29 but forehead and face black and dewlap mostly red.

32. SICKLE-WINGED GUAN **MH-F**
Chamaepetes goudotii 57

Large bare facial area blue. No knob, wattle or dewlap. Upperparts brown (neck scaled gray in s). Breast, belly, flanks and crissum chestnut. Legs red.

33. RUFOUS-VENTED CHACHALACA **L-TS**
Ortalis ruficauda 49

Head,face and neck gray. Above brown Breast brown. Belly buffy. Crissum rufous. Legs dusky.

34. RUFOUS-HEADED CHACHALACA **L-SA**
Ortalis erythroptera 50

Like 3-33 but head rufous and primaries chestnut.

35. CHESTNUT-WINGED CHACHALACA **L-TS**
Ortalis garrula 48

Like 3-33 but head rufous or gray and primaries chestnut. Underparts and tail tips white.

36. CHACO CHACHALACA **L-TS**
Ortalis canicollis 50

Forehead black Head gray. Back olive-brown Below buffy. Flanks rufous.

LARGE LAND BIRDS - IV - CHACHALACAS 2, SERIEMAS, TRUMPETERS.
MID-SIZE LAND BIRDS -I- TINAMOUS 1.

Ortalis: Red skin on throat, no dewlap.
Cariama
Chunga
Psophia
Burhinus
Tinamus

37. VARIABLE (LITTLE) CHACHALACA **LM-TS**
Ortalis motmot 47

Head and neck chestnut or gray speckled white. Above brownish. Below grayish.

38. RED-LEGGED SERIEMA **L-O**
Cariama cristata 69

Brownish gray
Conspicuous crest.
Legs long, reddish.

39. BLACK-LEGGED SERIEMA **L-O**
Chunga burmeisteri 69

Grayish. Belly white. Black bands near end of tail. Legs long, black.

40. PALE-WINGED TRUMPETER **L-F**
Psophia leucoptera 55

Like 4-41 but inner wing coverts white or buff.

41. GRAY-WINGED TRUMPETER **L-F**
Psophia crepitans 55

Mainly black. Extensive inner wing coverts gray.

42. DARK-WINGED TRUMPETER **L-F**
Psophia viridis 55

Like 4-41 but browner with inner wing coverts green.

43. DOUBLE-STRIPED THICK-KNEE **L-0**
Burhinus bistriatus 43

RIDGELY

Dark brown streaked buff. Broad eyebrow white, bordered above with black line.Throat and belly white.
Legs long, olive.

44. PERUVIAN THICK-KNEE **L-0A**
Burhinus superciliaris 36

Like 4-43 but back vermiculated buff and dusky.

1. GREAT TINAMOU **L-F**
Tinamus major 42

Like 5-5 but browner. Flanks prominently barred. Belly white.

Tinamus: Compact, seem tailless.
Tinamotis: Compact seem tailless.
Eudromia: Long, forward-curving crest.
Nothocercus: Compact, seem tailless.
Rhynchotus

2. SOLITARY TINAMOU **L-F**
Tinamus solitarius 42

Above brown, barred black. Buff line down sides of neck. Throat white. Breast gray. Center of under parts gray.

3. GRAY TINAMOU **L-F**
Tinamus tao 42

Head and neck gray speckled white. Above dark gray barred black. Throat white. Below olive-gray. Crissum cinnamon.

4. BLACK TINAMOU **L-F**
Tinamus osgoodi 42

Upperparts and breast black. Throat and belly gray. Crissum cinnamon.

5. WHITE-THROATED TINAMOU **L-F**
Tinamus guttatus 30

Crown gray. Above brownish speckled white. Throat white. Below light brown. Crissum chestnut.

6. PUNA TINAMOU **H-O**
Tinamotis pentlandii 41

Crown and nape buff. Above barred. Rump and tail yellowish. Breast buff barred gray. Below mostly rufous.

7. PATAGONIAN TINAMOU **L-O**
Tinamotis ingoufi 35

Face and throat white. Back gray with large black, white-edged spots. Breast gray. Belly cinnamon.

8. ELEGANT CRESTED-TINAMOU **L-SO**
Eudromia elegans 39

Above brown, thickly spotted white. Below buff barred black.

9. QUEBRACHO CRESTED-TINAMOU **L-SO**
Eudromia formosa 39

Above dark brown thinly spotted white. Below whitish barred black

10. HIGHLAND TINAMOU **M-F**
Nothocercus bonapartei 36

Above brown waved black, rear dotted buff. Below cinnamon waved black.

11. TAWNY-BREASTED TINAMOU **H-F**
Nothocercus julius 36

Head bright chestnut. Above brown waved black, inner wing coverts spotted buff. Throat white. Breast tawny. Belly rufous.

12. HOODED TINAMOU **M-F**
Nothocercus nigrocapillus 33

Head gray. Above light brown waved black. Below cinnamon waved black.

13. RED-WINGED TINAMOU **L-O**
Rhynchotus rufescens 37

Above barred brown, black and buff. Primaries rufous. Breast buff or gray. Bill long.

Crypturellus: Compact, seem tailless.

14. VARIEGATED TINAMOU **L-F**
Crypturellus variegatus 30

Bright rufous, barred on rump and flanks. Crown blackish. Bill very long.

15. BARTLETT'S TINAMOU **L-F**
Crypturellus bartletti 28

Bright rufous, barred on rump and flanks. Crown blackish.

16. RUSTY TINAMOU **L-F**
Crypturellus brevirostris 28

Bright rufous, barred on rump and flanks. Crown chestnut.

17. UNDULATED TINAMOU **L-FTS**
Crypturellus undulatus 28

Upperparts barred (usually including crown) Throat white. Breast gray. Below whitish. Flanks and crissum barred.

18. RED-LEGGED TINAMOU **L-TS**
Crypturellus erythropus (atrocapillus) 28

Crown black. Above brown barred black. Throat rufous. Breast gray. Below cinnamon. Legs red.

19. YELLOW-LEGGED TINAMOU **L-FTS**
Crypturellus noctivagus 28

Cap blackish. Broad eyebrow buffy. Above gray, wings and rump barred black. Throat white. Breast rufous. Belly buffy. Legs yellow.

20. GRAY-LEGGED TINAMOU **L-T**
Crypturellus duidae 28

Head, neck and breast rufous. Throat white. Back dark brown, barred blackish. Legs grayish.

21. PALE-BROWED TINAMOU **L-F**
Crypturellus transfasciatus 26

Crown brown. Eyebrow and throat white. Above grayish barred black.Below buffy. Flanks barred. Legs pink.

22. BRAZILIAN TINAMOU **L-F**
Crypturellus strigulosus 26

Above reddish brown. (f. barred blackish.) Throat rufous. Breast gray. Belly white. Legs brown.

23. SLATY-BREASTED TINAMOU **L-F**
Crypturellus boucardi 25

Head chestnut. Back dark brown. Throat white. Below gray, flanks pale barred. Legs reddish.

24. BARRED TINAMOU **L-F**
Crypturellus casiquiare 23

Head and neck bright chestnut. Above boldly barred black and buff. Throat white. Breast gray. Belly white.

25. CHOCO TINAMOU **L-FT**
Crypturellus kerriae 25

Head blackish. Above dark red dish brown. Throat grayish. Below dark brown. Legs reddish.

26. TEPUI TINAMOU **M-F**
Crypturellus ptaritepui 25

Above reddish brown, lighter on crown and nape. Bill black, lower yellow tipped black. Below dusky.

Crypturellus: Compact, seem tailless.
Nothoprocta
Nothura: Compact, seem tailless.

27. CINEREOUS TINAMOU L-FT
Crypturellus cinereus 25

Uniform dark brown. No con trasting throat or belly

28. BROWN TINAMOU LM-F
Crypturellus obsoletus 25

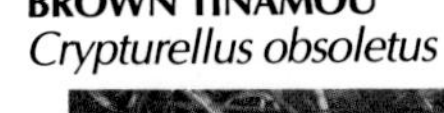

Head gray. Above varies from gray to dark brown to reddish brown. Below rufous. Legs gray.

29. LITTLE TINAMOU L-FTS
Crypturellus soui 21

Nearly uniform brown plumage, crown darker. Throat white. Flanks lightly barred.

30. TATAUPA TINAMOU LM-FTS
Crypturellus tataupa 21

Head, throat and breast gray. Above brown. Belly and crissum white barred black. Legs purplish.

31. SMALL-BILLED TINAMOU L-FS
Crypturellus parvirostris 19

Like 7-30 but bill smaller and breast buffier. Bill and legs red.

32. KALINOWSKI'S TINAMOU H-S
Nothoprocta kalinowskii 33

Above grayish brown barred black Below gray dotted buff.

33. ORNATE TINAMOU H-S
Nothoprocta ornata 33

Above barred buff and black. Throat buff spotted black. Breast gray. Belly rufous.

34. TACZANOWSKI'S TINAMOU H-S
Nothoprocta taczanowskii 32

Head brown. Above dusky. Throat white surrounded by black lines. Breast gray spotted white. Below buff. Legs yellow.

35. CHILEAN TINAMOU L-O
Nothoprocta perdicaria 27

Above grayish brown spotted black.Throat and belly whitish. Breast and sides gray.

36. BRUSHLAND TINAMOU L-SO
Nothoprocta cinerescens 27

Above brown barred black and streaked whitish. Below white, barred black on breast.

37. ANDEAN TINAMOU MH-O
Nothoprocta pentlandii 25

Upperparts brownish, narrowly streaked black. Throat and breast gray, pale-spotted. Below buff. Legs yellow.

38. CURVE-BILLED TINAMOU H-O
Nothoprocta curvirostris 23

Bill very curved. Above dark streaked white. Face and throat white. Breast rufous spotted black. Below buff. Legs yellow.

39. DARWIN'S NOTHURA LMH-SO
Nothura darwinii 23

Rather like 8-41 but darker above and breast grayer.

MID SIZE LAND BIRDS - V - NOTHURAS, SEEDSNIPE, WOOD QUAIL.

Nothura: Compact, seem tailless.
Taoniscus
Attagis: Finch-like bill.
Thinocorus
Odontophorus : Heavy, curved bill.

40. SPOTTED NOTHURA **L-TSO**
Nothura maculosa 23

Upperparts blackish and buff, all streaked white. Throat white. Belly buff. Legs brownish.

41. WHITE-BELLIED NOTHURA **L-SO**
Nothura boraquira 23

Above streaked. Eye white. Throat white. Below buffy in center. Legs yellow.

42. LESSER NOTHURA **L-TS**
Nothura minor 16

Upperparts buffy or chestnut marbled black. Wings evenly barred Throat white. Below tawny, sides barred dusky.

43. DWARF TINAMOU **L-TS**
Taoniscus nanus 14

Very small. Crown black. Above buff waved dusky. Below buff, barred brown on breast and flanks.

44. RUFOUS-BELLIED SEEDSNIPE **H-O**
Attagis gayi 27

Mostly grayish brown, barred and spotted black. Belly buff. Legs yellowish.

45. WHITE-BELLIED SEEDSNIPE **H-SO**
Attagis malouinus 25

Above dark brown. Throat white Breast brown scalloped black. Belly pure white. Legs grayish.

46. GRAY-BREASTED SEEDSNIPE **LMH-O**
Thinocorus orbignyianus 20

RIDGELY

Above dark brown and black. Head and neck gray. Throat white sharply outlined black. Breast gray with narrow black bar below. Belly white.

47. LEAST SEEDSNIPE **LMH-O**
Thinocorus rumicivorus 7

Like 8-46 but black stripe down center of breast (f: lacking).

48. BLACK-FRONTED WOOD-QUAIL **M-F**
Odontophorus atrifrons 27

Above brownish marked buff and black. Forehead, face and throat black. Breast brown speckled white. Belly buff streaked black.

49. MARBLED WOOD-QUAIL **L-T**
Odontophorus gujanensis 26

Above black and dark brown. Upper wing coverts streaked white.Bare orbital skin red. Below dark brown.

50. SPOT-WINGED WOOD- QUAIL **L-F**
Odontophorus capueira 26

Above brown marked buff. Crown and short crest reddish brown. Bare orbital skin red. Wings spotted white. Below uniform gray

51. RUFOUS-FRONTED WOOD-QUAIL **LM-F**
Odontophorus erythrops 26

Forehead and face rufous. Throat black with white crescent. Back mottled black and buff. Face and throat black (f: lacking). Below chestnut.

MANY WATER -EDGE BIRDS OCCUR FAR FROM WATER.
Odontophorus: Heavy, curved bill.
Colinus
Rhynchortyx

FLAMINGOS FLY WITH NECK EXTENDED.
Jabiru
Phoenicopterus: Neck and legs very long.

52. DARK-BACKED WOOD-QUAIL M-F
Odontophorus melanonotus 26

Skin around eye blackish. Above dark brown waved rufous. Throat and breast chestnut. Below brown waved black.

53. CHESTNUT WOOD-QUAIL M-F
Odontophorus hyperythrus 26

Above brown conspicuously spotted black. Eye stripe white. Underparts chestnut (f: gray).

54. RUFOUS-BREASTED WOOD-QUAIL L-F
Odontophorus speciosus 26

Above brown spotted black. Eye stripe speckled black and white. Face and throat black. Below bright rufous (f: belly gray).

55. STRIPE-FACED WOOD-QUAIL M-F
Odontophorus balliviani 26

Above mixed reddish and black. Crown chestnut. Stripe behind eye black bordered above and below by buffy stripes. Throat black. Below chestnut spotted white.

56. GORGETED WOOD-QUAIL H-F
Odontophorus strophium 24

Above mixed brown, black and white. Face white speckled black. Throat black with white crescent. Below chestnut spotted white.

57. VENEZUELAN WOOD-QUAIL M-F
Odontophorus columbianus 24

Above mixed brown, black and buff. Face dark. Throat white with black crescent. Below brown spotted white.

58. STARRED WOOD-QUAIL L-F
Odontophorus stellatus 24

Crown and crest bright chestnut. (f: blackish). Above brownish. Skin around eye red. Throat gray. Below rufous. Crissum barred black.

59. CRESTED BOBWHITE LMH-SO
Colinus cristatus 21

Above brownish. Long, thin crest whitish. Nape spotted black and white. Below barred or spotted.

60. TAWNY-FACED QUAIL L-F
Rhynchortyx cinctus 17

Above brownish. Face bright rufous, stripe behind eye black (f: white). Below gray. Belly buffy, (F: white barred black).

1. JABIRU L-OW
Jabiru mycteria 130

White. Bare head and neck black, red at base of neck. Bill heavy, lower upcurved, black. Legs black.

2. CHILEAN FLAMINGO LMH-W
Phoenicopterus chilensis 110

Mostly whitish tinged pink, including underparts. Reddish on wings. Legs brownish, joints red. Bill black, yellow at base.

STORKS FLY WITH NECK EXTENDED. **HERONS AND EGRETS FLY WITH NECK RETRACTED.**

Phoenicopteras *Ardea* *Euxenura*
Phoenicoparrus: Neck and legs very long. *Mycteria* *Casmerodius*
Ajaia

3. AMERICAN FLAMINGO L-W
Phoenicopterus ruber 106

Rosy pink, neck darker. Bill pink with black tip. Primaries black. Legs pink.

4. ANDEAN FLAMINGO LMH-W
Phoenicoparrus andinus 115

Like 9-2 but face, breast and base of neck redder. Legs yellowish, joints not red.

5. PUNA FLAMINGO H-W
Phoenicoparrus jamesi 88

Like 9-2 but legs all dark brick red.

6. ROSEATE SPOONBILL L-W
Ajaia ajaja 76

Bill long, flattened at tip. Head, neck and back white. Rump and wings pink (imm: mostly white). Legs pink (imm: blackish).

7. WHITE-NECKED HERON L-W
Ardea cocoi 120

Like 10-8 but crown all black, bill all yellow, long crest black and legs yellow. Thighs white. Belly black.

8. GREAT BLUE HERON L-W
*Ardea herodias** 108

Crown white broadly bordered black. Back blue-gray. Below more or less streaked black and white. Legs dusky. Thighs rufous.

9. WOOD STORK (IBIS) L-W
Mycteria americana 96

Bill curved, black. Head and neck bare, blackish. Body white. Legs black, feet pink.

10. MAGUARI STORK L-W
Euxenura maguari 87

White. Edge of wings black. Bill straight, orange, yellow at base. Legs red. Tail white.

11. GREAT EGRET L-W
Casmerodius albus 91

All white. Bill yellow. Legs and feet black.

HERONS AND EGRETS FLY WITH NECK RETRACTED.

Anhima *Agamia* *Cochlearius*
Chauna *Tigrisoma* *Nyticorax*

12. HORNED SCREAMER **L-W**
Anhima cornuta 81

Mostly black, mottled white on crown and neck. Long thin quill on head. Legs short, heavy.

13. SOUTHERN SCREAMER **M-W**
Chauna torquata 79

Narrow white line circles neck. Above dark gray. Below lighter gray. Legs short, heavy.

14. NORTHERN SCREAMER **L-W**
Chauna chavaria 79

Very like 11-13 but usually no black above neck ring and underparts dark gray. Legs short, heavy.

15. CHESTNUT-BELLIED HERON **L-W**
Agamia agami 67

Bill long. Long crest gray. Above shiny dark green. Sides of neck chestnut. Throat white. Belly chestnut.

16. BARE-THROATED TIGER-HERON **L-W**
Tigrisoma mexicanum 68

Like 11-17 but throat extensively bare, yellow.

Note: No. 17 should read "adult" instead of "male" above picture on left.

17. RUFESCENT TIGER-HERON **L-TW**
Tigrisoma lineatum 66

Crown, back of neck and mantle chestnut. Back and wings brown vermiculated black Below white in center. Belly brown Imm:Above brown banded black. Below brown broadly streaked white.

male immature

18. FASCIATED TIGER-HERON **LM-FW**
Tigrisoma fasciatum 61

Like 11-17 but above black barred buff. Below brown streaked white.

19. BOAT-BILLED HERON **L-W**
Cochlearius cochlearius 53

Rather like 11-20 in shape but bill very broad and flat. Forehead white.Crown and crest black. Above gray. Breast buff. Belly chestnut.

20. BLACK-CROWNED NIGHT-HERON **L-TW**
Nycticorax nycticorax 52

Crown, nape and back black. Forehead and underparts white. Wings gray.

HERONS AND EGRETS FLY WITH NECK RETRACTED.

Nyctanassa *Pilherodius* *Bubulcus*
Egretta *Syrigma* *Butorides*

21. YELLOW-CROWNED NIGHT-HERON **L-TW**
Nyctanassa violacea 55

Like 11-20 but center of crown buffy yellow and face black with broad white malar streak.

22. TRICOLORED HERON **L-W**
Egretta (Hydranassa) tricolor 57

Mostly dark gray. Throat and line down center of neck rufous. Belly white.

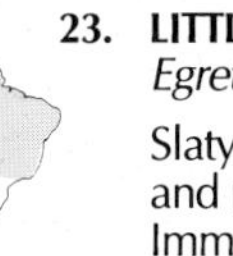

23. LITTLE BLUE HERON **L-W**
Egretta (Florida) caerulea 54

Slaty blue tinged maroon on head and neck. Bill pale, tipped black Imm: All white, legs greenish.

24. CAPPED HERON **L-W**
Pilherodius pileatus 51

White, crown black. Face and bill bluish. Legs gray.

25. WHISTLING HERON **L-W**
Syrigma sibilatrix 48

Bill pink, tipped black. Crown black. Bare skin around eye blue. Neck buffy. Back and tail white. Usually far from water.

26. SNOWY EGRET **L-W**
Egretta thula 54

All white. Bill black. Legs black. Feet yellow. Bare skin around eye yellow. Cf. 12-27.

27. CATTLE EGRET **L-OW**
Bubulcus ibis 44

nb plumage

White (crown, neck and breast buff in breeding plumage). Bill yellow. Lacks contrasting yellow feet of 12-26. Usually feeds with cattle.

28. GREEN HERON **L-W**
*Butorides virescens** 40

Crown and nape black. Eye-ring and lores whitish. Neck chestnut on sides, white in front. Back striped. Below streaked to brown belly.

29. STRIATED (GREEN-BACKED) HERON **L-W**
Butorides striatus 40

Like 12-28 but neck gray on sides. Considered conspecific by some.

IBISES HAVE SLENDER CURVED BILL AND FLY WITH NECK EXTENDED.

Harpiprion *Aramus* *Plegadis*
Theristicus *Eudocimus* *Phimosus*
Cercibis *Mesembrinibis* *Opisthocomus*

30. PLUMBEOUS IBIS L-W
Harpiprion caerulescens 74

The only ibis almost entirely gray. Bill black. Feet and legs salmon color.

31. BUFF-NECKED IBIS L-W
Theristicus caudatus 66

Head and neck buff. Back gray. Wing coverts white. Breast and belly black. Tail black.

32. SHARP-TAILED IBIS L-W
Cercibis oxycerca 66

Like 13-39 but bare red face goes around eye. Legs red. Tail extends about 8cm beyond folded wings.

33. LIMPKIN L-W
Aramus guarauna 61

Brown, streaked white on nape, back and sides of neck. Bill long, slightly curved.

34. WHITE IBIS L-W
Eudocimus albus 56

White. Wing tips black (often concealed). Bill, face and legs red. Imm: Cf. 13-38.

35. GREEN IBIS L-W
Mesembrinibis cayennensis 53

Rather like 13-39 but bill green and bare face slaty. Feet and legs greenish. Bushy crest green.

36. PUNA IBIS H-W
Plegadis ridgwayi 5l

Above blackish. Head, neck and underparts rufous. Face without white markings. Only ibis at high elevation.

37. WHITE-FACED IBIS L-W
Plegadis chihi 46

Head, neck and underparts reddish. Face whitish in breeding plumage. Above glossy purple Legs long, dark.

38. SCARLET IBIS L-W
Eudocimus ruber 51

Scarlet. Wing tips black (often concealed). Imm: Head and neck pale brown. Wings and tail dark brown. Rump and belly white.

39. BARE-FACED IBIS L-W
Phimosus infuscatus 43

Blackish. Bare skin on face red. Bill and legs reddish. Tail about even with folded wings.

40. HOATZIN L-TSW
Opisthocomus hoazin 58

Long crest rufous. Face bare, blue. Above bronzy olive streaked buff. Throat and breast buff, belly chestnut. In trees and bushes at water edge.

Botaurus	*Zebrilus*	*Limosa*
Eurypyga	*Himantopus*	*Catoptrophorus*
Ixobrychus	*Recurvirostra*	

41. PINNATED BITTERN L-W
Botaurus pinnatus 56

Crown black. Above brown barred buff. Throat white. Below buffy streaked brown.

42. SUNBITTERN L-W
Eurypyga helias 46

Head black with long strong white eyebrow and malar stripe Throat white. Tail much longer than a bittern. Broad chestnut bars on back.

1. STRIPE-BACKED BITTERN L-W
Ixobrychus involucris 30

Line down center of crown and broad streaks on back black. Throat white. Below buffy white narrowly streaked brown.

2. ZIGZAG HERON L-W
Zebrilus undulatus 30

A small, dark heron. Crown and large crest black. Face and neck chestnut. Above black, waved buff. Below buff.

3. LEAST BITTERN L-W
*Ixobrychus exilis** 25

Tiny. Upperparts blackish, a white stripe at each side of back. Face, mantle and breast chestnut. Shoulders extensively pale buff. Belly whitish.

4. COMMON STILT L-W
Himantopus himantopus 41

Bill thin, 1-1/2x head. Upperparts black, forecrown white. Under-parts all white. Legs very long, red.

5. ANDEAN AVOCET H-W
Recurvirostra andina 41

White. Mid-back, rump, wings and tip of tail blackish. Bill sharply upturned.

6. HUDSONIAN GODWIT LM-W
Limosa haemasticas 36

Non-breeding plumage. Quite like 14-7 but bill 2x head, upturned, reddish with black tip. Tail black.

7. WILLET L-OW
*Catoptrophorus semipalmatus**32

Gray. Bill 2x head, straight. Rump and underparts white. Tail whitish. Legs grayish.

Limnodromus
Gallinula
Porphyrula
Porphyriops
Jacana
Gallinago

8. SHORT-BILLED (COMMON) DOWITCHER L-W
*Limnodromus griseus** 25

Non-breeding plumage. Rather like 14-7 but above gray, rump and tail extensively white extending in a point to back.

9. COMMON GALLINULE LMH-W
Gallinula chloropus 36

Dark gray. Head blackish. Bill and frontal shield red, bill tipped yellow. White on sides of body. Crissum black, edged white. Legs yellow.

10. PURPLE GALLINULE LM-OW
Porphyrula martinica 30

Above bronzy green. Bill red tipped yellow Forecrown pale blue. Head, neck and underparts bluish purple. Crissum all white.

11. AZURE GALLINULE L-W
Porphyrula flavirostris 23

Like 15-10 but blue replaced by purple and crown, mantle and breast brownish.

12. SPOT-FLANKED GALLINULE MH-W
Porphyriops melanops 28

Head, mantle, neck and breast gray. Wings chestnut. Belly white. Flanks brown with large white spots.

13. WATTLED JACANA L-W
Jacana jacana 25

Bill yellow. Bare forehead and knobs red Head, neck, mantle and underparts black. Back chestnut Wings yellow in flight. Toes very long.

14. GIANT SNIPE LM-W
Gallinago undulata 41

Above like 16-17 but much larger and with primaries barred. Throat and belly white, breast marked buffy.

15. CORDILLERAN SNIPE H-W
Gallinago stricklandii 33

Like 16-17 but tail without rufous and underparts more strongly barred.

16. NOBLE SNIPE H-W
Gallinago nobilis 28

Very like 16-17 but bill much longer.

Gallinago
Nycticryphes
Tringa
Bartramia
Calidris
Micropalama
Vanellus

17. COMMON SNIPE L-W
Gallinago gallinago 25

Central crown stripe and eyebrow whitish. Back striped and spotted buff. Throat and belly white. Breast white speckled brown. Includes Paraguayan Snipe.

18. PUNA SNIPE H-W
Gallinago andina 20

Very like 16-17 but found in high Andes only.

19. SOUTH AMERICAN PAINTED SNIPE L-OA
Nycticryphes semicollaris 20

Bill green and yellow, curved. Head brown, crown stripe whitish. Above brown and black, Large round white spots on wings. Throat and breast brown. Belly white.

20. LESSER YELLOWLEGS L-W
*Tringa flavipes** 23

Bill 1-1/4x head, straight. Above dark brown spotted white and black. Rump white. Below white streaked brown on breast. Tail barred black and white. Nb: Above grayer, below whiter.

21. GREATER YELLOWLEGS LMH-W
*Tringa melanoleuca** 28

Very like 16-20 but bill 1-1/2 x head, slightly upturned. Legs long, yellow. Nb: Above grayer, below whiter.

22. UPLAND SANDPIPER LM-O
*Bartramia longicauda** 28

Bill 3/4x head. Above dark brown, feathers edged buff. Rump black. Eyebrow whitish. Below white, sides barred blackish. Usually far from water.

23. PECTORAL SANDPIPER LM-OW
*Calidris melanotos** 21

Bill 3/4x head. Upperparts blackish scaled rufous. Rump black. Throat and belly white sharply contrasting with streaked breast.

24. STILT SANDPIPER L-OW
*Micropalama himantopus** 20

Bill=head, straight. Nb: Somewhat like 14-7 but little or no black on wings. Legs olive.

25. SOUTHERN LAPWING M-O
Vanellus chilensis 30

Above gray, upper wing tinged reddish and green. Forehead and long thin crest black. Breast and front of neck black. Belly white.

LAPWINGS, PLOVERS, RAILS AND CRAKES OFTEN OCCUR FAR FROM WATER.

Vanellus
Oreopholus
Zonibyx
Pluvialis
Charadrius
Hoploxypterus
Phalaropus
Aramides: Primaries rufous. Legs red.

26 ANDEAN LAPWING **H-W**
Vanellus resplendens 30

Quite like 16-25 but no crest and no black on head and breast. Upperparts and breast grayish. Belly white.

27. TAWNY-THROATED DOTTEREL **LMH-W**
Oreopholus ruficollis 25

Crown, neck and breast light brown. Back streaked black and tawny. Throat cinnamon. Belly buff with black patch in center.

28. RUFOUS-CHESTED DOTTEREL **L-OW**
Zonibyx modestus 20

Forehead and broad eye stripe white. Upper parts uniform brown. Throat gray. Breast rufous with black band below. Belly white. Nb: Mostly dull brown. Throat and belly white.

29. LESSER (AMERICAN) GOLDEN PLOVER **L-OA**
*Pluvialis dominica** 25

Bill 3/4x head. Nb: Above brown spotted yellow. Below white. Tail brown barred black.

30. KILLDEER **L-O**
Charadrius vociferus 23

Forehead white with narrow black line above. Above brown. Below white with two black breast bands.

31. PIED PLOVER **L-OW**
Hoploxypterus cayanus 20

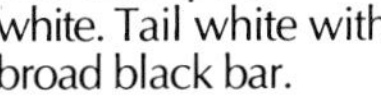

Crown white, brown in center. Forehead, face and breast black. Rump, throat and underparts white. Tail white with broad black bar.

32. WILSON'S PHALAROPE **L-OW**
*Phalaropus (Steganopus) tricolor** 20

Bill = head, needlelike. Nb. Crown and back uniform, grayish. Face white, eye-stripe dusky. Wings browner, no bars. Rump white. Underparts white. Often swims. Two other Phalaropes usually not inland.

33. GIANT WOOD-RAIL **L-TOW**
Aramides ypecaiha 43

Like 17-35 but face whiter, and nape cinnamon. Bill yellowish. Legs pink. Breast gray. Belly cinnamon.

34. SLATY-BREASTED WOOD-RAIL **L-F**
Aramides saracura 38

Like 17-35 but crown and underparts dark gray, nape reddish brown.

35. GRAY-NECKED WOOD-RAIL **LM-TS**
Aramides cajanea 36

Head, neck and thighs gray. Back olive, rump black Throat white. Breast rufous. Belly and tail black.

WOODRAILS, RAILS AND CRAKES HAVE SHORT TAILS USUALLY HELD UPRIGHT.

Aramides: Primaries rufous. Legs red. *Porzana*

Rallus

36. RED-WINGED WOOD-RAIL L-W
Aramides calopterus 33

Rear crown brown. Back olive, rump and tail black. Wing coverts and sides of neck red. Below gray.

37. BROWN WOOD-RAIL L-FW
Aramides wolfi 30

Head and back of neck gray. Back reddish brown. Wings olive.Throat white. Below pale reddish brown, center of belly black.

38. LITTLE WOOD-RAIL L-FT
Aramides mangle 30

Head, neck and mantle gray. Back olive. Underparts light chestnut. Bill greenish, red at base.

39. RUFOUS-NECKED WOOD-RAIL L-FTW
Aramides axillaris 28

Head and neck rufous chestnut. Back olive. Underparts chestnut.

40. PLUMBEOUS RAIL LMH-W
Rallus sanguinolentus 25

Bill long, green, red at base. Forecrown, face and all underparts dark gray. Above (including tail) olive brown.

41. BLACKISH RAIL L-W
Rallus nigricans 25

Bill long, yellowish green. Forecrown and face gray. Above olive brown. Throat white. Below dark gray. Tail black.

42. SUNGREBE L-W
Heliornis fulica 25

Head black. Stripe behind eye white. Cheeks, neck and underparts white, line down neck black. Above olive brown. Tail tipped white.

43 BOGOTA RAIL H-W
Rallus semiplumbeus 23

Bill red, tip black. Above brown streaked black, wing coverts rufous. Face and throat pale gray. Broad eyebrow pale buff. Underparts gray. Flanks barred black and white.

44. AUSTRAL RAIL L-OW
Rallus antarcticus 23

Bill bright red. Upperparts brown streaked black Below dark gray. Legs dark purple.

45. SPOTTED RAIL L-OW
Rallus maculatus 23

Bill yellow, red at base. Back brown streaked white. Neck, mantle and breast heavily spotted black. Belly white barred dark brown.

46. VIRGINIA RAIL L-OW
*Rallus limicola** 23

Bill 1-1/4x head, slender, slightly decurved. Above black streaked tawny. Face gray. Underparts chestnut (imm: mottled black).

47. SORA RAIL LMH-W
*Porzana carolina** 20

Quite like 19-1 but face and throat black (imm: no black). Gray back of eye. Above brown streaked white. Breast gray. Belly white.

CRAKES OFTEN OCCUR IN FIELDS FAR FROM WATER.
Porzana: Flanks barred black and white.
Anurolimnas
Amaurolimnas
Neocrex
Laterallus: Flanks barred black and white.

1. ASH-THROATED CRAKE L-O
Porzana albicollis 23

Upperparts brownish, broadly streaked black. Center of throat white. Below all pale gray, flanks barred black and white.

2. CHESTNUT-HEADED CRAKE L-F
Anurolimnas castaneiceps 20

Bill yellowish green. Face, neck and breast rufous chestnut (not pale gray). Rest of plumage dark olive. Flanks not barred. Legs orange red.

3. UNIFORM CRAKE L-F
Amaurolimnas concolor 21

Bill yellowish green. Eye red. Above dark chestnut brown. Throat whitish. Below rufous brown. Legs pinkish

4. PAINT-BILLED CRAKE L-OW
Neocrex erythrops 19

Like 19-1 but back not streaked and bill yellow, bright red at base.

5. RED-AND-WHITE CRAKE L-OW
Laterallus leucopyrrhus 16

Crown, face, mantle and sides of rufous chestnut. Underparts white, barred black on flanks. Legs red.

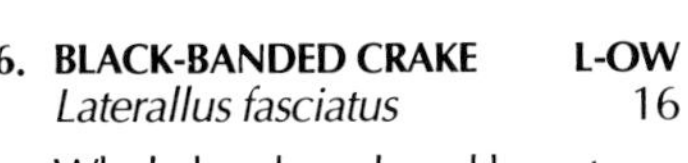

6. BLACK-BANDED CRAKE L-OW
Laterallus fasciatus 16

Whole head, neck and breast rufous chestnut. Rest of under parts orange rufous banded black.

7. RUFOUS-SIDED CRAKE L-OW
Laterallus melanophaius 15

Quite like 19-1 but face, neck and breast orange rufous. Crissum chestnut. Bill and legs pale yellowish.

8. RUSTY-FLANKED CRAKE L-OW
Laterallus levraudi 15

Quite like 19-1 but above dark brown, not streaked. Forecrown, face and unbarred sides rufous. Below white in center.

9. RUSSET-CROWNED CRAKE L-OW
Laterallus viridis 15

Above olive. Crown rufous. Face gray. Underparts all orange. Legs salmon color.

10. DOT-WINGED CRAKE L-OW
Laterallus spilopterus 14

Very like 19-1 but wings spotted white and breast darker gray.

11. BLACK CRAKE L-OW
Laterallus jamaicensis 14

Like 19-1 but darker and bill and legs blackish. Lower back dotted white.

12. GRAY-BREASTED CRAKE LM-OW
Laterallus exilis 14

Like 19-1 but prominent chestnut patch on hindneck.

Micropygia
Coturnicops
Porzana
Tringa
Tryngites
Actitis
Calidris

13. OCELLATED CRAKE **L-OW**
Micropygia schomburgkii 13

Mostly ochraceous. Crown black dotted white. Wing coverts and sides of breast with round white, black-encircled spots. Center of belly white.

14. SPECKLED CRAKE **L-OW**
Coturnicops notata 13

Upperparts dark olive brown dotted black and white. Throat white. Neck and breast olive, narrowly streaked white. Belly olive barred white. Eye red.

15. YELLOW-BREASTED CRAKE **L-OW**
Porzana flaviventer 13

Crown and stripe through eye black. Back black streaked white. Wing brownish barred and mottled black and white. Breast buffy. Belly white, sides barred black and white. Legs yellow.

16. SOLITARY SANDPIPER **L-W**
*Tringa solitaria** 20

Above dark olive-brown speckled white. Below white,narrowly streaked dusky brown on throat and breast.Edges of tail white,barred black. Cf. 20-18.

17. BUFF-BREASTED SANDPIPER **L-TW**
*Tryngites subruficollis** 20

Upperparts black, scaled buff. Underparts uniform buff. Bill rather short. Legs greenish yellow.

18. SPOTTED SANDPIPER **LM-W**
*Actitis macularia ** 18

non-breeding

Above grayish brown, eyebrow white. Nb: Below all white, wedge before shoulder white. Teeters constantly. Flies on stiff wings.

19. BAIRD'S SANDPIPER **L-W**
*Calidris bairdii** 18

Somewhat like 20-21 but grayer and legs black, not yellowish. Above brown streaked buffy. Rump white with dark center. Eyebrow white. Below whitish, lightly streaked dusky on sides of neck and breast

20. WHITE-RUMPED SANDPIPER **L-W**
*Calidris fuscicollis** 18

Above rather like 20-21. Rump all white Below whitish lightly streaked on sides of neck and breast. Legs dark greenish.

21. LEAST SANDPIPER **L-W**
*Calidris minutilla** 14

non-breeding

Above dark brownish, feathers rufous-edged. Rump black. Below white, breast streaked brown. Legs yellowish. (Nb: Upper-parts grayish brown, no rufous on feathers).

Phegornis
Charadrius
Cinclus
Pelecanus
Cygnus

22. DIADEMED SANDPIPER-PLOVER **H-O**
Phegornis mitchellii 17

Hindcrown gray encircled by white line. Mantle orange-rufous. Back brown. Forehead and face brown.Throat white. Below barred gray and white.

23. PUNA PLOVER **H-OW**
Charadrius alticola 17

Above like 21-25 but imm. lacks black bar across breast. Legs black.

24. TWO-BANDED PLOVER **M-W**
Charadrius falklandicus 17

Above like 21-25. Underparts white with two black bands across breast. Legs black.

25. COLLARED PLOVER **L-OW**
Charadrius collaris 15

Forehead white. Forecrown black, bordered in back by more or less cinnamon. One narrow black band across breast. Legs orange.

26. SEMIPALMATED PLOVER **L-W**
*Charadrius semipalmatus** 16

Bill yellow, tipped black (nb. all black). Very like 21-25 with single breast band black (nb. brown) and forehead white.

27. WHITE-CAPPED DIPPER **MH-W**
Cinclus leucocephalus 14

Cap and mantle white. Collar, eyestripe, back, wings and sides brownish. Below white (breast brown in s). Dives in water. Bobs tail.

28. RUFOUS-THROATED DIPPER **MH-W**
Cinclus schultzi 14

Uniform dark gray except throat cinnamon. Dives in water.

1. BROWN PELICAN **L-W**
Pelecanus occidentalis 96-150

Extremely large heavy bill. Head white. Back gray. Neck chestnut. Below brown (Imm. brown above and below)

2. BLACK-NECKED SWAN **L-W**
Cygnus melancoryphus 91

White, neck black. Base of bill red. Legs red.

CORMORANTS FLY WITH NECK EXTENDED.
SWANS: VERY LONG NECK.
GEESE: LONG NECK.

Coscoroba
Chloephaga
Neochen

Anhinga
Phalacrocorax:
Feeds under water.

3. COSCOROBA SWAN **L-W**
Coscoroba coscoroba 66

White. Wings tipped black. Bill and legs bright pink. Black wing tips prominent when flying.

4. ANDEAN GOOSE **H-W**
Chloephaga melanoptera 68

White with few black streaks on back. Wings and tail black. Legs red.

5. UPLAND GOOSE **M-OW**
Chloephaga picta 63

Head, neck, shoulders and underparts white, more or less barred black. Lower back and wings brown. Tail black with broad white bar. F: Neck, back and breast barred.

6. ASHY-HEADED GOOSE **L-W**
Chloephaga poliocephala 56

Head and neck gray. Mantle chestnut. Shoulder white. Rump and tail black. Breast chestnut (f. barred black). Below white, barred black on sides.

7. RUDDY-HEADED GOOSE **L-OA**
Chloephaga rubidiceps 56

Head and neck cinnamon. Shoulder white. Mantle and breast cinnamon finely barred black. Belly reddish.

8. ORINOCO GOOSE **L-W**
Neochen jubata 53

Head, neck and breast whitish. Back and belly brown. Rump, wings and tail black. Wing speculum white. Belly chestnut. Legs pink.

9. ANHINGA **L-W**
Anhinga anhinga 79

Bill long, thin, pointed. Glossy black (f: head, neck and breast buff). Wing coverts extensively white. Often perches with wings spread. Feeds under water. Cf: 22-10

10. OLIVACEOUS CORMORANT **LMH-W**
Phalacrocorax olivaceus 63

Black. Bill long, narrow, hooked. Flies with neck extended. Sometimes perches with wings dangling. Cf. 22-9

11. KING CORMORANT **L-W**
Phalacrocorax albiventer 63

Upperparts black, glossed greenish. Face reddish. Underparts white. Legs red. On large lakes.

Sarkidiornis	*Tachyeres*
Cairina	*Anas:* Very pointed tail.
Lophonetta	*Mergus*

12. COMB DUCK L-FW
Sarkidiornis melanotos m:68 f:51

Bill black with large red knob at base (f: lacking). Above black. Face and neck white spotted black. Below white.

13. MUSCOVY DUCK L-FW
Cairina moschata m:68 f:52

Mostly black (some white below on some birds). Large wing patch white. Face black with small red knobs (f: lacking). Usually with no white below which this photo shows.

14. CRESTED DUCK H-W
Lophonetta specularioides 56

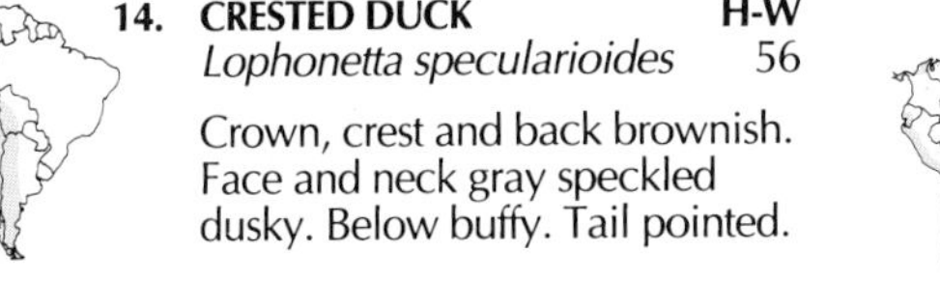

Crown, crest and back brownish. Face and neck gray speckled dusky. Below buffy. Tail pointed.

15. FLYING STEAMER-DUCK L-W
Tachyeres patachonicus 51

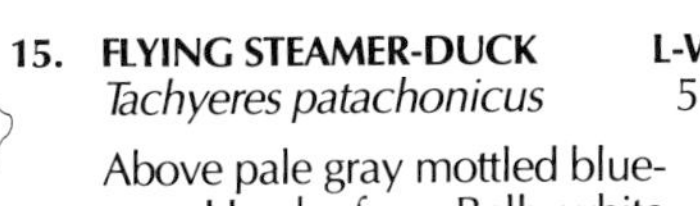

Above pale gray mottled blue-gray. Head rufous. Belly white.

16. NORTHERN (COMMON) PINTAIL L-W
*Anas acuta** 58

Very like 23-17 but bill gray (not yellow).

17. YELLOW-BILLED PINTAIL LM-W
*Anas georgica** 56

Bill yellow. Upperparts brown. Face and neck speckled dusky. Underparts whitish or brown spotted dusky.

18. AMERICAN WIGEON L-OW
*Anas americana** 46

Crown and shoulders white. Line back of eye green. Face and neck freckled black and buff. Back brownish vermiculated buff. Underparts white.

19. SOUTHERN WIGEON L-M
Anas sibilatrix 43

Forecrown and broad crescent in front of eye white. Broad streak behind eye green (f: lacking). Neck black. Back and breast white barred black. Belly white.

20. WHITE-CHEEKED PINTAIL L-W
Anas bahamensis 41

Brown spotted black. Crown, lower face, forehead and throat white. Bill black, red spot at base.

21. BRAZILIAN MERGANSER L-W
Mergus octosetaceus 51

Head, neck and long, thin crest black. Above brown. Wings black with white patch. Below barred brown and white.

Netta
Dendrocygna
Anas

22. ROSY-BILLED POCHARD L-W
Netta peposaca 46

male

Bill and knob at forehead pink. Head, neck and breast black. Back black vermiculated white. Belly and crissum white vermiculated black. F: Brown. Throat white. No knob.

female

23. SOUTHERN POCHARD LM-W
Netta erythrophthalma 38

All blackish with gray bill. F: Brown with white on face.

24. FULVOUS WHISTLING-DUCK L-W
Dendrocygna bicolor 43

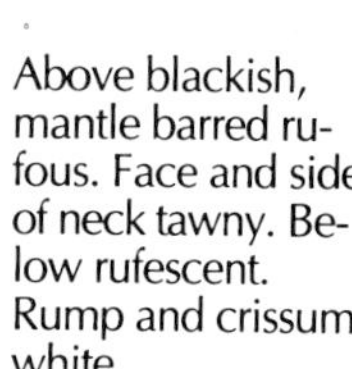

Above blackish, mantle barred rufous. Face and sides of neck tawny. Below rufescent. Rump and crissum white.

25. BLACK-BELLIED WHISTLING-DUCK L-W
Dendrocygna autumnalis 43

Bill pink. Face, neck and lower breast gray. Back rufous brown. Prominent broad white stripe on wings. Rump and belly black.

26. WHITE-FACED WHISTLING DUCK L-W
Dendrocygna viduata 38

Face and foreneck white. Nape black Back brown, narrowly streaked white. Rump and belly black, sides barred.

27. NORTHERN SHOVELER LM-W
*Anas clypeata** 41

Bill broad at tip. Head and neck green. Shoulder blue. Much white on back. Breast white. Below dark chestnut.

28. RED SHOVELER LM-W
Anas platalea 41

Bill broad at tip. Head whitish spotted black. Upperparts, breast and sides cinnamon (f. brown) spotted black. Rump black. Shoulders blue. Below cinnamon.

29 SPECTACLED DUCK L-TW
Anas specularis 41

Head and back of neck brown, vertical white spot in front of eye. Front of neck white. Above blackish spotted buff. Below brownish, with prominent black spots on sides.

Oxyura
Heteronetta
Merganetta
Aythya
Amazonetta
Anas

30. RUDDY DUCK **H-W**
Oxyura jamaicensis 38

Head black, (white spots on cheeks in n.) Above, breast and belly mottled brownish and black. Tail black. F: Brown

31. LAKE DUCK **L-W**
Oxyura vittata 33

Bill blue. Head black. Above and below mottled brown and black. Tail black. F: Brown.

32. MASKED DUCK **L-W**
Oxyura dominica 33

Bill blue. Face and forecrown black. Above chestnut. Large wing patch white. Below light brown. Tail black. F: Brown. Face striped.

33. BLACK-HEADED DUCK **L-W**
Heteronetta atricapilla 33

Head, neck and back blackish. Breast brown. Below white. Sides brown and whitish. F: Head paler and throat whitish.

34. TORRENT DUCK **MH-W**
Merganetta armata 36

Bill red. Face and sides of neck striped black and white. Back brownish streaked black. Below whitish or brown, streaked black. Andean torrents. F: Above gray. Below rufous.

35. LESSER SCAUP **L-W**
*Aythya affinis** 36

Head, neck, rump and breast black. Back gray waved black. Belly white. F: Brown. White at base of bill.

36. BRAZILIAN DUCK **L-W**
Amazonetta brasiliensis 33

Brown. Bill pink Crown, back of neck, rump and tail black. Speculum white.

37. PUNA TEAL **H-W**
Anas puna 43

Quite like 25-39 but rump uniform grayish brown, sides narrowly barred and tail with little or no barring.

38. SPECKLED TEAL **L-W**
Anas flavirostris 41

Head and neck freckled black and brown. Above brown mottled darker (paler in n). Below whitish mottled blackish on breast. Speculum black.

39. SILVER TEAL **L-W**
Anas versicolor 38

Bill blue, upper yellow at base. Cap and nape blackish. Back blackish, feathers edged buff. Rump, tail and sides broadly barred black and white. Throat and lower face whitish. Below spotted black.

Anas
Fulica: Frontal shield above bill.
Podiceps: Appear tailless.

40. CINNAMON TEAL L-W
Anas cyanoptera 38

Head, neck and underparts chestnut (lightly spotted black on some). Shoulders blue. Speculum green. F: Most all brown.

41. BLUE-WINGED TEAL L-W
*Anas discors** 36

Head gray with white crescent in front of eye. Above brown. Shoulders blue. F: Most all brown. Eyebrow gray. No white crescent.

42. RINGED TEAL L-W
Anas leucophrys 33

female

Crown and hindneck black. Face, throat and neck whitish. Mantle brown. Back black. White patch on wings. Breast pink with round black spots. Tail black. F: Browner.

43. GIANT COOT H-W
Fulica gigantea 58

Blackish. Bill dark red tipped white. Frontal shield white. Legs red.

44. HORNED COOT H-W
Fulica cornuta 53

Black. Bill yellowish green, ridge black. Frontal shield horn-shaped.

45. RED-FRONTED COOT L-W
Fulica rufifrons 43

Black. Bill yellow, red at base. Frontal shield dark red.

46. RED-GARTERED COOT LM-W
Fulica armillata 38

Black. Bill yellow, red at base of upper bill. Frontal shield red, bordered yellow.

47. AMERICAN COOT H-W
Fulica americana 41

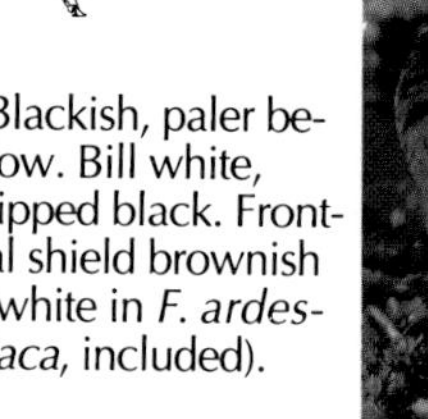

Blackish, paler below. Bill white, tipped black. Frontal shield brownish (white in *F. ardesiaca*, included).

48. CARIBBEAN COOT L-W
Fulica caribaea 36

Like 26-47 but with large white frontal shield.

49. WHITE-WINGED COOT L-W
Fulica leucoptera 30

Slate-colored. Bill and frontal shield lemon-yellow.

50. GREAT GREBE LM-W
Podiceps major 53

Brownish. Face and throat gray. Foreneck chestnut. Underparts white. Nb: Throat white.

51. PUNA GREBE H-W
Podiceps taczanowskii 33

Upperparts gray, blackish on nape. Below white. Plumes back of eye gray. Nb: No plumes or black on nape.

Podilymbus
Podiceps
Heliornis
Centropelma
Larus

52. PIED-BILLED GREBE **LMH-W**
Podilymbus podiceps 30

Bill yellowish, black ring in center. Throat black. (Nb: Lacks black on bill and throat is white). Upperparts and neck grayish brown.

53. WHITE-TUFTED GREBE **LMH-W**
Podiceps rolland 28

Above black, white tuft back of eye. Neck black. Underparts rufescent.

54. EARED GREBE **H-W**
Podiceps nigricollis 28

Above blackish. Plumes back of eye buff. Throat black, foreneck and sides of body chestnut. Below white. (Nb: Below all white and no plumes).

55. SILVERY GREBE **H-W**
Podiceps occipitalis 25

Above gray, blackish on nape and hindneck. Plumes back of eye gray. Below white, faint cinnamon patch on breast (f: lacking).

56. SHORT-WINGED GREBE **M-W**
Centropelma micropterum 25

Crown blackish. Nape chestnut. Plume back of eye black. Throat and foreneck white.Rest of plumage dark brownish, paler below. No white below. No plumes.

57. LEAST GREBE **LMH-W**
Podiceps (Tachybaptus) dominicus 20

Eye white. Upperparts, neck and upper breast gray. Crown darker. Bill with light tip. Throat black (nb: white). Below whitish.

58. KELP GULL **LH-W**
Larus dominicanus 48

White. Back and wing black. Bill yellow tipped red. Legs greenish yellow. Tail all white. Juv: Brown spotted black.

59. ANDEAN GULL **LMH-W**
Larus serranus 41

Head black, white mark back of eye. Mantle, underparts and tail white. Back and wings pale gray. Bill and feet dark red. Nb: Head white marked gray.

60. GRAY-HOODED GULL **L-W**
Larus cirrocephalus 36

Head gray. Eye yellow. Back pale gray. Rump, underparts and tail white. Bill and feet red. Nb: Head white.

61. GRAY GULL **L-W**
Larus modestus 36

Mostly pale gray, front of head white. Bill and feet black. Tail with black sub-terminal bar. Nb: Head light brown.

62. BROWN-HOODED GULL **L-W**
Larus maculipennis 33

Head brownish black. Back and underparts white. Bill and feet red.

Phaetusa
Sterna
Gelochelidon
Rynchops
Vultur
Sarcoramphus
Cathartes

63. LARGE-BILLED TERN **L-W**
Phaetusa simplex 33

Forehead, neck and underparts white. Cap black. Back and tail gray. Bill greenish yellow.

64. SNOWY-CROWNED TERN **L-W**
Sterna trudeaui 33

Light gray. Crown white. Eye stripe black. Rump white. Bill yellow tipped black.

65. YELLOW-BILLED TERN **L-W**
Sterna superciliaris 23

Bill yellow. Crown and nape black. (nb: streaked). Above pale gray. Underparts white. Legs yellow.

66. GULL-BILLED TERN **L-W**
*Gelochelidon nilotica** 33

Bill thick, black. Crown black. Above grayish. Underparts white. Tail short, forked. Nb: Patch behind eye black.

67. BLACK SKIMMER **LM-W**
*Rynchops niger (nigra)** 41

Bill blade-like, lower longer, red, black at end. Above black. Forehead, sides of neck and all underparts white. Flies low with bill cutting water.

1. ANDEAN CONDOR **LMH-O**
Vultur gryphus 96

Black. Head bare surmounted by a flashy comb (f: lacking). Downy white ruff around neck. Much white in wings.

2. KING VULTURE **L-FO**
Sarcoramphus papa 68

Creamy white. Head, knob and neck bare, bright orange. Underwing coverts white. Imm: Mostly blackish.

3. GREATER YELLOW-HEADED VULTURE **L-F**
Cathartes melambrotus 76

Like 29-5. Glossy black. Bare head mostly yellow, crown grayish. No white on underside of wing. Flies only over forest.

4. LESSER YELLOW-HEADED VULTURE **L-O**
Cathartes burrovianus 66

Like 29-5. Dull black. Bare head orange-yellow. Crown grayish. White patch on underside of wing shows in flight. Flies only over open areas.

VULTURES: BLACK WITH NAKED HEAD. APPEAR NECKLESS.

Cathartes	*Leptodon*	*Rostrhamus*
Coragypus	*Chondrohierax*	*Helicolestes*
Elanoides	*Elanus*	*Ictinia*

5. TURKEY VULTURE **LM-FTSO**
Cathartes aura 63

RIDGELY

Black. Head bare, reddish. In flight wings held above horizontal and tail reaches much past legs. Much sailing, little flapping. Cf. 29-6.

9. HOOK-BILLED KITE **LM-FH**
Chondrohierax uncinatus 36-41

Very variable. Above mostly dark blue-gray. Below usually barred. F: Browner. Tail black, two broad bars and tip whitish.

10. BLACK-SHOULDERED (WHITE-TAILED) KITE **L-TA**
Elanus leucurus 36

Head white. Above pale gray. Large shoulder patch black. Under-parts white. Tail long, square, white.

6. BLACK VULTURE **LM-TSO**
Coragyps atratus 56

Head and neck bare, grayish black. Legs gray. In flight legs extend to end of short rounded tail. Fast flapping, little sailing. Cf. 29-5.

11. SNAIL (EVERGLADE) KITE **L-W**
Rostrhamus sociabilis 36

immature

Bill slender, very hooked, red at base. Blackish. Rump, and base of tail white. F: Brown. Broad eyebrow white. Broadly streaked below.

7. SWALLOW-TAILED KITE **LM-F**
Elanoides forficatus 56

Tail very long, deeply forked. Head and underparts white. Back, wings and tail black.

8. GRAY-HEADED KITE **L-F**
Leptodon cayanensis 43

RIDGELY

Crown and nape gray. Back blackish gray. Underparts white. Tail black with two visible broad bars and small tip white.

12. SLENDER-BILLED KITE **L-FW**
Helicolestes hamatus 33

Like 29-11 but eye pale and tail all black. (Imm: Tail barred).

13. MISSISSIPPI KITE **L-O**
*Ictinia misisippiensis** 33

Head and underparts pale gray. Back dark gray. Tail black. Legs dusky. Imm: Throat white. Under-parts white broadly streaked rufous brown.

HAWKS: ONLY TAIL BARS WHICH SHOW WHEN PERCHED ARE MENTIONED.
EAGLES: BROAD WINGS, SHORT TAIL.

Ictinia *Gampsonyx* *Morphnus* *Spizaetus*
Harpagus *Harpia* *Oroaetus*

14 PLUMBEOUS KITE **L-FT**
Ictinia plumbea 33

Head and underparts gray. Throat paler. Back dark gray. Primaries show rufous edges and extend beyond tail at rest. Tail dark gray, plain above, banded white below. Imm: Head and underparts white streaked gray.

15. RUFOUS-THIGHED KITE **L-FT**
Harpagus diodon 30

Above slaty gray. Throat whitish, black in center. Below pale gray. Thighs bright rufous. Imm: Above brown mottled white. Below white streaked brown.

16. DOUBLE-TOOTHED KITE **L-FT**
Harpagus bidentatus 30

Above slaty gray. Throat white, dark stripe down center. Below rufous barred with whitish or grayish. Tail blackish with few gray bars. Imm: Above brown mottled white. Below white streaked brown.

17 PEARL KITE **L-SO**
Gampsonyx swainsonii 23

Forehead and sides of head yellowish buff. Crown and upperparts slaty. Collar and most of underparts white. Thighs rufous.

1. HARPY EAGLE **LM-F**
Harpia harpyja 84

Divided crest blackish. Head gray, upperparts and breast black. Belly white, thighs barred black. Long tail black with three pale gray bands. Underwing boldly banded. Imm: Head whitish.

2. CRESTED EAGLE **L-F**
Morphnus guianensis 76

Prominent pointed crest black. Head and breast light gray. Upperparts black, pale gray marbling on wings. Below whitish. Long tail black with three pale grayish bands. Imm: Head, neck and underparts whitish.

3. BLACK-AND-CHESTNUT EAGLE **MH-F**
Oroaetus isidori 64

Black crest long, pointed. Head, throat and upperparts black. Below chestnut, lightly streaked black. Large pale area on wing. Imm: Above mottled. Below white.

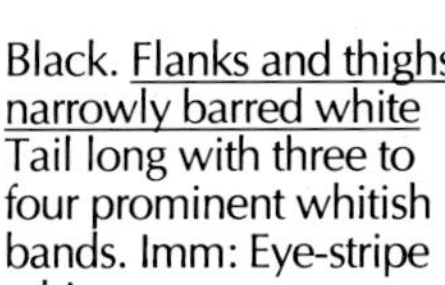

4. BLACK HAWK-EAGLE **L-F**
Spizaetus tyrannus 55

Black. Flanks and thighs narrowly barred white Tail long with three to four prominent whitish bands. Imm: Eye-stripe white.

Spizaetus	*Spizastur*
Geranoaetus	*Buteogallus*
Harpyhaliaetus	*Buteo:* Broad wings, short, wide tail.

5. ORNATE HAWK-EAGLE L-F
Spizaetus ornatus 55

Crown and long crest black. Sides of head and neck bright rufous. Upperparts blackish. Below white barred rufous on breast and black on belly. Imm: White head, neck and underparts.

6. BLACK-CHESTED BUZZARD-EAGLE LMH-SO
Geranoaetus melanoleucus 58

Dark gray. Large shoulder patch pale gray, lightly barred dusky. Breast black. Belly white. Tail blackish.

7 SOLITARY EAGLE LM-FTS
Harpyhaliaetus solitarius 58

Blackish. Lores and legs yellow. Tail black with broad white band. In flight shows no white in wing.

8. CROWNED EAGLE LM-TS
Harpyhaliaetus coronatus 59

Brownish. Prominent pointed crest. Primaries barred black and white. Underparts light brown. Tail black with one white bar.

9. BLACK-AND-WHITE HAWK-EAGLE L-FT
Spizaster melanoleucus 53

Head, neck and underparts white. Short crest, orbital area and back black. Tail black evenly barred grayish brown. Legs feathered.

10. GREAT BLACK-HAWK L-FTS
Buteogallus urubitinga 58

Black. Tail short, white at base and tip. Imm Browner above. Below buffy broadly streaked dusky. Tail narrowly barred black. Imm: Brown marked buff on head.

11. COMMON BLACK-HAWK L-TW
Buteogallus anthracinus 43

Like 31-10 but yellow facial skin more extensive. Rump black. White on base of tail less extensive. Imm: Like imm. 31-10.

12. WHITE-TAILED HAWK LM-SO
Buteo albicaudatus 58

Head blackish. Above light gray, shoulders rufous (or all dark gray). Underparts white. Tail mostly white with single broad black bar near end. Imm: Heavily blotched below. Cf. 32-15.

13. RUFOUS-TAILED HAWK L-T
Buteo ventralis 56

Above dark brown. Throat white. Below cinnamon streaked black. Thighs rufous. Tail rufous with many black bars. Dusky phase all blackish.

14 PUNA (VARIABLE) HAWK H-O
Buteo poecilochrous 52

Very like 32-15 in all phases, but larger. Only very high altitude.

Buteo: Broad wings, short wide tail.

15. RED-BACKED HAWK **LMH-OS**
Buteo polyosoma 47

Varies from little to extensive rufous on back. No rufous on shoulder.Below white, narrowly barred on belly. In all phases tail is white with broad black bar near end.

male

immature

16. ZONE-TAILED HAWK **L-TS**
Buteo albonotatus 48

Black. Tail with three pale gray bands and narrow tip. Imm: Underparts spotted white.

17. SWAINSON'S HAWK **L-O**
*Buteo swainsoni** 48

Above dark brown. Tail brown barred dusky. Underparts: Light phase: Throat white, breast reddish brown, belly buffy. Dark phase: Below all brown

18. WHITE-THROATED HAWK **MH-FTS**
Buteo albigula 42

Upperparts and face dark brown. Below white lightly streaked brown.Tail short with narrow dusky bars.

NOTE: Photographs under No. 15 are incorrectly labelled. Bird on left is immature. Bird on right is female.

19. SHORT-TAILED HAWK **LM-TW**
Buteo brachyurus 41

Upperparts and face dark brown with broad white forehead. Below white. Tail short, black, narrowly barred whitish.

20. GRAY HAWK **L-TS**
Buteo nitidus 38

Gray (lighter below) all narrowly barred dusky. Above pale gray. Below white, narrowly barred. Tail black with one or two prominent white bands. Imm: Brown above. Below streaked.

21. BROAD-WINGED HAWK **LM-T**
*Buteo platypterus** 38

Above brown, head lightly streaked whitish. Throat whitish. Below barred (imm. streaked). Tail with two or three prominent white bands. Underwing white.

22. ROADSIDE HAWK **LM-TO**
Buteo magnirostris 36

Above varies from gray to brown to almost black. Rufous patch in primaries. Breast gray. Below barred cinnamon. Tail brown with four or five gray or buff bars.

Buteo
Parabuteo
Leucopternis

23. WHITE-RUMPED HAWK LM-FT
Buteo leucorrhous 36

Black. Thighs rufous. Rump white. Tail with few white bars. In flight distinctive white underwing coverts contrast with black body and flight feathers. Imm: Blackish streaked rufous.

24. BAY-WINGED HAWK LM-TSO
Parabuteo unicinctus 46

immature

Dark brown. Shoulders and thighs rufous. Base and tip of tail white. Imm: Head and underparts streaked or mottled whitish.

25. MANTLED HAWK LM-FT
Leucopternis polionota 51

Head, neck, upper back and underparts pure white. Upper wing coverts partly white. Lower back and wings slaty gray. Tail mostly white, black band near base.

26. WHITE HAWK L-FT
Leucopternis albicollis 48

White. Lores and wings black. Crown and back more or less spotted black. Tail white with single broad black band.

27. WHITE-NECKED HAWK L-F
Leucopternis lacernulata 48

Crown and hind neck white tinged pale gray. Back dark slaty gray. Below white. Tail white with black base and narrow black band near tip.

28. GRAY-BACKED HAWK LM-FT
Leucopternis occidentalis 46

Upperparts dark gray, crown and nape streaked white. Below white.Underwing mostly white. Tail white with single broad black band.

29. BARRED HAWK LM-F
Leucopternis princeps 46

Upperparts black. Throat and breast black. Below whitish narrowly barred dusky. Tail black with one white band. Legs and base of bill yellow.

30. SLATE-COLORED HAWK L-FT
Leucopternis schistacea 38

Uniform slaty gray. Eye pale. Tail black with one white band. Legs and base of bill orange-red. Imm: Belly and underwing narrowly barred white.

31. PLUMBEOUS HAWK L-F
Leucopternis plumbea 33

Uniform dark slaty gray. Tail black with one white band. Under-wing coverts white. Legs and base of bill orange.

32. BLACK-FACED HAWK L-F
Leucopternis melanops 36

Crown and hindneck whitish narrowly streaked black. Upperparts slaty black, back spotted white. Below white. Tail black with single narrow white band. Legs and base of bill orange.

33. WHITE-BROWED HAWK L-F
Leucopternis kuhli 33

Crown and hindneck blackish narrowly streaked white. Eyebrow white. Upperparts slaty black. Below white. Tail black with single narrow white band. Legs and base of bill orange.

HARRIERS FLY LOW OVER GROUND.

Leucopternis
Heterospizias
Busarellus

Circus: Long narrow tail.
Pandion
Geranospiza

Accipiter: Short, rounded wings, long tail.

34. SEMI-PLUMBEOUS HAWK L-F
Leucopternis semiplumbea 33

Above uniform lead gray. Below white. Tail black with one (rarely two) narrow white tail band. Legs and base of bill orange.

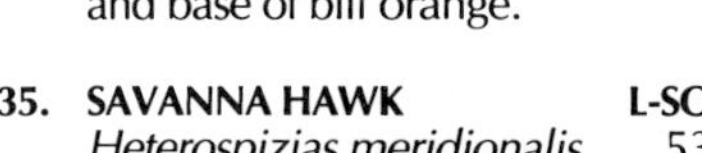

35. SAVANNA HAWK L-SO
Heterospizias meridionalis 53

Mostly rufous. Underparts rufous barred blackish. Tail black with one broad band and tip white.

36. BLACK-COLLARED HAWK L-SWO
Busarellus nigricollis 43

Head whitish. Above and below bright rufous chestnut with black patch on upper breast. Tail rufous barred black. Imm: Buffy below.

37. LONG-WINGED HARRIER L-O
Circus buffoni 51

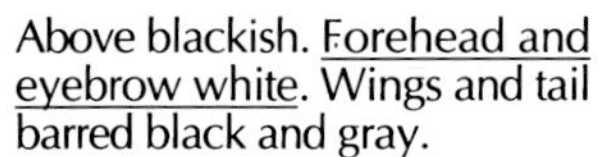

Above blackish. Forehead and eyebrow white. Wings and tail barred black and gray.

38. CINEREOUS HARRIER LMH-O
Circus cinereus 43

Head, back, wings, throat and breast pale gray. Rump white. Belly barred rufous-brown and white. F: Browner.

39. OSPREY LMH-W
*Pandion haliaetus** 48

Above dark brown. Head white with prominent dark eye stripe. Below white (f: breast streaked dusky). Wings and tail banded blackish. Wings long, usually "kinked" back showing black patch at bend of wing from below.

40. CRANE HAWK L-FSO
Geranospiza caerulescens 43

Gray. Bill dark. In e and s underparts barred with white. Tail black with two white bands. Legs long, orange-red. Wings from below have white band near end.

41. GRAY-BELLIED HAWK L-F
Accipiter poliogaster 46

Upperparts dark gray. Below gray. Tail with three pale gray bands. Imm: Face and collar rufous. Below white barred black.

CARACARAS AND FALCONS: WINGS GENERALLY MORE POINTED.
CARACARAS: FACE SKIN BARE, BRIGHTLY COLORED.

Accipter *Polyborus* *Phalcoboenus*

42 BICOLORED HAWK **LM-FT**
Accipiter bicolor 38

Crown black, above dark gray. Below gray with contrasting rufous thighs. Tail with three pale gray bars. Imm: Varies from creamy white to rufous below.

43. SEMICOLLARED HAWK **M-F**
Accipiter collaris 30

Like 35-46 but collar whitish and coarser barring on breast.

44. RUFOUS-THIGHED (SHARP-SHINNED) HAWK **LMH-FT**
Accipiter erythronemius (striatus) 28

Above dark gray. Eye pale. Below white with irregular brownish bars on breast and sides. Thighs rufous. Tail with three broad grayish bars.

45. PLAIN-BREASTED (SHARP-SHINNED) HAWK **LMH-FT**
Accipiter ventralis (striatus) 28

Above dark gray. Eye pale. Below white finely (sometimes faintly) streaked dusky on breast. Thighs rufous. Tail blackish with three broad gray bars.

46. TINY HAWK **LM-FT**
Accipiter superciliosus 23

Upperparts slaty gray. Throat white. Below narrowly barred grayish brown. Legs yellow. Tail black with three or four broad gray bars showing.

1. CRESTED CARACARA **LMH-TO**
Polyborus plancus 51

Face red. Crown black. Rump white. Crissum barred. Breast and tail white barred black. White wing-tips show in flight.

2. MOUNTAIN CARACARA **H-O**
Phalcoboenus megalopterus 46

Black. Shoulders, rump and belly white. Face orange. Imm: Pale brown.

3. CARUNCULATED CARACARA **H-O**
Phalcoboenus carunculatus 48

Like 35-2 but breast striped white.

Phalcoboenus
Daptrius
Milvago
Herpetotheres
Micrastur

4. WHITE-THROATED CARACARA **LMH-O**
Phalcoboenus albogularis 46

Like 35-2 but rump and all underparts white.

5. RED-THROATED CARACARA **L-F**
Daptrius americanus 46

Black. Ear coverts finely streaked white. Bare face and throat red. Belly and crissum white. Tail all black.

6. BLACK CARACARA **L-FTW**
Daptrius ater 43
Black. Tail white at base. Bare skin of face and throat orange-red.

7. YELLOW-HEADED CARACARA **LM-TO**
Milvago chimachima 38

Black stripe behind eye. Back brown. Tail long, buffy, barred and tipped black. Imm: Head, neck and underparts streaked dusky.

8. CHIMANGO CARACARA **L-O**
Milvago chimango 36

Brown. Feathers of upperparts pale-edged. Crown streaked dark brown. Rump white Tail white barred dusky, broad black band near end.

9. LAUGHING FALCON **LM-TO**
Herpetotheres cachinnans 46

RIDGELY

Crown white, narrowly streaked black. Nape and underparts white. Conspicuous broad black mask extends around back of head. Back brown. Rump white. Tail black, narrowly barred white.

10. COLLARED FOREST-FALCON **LM-FT**
Micrastur semitorquatus 46

Rather like 36-12 but white under eye more extensive and forming collar. Below white or tawny. Outer tail feathers with six bars.

11. BUCKLEY'S FOREST-FALCON **LM-FT**
Micrastur buckleyi 42

Above black with white cheeks and white collar. Underparts white or tawny.Tail black with three bars and tip white. Outer feather with four instead of six bars.

12. SLATY-BACKED FOREST-FALCON **L-F**
Micrastur mirandollei 36

Above dark gray. No collar. Below white. Tail black with three narrow white bars and white tip.

Micrastur
Falco
Spiziapteryx

13. BARRED FOREST-FALCON LM-F
Micrastur ruficollis 35

Upperparts, throat and breast gray (rufous in rufous phase). Rest of underparts evenly banded black and white. Tail black with three or four narrow white bands.

14. PLUMBEOUS FOREST-FALCON L-F
Micrastur plumbeus 35

Above gray. Below pale gray finely barred black. Tail black with one conspicuous white bar. Imm: Similar but with barring on sides only.

15. PEREGRINE FALCON LM-SO
*Falco peregrinus** 46

Crown, nape and broad whisker black. Back dark gray. Throat and sides of neck white. Below white barred black.

16. PALLID FALCON LM-O
Falco kreyenborgi 41
Head whitish streaked gray. Narrow whisker black. Above pale gray, bar-red blackish. Below white. Tail narrowly barred black and gray.

17. ORANGE-BREASTED FALCON LM-FT
Falco deiroleucus 36

Very like 37-20 but larger and has chestnut breast.

18. MERLIN LMF-TW
*Falco columbarius** 25

Above bluish gray (f: brown, rump gray). Tail with three or four gray bars and tip. Below whitish prominently streaked brown.

19. APLOMADO FALCON LM-OA
Falco femoralis 36

Above slaty gray White eyestripe circling crown. Prominent whisker black. Lower breast irregular black.

20. BAT FALCON L-FT
Falco rufigularis 25

Above black with whitish semi-collar. Throat white. Breast black, narrowly barred white. Thighs and crissum chestnut.

21. SPOT-WINGED FALCONET L-TOA
Spiziapteryx circumcinctus 25

Above ashy brown, streaked black Wings spotted white. Breast whitish streaked black. Rump, flanks and crissum white. Tail black, white bars on outers.

22. AMERICAN KESTREL LMH-TO
Falco sparverius 23

Crown gray. Face white with two vertical black stripes. Wings blue-gray (f. chestnut). Tail rufous tipped black.

male

female

Columba: Legs red.

1. **CHILEAN PIGEON** L-F
Columba araucana 34

Head, mantle and underparts reddish chestnut. Narrow band across hind-neck buff. Back and wings gray. Tail gray with black subterminal band.

2. **BAND-TAILED PIGEON** MH-FT
Columba fasciata 33

Bill and legs yellow. Eye-ring red. Head and underparts gray tinged purplish. Narrow band across nape white. Tail gray, paler at end.

3. **PICAZURO PIGEON** L-TSO
Columba picazuro 30

Head and underparts purplish brown, belly paler. Skin around eye dark red. Back gray. Tail gray, tipped dusky.

4. **BARE-EYED PIGEON** L-OA
Columba corensis 29

Bill yellow. Orbital area pale blue. Head and underparts light pinkish brown. Above grayish brown, nape scaled whitish. Wing coverts with white patch conspicuous both at rest and in flight.

5. **SPOT-WINGED PIGEON** LMH-TS
Columba maculosa 29

Mostly uniform grayish. Bill black. Wings brown, conspicuously and evenly spotted white. White wing band in flight.

6. **RUDDY PIGEON** LM-F
Columba subvinacea 28

Above and below reddish brown, wings darker, feathers lined dull chestnut. Short bill black. Tail rather long, bronzy brown.

7. **SCALED PIGEON** L-FT
Columba speciosa 28

Bill, legs and orbital skin red. Head and back dark purplish chestnut. Nape, neck and throat. conspicuously scaled white becoming buff on breast and belly.

8. **PALE-VENTED PIGEON** L-TS
Columba cayennensis 28

Mostly purplish brown, head and rump gray. Bill black. Throat and vent white. Tail brown, outer half contrastingly gray.

9. **PERUVIAN PIGEON** M-T
Columba oenops 28

Bill red tipped dark blue. Mostly purplish chestnut. Rump and belly dark gray, tail blackish.

10. **PLUMBEOUS PIGEON** LM-F
Columba plumbea 28

Above purplish brown. Wings darker with no chestnut linings. Underparts grayish brown. Tail bronzy brown. Cf. 38-6.

11. **SHORT-BILLED PIGEON** L-F
Columba nigrirostris 27

Back and wings bronzy brown. Wing linings dull cinnamon. Below grayish brown. Tail bronzy brown.

Columba: Legs red.
Geotrygon: Stocky build. Tail short, not tipped.

12. DUSKY PIGEON L-F
Columba goodsoni 25

Bill black. Eye white. Head, neck,nape and breast light gray. Back,wings and tail bronzy. Belly pale chestnut.

13. WHITE-THROATED QUAIL-DOVE LM-F
Geotrygon frenata 30

Crown and breast gray. Malar stripe black. Back dark brown. Throat white. Below brownish.

14. LINED QUAIL-DOVE L-F
Geotrygon linearis 29

Forehead rufous Broad gray band behind eye. Long, narrow malar stripe black. Above brown. Throat white. Below buff becoming deeper on belly.

15. RUSSET-CROWNED QUAIL-DOVE L-F
Geotrygon goldmani 29

Rather like 39-14 but crown and nape rufous.

16. SAPPHIRE QUAIL-DOVE L-F
Geotrygon saphirina 24

Forehead and malar stripe white. Crown pale gray. Mantle bronzy. Back purple. Below white.

17. RUDDY QUAIL-DOVE LM-FT
Geotrygon montana 23

female

Upperparts and tail rich rufous Malar stripe buffy. Throat white. Below brownish. F: Olive brown above.

18. VIOLACEOUS QUAIL-DOVE L-F
Geotrygon violacea 23

Forehead white. No malar stripe. Upperparts brown. Wings rufous. Breast gray. Below white. Tail purplish brown.

19. OLIVE-BACKED QUAIL-DOVE L-F
Geotrygon veraguensis 23

Forehead and malar stripe white. Above olive brown, tinged violet on nape and breast. Belly white. Tail like back.

Leptotila
Zenaida
Scardafella

20. LARGE-TAILED DOVE M-F
Leptotila megalura 28

Like 40-21 but white throat more extensive, extending to face.

21. WHITE-TIPPED DOVE LMH-TS
Leptotila verreauxi 27

Head light gray, forehead paler. Skin around eye blue. Above varies from grayish brown to brownish gray. Outer tail black, broadly tipped white.

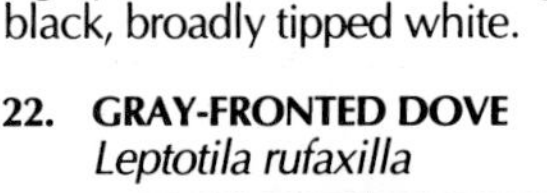

22. GRAY-FRONTED DOVE L-FT
Leptotila rufaxilla 25

Crown gray. Forehead whitish. Skin around eye red. Above dark olive brown.

23. PALLID DOVE L-F
Leptotila pallida 25

Very like 40-22 but head more whitish and back darker and redder brown. Breast somewhat whiter.

24. GRAY-HEADED DOVE LM-TS
Leptotila plumbeiceps 23

Like darker forms of 40-22 but cape and nape obviously gray.

25. TOLIMA DOVE M-T
Leptotila conoveri 23

Like 40-22 but back bronzy brown. Breast dark tawny pink. Below pale brown. Outer tail feathers with small white tip.

26. GRAY-CHESTED DOVE L-F
Leptotila cassinii 23

Like 40-22 but breast darker gray. Throat and crissum white. Tail outer feathers with small white tip.

27. OCHRE-BELLIED DOVE LM-F
Leptotila ochraceiventris 22

Like 40-21 but crown brown. Face and underparts tawny.

28. WHITE-WINGED DOVE L-SOA
Zenaida asiatica 25

Upperparts pale olive brown, wing coverts broadly edged white. Wings not spotted. Below pale sandy, belly grayer. Tail with dusky bar.

29. EARED DOVE LMH-TA
Zenaida auriculata 23

Head pinkish, crown gray. Two black lines on cheeks. Above olive brown. Wings spotted black. Underparts pinkish. Tail edged buff or white.

30. SCALED DOVE L-SOA
Scardafella squammata 20

Above sandy gray, below white, all scalloped dusky. Tail edged white.

Claravis
Metriopelia
Uropelia

Columbina

31. MAROON-CHESTED GROUND-DOVE M-TS
Claravis mondetoura 20

Rather like 41-33 but breast maroon and tail edged white.

32. PURPLE-WINGED GROUND-DOVE L-T
Claravis godefrida 20

Like 41-33 but wing coverts with three broad purple bars and outer tail feather white. F: Brown.

33. BLUE GROUND-DOVE LM-TS
Claravis pretiosa 20

Upperparts blue-gray. Crown and nape paler. Wings spotted-black Underparts pale gray becoming darker on crissum.Tail edged black.
F: Above brown, rump rufous. Tail rufous, outers black.

female

34 BLACK-WINGED GROUND-DOVE H-SO
Metriopelia melanoptera 20

Uniform light grayish brown, wings unspotted. Small bare orange patch below eye. Bend of wing white. Primaries black. Outer feathers and end of tail black.

35. GOLDEN-SPOTTED GROUND-DOVE H-O
Metriopelia aymara 18

Uniform light grayish brown Wings spotted golden bronze.No white on wings. Tail edged black.

36. BARE-FACED GROUND-DOVE H-O
Metriopelia ceciliae 18

Above grayish, spotted whitish on wings. Bare skin around eye orange. Throat white. Below buffy

37. BARE-EYED GROUND-DOVE M-O
Metriopelia morenoi 17

Above grayish brown, head and mantle grayer. Skin around eye orange. Below pale brownish gray Crissum reddish brown. Legs flesh color.

38. LONG-TAILED GROUND-DOVE LM-O
Uropelia campestris 17

Base of bill orange. Upperparts brown, forecrown gray. Eye-ring yellow. Wing coverts with purple spots bordered behind by white. Below whitish, gray on breast. Tail broadly edged white.

39. RUDDY GROUND-DOVE LM-SOA
Columbina talpacoti 17

Rufous. Head gray. Wing coverts spotted black. Tail edged black, tipped cinnamon.

Columbina
Anodorhynchus
Ara: Bare facial skin whitish. Tail very long.

40. PICUI GROUND-DOVE L-TO
Columbina picui 17

Upperparts grayish brown. Wing coverts with a few short purple streaks, some black spots and prominent white lower edging. Underparts whitish. Tail like back, outer feathers white.

41. CROAKING GROUND-DOVE L-SOA
Columbina cruziana 17

Bill bright yellow tipped black. Wings grayish brown with dark brown stripe on shoulder. Below pinkish.

42. SCALY (COMMON) GROUND-DOVE L-OA
Columbina passerina 15

Bill pink tipped black. Head, neck and breast scaled black and whitish. Above grayish. Wings spotted black. Belly whitish. Tail gray or black, outers tipped white.

43. PLAIN-BREASTED GROUND-DOVE L-SO
Columbina minuta 14

Head and nape blue gray. Back pale grayish brown. Wings spotted steel blue. Below plain pinkish brown without spotting.

44. BLUE-EYED GROUND-DOVE L-SO
Columbina cyanopis 14

Head chestnut. Back olive brown, rump rufous. Throat white. Breast and sides ochraceous. Belly buff. Crissum white.

1. HYACINTH MACAW L-FT
Anodorhynchus hyacinthinus 100

Uniform deep blue. Bare skin around eye and at base of lower bill yellow.

2. RED-AND-GREEN MACAW L-F
Ara chloroptera 82

Like 43-4 but patch on wings green instead of yellow. Bare face lined red.

3. GREAT GREEN MACAW L-F
Ara ambigua 82

Very like 43-5 but tail paler blue.

Ara: Bare facial skin whitish. Tail very long, pointed.

4. SCARLET MACAW L-FT
Ara macao 80

Mostly scarlet. Wings blue with large yellow patch. Rump light blue. Tail red tipped blue. Bare face white.

5. MILITARY MACAW L-FT
Ara militaris 65

Tail in molt

Green. Rump and primaries blue. Tail blue, red in center. Bare face white lined red.

6. BLUE-AND-YELLOW MACAW L-FT
Ara ararauna 80

Upperparts blue. Bare face white sharply lined black. Below all bright yellow.

7. RED-FRONTED MACAW M-F
Ara rubrogenys 56

Mostly pale green. Crown, ear coverts, shoulders and thighs orange. Tail red and blue.

8. RED-BELLIED MACAW L-TO
Ara manilata 48

Green. Forecrown and cheeks blue. Underwing yellowish. Center of belly red. Rather like 43-10 but rump not red. Usually in palms.

9. CHESTNUT-FRONTED MACAW L-F
Ara severa 46

Green. Forehead chestnut. Crown bluish green. Underside of wings and tail dull red. Base of tail green.

10. BLUE-WINGED MACAW L-FT
Ara maracana 48

Green. Head tinged bluish, forehead and rump orange red and central tail feathers red at base. Wings blue, but underwing green (unlike 43-9).

11. GOLDEN-COLLARED MACAW L-T
Ara auricollis 36

Green. Crown and cheeks black. Collar on hindneck golden yellow. Flight feathers blue.

Cyanopsitta	*Ognorhynchus*	*Nandayus*
Ara: Bare facial skin whitish	*Leptosittaca*	*Myiopsitta*
Tail very long, pointed.	*Enicognathus*	*Aratinga*

12. LITTLE BLUE MACAW L-T
Cyanopsitta spixii 50

Blue, upperparts darker. Bare facial skin black. Head dusty bluish gray.

13. BLUE-HEADED MACAW L-FT
Cyanopsitta spixiii 38

Like 43-10 but no red on forehead, back or belly

14. RED-SHOULDERED MACAW L-TS
Ara nobilis 33

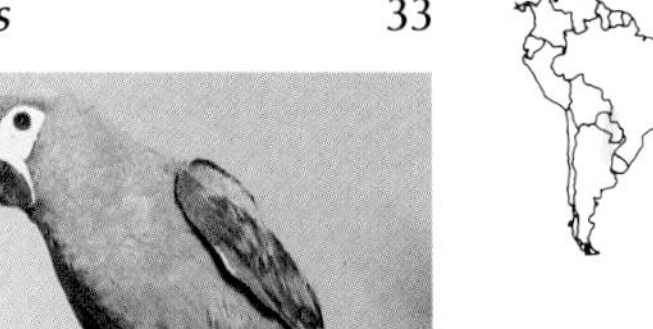

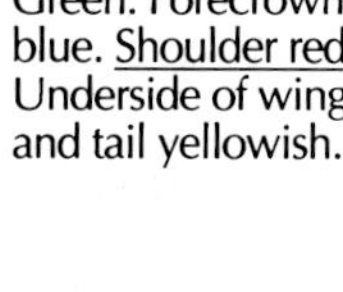

Green. Forecrown blue. Shoulder red. Underside of wing and tail yellowish.

15. BURROWING PARROT LMH-O
Cyanoliseus patagonus 43

Above olive. Rumps and flanks yellow in some races. Breast brownish. Belly red in center. Tail olive.

16. YELLOW-EARED PARROT H-F
Ognorhynchus icterotis 38

Forehead and face bright yellow. Above dark green. Below yellowish green. Underside of tail reddish.

17. GOLDEN-PLUMED PARROT L-F
Eleptosittaca branickii 36

Mostly green. Forehead orange. Malar stripe dull yellow. Center of belly dull orange.

18. SLENDER-BILLED PARAKEET L-F
Enicognathus fleptorhynchus 38

Green. Red lores extend back to encircle eyes. Bill very straight and slender. Tail red.

19. AUSTRAL PARAKEET L-FT
Enicognathus ferrugineus 33

Green, scaled black. Forehead and face red. Tail and center of belly red.

20. BLACK-HOODED PARAKEET L-T
Nandayus nenday 36

Green, rump and belly paler. Head black. Thighs red.

21. MONK PARAKEET LM-TO
Myiopsitta monachus 26

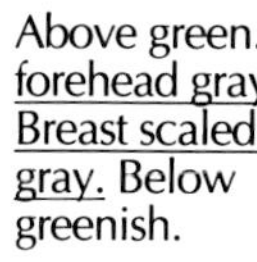

Above green. forehead gray. Breast scaled gray. Below greenish.

22. BLUE-CROWNED PARAKEET LM-T
Aratinga acuticauda 36

Green, forecrown tinged blue. Bill pinkish. Tail red on outer feathers.

23. GOLDEN PARAKEET L-F
Aratinga guarouba 36

Golden yellow. Primaries green.

Aratinga

24. SCARLET-FRONTED PARAKEET **L-TSO**
Aratinga wagleri 36

Green. Face, fore-crown (and bend of wing in s) red. A few red spots on neck or under-parts. Underwing coverts green.

25. MITRED PARAKEET **L-F**
Aratinga mitrata 36

Green. Only forehead and face red.

26. WHITE-EYED PARAKEET **L-TO**
Aratinga leucophthalmus 33

Green. Shoulders red. More or less red spotting on neck. Prominent eye-ring white.

27. RED-MASKED PARAKEET **L-SO**
Aratinga erythrogenys 30

Green. Forehead, face and cheeks red. Underwing coverts red and green.

28. SUN PARAKEET **L-T**
Aratinga solstitialis 30

Head yellow, face strongly tinged orange. Back yellow. Wings more or less yellow or green. Primaries blue. Tail olive tipped blue.

29. JANDAYA PARAKEET **L-T**
Aratinga (solstitialis) jandaya 30

Head, neck and throat yellow, face orange. Above green (no yellow on back or wings) Belly red. Tail olive.

30. FLAME-CAPPED PARAKEET **L-FT**
Aratinga (solstitialis) auricapilla 30

Forehead flaming red. Forecrown red spotted yellow. Above green, primaries blue. Throat and breast green. Center of belly dull red. Tail olive.

31. PEACH-FRONTED PARAKEET **L-TS**
Aratinga aurea 27

Rather like 45-32 but forecrown peach color. Hindcrown blue.

32. BROWN-THROATED PARAKEET **L-SO**
Aratinga pertinax 25

Green. Crown blue to greenish. Cheeks, throat and breast brownish. Below yellowish green.

Aratinga
Pyrrhura: Breast usually scaled.

33. DUSKY-HEADED PARAKEET **L-FT**
Aratinga weddellii 25

Green, belly somewhat yellower. Head bluish gray. Tail partly blue.

34. CACTUS PARAKEET **L-TS**
Aratinga cactorum 25

Like 45-32 but belly dull orange.

35. BLUE-BREASTED (OCHRE-MARKED) PARAKEET **L-F**
Pyrrhura cruentata 25

Green. Crown and nape brown Collar on hindneck blue. Behind ear coverts buff. Shoulder, rump and belly red. Breast blue.

36. REDDISH-BELLIED PARAKEET **LM-T**
Pyrrhura frontalis 25

Mostly green. Ear coverts gray Breast brown scaled whitish Narrow forehead maroon. Center of belly red. Tail olive above, reddish below.

37. GREEN-CHEEKED PARAKEET **LM-FT**
Pyrrhura molinae 25

Above green. Crown and nape dull brown. Green patch below eye. Belly red. Tail reddish.

38. BLACK-CAPPED (ROCK) PARAKEET **L-FT**
Pyrrhura rupicola 25

Above green. Crown and nape blackish. Patch below eye green. Breast blackish scaled buff. Below green.

39. PEARLY PARAKEET **L-F**
Pyrrhura perlata 23

Crown brown. Nape scaled white. Ear spot brownish. Back and patch below eye green. Belly green. Tail reddish above, black below.

40. BLOOD-EARED PARAKEET **M-F**
Pyrrhura hoematotis 23

Green, crown brownish. Dull red patch back of eye. Breast brownish. Back green. Below green scaled dusky. Tail reddish.

41. SANTA MARTA PARAKEET **M-FT**
Pyrrhura viridicata 23

Green. Shoulder orange. Ear patch, bill, tail and narrow forehead red. Some fiery orange on wing coverts. Limited range.

42. MAROON-TAILED PARAKEET **LM-F**
Pyrrhura melanura 23

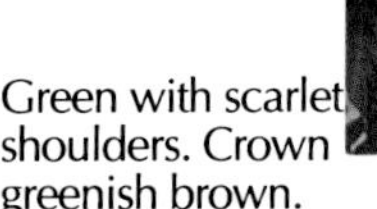

Green with scarlet shoulders. Crown greenish brown. Breast scaled whitish. Tail dark red.

Pyrrhura: Breast usually scaled.
Bolborhynchus: Tail short, pointed.

43. FIERY-SHOULDERED PARAKEET **LM-FT**
Pyrrhura egregia 23

Very like 46-42 but shoulders orange and yellow.

44. WHITE-NECKED (BREASTED) PARAKEET **LM-FT**
Pyrrhura albipectus 23

Green. Crown brown. Ear coverts orange. Broad collar and throat white. Breast yellowish. Tail red dish.

45. FLAME-WINGED PARAKEET **M-F**
Pyrrhura calliptera 23

Green. Crown brown. Ear patch maroon. Collar and breast brown scaled paler. Shoulder orange. Tail maroon.

46. ROSE-CROWNED (HEADED) PARAKEET **M-F**
Pyrrhura rhodocephala 23

Green. Crown rosy red. Ear coverts maroon. Primary coverts white. Tail reddish.

47. BLAZE-WINGED PARAKEET **L-FT**
Pyrrhura devillei 23

Green. Crown and nape brown. Below olive, scaled buff. Small red patch on belly. Tail green. Only species with red crissum and green tail.

48. CRIMSON-BELLIED PARAKEET **L-F**
Pyrrhura rhodogaster 21

Crown, nape and breast dark brown scaled pale. Forehead blue. Belly bright red. Tail dark reddish above, blackish below.

49. PAINTED PARAKEET **L-FT**
Pyrrhura picta 20

Forecrown blue or red. Shoulder red (green in some races). Breast scaling U-shaped.

50. MAROON-FACED PARAKEET **MH-T**
Pyrrhura leucotis 18

Very like illustrated race of 47-49 but breast feathers edged with pale straight bars (not V- or U-shaped).

51. GRAY-HOODED PARAKEET **MH-T**
Bolborhynchus aymara 21

Head brown. Above green. Throat gray becoming green on belly.

52. MOUNTAIN PARAKEET **LMH-SO**
Bolborhynchus aurifrons 18

Bright green. Forehead and throat yellow in n. Wings blue.

53. RUFOUS-FRONTED PARAKEET **H-S**
Bolborhynchus ferrugineifrons 18

Green. Forehead and chin dull orange. Below green tinged olive.

54. BARRED PARAKEET **M-F**
Bolborhynchus lineola 15

Mostly green, feathers above narrowly barred black. Shoulders black.

55. ANDEAN PARAKEET **H-S**
Bolborhynchus orbygnesius 15

All dark green except shaded olive below.

Brotogeris jugularis

56. PLAIN PARAKEET **L-FT**
Brotogeris tirica 23

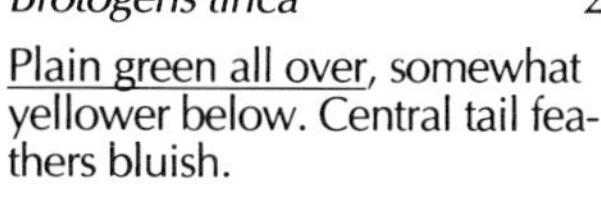

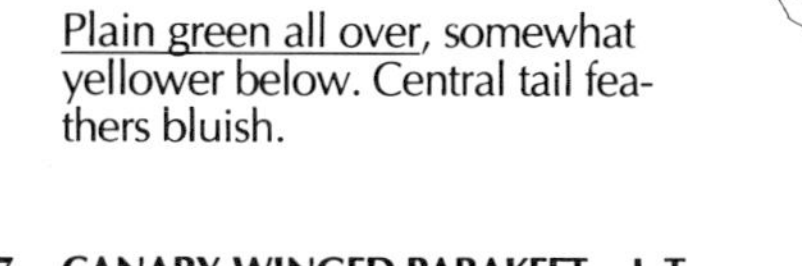

Plain green all over, somewhat yellower below. Central tail feathers bluish.

57. CANARY-WINGED PARAKEET **L-T**
Brotogeris versicolurus 20

Green. Large yellow patch (also white patch in some races) in wing coverts.

58. GRAY-CHEEKED PARAKEET **L-FSA**
Brotogerls pyrrhopterus 19

Green. Crown pale blue. Cheeks and throat whitish. Shoulder orange.

59. COBALT-WINGED PARAKEET **L-FT**
Brotogeris cyanoptera 18

Green. Forehead yellowish, small chin spot orange. Wings dark blue. Bend of wing yellow.

60. ORANGE-CHINNED PARAKEET **L-FT**
Brotogeris jugularis 15

Green. Crown all green. Small chin spot orange. Wing coverts tinged brown in w.

61. GOLDEN-WINGED PARAKEET **L-FT**
Brotogeris chrysopterus 15

Like 48-59 but primary coverts bright orange.

62. TUI PARAKEET **L-TW**
Brotogeris sanctithomae 14

Like 48-59 but has no orange chin spot and has more yellow on forecrown.

Amazona: Mostly green with colorful face patterns. Plumage often scaly.

1. MEALY PARROT L-F
Amazona farinosa 38

Green with whitish bloom. Center of crown yellow or red or all green. Conspicuous large, bare eye-ring. Tail dark green at base, end half light green.

2. FESTIVE PARROT L-FT
Amazona festiva 36

Green. Forehead dark red. No color patch on wing. Only species with red rump. Tail. tipped dusky.

3. TURQUOISE-FRONTED PARROT L-TS
Amazona aestiva 36

Green, scaled blackish. Forehead light blue. Face yellow. Shoulders red and yellow. Speculum red.

4. BLUE-CHEEKED PARROT L-F
Amazona brasiliensis 33

Green, cheeks blue. Variable crown red or yellow. Speculum red or orange.

5. VINACEOUS-BREASTED PARROT L-F
Amazona vinacea 33

Above green scaled dusky. Forehead red. Breast plum color Throat and belly green. Crissum yellowish green.

6. YELLOW-CROWNED (-HEADED) PARROT L-FTO
Amazona ochrocephala 33

Green. Crown yellow. Shoulder and speculum red.

7. RED-LORED PARROT L-FT
Amazona autumnalis 30

Green. Forehead and speculum red. Crown bluish.

Amazona
Deroptyus
Pionus

8. RED-SPECTACLED PARROT L-FT
Amazona pretrei 30

Green, feathers edged black. Forecrown, shoulders and thighs red Tail green tipped yellowish.

9. ALDER PARROT LM-FT
Amazona tucumana 30

Green, feathers edged black. Forehead and speculum red. Shoulder not red.

10. YELLOW-SHOULDERED PARROT L-TSA
Amazona barbadensis 30

Green, feathers edged black. Head, face and shoulder yellow. Speculum red.

11. ORANGE-WINGED PARROT L-FT
Amazona amazonica 30

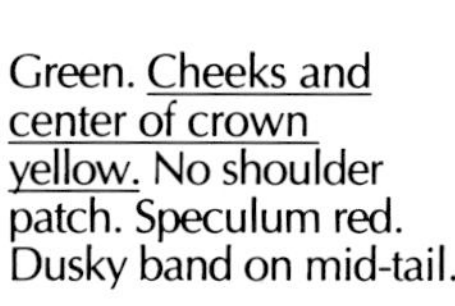

Green. Cheeks and center of crown yellow. No shoulder patch. Speculum red. Dusky band on mid-tail.

12. SCALY-NAPED PARROT MH-F
Amazona mercenaria 30

Green, nape and breast scaled. Edge of wing red. Tail with variable amount of red, and yellowish tip.

13. YELLOW-FACED PARROT L-F
Amazona xanthops 25

Mainly green. Crown and face yellow tinged reddish on ear coverts. Below light green lightly barred darker green. Yellow band across belly.

14. RED-FAN PARROT L-F
Deroptyus accipitrinus 33

Forehead white Back green. Nape and underparts dark red, feathers edged blue. Tail dark, very long.

15. BLUE-HEADED PARROT L-FT
Pionus menstruus 25

Head, neck and breast blue. Dusky ear patch Back and belly green. Crissum red. Tail green and red.

Pionus: Crissum red
Hapalopsittaca
Graydidascalus
Pionopsitta

16. SCALY-HEADED PARROT L-FT
Pionus maximiliani 28

Dull green. Crown dusky. Nape scaly Throat blue. Bill black and yellow.

17. RED-BILLED PARROT LM-FT
Pionus sordidus 28

Rather like 51-16 but bill all red.

18. PLUM-CROWNED (SPECKLED-FACED) PARROT M-F
Pionus tumultuosus 25

Dark green. Crown plum color. Face speckled. Breast purplish. Bill olive-yellow.

19. WHITE-CAPPED PARROT MH-F
Pionus seniloides 25

Like 51-18 but crown whitish and below browner.

20. BRONZE-WINGED PARROT LM-F
Pionus chalcopterus 25

A very dark parrot. Upperparts dark green. Wing coverts bronzy brown, Large throat patch whitish. Below dark brown. Tail dark blue.

21. DUSKY PARROT L-F
Pionus fuscus 23

Above dark brown Head, neck and throat speckled white. Below brown.

22. BLACK-EARED PARROT MH-F
Hapalopsittaca melanotis 23

Head and neck pale blue, mixed with green on crown and nape. Bright green around eye. Wings mostly black. Tail broadly tipped blue.

23. RUSTY-FACED PARROT MH-F
Hapalopsittaca amazonina 20

Face and shoulders red. Above green. Breast light brown. Belly yellowish green. Tail tipped blue.

24. SHORT-TAILED PARROT L-T
Graydidascalus brachyurus 23

Mostly pale green. Wing covert feathers edged yellowish. Tail pale yellowish green, short.

25. ORANGE-CHEEKED PARROT L-F
Pionopsitta barrabandi 23

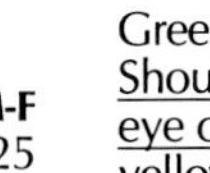

Green. Head black. Shoulder and below eye orange. Breast yellowish olive.

Gypopsitta
Pionopsitta
Triclaria

Pionites
Touit: Tail short. square.

26. VULTURINE PARROT L-F
Gypopsitta vulturina 21

Head bare, mostly black. Chin and shoulders orange. Back green.

27. BROWN-HOODED PARROT LM-T
Pionopsitta haematotis 21

Green. Head brown. Throat and semi-collar rose color. Below brownish olive.

28. SAFFRON-HEADED PARROT L-F
Pionopsitta pyrilia 21

Head and shoulders orange yellow. Above and belly green. Bend of wing red. Breast brownish.

29. PILEATED (RED-CAPPED) PARROT L-F
Pionopsitta pileata 20

Green. Cap and face red (f. only ear coverts red). Shoulder and tail outers blue.

30. CAICA PARROT L-F
Pionopsitta caica 20

Green. Head blackish. Nape orange. Throat and breast brownish olive. Outer tail feathers yellow, tipped blue.

31. BLUE-BELLIED PARROT LM-F
Triclaria malachitacea 20

Mossy green. Belly violet blue (f. all green).

32. BLACK-HEADED PARROT L-FT
Pionites melanocephala 20

Cap black. Broad collar yellow. Above green. Breast and belly white. Thighs and crissum orange.

33. WHITE-BELLIED PARROT L-FT
Pionites leucogaster 20

Back green. Crown and nape light orange. Cheeks and throat light yellow. Below white. Flanks, thighs and tail green (yellow in w).

34. RED-WINGED PARROTLET L-F
Touit dilectissima 18

Green. Forecrown blue. Around eye red. Wing coverts scarlet. Chin and throat yellow. Tail sides yellow, tip black.

35. SAPPHIRE-RUMPED PARROTLET L-F
Touit purpurata 15

Crown and nape brown. Back green. Rump blue. Below lighter green, sides yellow. Tail green, sides red.

36. SPOT-WINGED PARROTLET LM-F
Touit stictoptera 15

Green. Yellowish around eye. Wing coverts brownish, spotted white (f. all green). Tail green.

Touit : Tail short.
Nannopsittaca
Forpus: Sparrow-size. Tail short.

37. LILAC-TAILED PARROTLET L-F
Touit batavica 14

Back and shoulders black. Prominent wing coverts yellow. Throat and belly bright green Breast blue. Tail violet.

38. BROWN-BACKED (BLACK-EARED) PARROTLET M-F
Touit melanonota 14

Above dark brown. Below green, sides bluish. Tail green in center, sides red, black on end.

39. SCARLET-SHOULDERED PARROTLET L-F
Touit huetii 14

Green. Crown and nape brown. Shoulders red. Below green. Tail green, red (f. yellow) at sides.

40. GOLDEN-TAILED PARROTLET L-F
Touit surda 14

Green. Yellowish before eye. Inner wing coverts brownish. Tail green, outers golden, tipped black.

41. TEPUI PARROTLET M-F
Nannopsittaca panychlora 13

Uniform green. Around eye yellowish. Tail short, square.

42. YELLOW-FACED PARROTLET LM-SA
Forpus xanthops 14

Green. Crown and face yellow. Back gray. Wing coverts and rump blue.

43. GREEN-RUMPED PARROTLET L-TS
Forpus passerinus 11

Green. Bill pale. Wing coverts blue (f. no blue). Rump bright green.

44. BLUE-WINGED PARROTLET L-TS
Forpus xanthopterygius 11

Very like 53-43 but rump and wing coverts blue (f. no blue).

45. SPECTACLED PARROTLET L-TS
Forpus conspicillatus 11

Green. Wing coverts, rump and area around eye blue (f. little or no blue). Bill ivory.

46. DUSKY-BILLED PARROTLET L-T
Forpus sclateri 11

Very like 53-43 but billdusky above instead of pale. F: rump blue.

47. PACIFIC PARROTLET L-TSA
Forpus coelestis 11

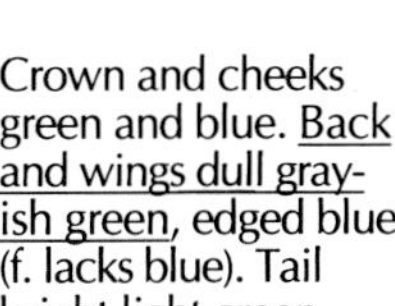

Crown and cheeks green and blue. Back and wings dull grayish green, edged blue (f. lacks blue). Tail bright light green.

CUCKOOS: SLENDER SHAPE, SLIGHTLY CURVED BILL, LONG TAIL.

Neomorphus: Terrestrial. Tail long. *Guira* *Piaya*
Crotophaga *Dromococcyx*

1. RUFOUS-VENTED GROUND-CUCKOO **L-FT**
Neomorphus geoffroyi 43

Crest dark blue. Head, neck, throat and breast brownish, feathers pale-edged. Back bronzy green to purple. Crissum chestnut. Includes Scaled Ground-Cuckoo, now considered conspecific.

2. BANDED GROUND-CUCKOO **L-F**
Neomorphus radiolosus 43

Long flat crest, hindneck and nape blue-black. Mantle barred black and buff. Back maroon. Rump green. Below banded black and buff.

3. RUFOUS-WINGED GROUND-CUCKOO **L-F**
Neomorphus rufipennis 43

Crest, head, neck and breast blackish. Back and tail purplish. Belly brown. Skin around eye red.

4. RED-BILLED GROUND-CUCKOO **L-F**
Neomorphus pucheranii 43

Upperparts dark metallic olive. Throat and breast ashy. Narrow black breast band. Belly white Flanks brown. Face bare, red.

5. GREATER ANI **L-TW**
Crotophaga major 38

All black. Eye white. Bill with high ridge.

6. GROOVE-BILLED ANI **L-SOA**
Crotophaga sulcirostris 28

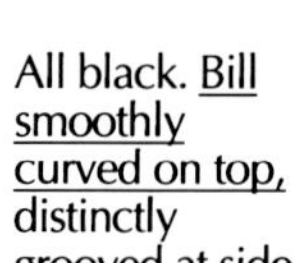

All black. Bill smoothly curved on top, distinctly grooved at sides (hard to see in field). Tail long, ragged-looking.

7. SMOOTH-BILLED ANI **L-TSO**
Crotophaga ani 30

Black, feathers edged paler. High, smooth thin ridge on bill producing "humped" look. Tail long, ragged-looking.

8. GUIRA CUCKOO **L-TO**
Guira guira 36

Crown and shaggy crest rufous. Above dark brown streaked white. Tail long, dark, broadly tipped white.

9. PHEASANT CUCKOO **L-FT**
Dromococcyx phasianellus 33

Crown and crest rufous. Above dark brown, wing coverts scaled buff. Throat and breast buff, spotted dusky. Belly white. Tail long and very broad.

10. PAVONINE CUCKOO **L-F**
Dromococcyx pavoninus 23

Crown and crest rufous. Above blackish, wing coverts scaled buff. Throat and breast uniform buffy brown. Belly white.

11. SQUIRREL CUCKOO **LM-T**
Piaya cayana 38

Very like 55-14 but much larger and breast and belly paler. Eye-ring red (yellow w of Andes). Cf. 55-14.

Piaya
Coccyzus
Tapera

12. BLACK-BELLIED CUCKOO L-F
Piaya melanogaster 33

Bill red, Crown gray. Loral spot yellow. Above and below chestnut. Belly blackish.

13. PEARLY-BREASTED CUCKOO L-TS
Coccyzus euleri 23

Very like 55-17 but no rufous in wings. Outer tail feathers blackish, broadly tipped white.

14. LITTLE CUCKOO L-T
Piaya minuta 23

Bill yellow. Eye-ring red Upperparts chestnut. Throat and breast chestnut becoming grayish olive on belly and crissum. Tail long broadly tipped white. Cf. 54-11.

15. STRIPED CUCKOO LM-TS
Tapera naevia 25

Rufous crest and brown back both streaked black. Throat and breast buffy. Narrow whisker black. Belly white.

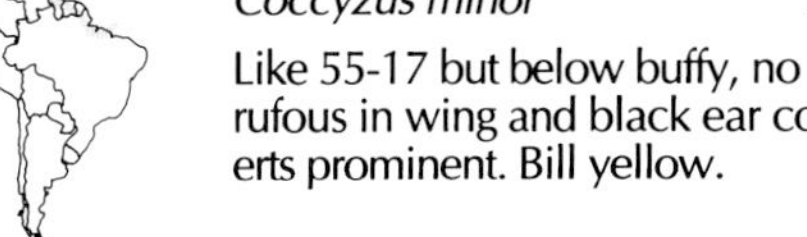

16. MANGROVE CUCKOO L-TS
Coccyzus minor 28

Like 55-17 but below buffy, no rufous in wing and black ear coverts prominent. Bill yellow.

17. YELLOW-BILLED CUCKOO LM-T
*Coccyzus americanus** 25

Bill lower yellow, upper black. Above brown. Below white. Prominent rufous in wings shows in flight. Tail feathers broadly tipped white.

18. BLACK-BILLED CUCKOO L-TS
*Coccyzus erythropthalmus** 25

Bill all black. Eye-ring red. Above brown. Undertail gray, feathers tipped white.

19. ASH-COLORED CUCKOO L-TS
Coccyzus cinereus 23

Above brown. Eye red. Throat and breast gray-brown. Belly white. Tail with narrow black bar and white tip.

20. GRAY-CAPPED CUCKOO L-S
Coccyzus lansbergi 23

Bill black. Crown gray. Above rufous brown. Below deep buff. Tail black, outer feathers tipped white.

MANY OWLS OCCUR IN BROWN AND RUFOUS PHASES. NO EAR TUFTS UNLESS MENTIONED.

Coccyzus	*Pulsatrix*	*Lophostrix*	*Ciccaba*
Bubo	*Asio*	*Tyto*	

21. DARK-BILLED CUCKOO L-S
Coccyzus melacoryphus 22

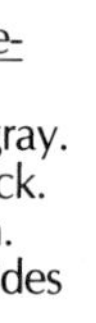

Bill black. Eye-ring yellow. Crown dark gray. Eye stripe black. Above brown. Below buff, sides of breast gray.

22. DWARF CUCKOO L-TS
Coccyzus pumilus 20

Bill black. Crown gray. Back browner. Throat and breast rufous. Below white.

1. GREAT HORNED OWL L-TO
Bubo virginianus 46

Above brown and white. Large throat patch white. Below barred dusky and whitish. Conspicuous ear tufts.

2. SPECTACLED OWL L-TO
Pulsatrix perspicillata 41

Above uniform dark brown. Face brown outlined white. Below buffy with broad brown breast band. Eye yellow

RIDGELY

3. TAWNY-BROWED OWL L-F
Pulsatrix koeniswaldiana 36

Like 56-2 but lines around face buffy instead of white.

4. BAND-BELLIED OWL L-F
Pulsatrix melanota 38

Like 56-2 but breast band broader and belly white, heavily barred brown.

5. STYGIAN OWL LMH-FT
Asio stygius 38

Above dark brown with few buff spots. Below mottled buff and dark brown. Ear tufts close together.

6. SHORT-EARED OWL LMH-FTO
*Asio flammeus** 38

Above dark brown lightly spotted buff. Below buff streaked brown. Small ear tufts.

7. CRESTED OWL L-F
Lophostrix cristata 36

Prominent long white ear tufts, usually laid flat. Above dark brown. Large white spots on wings. Below buff, faintly vermiculated brownish.

8. BARN OWL LMH-O
Tyto alba 36

Face white. Above brown dotted white. Underparts white to buff, dotted dusky. Tail barred buff and black.

9. BLACK-AND-WHITE OWL LM-FT
Ciccaba nigrolineata 36

Above uniform blackish with few white bars on nape. Below white evenly barred black.

Ciccaba
Strix: No ear tufts.
Rhinoptynx

Otus: Small ear tufts.

10. BLACK-BANDED OWL L-F
Ciccaba huhula 36

Black, narrowly banded whitish. Tail tipped white.

11. RUFOUS-BANDED OWL MH-F
Ciccaba albitarsus 36

Above black banded rufous. Face brown, outlined white. Below brown boldly spotted white. Tail barred.

12. MOTTLED OWL LM-FT
Ciccaba virgata 30

Above brown or reddish brown barred paler. Face brown outlined whitish. Breast brown vermiculated whitish. Below white streaked brown.

13. RUSTY-BARRED OWL LM-F
Strix hylophila 36

Above black banded rufous. Face brown lined buff. Breast barred brown and rufous. Belly white streaked brown.

14. RUFOUS-LEGGED OWL LM-FT
Strix rufipes 36

Dark brown barred white, orange bases of feathers showing through. Below white barred black. Tail blackish with 6-7 paler bars

15. STRIPED OWL L-SO
Rhinoptynx clamator 36

Buff streaked black. Face white outlined in black. Ear tufts prominent. Below white strongly streaked black.

16. WHITE-THROATED SCREECH-OWL MH-F
Otus albogularis 27

Upperparts and breast dark brown. Throat extensively white. Belly buff. Ear tufts very small.

17. RUFESCENT SCREECH-OWL M-F
Otus ingens 25

Like 57-20 but eye brown, above browner. Ear tufts and partly concealed collar whitish. Below buffy prominently streaked brown.

18. BARE-SHANKED SCREECH-OWL M-F
Otus clarkii 23

Like 57-20 but face cinnamon, rim indistinct. Breast spotted white.

19. LONG-TUFTED SCREECH-OWL L-F
Otus atricapillus 23

Very like 57-20 with ear tufts longer.

20. TROPICAL SCREECH-OWL LM-FTO
Otus choliba 22

Above brown streaked black and spotted buff. White stripe shows at sides of back. Below white streaked black. Thighs rufous. Ear tufts. Eye yellow.

21. WEST PERUVIAN SCREECH-OWL LMH-T
Otus roboratus 23

Very like 57-20 but center of belly white.

Otus: Small ear tufts.
Speotyto
Aegolius
Glaucidium: False "eyes" in back of head.
Steatornis: Stays in caves in daytime.
Nyctibius: Night flying.

22. TAWNY-BELLIED SCREECH-OWL **L-F**
Otus watsonii 20

Dark. Collar buffy. Below tawny streaked black. Ear tufts long.

23. VERMICULATED SCREECH-OWL **LM-F**
Otus guatemalae 18

Like 57-20 but below pale brown vermiculated but lacking streaks.

24. BURROWING OWL **LMH-OA**
Speotyto cunicularia 20

Active in daytime. Above brown spotted white. Below white sparsely barred brown. On or near ground.

25. BUFF-FRONTED OWL **MH-FT**
Aegolius harrisii 20

Above dark brown. Wings and tail spotted white. Face, collar and entire underparts rich buff.

26. AUSTRAL PYGMY-OWL **L-WS**
Glaucidium nanum 18

Like 58-29 but numerous white spots on wing coverts. Tail narrowly barred.

27. LEAST PYGMY-OWL **L-FT**
Glaucidium minutissimum 14

Rather like 58-29 but top of head brown minutely dotted white.

28. FERRUGINOUS PYGMY-OWL **LM-TS**
Glaucidium brasilianum 15

Crown with small buff streaks (not spots). Back like 58-29.

rufous phase

brown phase

29. ANDEAN PYGMY-OWL **MH-TS**
Glaucidium jardinii 15

Brown. Crown with small buff spots (not streaks). Back brown.

1. OILBIRD **LM-F**
Steatornis caripensis 43

Brown, spotted white. Tail brown narrowly barred dusky. Eye red. In cave during day.

2. GREAT POTOO **L-FT**
Nyctibius grandis 46

Like gray phase of 59-4 but tail appears whitish with numerous dusky bars.

Nyctibius: Night flying.
Uropsalis
Macropsalis
Hydropsalis
Caprimulgus

3. LONG-TAILED POTOO L-FO
Nyctibius aethereus 43

Like 59-4 but somewhat more rufous brown. Tail long, feathers pointed.

4. COMMON POTOO L-FT
Nyctibius griseus 36

Grayish brown, marbled black and white. Center of breast with broad black streaks. Two color phases – gray or brown. Voice melancholy, descending.

5. WHITE-WINGED POTOO M-F
Nyctibius leucopterus 23

Like dark brown phase of 59-4 but inner wing coverts white.

6. RUFOUS POTOO L-F
Nyctibius bracteatus 20

Rather like 59-4 in shape, but mostly rufous in color. Tail black, tipped white.

7. LYRE-TAILED NIGHTJAR M-FT
Uropsalis lyra 25+35

Like 59-11 but has very long extended tail feathers black, tipped white. Collar rufous.

8. SWALLOW-TAILED NIGHTJAR H-FT
Uropsalis segmentata 32+20

Like 59-11 but darker and outer tail feathers very long, black, notched. No collar. F: Tail normal.

9. LONG-TRAINED NIGHTJAR L-FT
Macropsalis creagra 25+27

Like 59-11 but darker and outer tail feathers very long, mostly white on inner web (f. tail normal). Collar pale rufous.

10. SCISSOR-TAILED NIGHTJAR LM-T
Hydropsalis brasiliana 25+17

Like 59-11 but darker and outer tail feathers very long broadly tipped white. (F: Tail forked, much shorter than m.) Collar rufous.

11. LADDER-TAILED NIGHTJAR L-FO
Hydropsalis climacocerca 25

Tail rather long, outer feathers with broad white tips. (f: lacking white tips). No collar.

12. CHUCK-WILLS-WIDOW LM-FT
*Caprimulgus carolinensis** 25

Like 60-22 but no white in wing, primaries black barred rufous. Three outer tail feathers mostly white (f. no white). Cf. 60-13.

13. RUFOUS NIGHTJAR L-T
Caprimulgus rufus 25

Like 60-22 but not white in wing, primaries black barred rufous. Three outer tail feathers with large white patch (f. no white).

Caprimulgus
Eleothreptus

14. SILKY-TAILED NIGHTJAR **L-T**
Caprimulgus sericocaudatus 25

Like 60-22 but band across throat buff. Primaries blackish notched rufous on outer web. Three outer tail feathers with wide diagonal white (f. rufous) ends.

15. BAND-WINGED NIGHTJAR **MH-TSO**
Caprimulgus longirostris 20

female

Four outermost primaries with broad white band. Narrow throat band white.

16. WHITE-TAILED NIGHTJAR **LM-TO**
Caprimulgus cayennensis 21

female

Throat and belly white (f. buff). Breast brownish. Much white (f. buff) on sides of tail.

17. WHITE-WINGED NIGHTJAR **L-O**
Caprimulgus candicans 22

Rather pale. Primaries black, with white base. Belly and outer tail feathers white.

18. CAYENNE NIGHTJAR **L-O**
Caprimulgus maculosus 21

A dark nightjar. Primaries black with white spot on web of four outermost feathers.

19. BLACKISH NIGHTJAR **L-SO**
Caprimulgus nigrescens 20

Very dark. No rufous on collar. Narrow throat band white.

20. RORAIMAN NIGHTJAR **L-TO**
Caprimulgus whiteleyi 20

No rufous on collar. Primaries blackish, outer three with white band. Small tail tips white.

21. SPOT-TAILED NIGHTJAR **L-TSO**
Caprimulgus maculicaudus 19

A small rufescent nightjar. Prominent pale eyebrow. No white in wings. Tail broadly tipped white (f. gray).

22. LITTLE NIGHTJAR **L-TSO**
Caprimulgus parvulus 19

Dark. Conspicuous throat patch white. Broad white wing band. Four outer tail feathers with small white tip.

23. PYGMY NIGHTJAR **L-T**
Caprimulgus hirundinaceus 17

Rather like 60-22 in appearance but folded wings do not reach end of tail.

24. SICKLE-WINGED NIGHTJAR **L-OW**
Eleothreptus anomalus 18

Primaries blackish, curved inward with large white tips. Tail very short. F: Wings normal shape and banded rufous.

NIGHT HAWKS FLY MOSTLY AT DUSK.

Nyctidromus	*Lurocalis*	*Nyctiphrynus*
Podager	*Chordeiles*	*Nyctiprogne*

25. PAURAQUE LM-TS
Nyctidromus albicollis 25

Common, often on road. Large black spots above. Rather long tail with much white on sides. F: Also has white wing band.

26. NACUNDA NIGHTHAWK L-O
Podager nacunda 25

Very large with long rounded wings. Above buffy brown speckled blackish. White wing bars. Below white. Tail notched.

27. SHORT-TAILED (SEMI-COLLARED) NIGHTHAWK LM-FT
Lurocalis semitorquatus 23

Above blackish speckled rufous No white in wings. Throat white, below dark brown, barred black. Tail short. Flies over forest canopy.

28. LESSER NIGHTHAWK L-O
Chordeiles acutipennis 19

Prominent white band near tip of wing (f. band buffy). Underparts whitish barred dusky. Cf. 61-29 but white wing band nearer tip.

29. COMMON NIGHTHAWK L-TO
*Chordeiles minor** 20

Very like 61-28 but broad white wing band mid-way between base and tip.

30. SAND-COLORED NIGHTHAWK L-OW
Chordeiles rupestris 20

Upperparts sandy gray mottled black and buffy. Below white, breast like back. Large white wing patch, white underside of tail. Usually on sandbars in rivers.

31. OCELLATED POORWILL L-F
Nyctiphrynus ocellatus 20

Dark reddish brown speckled black. Large black spots on shoul der, Large white spots on wing coverts. Throat and spots on belly white. (In flight wings uniform dark).

32. BAND-TAILED NIGHTHAWK L-O
Nyctiprogne leucopyga 17

Above dark brown speckled buff and rufous. No white in wing. Throat white. Below barred brown and white. Band across center of tail white. Flies at dusk low over rivers.

33. LEAST NIGHTHAWK L-O
Chordeiles pusillus 14

Above dark brown speckled buff and rufous. White band on primaries and pale trailing edge to inner flight feathers. Below barred brown and white.

SWIFTS: MUCH GLIDING ON STIFF BACK-CURVED WINGS. NEVER PERCH ON LIMBS OR WIRES.

Streptoprocne *Aeronautes* *Reinarda*
Cypseloides *Panyptila* *Chaetura*

1. WHITE-COLLARED SWIFT LMH-OW
Streptoprocne zonaris 19

Black with sharp white collar. Tail slightly forked.

2. BISCUTATE SWIFT LM-TO
Streptoprocne biscutata 18

Black with white bar on nape. Throat white. Tail square.

3. GREAT DUSKY SWIFT L-TO
Cypseloides senex 18

Sooty brown. Head and throat dark gray with black shaft streaks. Tail short, square.

4. SOOTY SWIFT LM-TO
Cypseloides fumigatus 16

Uniform sooty brown. Tail square.

5. WHITE-CHINNED SWIFT LM-TO
Cypseloides cryptus 14

Sooty brown. Usually with small white patch on chin. Tail very short.

6. WHITE-CHESTED SWIFT LM-TO
Cypseloides lemosi 14

Sooty black with triangular white patch on breast. Tail somewhat forked.

7. CHESTNUT-COLLARED SWIFT LM-TO
Cypseloides rutilus 14

Sooty black with broad rufous collar around neck (f. sometimes lacking collar). Tail notched.

8. SPOT-FRONTED SWIFT M-TO
Cypseloides cherriei 13

Sooty black. Small white streak before and behind eye. Tail very short.

9. ANDEAN SWIFT MH-O
Aeronautes andecolus 14

Above brown but collar and rump white. Underparts white. Tail long, forked.

10. WHITE-TIPPED SWIFT MH-TO
Aeronautes montivagus 13

Brownish black. Throat and small flanks white. Tail square, edged and tipped whitish.

11. LESSER SWALLOW-TAILED SWIFT L-TO
Panyptila cayennensis 13

Black. White spot before eye. Throat white, connected to white collar. Tail long, forked but usually held pointed.

12. FORK-TAILED PALM-SWIFT L-SO
Reinarda squamata 13

Above brown glossed bluish. Lores white. Throat white. Below mixed brown and white. Tail very long, forked, but held nearly pointed. Cf. 63-21.

13. ASHY-TAILED SWIFT LM-TO
Chaetura andrei 14

Above dark smoky brown, rump grayer. Throat pale gray, below contrastingly darker gray. Tail very short.

14. CHAPMAN'S SWIFT L-TO
Chaetura chapmani 13

Above glossy blue-black, rump only slightly contrasting. Below deep sooty. Tail short.

MARTINS AND SWALLOWS: SHORT GLIDES, RAPID FLAPPING.

Chaetura
Micropanyptila
Progne
Phaeoprogne

15. CHIMNEY SWIFT LM-TO
*Chaetura pelagica** 13

Above dark sooty olive, rump paler. Below grayish brown, noticeably paler on throat. Cf. 63-20.

16. PALE-RUMPED SWIFT L-TO
Chaetura egregia 11

Upperparts blue-black, rump whiter.

17. BAND-RUMPED SWIFT LM-TO
Chaetura spinicauda 11

Upperparts blue-black. Contrasting rump band paler. Contrasting throat whitish.

18. SHORT-TAILED SWIFT L-O
Chaetura brachyura 11

Glossy black. Rump and tail ashy gray. Tail very short.

19. GRAY-RUMPED SWIFT LM-TO
Chaetura cinereiventris 10

Crown, mantle and wings blue-black. Rump and underparts gray, paler on throat, Crissum black.

20. VAUX'S SWIFT LM-TO
Chaetura vauxi 9

Black, throat paler. Rump grayish brown. Tail short. Cf. 63-15.

21. PYGMY SWIFT L-O
Micropanyptila furcata 9

Above ashy brown. Below paler, whitish on center of throat and belly. Tail deeply forked, but usually held pointed, white at base. Cf. 62-12.

22. PURPLE MARTIN L-O
*Progne subis** 19

female

Shiny dark purplish. Tail quite forked. F: Above dull blackish. Forehead and narrow collar grayish. Breast brown. Below white lightly streaked dusky.

23. GRAY-BREASTED MARTIN LM-TO
Progne chalybea 19

Upperparts black-purple. Throat and breast gray. Belly white, sides ashy brown.

24. SOUTHERN MARTIN L-O
Progne modesta 15

Very like 63-22 but f. throat, breast and sides of body brown, feathers edged white.

25. BROWN-CHESTED MARTIN L-O
Phaeoprogne (Progne) tapera 17

Above brown, wings and tail darker. Below whitish, broad breast band brown. (Brown spots on belly in some races). Tail forked.

Hirundo
Atticora
Petrochelidon
Stelgidopteryx
Riparia

26. BARN SWALLOW **LMH-O**
*Hirundo rustica** 14

Upperparts and face shiny bluish black. Forehead and throat brown. Below buffy white to cinnamon. Tail black, deeply forked, outer feathers with white patch near end.

27. WHITE-BANDED SWALLOW **L-TW**
Atticora fasciata 14

Glossy steel blue, band across breast white. Thighs white. Tail long, deeply forked. Only along rivers.

28. BLACK-COLLARED SWALLOW **L-TW**
Atticora melanoleuca 13

Upperparts, face and neck dark steely blue. Below white with dark blue band across breast. Crissum dark. Tail long, deeply forked.

29. ANDEAN SWALLOW **H-O**
Petrochelidon andecola 14

Above blackish, brownish on rump. Throat ashy becoming white on belly. Tail slightly forked.

30. CLIFF SWALLOW **L-O**
*Petrochelidon pyrrhonota** 14

Forehead buffy white. Crown black. Back black streaked white. Face, neck, throat and rump rufous. Breast black. Below white. Tail square.

31. CAVE SWALLOW **L-SO**
Petrochelidon fulva 13

Forehead, collar, breast and rump chestnut. Crown black. Back glossy black streaked grayish. Face and throat whitish. Belly buffy white. Tail square.

32. ROUGH-WINGED SWALLOW **LM-TSO**
*Stelgidopteryx ruficollis** 13

Above brown, rump whitish. Throat cinnamon. Breast and sides grayish brown. Belly pale yellow. Tail notched.

33. BANK SWALLOW **L-O**
Riparia riparia * 13

Upperparts and face smoky brown. Below white with brownish band across breast. Tail brown, notched.

Notiochelidon: Tail forked.
Trachycineta: Tail slightly forked.
Alopochelidon
Neochelidon

34. BROWN-BELLIED SWALLOW **MH-O**
Notiochelidon murina 13

Above steely green or blue. Below uniform grayish brown. Wings and forked tail dark brown.

35. BLUE-AND-WHITE SWALLOW **LMH-OW**
Notiochelidon cyanoleuca 12

Upperparts glossy steel blue. Below white. Crissum black. Tail notched. Imm: Throat buffy.

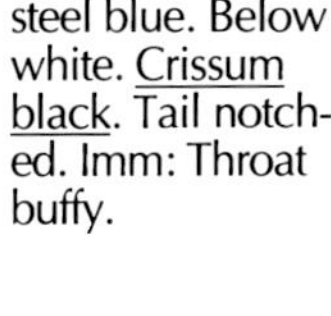

36. PALE-FOOTED SWALLOW **H-FT**
Notiochelidon flavipes 12

Like 65-35 but throat pinkish buff, sides brownish and feet pinkish white.

37. WHITE-WINGED SWALLOW **L-TOW**
Tachycineta albiventer 13

Above shiny blue-green. Large white patch on wings. Rump and underparts white. Tail black, slightly forked.

38. WHITE-RUMPED SWALLOW **L-O**
Tachycineta leucorrhoa 13

Above shiny bluish black. Narrow line on forehead white. Rump white. Underparts white. No white in wing or tail. Cf. 65-39.

39. CHILEAN SWALLOW **LM-TO**
Tachycineta leucopyga 12

Very like 65-38 but lacks narrow white line on forehead.

40. TAWNY-HEADED SWALLOW **L-TSO**
Alopochelidon fucata 12

Above grayish brown. Forehead, face, throat and collar tawny. Breast, belly and crissum white.

41. WHITE-THIGHED SWALLOW **L-FTS**
Neochelidon tibialis 12

Above uniform dark brown. Rump paler brown. Below grayish brown. Thighs white. Tail notched.

HERMITS: MOST HAVE LONG CURVED BILL.

Phaethornis: Central tail feathers elongated, white.

1. GREAT-BILLED HERMIT L-F
Phaethornis malaris 12+4

Bill long, heavy, lower red on underside. Underparts gray, tinged buff.

2. WHITE-WHISKERED HERMIT L-FT
Phaethornis yaruqui 11+4
female

Above dark green. Eyebrow and malar streak whitish. Below gray, greener on breast. Pale line down center of throat (f: and breast). Central white tail feathers extended very little. Cf. 66-3.

3. GREEN HERMIT LM-FT
Phaethornis guy 15

Very like 66-2 but central white tail feathers much extended beyond side feathers. Below gray with pale line down center of throat.

4. TAWNY-BELLIED HERMIT LM-FT
Phaethornis syrmatophorus 12+3

Above coppery green. Eyestripe white. Rump bright ochraceous. Underparts bright tawny broadly buff. Tail outers tipped buff.

5. LONG-TAILED HERMIT LM-FT
Phaethornis superciliosus 12+3

Bill 1-3/4x head, lower red at base Above bronzy green, feathers of uppertail coverts edged buffy. Eyebrow and malar stripe whitish. Broad line through eye black. Underparts grayish buff. Throat streak pale buff.

6. SCALE-THROATED HERMIT LM-FT
Phaethornis eurynome 12+3

Like 66-5 but throat feathers black edged buff appearing scaled. Crown blacker.

Phaethornis: Central tail feathers elongated, white.

7. BUFF-BELLIED HERMIT L-FT
Phaethornis subochraceus 10+2

Crown feathers dark coppery edged buffy. Below buffy.

8. NEEDLE-BILLED HERMIT L-F
Phaethornis philippi 11+3

Bill almost straight. Otherwise very like 66-4.

9. WHITE-BEARDED HERMIT L-FT
Phaethornis hispidus 11+3

Like 66-5 but grayer and white throat-streak more prominent.

10. SOOTY-CAPPED HERMIT L-FT
Phaethornis augusti 11+3

Like 66-5 but facial lines whiter and rump rufous.

11. PLANALTO HERMIT LM-FT
Phaethornis pretrei 11+3

Back greenish. Rump and upper tail coverts extensively rufous. Below tawny. Tail all broadly tipped white.

12. PALE-BELLIED HERMIT L-TS
Phaethornis anthophilus 10+3

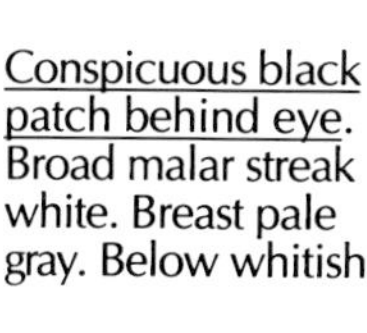

Conspicuous black patch behind eye. Broad malar streak white. Breast pale gray. Below whitish.

13. STRAIGHT-BILLED HERMIT L-F
Phaethornis bourcieri 10+3

Bill almost straight. Otherwise very like 66-5, but facial lines duller.

14. CINNAMON-THROATED HERMIT L-TS
Phaethornis nattereri 8+3

Like 67-11 but outer tail feathers pale cinnamon instead of white.

15. DUSKY-THROATED HERMIT LM-F
Phaethornis squalidus 9+2

Above dull olive. Throat dusky, below dull brownish yellow to whitish.

16. BROAD-TIPPED HERMIT L-S
Phaethornis gounellei 9+2

Above grayish green. Upper tail coverts fringed rufous. Underparts cinnamon. Tail with much white on edges.

17. WHITE-BROWED HERMIT L-FT
Phaethornis stuarti 10+1

Like 68-19 but tail greener and tips generally paler.

18. LITTLE HERMIT L-FT
Phaethornis longuemareus 10+1

Very like 68-19 but lacks black band on breast and central tail feathers more extended.

HERMITS: MOST HAVE LONG CURVED BILL.

Phaethornis: Central tail feathers elongated, white. *Threnetes*
Glaucis

19. REDDISH HERMIT L-FSO
Phaethornis ruber 8+0.5

Back reddish brown. Rump rufous. Below rufous with narrow black band across breast. Central tail feathers not much extended.

20. GRAY-CHINNED HERMIT LM-F
Phaethornis griseogularis 8+1

Very like 68-19 but lacks black band on breast and is generally paler.

21. MINUTE HERMIT L-FSO
Phaethornis idaliae 8+1

Upper tail coverts green. Chin black. Throat and breast reddish buff. Belly dark gray.

22. RUFOUS-BREASTED HERMIT L-F
Glaucis hirsuta 13

Above greenish bronze. Breast dull rufous, becoming more grayish on belly. Tail all tipped white, rufous at base.

23. BRONZY HERMIT L-FT
Glaucis aenea 10

Above coppery green. Below uniform cinnamon. Tail feathers (except centrals) black, cinnamon at base, tipped white.

24. SOOTY BARBTHROAT L-FT
Threnetes niger 12

Bill slightly curved. All dark olive bronze. Throat black with tawny band below. Tail dark bronzy above, blackish below.

25. PALE-TAILED BARBTHROAT L-T
Threnetes leucurus 13

Above bronze green. Throat black with rufous band below. Whiskers white. Breast dusky. Below buffy. Tail whitish at base.

26. BAND-TAILED BARBTHROAT L-T
Threnetes ruckeri 13

Like 68-25 but all except central tail feathers white with broad band of black near end.

Ramphodon
Campylopterus
Eutoxeres
Androdon
Rhodopis
Heliomaster

1. SAW-BILLED HERMIT LM-F
Ramphodon naevius 17

Bill straight, heavy, hooked at tip, lower yellow at base. (f: bill curved, not hooked at tip). Above dark olive. Streak back of eye buff. Throat tawny. Below buff, heavily streaked dusky. Tail bronzy, outer feathers broadly tipped tawny.

male 

female 

2. HOOK-BILLED HERMIT L-F
Ramphodon dohrnii 14

Like 69-1 but above more greenish and underparts cinnamon speckled dusky on flanks. Tail reddish bronze tipped white (f: no white). Bill of m and f as in 69-1

3. GRAY-BREASTED SABREWING L-FS
Campylopterus largipennis 14

Bill slightly curved. Above shining green to bronzy green. Below uniform gray Tail bluish, outers with very large white tips.

4. WHITE-TIPPED SICKLEBILL L-F
Eutoxeres aquila 14

Bill greatly curved. Above greenish. Underparts striped buff and black. Tail greenish, broadly tipped white.

5. BUFF-TAILED SICKLEBILL L-F
Eutoxeres condamini 14

Very like 69-4 but has small blue patch on sides of neck and outer tail feathers buff..

6. TOOTH-BILLED HUMMINGBIRD LM-F
Androdon aequatorialis 13

Bill 2x head, slightly upcurved. Above bronzy green. Broad white bar across rump. Below whitish streaked black becoming whiter on belly.

7. OASIS HUMMINGBIRD LMH-SA
Rhodopis vesper 13

Bill curved. Above shining olive green. Rump rufous. Throat glittering violet (f: lacking). Tail much (f: slightly) forked.

8. STRIPE-BREASTED STARTHROAT L-TSO
Heliomaster squamosus 13

Crown glittering green. Throat glit-tering violet. Above greenish. Below black with white line down center. Tail dull green, notched.

Heliomaster
Topaza: Extended tail feathers cross.
Taphrospilus
Heliodoxa: White spot behind eye.
Polyplancta

9. BLUE-TUFTED STARTHROAT **L-TSO**
Heliomaster furcifer 13

Above green. Below bluish, throa glittering violet. F: Below whitish.

male

female

10. LONG-BILLED STARTHROAT **L-TSO**
Heliomaster longirostris 12

Bill 2x head, straight. Crown glittering blue (f. lacking). Above green. Whisker white. Throat glittering violet. Below whitish.

1. CRIMSON TOPAZ **L-FW**
Topaza pella 11+5

Crown and face black. Above purple. Rump gold (f. green). Throat glittering green. Breast glittering crimson, Crissum green. Thighs white. Outer tail feathers protruding, crossed (f. shorter, not crossed).

2. FIERY TOPAZ **L-FW**
Topaza pyra 11+5

Crown, face and thighs black. Above purple. Throat green. Below orange. Tail purple, outer feathers protruding, crossed (f. shorter, not crossed).

3. MANY-SPOTTED HUMMINGBIRD **L-SA**
Taphrospilus hypostictus 14

Upperparts shining green. Underparts white, thickly spotted green everywhere except belly.

4. BLACK-THROATED BRILLIANT **L-TS**
Heliodoxa schreibersii 14

female

Upperparts shining green. Below black. Tail forked, steel blue. F: Like m. except it has whitish malar stripe.

5. PINK-THROATED BRILLIANT **L-F**
Heliodoxa gularis 13

Shining grass green. Throat patch glittering rosy red. Belly gray. Crissum white. F: Like f. 70-4 but lacks white malar stripe.

6. JEWEL-FRONT (GOULD'S JEWEL-FRONT) **L-FS**
Polyplancta aurescens 13

Forecrown glittering violet. Above shining grass green. Chin black. Throat glittering green. Breast band rufous. Below greenish. Tail sides chestnut.

Anthracothorax: Bill slightly curved.
Thalurania: Bill slightly curved.
Polytmus: Bill slightly curved.

7. BLACK-THROATED MANGO **L-TO**
Anthracothorax nigricollis 12

Above shining bronzy green. Below green, black down center. Tail purple. F: Below white, with black stripe down center. Tail tipped white.

male

female

8. GREEN-THROATED MANGO **L-SO**
Anthracothorax viridigula 12

female

Above bronzy green. Throat glittering green. Below black in center. Tail shining purple. F: Like f. 71-7 but line down center below mixed black and green.

9. GREEN-BREASTED MANGO **L-TS**
Anthracothorax prevostii 12

Very like 71-7 but sides more bluish. F: Very like f. 71-7.

10. LONG-TAILED WOODNYMPH **L-FT**
Thalurania watertonii 13

Crown green. Back glittering purple. Underparts glittering green. Tail forked. F: Like f. 71-12 but tail longer.

11. FORK-TAILED WOODNYMPH **LM-FT**
Thalurania furcata 12

Crown glittering purple or green. Upperparts greenish, shoulders purple. Throat and upper breast glittering green. Below glittering purple. F: Like f. 71-12.

12. VIOLET-CAPPED WOOD NYMPH **LM-FT**
Thalurania glaucopis 12

Crown glittering violet blue. Back bronzy green. Underparts glittering golden green. Tail forked, steel blue. F: Below light gray, often spotted on sides.

male

female

13. WHITE-TAILED GOLDENTHROAT **L-SO**
Polytmus guainumbi 11

imm. male

Golden above. White stripes above and below eye. Tail tipped white, increasing to outer feathers. F: Chin white. Below pale gray tinged rufous. Imm: Throat spotted

Polytmus
Chalybura
Leucippus: Bill longer and straighter than *Amazilia.*

14. GREEN-TAILED GOLDENTHROAT **L-SO**
Polytmus theresiae 10

Above golden bronze. Eye stripe white. Below glittering golden green. Tail green. F: Below white, spangled green. Cf. 71-13.

15. WHITE-VENTED PLUMELETEER **L-FO**
Chalybura buffonii 12

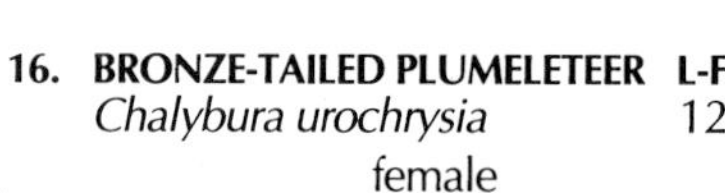

Above shining bronzy green. Below glittering green. Crissum white, feathers long, plume-like. Feet black. F: Very like f. 72-16 but feet black and tail blue-black

16. BRONZE-TAILED PLUMELETEER **L-F**
Chalybura urochrysia 12

female

Like m 72-15 but tail bronzy and feet pink, nails black. F: Above like m. Below grayish.

17. SPOT-THROATED HUMMINGBIRD **L-OA**
Leucippus taczanowskii 12

Like 72-20 but throat with small glittering green spots.

18. TUMBES HUMMINGBIRD **L-OA**
Leucippus baeri 11

Back dusty, dull green. Underparts pale gray (no spots). Undertail coverts long, white.

back view

front view

19. BUFFY HUMMINGBIRD **L-SA**
Leucippus fallax 10

Forecrown, face and neck brown. Above grayish green. Below uniform buff. Crissum white. Tail centrals green, outers with broad white tip.

20. OLIVE-SPOTTED HUMMINGBIRD **L-S**
Leucippus chlorocercus 10

Above dull dusty green. Underparts whitish faintly spotted dusky. Tail greenish, tipped gray. Usually on river islands.

Florisuga
Melanotrochilus
Phaeochroa

Hylocharis: Bill red, tipped black.

21. WHITE-NECKED JACOBIN L-FT
Florisuga mellivora 11

Head, throat and breast shining blue. Back greenish with broad white crescent across mantle. Tail mostly white. F: Upperparts green. Below white scaled green on breast. Tail green.

male

female

25. RUFOUS-THROATED SAPPHIRE L-FS
Hylocharis sapphirina 11

Upperparts and belly dark green. Chin rufous. Breast glittering violet. Tail coppery rufous. F: Throat rufous. Below grayish. Tail outers tipped white.

male

female

22. BLACK JACOBIN LM-FTS
Melanotrochilus fuscus 11

Black. Rump and wing coverts bronzy olive. Central tail feathers black, rest white tipped black.

23. SCALY-BREASTED HUMMINGBIRD L-T
Phaeochroa cuvierii 12

Above shining green. Below whitish all covered with green disks producing a scaled effect. Outer tail feathers broadly tipped white.

24. GILDED SAPPHIRE (HUMMINGBIRD) L-SO
Hylocharis chrysura 12

Shining greenish gold. Chin pale rufous

26. WHITE-CHINNED SAPPHIRE L-FT
Hylocharis cyanus 11

Head, throat and breast purple. Back and belly dark green. Chin white. Tail blue black. F: Like f. 73-25 but throat white.

27. BLUE-HEADED SAPPHIRE L-FS
Hylocharis grayi 10

Entire head glittering blue. Above and below shining green. Tail dark blue or green.

male

female

Chrysuronia
Chlorestes
Leucochloris
Aphantochroa
Clytolaema
Avocettula

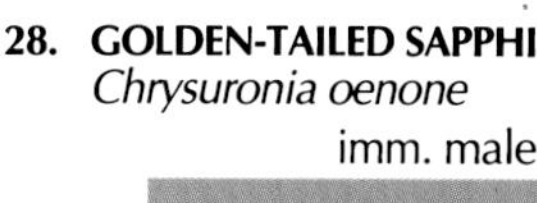

28. GOLDEN-TAILED SAPPHIRE L-FS
Chrysuronia oenone 10

imm. male

All dark green but head and throat purple. Tail shining golden copper F: Like f. 73-27 but tail golden bronze.

29. BLUE-CHINNED SAPPHIRE L-FS
Chlorestes notatus 10

Above shining bronze green. Below glittering green, bluer on throat. Thighs white. Tail steel blue. Crissum green. F: Below white, speckled green on breast.

male

female

30. WHITE-THROATED HUMMINGBIRD LM-FT
Leucochloris albicollis 12

Upperparts shining green. Below white with broad green band across breast Crissum long, white. Tail steel blue broadly tipped white.

31. SOMBRE HUMMINGBIRD L-FS
Aphantochroa cirrhochloris 11

Upperparts gray speckled green. Underparts dull gray. Tail bronzy black.

32. BRAZILIAN RUBY LM-FT
Clytolaema rubricauda 11

Crown glittering green. Above green shading to purple on rump. Throat glittering red. Breast shining green. Below gray. Tail chestnut. F: Above shining green. Below uniform cinnamon.

male female

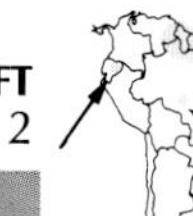

33. FIERY-TAILED AWLBILL L-F
Avocettula recurvirostris 9

Bill tip upturned. Above shining green. Throat and breast glittering green. Center of belly black. Tail dull violet above, bright copper below.

Damophila
Lepidopyga
Goethalsia

Leucippus: Bill longer and straighter than *Amazilia*.
Amazilia: Bill curved, lower red at base. No tail tips.

34. VIOLET-BELLIED HUMMINGBIRD L-FT
Damophila julie 8

Upperparts shining green. Throat glittering green. Below glittering violet blue. Tail steel blue. F: Below grayish. Tail with outer feather pale-tipped.

male

female

35. SHINING-GREEN HUMMINGBIRD L-T
Lepidopyga goudoti 9

Upperparts shining green. Underparts glittering green. Thighs white. Tail blue-black, forked. F: Like m.

36. SAPPHIRE-THROATED HUMMINGBIRD L-TS
Lepidopyga coeruleogularis 9

Like 75-35 but throat glittering purple. F: Underparts white, green spangles on breast and sides.

37. SAPPHIRE-BELLIED HUMMINGBIRD L-T
Lepidopyga lilliae 9

Like 75-35 but throat glittering purple. Below glittering blue. F: Unknown.

38. PIRRE HUMMINGBIRD L-F
Goethalsia bella 10

Green. Forehead, lores and chin rufous. Conspicuous wing-bar and outer tail feathers cinnamon. F: Below buff.

39. WHITE-CHESTED HUMMINGBIRD (EMERALD) L-FS
Leucippus (Amazilia) chionopectus 9

Bill straight, black. Upperparts shining green. Throat and breast white in center, greenish on sides. Belly grayish.

40. VERSICOLORED EMERALD L-TS
Amazilia versicolor 9

Upperparts greenish. Below white, sides greenish. Tail dull olive with dusky band near end.

41. GLITTERING-THROATED EMERALD L-TS
Amazilia fimbriata 10

Upperparts shining green. Below glittering green with white line down center of breast and belly. F: Belly white.

Amazilia: Bill curved, lower red at base. No tail tips.

42. TACHIRA EMERALD L-F
Amazilia distans 9

Rather like 75-41 but crown bluish green, breast blue and line on belly gray.

43. SAPPHIRE-SPANGLED EMERALD L-FSO
Amazilia lactea 10

Like 75-41 but throat and breast glittering purple.

44. BLUE-CHESTED EMERALD (HUMMINGBIRD) L-FT
Amazilia amabilis 9

female

Like 76-45 but crown glittering green. Belly gray. F: Throat with green disks. No purple.

45. PURPLE-CHESTED EMERALD L-S
Amazilia rosenbergi 9

Above shining green, crown not glittering. Throat all glittering green. Breast glittering purple. Below gray. Crissum white. F: Like f. 76-44 but throat and breast with glittering green disks.

46. PLAIN-BELLIED EMERALD L-TO
Amazilia leucogaster 10

Like green-capped form of 86-26 but only center of underparts white and tail centrals purple.

47. INDIGO-CAPPED EMERALD (HUMMINGBIRD) LM-F
Amazilia cyanifrons 10

Crown glittering dark blue Back like 76-48. Below all glittering green. Tail steel blue.

48. STEELY-VENTED EMERALD (HUMMINGBIRD) LM-TS
Amazilia saucerottei 10

Crown and back shining green becoming bronzy on rump. Underparts all glittering green. Tail bright steel blue, strongly contrasting with green back.

49. COPPER-RUMPED EMERALD (HUMMINGBIRD) LM-TSO
Amazilia tobaci 9

Above bronzy green becoming copper-colored on rump. Below glittering green. Crissum rufous. Tail steel blue.

50. GREEN-BELLIED EMERALD (HUMMINGBIRD) LM-TS
Amazilia viridigaster 10

Very like 76-49 but tail shining rosy purple instead of blue.

Amazilia: Bill slightly curved, lower red at base. No tail tips.	*Phlogophilus* *Popelairia*: White rump-band.	*Thaumastura* *Heliothryx*

51. RUFOUS-TAILED EMERALD (HUMMINGBIRD) **LM-TS**
Amazilia tzacatl 10

Bill pink, tipped dark. Above bronzy green. Throat and breast glittering green. Belly gray. Tail rufous edged dusky.

52. AMAZILIA EMERALD (HUMMINGBIRD) **L-TSA**
Amazilia amazilia 10

Upperparts bronzy green. Throat green. Breast green. Belly rufous. Thighs white.

53. ECUADORIAN PIEDTAIL **L-F**
Phlogophilus hemileucurus 9

Upperparts shining grass green. Below white spotted green, a pure white band across breast. Tail centrals green, rest dark blue broadly tipped white.

54. PERUVIAN PIEDTAIL **L-F**
Phlogophilus harterti 8

Above shining green. Below pale buff, whitish on throat and center of belly. Tail outers buff with broad black diagonal median band.

1. BLACK-BELLIED THORNTAIL **L-FT**
Popelairia langsdorffi 8+6

Above dark green with white band on rump. Throat and breast glittering green. Belly black. Extended tail feathers wire-like. F: Malar white. Below black. Tail normal.

2. WIRE-CRESTED THORNTAIL **LM-FT**
Popelairia popelairii 8+4

Crest of thin wire-like feathers. Crown glittering green. Back bronzy green. Rump blue-black with white band. Underparts black, flanks white. Tail long, wire-like. F: Tail normal, tipped white.

3. GREEN THORNTAIL **L-FT**
Popelairia conversii 8+4

Above dark green with white band on rump. Flanks white. Crown and throat glittering green. Breast green with blue spot in center. Below green. Extended tail wire-like. F: Below gray. Malar stripe white. Tail normal.

4. PERUVIAN SHEARTAIL **LMH-A**
Thaumastura cora 9+4

Upperparts shining green. Throat rosy. Breast white. Below grayish with green disks. Extended tail feathers very long, whitish. F: Tail normal.

WOODSTARS: EXTENSIVE GLITTERING RED THROAT.

Heliothryx *Discosura* *Philodice*
Heliactin *Lophornis:* White rump-bar.

5. BLACK-EARED FAIRY L-FT
Heliothryx aurita 10

Crown glittering green. Above shining green. Lower face black. Underparts pure white (throat green in se).

6. PURPLE-CROWNED FAIRY L-TF
Heliothryx barroti 10

Very like 78-5 but crown and ear coverts glittering purple.

7. HORNED SUNGEM L-SO
Heliactin cornuta 8+2

female

Above green. "Horns" at sides of crown glittering red. Face and throat black. Below white. F: Lacks horns and black throat. Face brown.

8. RACKET-TAILED COQUETTE L-FSO
Discosura longicauda 8+2

Head and throat glittering green. Back green with buff band across rump. Below blackish spotted coppery.Tail extended, outers ending in black rackets. F: Throat black, whiskers white.

9. PEACOCK COQUETTE LM-F
Lophornis pavonina 10

Crown sides glittering green, center black. Cheek tufts and back green. Below dark green. Tail bronze. F: No cheek plumes. Below streaked brown and white.

10. FESTIVE COQUETTE L-TS
Lophornis chalybea 9

Forehead and plumes from cheeks green. Crown brown. Back green. Throat and belly green. Tail purple. F: Chin and whiskers white.

11. TUFTED COQUETTE L-FS
Lophornis ornata 8

female

Head and throat glittering green with rufous crest. Plumes from cheeks cinnamon. Mantle and underparts green. F: No plumes. Above green. Underparts cinnamon.

12. DOT-EARED COQUETTE LM-TS
Lophornis gouldii 8

Like m. 78-11 but plumes from cheeks white. F: Like f. 78-11.

13. FRILLED COQUETTE L-FS
Lophornis magnifica 8

Like m. 78-11 but plumes from cheeks white, much shorter, with green tip. F: Like f. 78-1 but breast and belly greenish.

14. RUFOUS-CRESTED COUQUETTE LM-TS
Lophornis delattrei 8

Green. Crown and crest rufous. No cheek plumes. Tail mostly rufous. F: Like f. 78-11.

Lophornis	*Calliphlox*	*Chrysolampis*	*Acestrura:* No rump band.	*Ensifera*
Philodice	*Eulidia*	*Myrmia*	*Chlorostrilbon*	*Patagona*

15. SPANGLED COQUETTE **LM-S**
Lophornis stictolopha 8

Crown and long crest rufous. Back bronze green. Throat glittering green. Below bronzy green.
F: Rather like f. 78-11.

16. PURPLE-THROATED WOODSTAR **LM-FO**
Philodice mitchellii 9

Above dark green. Throat glittering violet. Breast white. Belly bronze. Flanks chestnut. F: Throat white. Eye stripe white. Belly rufous.

17. AMETHYST WOODSTAR **L-TS**
Calliphlox amethystina 9

Above dark green. Throat rosy violet bordered below by white band. Below gray with green disks. Tail rather long, deeply forked.
F: Throat whitish. Below cinnamon. Tail short, square.

18. CHILEAN WOODSTAR **L-TA**
Eulidia yarrellii 9

Above shining olive green. Throat red. Underparts white.

19. RUBY-TOPAZ HUMMINGBIRD **L-FSO**
Chrysolampis mosquitus 8

Crown and nape red. Back dark brown. Throat and breast glittering orange. Belly brown. Tail rufous tipped black. F: Back green. Below gray.

female

20. SHORT-TAILED WOODSTAR **L-A**
Myrmia micrura 7

Above pale green. Chin and malar stripe white. Below white. Tail short. F: Below buffy.

21. LITTLE WOODSTAR **LM-FS**
Acestrura bombus 7

Above bronzy green. Throat rosy. Buff line behind eye. Below bronzy green. F: Cinnamon buff below. Outer tail feathers cinna mon with broad black band near end.

22. ESMERALDAS WOODSTAR **L-T**
Acestrura berlepschi 7

Above coppery green. Eye stripe white. Breast grayish white.
F: Underparts white.

23. RED-BILLED EMERALD **LM-TS**
Chlorostilbon gibsoni 7

Like 93-52 but lower bill reddish, tipped black. F: Eyebrow white.

1. SWORD-BILLED HUMMINGBIRD **MH-TF**
Ensifera ensifera 21

Amazingly long bill unmistakeable. Above greenish. Belly grayish. Usually perches with bill pointed nearly straight up.

2. GIANT HUMMINGBIRD **H-TA**
Patagona gigas 21

Above brownish. Rump whitish. Below cinnamon. Slow wingbeat.

Pterophanes
Oreonympha
Campylopterus: Bill curved.

Coeligena: Long straight bill.

3. GREAT SAPPHIREWING **H-O**
Pterophanes cyanopterus 18

Dark green. Wings blue. F: Below cinnamon. Tail edged white.

male female

4. BEARDED MOUNTAINEER **H-O**
Oreonympha nobilis 15

Crown maroon, bordered blue. Face black. Back olive. Narrow throat patch glittering green. Below white. Tail forked.

5. WHITE-TAILED SABREWING **LM-F**
Campylopterus ensipennis 14

Green. Throat glittering violet. Tail centrals black, rest mostly white.

6. SANTA MARTA SABREWING **MH-FO**
Campylopterus phainopeplus 14

All glittering green except crown, throat and breast glittering dark blue. Tail steel blue. F: Underparts and tail tips gray.

7. NAPO SABREWING **L-F**
Campylopterus villaviscensio 13

Upperparts shining green. Throat and breast glittering violet. Below dark gray with green disks. F: Below all gray.

8. LAZULINE SABREWING **MH-FS**
Campylopterus falcatus 13

Crown blue. Above glittering green. Throat and breast glittering dark violet blue becoming greener on belly. Tail chestnut. F: Breast and belly gray.

male female

9. RUFOUS-BREASTED SABREWING **M-FS**
Campylopterus hyperythrus 11

Like 69-3 but underparts rufous. Tail centrals bronze, outers rufous (all rufous below).

10. BUFF-BREASTED SABREWING **M-FS**
Campylopterus duidae 11

Like 69-3 but underparts buffy.

11. BRONZY INCA **LM-FT**
Coeligena coeligena 14

Upperparts shiny reddish brown, obscurely scaled green. Below dark brown scaled whitish on throat and breast. Tail bronze. Cf. 81-12.

Coeligena: Long straight bill.
Sternoclyta: Bill curved.

12. BROWN INCA LM-FT
Coeligena wilsoni 14

Upperparts dark shiny bronzy brown. Throat purplish. Below dark grayish brown. A conspicuous white spot at each side of breast. Cf. 80-11.

13. BLACK INCA MH-F
Coeligena prunellei 13

Black. Lesser wing coverts glittering blue. Patch at each side of breast white. Throat glittering greenish blue.

14. COLLARED INCA MH-FTS
Coeligena torquata 13

Above black. Crown purple. Throat blackish. Breast white. Belly black. Tail white tipped black. F: Throat white. Belly gray.

15. VIOLET-THROATED STARFRONTLET M-F
Coeligena violifer 14

Above dark green. Forehead glittering green in nw. Throat and breast green, glittering violet spot on throat. White band on breast in nw. Belly cinnamon.

16. BUFF-WINGED STARFRONTLET H-FT
Coeligena lutetiae 14

Above black, glossed purple on rump. Large patch on wing pale buff. Below glittering green, spot on throat blue. Tail dark green.

17. DUSKY STARFRONTLET H-F
Coeligena orina 14

Uniform dark shining green. Spot on throat glittering blue.

18. VIOLET-CHESTED HUMMINGBIRD M-F
Sternoclyta cyanopectus 13

Upperparts shining grass green. Throat glittering green. Breast glittering violet. Belly gray spotted green. Tail bronzy. F: Throat and breast grayish white with green disks. Belly buffy.

19. RAINBOW STARFRONTLET MH-F
Coeligena iris 14

Crown glittering green to orange. Mantle dark green. Back, belly, wings and tail chestnut. Throat and breast glittering green. Blue spot on throat.

20. GOLDEN-BELLIED STARFRONTLET MH-F
Coeligena bonapartei 13

Crown and nape black. Forehead and back green. Rump orange. Large chestnut patch on wings. Throat glittering purple. Breast green. Belly orange. F: Underparts cinnamon.

Coeligena: Long straight bill.
Doryfera: Bill very long, thin, straight.
Lafresnaya

21. BLUE-THROATED STARFRONTLET **MH-FS**
Coeligena helianthea 13

Above dark green. Frontlet glittering green. Throat patch purple. Belly and crissum violet. F: Throat cinnamon. Breast buff with green disks.

male

female

22. WHITE-TAILED STARFRONTLET **MH-FT**
Coeligena phalerata 13

Crown glittering green. Back shining dark green. Throat glittering purple. Below blue green. Tail white. F: Below uniform cinnamon. Tail bronzy.

male

female

23. GREEN-FRONTED LANCEBILL **MH-F**
Doryfera ludoviciae 13

Forehead glittering green. Above bronzy green. Below brownish green. Cf. 82-24
Often near streams.

24. BLUE-FRONTED LANCEBILL **LM-SO**
Doryfera johannae 11

Very dark bird
Forehead glittering violet.
Back dark bronzy green, rump bluish.
Below black.
Often near streams. F: Like 82-23

25. MOUNTAIN VELVETBREAST **MH-FS**
Lafresnaya lafresnayi 10

Bill thin, curved, Upperparts shining grass green. Throat and breast glittering green (f. buff spotted green). Belly black (f. white). Tail white, tipped and edged black, central feathers green.

male

female

Urochroa	*Eupetomena*	*Colibri*
Oreotrochilus	*Hylonympha*	*Taphrolesbia*

26. WHITE-TAILED HILLSTAR LM-F
Urochroa bougueri 14

Upperparts shining bronzy green. Throat and breast glittering blue. Malar rufous (lacking in s). Central and outermost tail feathers black, rest white edged black.

27. WEDGE-TAILED HILLSTAR H-T
Oreotrochilus adela 13

Crown dull brown. Back olive, feathers pale-edged. Throat glittering green (f. white spotted dusky). Below black in center, sides chestnut. Tail dark brown, feathers edged buff.

1. SWALLOW-TAILED HUMMINGBIRD L-SO
Eupetomena macroura 11+6

Head, neck, throat and breast purple blue. Rest of body shining green. Tail blackish, long, deeply forked. Imm: Throat white.

2. SCISSOR-TAILED HUMMINGBIRD M-FT
Hylonympha macrocerca 11+6

Crown glittering purple. Back shining dark green. Throat and breast glittering green. Below black, sides with green disks. Tail very long, deeply forked. F: Very like f. 88-5.

3. SPARKLING VIOLET-EAR MH-SO
Colibri coruscans 15

Upperparts shining green Ear tufts glittering purple Below glittering green with purple patch on center of belly. Tail green with black bar.

4. WHITE-VENTED VIOLET-EAR LM-SO
Colibri serrirostris 13

Much like 83-3 but no violet on chin or belly and crissum white.

5. BROWN VIOLET-EAR LM-TSO
Colibri delphinae 13

Brown, tinged rufous on rump. Throat green. Whisker whitish. Tail with dusky bar near end.

6. GREEN VIOLET-EAR MH-O
Colibri thalassinus 12

Very like 83-3 but has no purple patch on belly.

7. GRAY-BELLIED COMET H-TS
Taphrolesbia griseiventris 15

Upperparts shining green. Throat glittering blue (f. lacking). Below pale gray. Tail rather long, forked.

Heliodoxa
Oreotrochilus

8. EMPRESS BRILLIANT M-F
Heliodoxa imperatrix 15

female

Male very like m. 84-9 but tail bronzy green and longer. F: Upperparts dark bronzy green. Below like m. 84-9. Tail long, forked, contrastingly bronze.

9. GREEN-CROWNED BRILLIANT LM-F
Heliodoxa jacula 13

Green. Crown glittering green. Glittering purple spot on throat. Tail steel blue. F: Below white, spotted green. Tail tipped white.

male

female

10. VIOLET-FRONTED BRILLIANT M-FT
Heliodoxa leadbeateri 13

Like m. 84-9 but crown violet and throat green. F: Like f. 84-9 but belly tinged buff.

11. VELVET-BROWED BRILLIANT M-TS
Heliodoxa xanthogonys 11

Quite like 84-9 but crown black, only forehead green and base of lower bill orange.

12. FAWN-BREASTED BRILLIANT M-FT
Heliodoxa rubinoides 11

Above green to coppery green. Below light brown. Spot on throat glittering violet (f. lacking).

13. RUFOUS-WEBBED BRILLIANT L-F
Heliodoxa branickii 11

Dark shining green. Wing feathers edged rufous. Line from bill through center of crown glittering green. Throat glittering rosy red. Tail dark.

14. ANDEAN HILLSTAR H-SO
Oreotrochilus estella 13

Whole head and throat glittering violet or green. Above olive green. Below white with brown stripe down center. Tail green, outer feathers white. F: Throat white. Below gray.

15. WHITE-SIDED HILLSTAR H-S
Oreotrochilus leucopleurus 13

Whole head and throat glittering green. Above olive green. Below white with black stripe down center. Tail centrals green, outers mostly white.

16. BLACK-BREASTED HILLSTAR H-S
Oreotrochilus melanogaster 10

Upperparts dark shining green. Throat glittering emerald green. Below black, sides brown. Tail dark blue-green (f. outers tipped white).

Polytmus
Aglaeactis
Urosticte

Leucippus: Bill nearly straight, all black.
Amazilia: Bill slightly curved, lower red at base. No tail tips.

17. TEPUI GOLDENTHROAT M-SO
Polytmus milleri 13

Like 71-13 but no white at eye. Tail bronze green above, shining green below, all outers with broad white band at base and white tips.

18. PURPLE-BACKED SUNBEAM H-S
Aglaeactis aliciae 13

Like 85-19 but darker brown. Rump violet becoming golden green on upper tail coverts. Lores, throat and patch on breast white. Tail white at base.

19. SHINING SUNBEAM H-OS
Aglaeactis cupripennis 12

Mostly brown. Rump glittering purple to glittering green. Face and throat paler brown with some dusky marks. Below rufous or brown.

20. WHITE-TUFTED SUNBEAM H-S
Aglaeactis castelnaudii 12

Like 85-19 but darker brown below. Breast patch white. Rump glittering purple without green.

21. BLACK-HOODED SUNBEAM H-S
Aglaeactis pamela 12

Black. Patch on breast white. Rump and upper tail coverts green. Tail and crissum rufous.

22. WHITETIP M-FT
Urosticte benjamini 11

Upperparts shining grass green. Spot behind eye white. Throat shining purple. Below whitish.
F: Underparts all spotted green.

23. WHITE-BELLIED HUMMINGBIRD MH-SO
Leucippus (Amazilia) chionogaster 10

Upperparts shining green. Underparts white. Tail centrals green, outers with white tips increasing in size to edge.

24. GREEN-AND-WHITE HUMMINGBIRD LM-FT
Leucippus (Amazilia) viridicauda 11

Upperparts shining green. Below white, sides broadly green.

25. CHESTNUT-BELLIED EMERALD M-TS
Amazilia castaneiventris 10

Like 77-51 but belly chestnut instead of gray.

Amazilia: Bill curved, lower red at base. No tail tips.
Sephanoides
Goldmania
Eriocnemis: Leg puffs white.
Haplophaedia: Leg puffs white.

26. ANDEAN EMERALD **M-FTS**
Amazilia franciae 10

Above shining green (blue in w), becoming coppery on tail. Below white, green on sides.

27. GREEN-BACKED FIRECROWN **LM-TSO**
Sephanoides sephanoides 11

Crown glittering red (f. lacking). Above bronzy green. Below whitish, speckled on throat and breast with bronze.

28. VIOLET-CAPPED HUMMINGBIRD **M-F**
Goldmania violiceps 10

Above green, crown violet blue. Underparts glittering green. Tail rich chestnut tipped bronzy. F: Below white spotted gray. Tail tipped whitish.

29. GOLDEN-BREASTED PUFFLEG **MH-F**
Eriocnemis mosquera 11

Upperparts shining coppery green. Throat green. Breast golden green. Crissum dark gray Tail long, deeply forked.

30. LONG TAILED (SAPPHIRE-VENTED) PUFFLEG **M-F**
Eriocnemis luciani 11+2

Forecrown shining dark blue. Above bronze green. Throat and breast glittering green. Crissum glittering purple. Tail long, blue-black, deeply forked.

31. BLACK-THIGHED PUFFLEG **H-TS**
Eriocnemis derbyi 10

Shining green. Rump and crissum glittering green. Leg puffs black. Tail short, slightly forked. F: Underparts white, spangled green.

32. GREENISH PUFFLEG **M-FT**
Haplophaedia aureliae 9

female

Crown coppery. Above and below all coppery green. Rump bright copper. Tail blue-black. F: Below gray with green disks.

33. HOARY PUFFLEG **MH-FT**
Haplophaedia lugens 10

Above dark grayish green. Below dark gray, feathers of throat and upper breast scaled whitish.

Eriocnemis: Leg puffs white.

34. TURQUOISE-THROATED PUFFLEG H-FT
Eriocnemis godini 9

Male like m. 87-36 but crissum green like rest of underparts.

35. BLACK-BREASTED PUFFLEG H-F
Eriocnemis nigrivestis 9

Above dark green. Rump shining dark blue. Throat and crissum glittering purple. Breast black.

36. GLOWING PUFFLEG H-TS
Eriocnemis vestitus 10

Upperparts shining dark green. Below green, crissum and spot on throat glittering purple. F: Malar buff. Breast buff spotted with green disks.

male

female

37. BLUE-CAPPED PUFFLEG H-F
Eriocnemis glaucopoides 10

Shining bronze green. Forecrown and crissum glittering blue. Tail black. F: No blue on crown. Below cinnamon.

38. COPPERY-BELLIED PUFFLEG H-S
Eriocnemis cupreoventris 10

Upperparts shining green. Throat and breast glittering green. Belly golden copper. Crissum glittering purple.

39. COLORFUL PUFFLEG M-F
Eriocnemis mirabilis 9

Above green. Below glittering green. Belly glittering blue. Crissum glittering red. F: Below whitish with green disks on breast, reddish bronze disks on belly.

male

female

40. EMERALD-BELLIED PUFFLEG M-F
Eriocnemis alinae 9

Above bronzy green. Below glittering green with white patch on center of breast. Tail short, notched.

Lesbia: Tail very long, thin.
Polyonymus
Sappho
Agaiocercus: Very long tail.

1. BLACK-TAILED TRAINBEARER **MH-SO**
Lesbia victoriae 13+10

Tail about 2x length of body, deeply forked, black. Above shining green. Center of throat glittering green. Below buff with green disks. F: Below white with green disks. Tail much shorter.

male female

2. GREEN-TAILED TRAINBEARER **MH-TS**
Lesbia nuna 11+6

Tail about 1-1/2x length of body, shorter tail feathers green. Above green. Below like 88-1. F: Like f. 88-1 but greener on body. Tail about length of body and quite green above.

male female

3. BRONZE-TAILED COMET **MH-TS**
Polyonymus caroli 13+6

Bronzy green. Throat glittering rosy violet. Tail forked. F: Throat with glittering orange disks. Tail much shorter.

4. RED-TAILED COMET **H-S**
Sappho sparganura 13+7

Tail long, deeply forked, rosy red. Below green. F: Above shining green, rump purple. Tail broadly edged white.

male female

5. LONG-TAILED SYLPH **LM-FT**
Aglaiocercus kingi m. 9+9 f. 9

Above shining green. Throat glittering violet blue. Below greenish olive. F: Throat white. Below cinnamon.

male female

6. VIOLET-TAILED SYLPH **L-TS**
Aglaiocercus coelestis m. 9+9 f. 9

female

Male very like 88-5 but throat patch larger and lower back bluer. F: Above dark green. Crown glittering blue. Throat and breast speckled green.

Loddigesia *Boissonneaua*
Ocreatus
Chalcostigma: Throat patch narrow, pointed.

7. MARVELOUS SPATULETAIL **M-FT**
Loddigesia mirabilis 9+5

Tail deeply forked, crossing and ending in two very large rackets. Crown purple. Back green. Throat glittering blue. Below white with black stripe down center.

8. BOOTED RACKET-TAIL **MH-FT**
Ocreatus underwoodii 9+5

Tail very forked ending in two black rackets. Upperparts shining green. Throat and breast glittering green. Leg puffs white or buff. F: Underparts white spotted green. Tail normal.

male female

9. OLIVACEOUS THORNBILL **H-O**
Chalcostigma olivaceum 14

Uniform dark grayish olive. Throat patch glittering green becoming violet. Tail shining olive.

10. BRONZE-TAILED THORNBILL **H-O**
Chalcostigma heteropogon 13

Above green becoming reddish on rump. Throat patch glittering green becoming rosy on breast. Belly dull olive. Tail coppery bronze.

11. VELVET-PURPLE CORONET **LM-FT**
Boissonneaua jardini 12

Crown glittering violet. Above glittering blue-green, wing coverts glittering golden green. Face, throat and breast black. Below mixed purple and green. Tail outer feathers white edged bronzy.

12. BUFF-TAILED CORONET **MH-FT**
Boissonneaua flavescens 12

Back shining green. Crown, throat and breast glittering green. Tail buffy, edged and tipped bronze. F: Below less solidly dark.

male female

13. CHESTNUT-BREASTED CORONET **M-FT**
Boissonneaua matthewsii 12

Upperparts shining green. Below chestnut, throat thickly speckled with glittering green disks. Tail centrals bronze, outers buff edged and tipped bronze.

14. BLUE-MANTLED THORNBILL **H-O**
Chalcostigma stanleyi 11

Crown greenish blue. Back purplish blue. Throat patch narrow, glittering green becoming violet or steel blue on breast. Below green. F: No throat patch.

15. RUFOUS-CAPPED THORNBILL **MH-TS**
Chalcostigma ruficeps 10

Crown rufous. Back green. Throat patch blue-green becoming glittering green on breast. Below buffy with green disks. Tail bronzy.

Chalcostigma
Heliangelus: Large throat patch violet.
Ramphomicron: Tiny bill.

16. RAINBOW-BEARDED THORNBILL **H-SO**
Chalcostigma herrani 10

Crown rufous bordered black. Back green. Throat stripe green becoming red on breast. Tail violet, outer feathers with broad white tips.

17. PURPLE-THROATED SUNANGEL **MH-FT**
Heliangelus viola 12

Very like 90-18 but forecrown glittering blue-green and throat more violet.

18. TOURMALINE SUNANGEL **MH-F**
Heliangelus exortis 10

Upperparts dark shining green. Throat glittering violet (f. white spotted dusky). Breast glittering green. Belly dark gray.

male

female

19. ORANGE-THROATED SUNANGEL **MH-TS**
Heliangelus mavors 10

Upperparts shining green. Throat glittering orange. Breast band buff. Below buff with green disks.

20. AMETHYST-THROATED SUNANGEL **MH-FT**
Heliangelus amethysticollis 10

Above green. Large throat patch glittering violet. Breast band white. Below grayish buff with greendisks. Crissum white. Central tail feathers bronzy, others blue-black.

21. GORGETED SUNANGEL **M-FT**
Heliangelus strophianus 10

Like 90-20 but belly dark gray with green disks and tail dark steel blue, somewhat forked.

22. MERIDA SUNANGEL **MH-FT**
Heliangelus spencei 10

Like 90-20 but forehead glittering green and crissum bronze green.

23. PURPLE-BACKED THORNBILL **MH-FT**
Ramphomicron microrhynchum 9

Upperparts shining purple. Throat golden green. Below bronzy green. Tail rather long, forked, blackish. F: Bronzy green above. Below white with green disks. Tail outers tipped white.

male

female

Ramphomicron *Oxypogon*
Lophornis
Metallura: Tail shining above, glittering below.

24. BLACK-BACKED THORNBILL H-FT
Ramphomicron dorsale 10

Above mostly black. Rump tipped purplish. Throat glittering golden olive. Below dark gray with green disks. Tail long, forked, blackish. F: Above green. Below whitish.

25. BLACK METALTAIL MH-SO
Metallura phoebe 13

Brownish black. Wings bronzy. Throat patch glittering blue.

26. VIOLET-THROATED METALTAIL H-TS
Metallura baroni 12

Mostly bronzy green. Large throat patch glittering violet. Below glittering green.

27. SCALED METALTAIL MH-FT
Metallura aeneocauda 11

Mostly bronzy green. Throat glittering green. Below green scaled buff. Tail bluish.

28. PERIJA METALTAIL MH-ST
Metallura iracunda 10

Black glossed coppery. Crown shining dark green. Throat glitter ing green.

29. COPPERY METALTAIL H-T
Metallura theresiae 10

Mostly reddish copper green, reddest on head. Throat glittering green. Tail bluish.

30. FIRE-THROATED METALTAIL H-T
Metallura eupogon 10

Bronzy green. Throat patch fiery red. Tail bluish.

31. TYRIAN METALTAIL MH-TS
Metallura tyrianthina 9

Above shining green. Throat glittering green. Tail upper base shining copper color, below purple.
F: Throat and breast rufous.

male female

32. VIRIDIAN METALTAIL H-O
Metallura williami 9

Coppery green. Throat glittering green. Tail above purplish blue, below coppery green.

33. BEARDED HELMETCREST H-O
Oxypogon guerinii 11

Crest white. Back olive Face black. Narrow throat patch green or blue bordered by long white feathers forming a beard. Tail forked. F: No crest or beard.

male female

Opisthoprora	*Stephanoxis*	*Schistes*
Augastes	*Adelomyia*	*Acestrura*
Klais	*Anthocephala*	*Myrtis*

34. MOUNTAIN AVOCETBILL **H-FT**
Opisthoprora euryptera 10

Bill upturned at tip. Above shining green. Crown and face coppery. Below, white thickly streaked green.

35. HOODED VISORBEARER **L-TS**
Augastes lumachellus 10

Bronzy green.Crown and face black (f. lacking). Throat glittering green with fiery red spot.

36. HYACINTH VISORBEARER **L-TS**
Augastes scutatus 9

Upperparts green. Throat glittering green edged black. Sides of neck blue. Band on breast white. Belly dark blue.

37. VIOLET-HEADED HUMMINGBIRD **LM-FS**
Klais guimeti 9

Head and throat shining purple. Spot behind eye white. Above shining green. Below gray. F: Less purple. Throat gray.

38. BLACK-BREASTED PLOVERCREST **LM-FT**
Stephanoxis lalandi 9

Crown and long thin crest green (violet in s). Spot behind eye white. Back shining green. Breast glittering purple. Belly gray. F: Below gray.

39. BLOSSOM CROWN **LM-FT**
Anthocephala floriceps 8

Forecrown buffy. Hindcrown chestnut. Spot behind eye white. Above green. Below grayish.

40. SPECKLED HUMMINGBIRD **M-FT**
Adelomyia melanogenys 9

Above bronzy green. Eye stripe whitish. Cheeks dusky. Below buff, speckled bronze on throat. Tail bronzy brown, tipped buff.

41. WEDGE-BILLED HUMMINGBIRD **MH-FT**
Schistes geoffroyi 9

Upperparts bronzy green. Throat glittering green (f. white). Patches at side of breast white. Below gray, disked green. Crissum white (green in w).

42. WHITE-BELLIED WOODSTAR **MH-FS**
Acestrura mulsant 8

female

Upperparts dark green. Eye stripe white. Throat red. Below white. F: Above bronzy green. Below buffy, rufous on sides.

43. PURPLE-COLLARED WOODSTAR **LMH-TA**
Myrtis fanny 9

Above bronze green. Throat glittering bluish green bordered below by glittering violet band. Underparts whitish. Tail dull brownish. F: Below buffy.

Chaetocercus
Microstilbon
Acestrura
Chlorostilbon

44. RUFOUS-SHAFTED WOODSTAR **LM-FS**
Chaetocercus jourdanii 9

Bronzy green. Throat red. Breast band white. Tail partly rufous
F: Underparts cinnamon.

45. SLENDER-TAILED WOODSTAR **LM-FT**
Microstilbon burmeisteri 8

Upperparts dark shining green. Face black. Throat and long tufts at sides of throat glittering rosy. Below gray. Tail rather long, deeply forked (f. square).

46. GORGETED WOODSTAR **M-FS**
Acestrura heliodor 7

Upperparts dark green or blue. Throat glittering violet, bordered below by white bar. Breast gray (white in s). Tail black, central feathers very short. F: Like f. 92-42.

47. GLITTERING-BELLIED EMERALD **LM-SO**
Chlorostilbon aureoventris 10

Bill mostly reddish. Above bronzy green. Crown and underparts glittering green. Tail steel blue, somewhat forked. F: Line behind eye white. Below grayish.

male

female

48. GREEN-TAILED EMERALD **M-ST**
Chlorostilbon alice 8

Very like 93-50 but tail slightly longer.

49. NARROW-TAILED EMERALD **LMH-ST**
Chlorostilbon stenura 8

Very like 93-51 but outer tail feathers pointed.

50. SHORT-TAILED EMERALD **LM-S**
Chlorostilbon poortmanni 9

Upperparts and underparts glittering golden green. Tail short, shining green, somewhat forked.

51. COPPERY EMERALD **LM-TS**
Chlorostilbon russatus 7

Above shining green. Below glittering golden green. Rump and upper tail coppery, in sharp contrast to back.
(F: With purple band near end).

52. BLUE-TAILED EMERALD **LM-SO**
Chlorostilbon mellisugus 7

Above and below glittering green Tail steel blue, slightly forked. Bill all black. Cf. 79-23. F: Above shining green.

male

female

TROGONS: BRIGHTLY COLORED, SLUGGISH BIRDS.

Pharomachrus: Belly red. No white breast band.
Trogon: Face and throat (mask) black.

1. CRESTED QUETZAL M-F
Pharomachrus antisianus 28

Bill yellow. Upperparts, throat and breast green. Tail centrals black, three outers mostly white. F: Bill black. Head and breast brown. Tail underside barred black and white. Cf. 94-3.

2. WHITE-TIPPED QUETZAL M-F
Pharomachrus fulgidus 28

Bill yellow. Upperparts, throat and breast green. Tail mostly black, outers barred white. F: Tail outers only tipped white.

3. GOLDEN-HEADED QUETZAL LM-F
Pharomachrus auriceps 30

Bill yellow. Upperparts, throat and breast green. Tail all black. F: Bill brown, ridge black.

4. PAVONINE QUETZAL L-F
Pharomachrus pavoninus 30

Bill red Upperparts, throat and breast green. F: Bill dusky, red at base. Head and breast brown. Tail notched black and white.

5. BLACK-TAILED TROGON L-FT
Trogon melanurus 28

Bill yellow. Above green. Wings blackish. Breast green, white band below. Red belly. Tail all black. F: Above and breast brown.

6. SLATY-TAILED TROGON L-FT
Trogon massena 28

Bill red. Above and breast green (no bar). Wings grayish. Belly red. Tail all blackish.

7. BLUE-TAILED TROGON L-F
Trogon comptus 27

Bill yellow. Eye white. Above and breast green (no bar). Wings blackish. Belly red. Tail all bluish black.

8. MASKED TROGON MH-FT
Trogon personatus 25

Upperparts golden green Underside of tail finely barred. F: Distinct black mask. Upperparts uniform brown. Prominent white back part of eye-ring. Belly light crimson. Outer tail feathers finely barred.

9. COLLARED TROGON LM-FT
Trogon collaris 25

Above green. Breast bar white
F: Brown. Face mask indistinct.

male

female

Trogon: Face and throat (mask) black.
Baryphthengus

10. SURUCUA TROGON L-FT
Trogon surrucura 25

female

Head and breast bluish (f. gray). Back greenish No white breast band Belly red. Tail outers white. F: Throat and breast gray.

11. BLACK-THROATED TROGON L-F
Trogon rufus 25

Above and breast green. Narrow breast bar. Belly yellow. F: is only brown trogon with yellow belly.

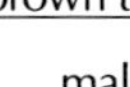

male female

12. BLUE-CROWNED TROGON L-FT
Trogon curucui 23

Head and breast blue. Back green. White breast bar indistinct. Belly red. F: Mostly gray. Tail notched.

13. WHITE-TAILED TROGON LM-TS
Trogon viridis 26

Eye-ring pale blue. Back dark green. Head and breast violet (no bar). Below yellow. Tail broadly tipped white underneath.

male female

14. VIOLACEOUS TROGON L-FT
Trogon violaceus 22

Very like 95-13 but eye-ring yel low and outer tail feathers white, underside barred. F: Like f. 95-13 but has conspicuous ring of white around eye.

15. RUFOUS MOTMOT L-FT
Baryphthengus ruficapillus (martii) 41

Bill serrated, not flat Head rufous with broad black mask. Below ru- fous, belly green. Tail with rackets.

KINGFISHERS: LONG, SHARP BILL.

Baryphthengus	*Electron*	*Ceryle*
Momotus	*Hylomanes*	

16. RUFOUS-CAPPED MOTMOT **L-FT**
Baryphthengus ruficapillus 41

Black mask. Crown and nape rufous. Back green. Throat whitish. Breast greenish olive with small black spots in center. Belly rufous. Crissum green. Tail long, without rackets. Included with 95-15 in BSA.

17. BLUE-CROWNED MOTMOT **L-FTS**
Momotus momota 38

Bill serrated. Crown and face black, surrounded by shining blue. Above green. Below olive-green to cinnamon. Usually has small black spot on breast. Tail green or blue with large rackets at end.

18. BROAD-BILLED MOTMOT **L-FT**
Electron platyrhynchum 33

Bill flat, broad, not serrated. Head, throat and breast rufous. Mask and small spot on breast black. Back green Belly blue-green. Tail without rackets e of Andes.

19. TODY MOTMOT **L-F**
Hylomanes momotula 17

Bill heavy. Crown and nape chestnut. Back, wings and tail dull green. Eyebrow blue. Cheeks black. Throat and malar stripe white. Breast brownish. No spots on breast. Belly whitish.

1. RINGED KINGFISHER **L-W**
Ceryle torquata 38

Bushy crest. Upperparts blue-gray. Throat and semicollar white. Breast and belly chestnut. Tail black banded white. F: Broad gray band across breast.

female

Chloroceryle

2. AMAZON KINGFISHER L-W
Chloroceryle amazona 25

Above oily green Collar white. No white on wings. Broad chest band rufous (f. green)

female

3. GREEN KINGFISHER LM-W
Chloroceryle americana 18

Above dark green with several round white spots on wings. Breast chestnut. Belly spotted green. Tail with much white on sides which flashes conspicuously in flight. F:Lacks chestnut band, has instead two narrow green bands across breast.

female

4. GREEN-AND-RUFOUS KINGFISHER L-FTW
Chloroceryle inda 20

Above oily green, speckled whitish on wings. Spot above lores cinnamon. Collar and underparts chestnut (f. with green band across breast).

female

5. PYGMY KINGFISHER L-FTW
Chloroceryle aenea 12

Tiny size. Upperparts dark oily green. Below rufous, crissum and center of belly white (f. with green and white breast band).

female

JACAMARS: LONG, THIN, SHARP BILL. THROAT WHITE.

Jacamerops
Galbula: Throat white, female.

6. GREAT JACAMAR L-F
Jacamerops aurea 28

Bill thick, black, slightly curved. Upperparts, face and chin green. Short white bar on throat (f. lacking). Below rufous.

7. PARADISE JACAMAR L-FT
Galbula dea 27

Crown brown. Throat white. Rest of plumage bronzy black. Central tail feathers long, narrow. F: Like male.

8. RUFOUS-TAILED JACAMAR L-FTS
Galbula ruficauda 21

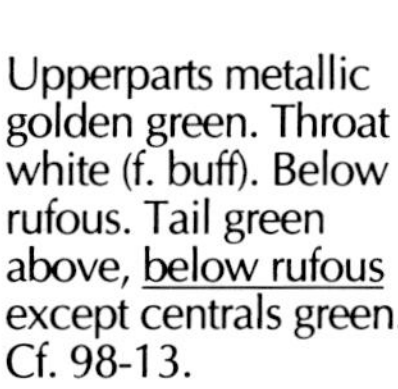

Upperparts metallic golden green. Throat white (f. buff). Below rufous. Tail green above, below rufous except centrals green. Cf. 98-13.

9. WHITE-CHINNED JACAMAR L-FW
Galbula tombacea 20

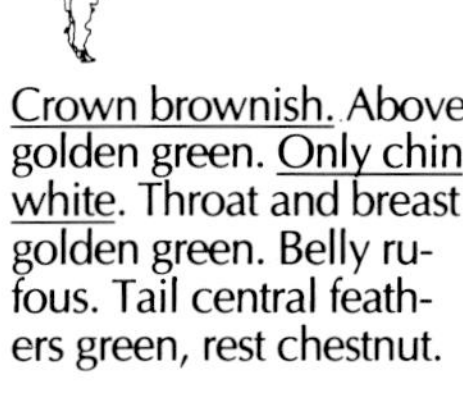

Crown brownish. Above golden green. Only chin white. Throat and breast golden green. Belly rufous. Tail central feathers green, rest chestnut.

10. BLUISH-FRONTED JACAMAR L-FT
Galbula cyanescens 20

Very like 98-9 but crown blue.

11. COPPERY-CHESTED JACAMAR M-FT
Galbula pastazae 23

Very like 98-9 but tail more coppery and bill heavier. Often shows yellow eye-ring.

12. BRONZY JACAMAR L-FT
Galbula leucogastra 20

female

A very dark jacamar. Head bronzy. Back purplish and green. Throat and belly white (f. buff). Breast mixed purplish green. Tail greenish, outermost feathers edged and tipped white.

13. GREEN-TAILED JACAMAR L-FT
Galbula galbula 20

Upperparts metallic green. Throat white (f. cinnamon). Breast green. Belly chestnut. Tail above bluish green, below blackish. Cf. 98-8.

Galbula: Throat white (f. buff). *Jacamaralcyon*
Galbalcyrhynchus
Brachygalba

14. YELLOW-BILLED JACAMAR L-FT
Galbula albirostris 18

Bill lower, lores, and eye-ring yellow. Crown purple brown. Above bronzy green. Breast, belly and underside of tail rufous.

15. CHESTNUT JACAMAR L-FT
Galbalcyrhynchus leucotis 19

Bill relatively heavy, pink with dark tip. Mostly dark chestnut. Ear coverts white (chestnut in e). Wings and tail black, tinged greenish.

16. BROWN JACAMAR L-FT
Brachygalba lugubris 16

Above dull brown. Wings, rump and tail blackish. Throat whitish. Breast brown. Belly white. Crissum brown.

17. PALE-HEADED JACAMAR L-TS
Brachygalba goeringi 15

Like 99-16 but head very pale and underparts white with broad chestnut band across belly.

18. DUSKY-BACKED JACAMAR L-FT
Brachygalba salmoni 17

Upperparts, wings and tail dark brown tinged green. Throat white Breast like back. Belly brownish rufous.

19. WHITE-THROATED JACAMAR L-FT
Brachygalba albogularis 15

Bill pale. Above blackish glossed greenish. Crown brownish. Face and throat white. Breast like back Belly rufous.

20. THREE-TOED JACAMAR L-FT
Jacamaralcyon tridactyla 15

Above blackish, glossed green. Crown streaked buff, some streaks under eye and on neck. Chin black. Below dusky, white in center. Crissum black. Has only three toes.

PUFFBIRDS: SLUGGISH BIRDS WITH LARGE HEADS

Monasa: Bill slender, curved.
Hapaloptila
Notharcus: Bill thick hooked.

1. BLACK-FRONTED NUNBIRD L-F
Monasa nigrifrons 29

Bill red. Dark gray, forehead, lores and chin black. Wings and tail blackish.

2. WHITE-FRONTED NUNBIRD L-F
Monasa morphoeus 28

Bill red. Slaty gray. Forehead, lores and chin white. Wings and tail black.

3. BLACK NUNBIRD L-F
Monasa atra 25

Bill red. Above black. Inner wing coverts white, outer ones gray. Underparts blackish gray.

4. YELLOW-BILLED NUNBIRD L-F
Monasa flavirostris 25

Bill yellowish white. Black. Upper and under wing coverts with much white.

5. WHITE-FACED NUNBIRD M-F
Hapaloptila castanea 24

Bill black. Above olive grayish. Forehead and lores white outlined in black. Throat white. Below chestnut.

6. WHITE-NECKED PUFFBIRD L-TS
Notharchus macrorhynchus 24

Crown and line through eye black. Back black. Forehead, cheeks, throat and collar white. Below white with broad black band across breast.

7. BLACK-BREASTED PUFFBIRD L-F
Notharchus pectoralis 19

Cap black. Ear coverts and narrow collar white. Above black. Throat white. Broad blue-black band across breast. Belly white.

Notharchus
Hypnelus
Nystalus

Malacoptila: White whiskers

8. BROWN-BANDED PUFFBIRD L-F
Notharchus ordii 19

Rather like 100-6 but white forehead narrow, lower part of breast band brown and upper belly barred brown.

9. RUSSET-THROATED PUFFBIRD L-TSO
Hypnelus ruficollis 21

Above brown somewhat spotted white. Narrow collar white. Below buff with one or two black bars.

10. BARRED PUFFBIRD L-FT
Nystalus radiatus 21

Bill gray. Broad collar buff. Back rufous-brown barred black. Below cinnamon-buff narrowly barred black on breast and sides.

11. WHITE-EARED PUFFBIRD L-SO
Nystalus chacuru 21

Bill red. Above brown spotted blackish. Ear patch, collar and underparts white.

12. STRIOLATED PUFFBIRD L-FT
Nystalus striolatus 21

Upperparts dark brown with buff collar. Throat and belly white. Rest of underparts buffy, narrowly streaked black. Tail black barred cinnamon.

13. SPOT-BACKED PUFFBIRD L-TS
Nystalus maculatus 20

Bill orange tipped black. Upperparts dark brown spotted buff. Collar buff. Throat white. Breast deep buff. Belly white spotted black.

14. MOUSTACHED PUFFBIRD LM-F
Malacoptila mystacalis 21

Bill upper black, lower gray. Head, nape and neck reddish brown. Back and wings brown spotted white. Lores and whisker white. Below rufous. Belly white.

15. BLACK-STREAKED PUFFBIRD M-F
Malacoptila fulvogularis 21

Head black narrowly streaked whitish. Whiskers white. Throat and breast uniform buff with no white crescent. Belly white heavily streaked black.

Malacoptila: White whiskers.
Bucco: Bill heavy, hooked.

16. WHITE-WHISKERED PUFFBIRD L-TS
Malacoptila panamensis 19

Lores buff. Whiskers white. Above reddish brown to brown, spotted buff on back and wings. Breast cinnamon. Belly whitish streaked dusky.

17. CRESCENT-CHESTED PUFFBIRD L-F
Malacoptila striata 19

Upperparts dark brown streaked buff. Lores buffy. Whisker white. Crescent across breast white bordered below by narrow black band. Below dull brownish.

18. WHITE-CHESTED PUFFBIRD L-F
Malacoptila fusca 18

Very like 102-17 but bill orange, ridge black and has no black band below white crescent on breast.

19. RUFOUS-NECKED PUFFBIRD L-F
Malacoptila rufa 18

Crown and face gray streaked white. Cheeks and narrow collar rufous. Back brown. Whiskers and breast white. Rest of underparts brown. Bill bluish gray.

20. SEMICOLLARED PUFFBIRD L-F
Malacoptila semicincta 18

Bill orange, ridge black. Head and back streaked. Collar on hindneck rusty. Underparts white streaked dusky.

21. COLLARED PUFFBIRD L-F
Bucco capensis 18

Bill orange with black ridge. Head and face rufous. Collar black. Back reddish brown narrowly banded black. Throat white. Breast band black. Below buff.

22. SOOTY-CAPPED PUFFBIRD L-FT
Bucco noanamae 18

Above dark brown Forehead and face grayish. Throat white. Broad blackish band across breast. Below buffy spotted black.

23. SPOTTED PUFFBIRD L-F
Bucco tamatia 17

Above brown spotted buff. Crown, throat and breast orange rufous. Narrow white malar stripe. Cheeks black. Belly white heavily spotted black.

Bucco: Bill heavy, hooked.
Notharchus
Nonnula: Bill rather long, slender, curved.
Micromonacha
Chelidoptera

24. CHESTNUT-CAPPED PUFFBIRD L-FT
Bucco macrodactylus 14

Crown chestnut. Back brown speckled white and buff. Broad black band across upper breast. Below buffy lightly barred.

25. PIED PUFFBIRD L-FT
Notharchus tectus 14

Like 100-6 but much smaller. Crown black speckled white. Long narrow eyebrow white.

26. GRAY-CHEEKED NUNLET L-FT
Nonnula ruficapilla 14

Crown and nape rufous. Back brown. Eye-ring red. Face and sides of neck gray. Below cinnamon. Belly whitish.

27. RUSTY-BREASTED NUNLET L-F
Nonnula rubecula 15

Like 103-26 but face brown, lores whitish. Throat and breast cinnamon. Eye-ring white.

28. FULVOUS-CHINNED NUNLET L-F
Nonnula sclateri 14

Like 103-26 but forehead, lores and chin buff. Cheeks brown.

29. BROWN NUNLET L-F
Nonnula brunnea 14

Like 103-26 but all dull brown. Eye-ring orange.

30. CHESTNUT-HEADED NUNLET L-F
Nonnula amaurocephala 14

Like 103-26 but entire neck and head rufous chestnut.

31. LANCEOLATED MONKLET LM-F
Micromonacha lanceolata 13

Bill short, rather thick. Narrow forehead and lores white. Above brown, feathers fringed whitish. Below white boldly streaked black.

32. SWALLOW-WING LM-TSO
Chelidoptera tenebrosa 14

Blackish. Belly cinnamon. Crissum grayish. Wings long, swallow-like. Bill broad, short, curved. White rump prominent in flight. Tail short.

Semnornis
Capito: Heavy bill.

33. TOUCAN BARBET LM-F
Semnornis ramphastinus 19

Bill heavy, short. Back olive brown. Crown and face shining black. White patch back of eye. Throat and sides of neck gray. Breast scarlet. Crissum olive.

34. BLACK-SPOTTED BARBET L-FT
Capito niger 18

Crown yellow. Throat red . Above mostly black. F: Spotted above and below.

female

35. WHITE-MANTLED BARBET L-F
Capito hypoleucus 17

Forecrown crimson. Crown to center of mantle white. Rest of upperparts black. Throat and breast white. Bellyand flanks pale yellow. Bill whitish.

36. SCARLET-CROWNED BARBET L-T
Capito aurovirens 17

Crown and nape red (f. white). Throat and breast orange-yellow. Belly olive.

female

37. SPOT-CROWNED BARBET L-FT
Capito maculicoronatus 17

Crown black spotted white. Above black. Below white, breast band yellow. Flanks spotted black and some red. F: Throat and breast black.

female

Capito: Heavy bill.
Eubucco: Back bright green, belly yellow streaked green.

38. ORANGE-FRONTED BARBET L-FT
Capito squamatus 17

female

Forecrown orange. Crown and nape white. Back black (f. scaled white). Underparts mostly white (f. throat and breast black).

39. FIVE-COLORED BARBET L-F
Capito quinticolor 17

Crown and nape red (f. black finely streaked yellow). Above black striped yellowish. Throat whitish. Breast and belly orange. Flanks olive mottled black.

40. BLACK-GIRDLED BARBET L-F
Capito dayi 17

Crown scarlet (f. black). Back black, white patch on mantle. Rump olive. Cheeks and throat olive barred black. Breast whitish shading to greenish on belly. Crissum mostly scarlet.

41. SCARLET-HOODED BARBET LM-TS
Eubucco tucinkae 15

Like 105-44 but back golden olive and collar yellow. F: Like m. but with head red.

42. VERSICOLORED BARBET M-FT
Eubucco versicolor 15

Head scarlet. Broad whisker and band surrounding red of head blue or yellow. F: Face and throat blue. Throat bordered below by red crescent.

43. RED-HEADED BARBET LM-FT
Eubucco bourcierii 15

female

Bill yellow. Whole head scarlet. Narrow collar bluish. Back green. Throat scarlet becoming orange on breast. F: Forehead and chin black Cheeks pale blue. Below pale greenish yellow.

44. LEMON-THROATED BARBET L-F
Eubucco richardsoni 14

female

Crown and face red. Nape bluish. Back green. Throat yellow. Breast orange. Below streaked dusky. F: Above greenish. Eyebrow gray. Face black.Throat gray. Breast orange-yellow.

TOUCANS AND ARACARIS - BILL HUGE

Ramphastos: Above black. Bill very large.

1. TOCO TOUCAN L-T
Ramphastos toco 61

Bill orange with large oval black spot at tip. Throat white. No red on breast. Rump white. Crissum red.

2. CITRON-THROATED TOUCAN LM-F
Ramphastos citreolaemus 56

Bill black, upper ridge and base yellow. Face blue. Rump yellow. Throat and breast yellow with red band below. Crissum red. Cf. 106-9.

3. RED-BILLED TOUCAN L-FT
Ramphastos tucanus 53

Bill dark red, upper ridge and base yellow, lower base blue. Rump yellow. Crissum red. Includes Orange-billed Toucan and Cuvier'sToucan.

4. YELLOW-RIDGED TOUCAN LM-F
Ramphastos culminatus 46

Like 106-2 but throat white instead of yellow.

5. KEEL-BILLED TOUCAN LM-FT
Ramphastos sulfuratus 48

Bill greenish with red tip and orange stripe along cutting edge. Throat and breast yellow Band on breast red. Rump white. Crissum red.

6. CHOCO TOUCAN L-F
Ramphastos brevis 46

Like 106-5 but bill mostly black with yellow on ridge.

7. CHESTNUT-MANDIBLED TOUCAN L-FT
Ramphastos swainsonii 53

Like 106-5 but bill mostly chestnut with yellow on ridge. Throat yellow. Rump white.

8. BLACK-MANDIBLED TOUCAN LM-FT
Ramphastos ambiguus 53

Like 106-5 but bill mostly black with yellow on ridge.

9. CHANNEL-BILLED TOUCAN L-FT
Ramphastos vitellinus 46

Bill black, blue at base. Throat yellow. Broad band on breast red. Rump and crissum red. Bare skin around eye blue or red.

Ramphastos: Above black. Bill very large.
Andigens: Belly blue-gray. Bill very large.
Aulacorhynchus: Green. Bill large.

10. RED-BREASTED TOUCAN **L-FT**
Ramphastos dicolorus 42

Bill pea green narrowly bordered black at base. Rump red. Face red. Upper throat yellow becoming orange. Breast and below red.

11. BLACK-BILLED MOUNTAIN-TOUCAN **MH-F**
Andigena nigrirostris 51

Bill blackish, crown, nape black. Back brown. Rump pale yellow. Throat whitish. Below pale blue. Crissum crimson. Thighs chestnut.

12. PLATE-BILLED MOUNTAIN-TOUCAN **LMH-F**
Andigena laminirostris 46

Bill black, reddish at base. Raised ivory patch near base of upper bill. Back and wings brownish. Rump pale yellow. Underparts blue-gray.

13. HOODED MOUNTAIN-TOUCAN **H-F**
Andigena cucullata 48

Above like 107-14 but rump greenish. Throat and breast black ish. Belly blue-gray. Bill olive green with tip and spot at base black. Tail gray.

14. GRAY-BREASTED MOUNTAIN-TOUCAN **H-F**
Andigena hypoglauca 48

Upper bill mostly red, bordered black, yellow at base, Crown, nape and face black. Broad band across upper back blue-gray. Rump yellow. Flanks chestnut. Underparts blue-gray Tail black tipped chestnut..

15. CRIMSON-RUMPED TOUCANET **LM-FT**
Aulacorhynchus haematopygus 43

Bill dark red, base outlined in white. Rump crimson.

16. BLUE-BANDED TOUCANET **M-F**
Aulacorhynchus coeruleicinctis 41

Bill blue-gray, no white line at base. Rump dark red. Short line behind eye bluish white. Throat white. Breast band blue.

Aulacorhynchus: Green. Bill large.
Baillonius
Selenidera: Yellow ear tufts. Blue around eye.

17. YELLOW-BROWED TOUCANET M-F
Aulacorhynchus huallagae 41

Bill blue-gray, sharp white line at base. Short line behind eye yellow. Throat whitish. Blue band across belly. Crissum yellow.

18. CHESTNUT-TIPPED TOUCANET LM-F
Aulacorhynchus derbianus 38

Bill black, base and tip dark red. Around eye blue. Throat bluish white.

19. EMERALD TOUCANET MH-F
Aulacorhynchus prasinus 36

Bill blackish, top of upper yellow, sharp white line at base. Throat white, blue or gray. Crissum and under tail chestnut.

20. GROOVE-BILLED TOUCANET M-F
Aulacorhynchus sulcatus 33

Bill varies -- black, red or yellow. Around eye blue. Throat gray. Tail tipped bluish. Includes Yellow-billed Toucanet.

21. SAFFRON TOUCANET L-F
Baillonius bailloni 36

Above dark olive green. Bill olive, red at base. Forecrown yellow. Rump crimson. Underparts yellow.

22. YELLOW-EARED TOUCANET LM-F
Selenidera spectabilis 36

Bill black, top of upper yellowish. Crown and nape black (f. chestnut). Ear tufts golden yellow (f. lacking). Back and wings green. Throat, breast and center of belly black. Sides orange. Crissum red.

23. GUIANAN TOUCANET L-FT
Selenidera culik 33

Bill black, red at base. Crown and nape black. Band across upper back yellow. Back olive green. Wings and tail gray. Below black (f. gray). Crissum red.

24. GOLDEN-COLLARED TOUCANET L-F
Selenidera reinwardtii 33

Like 108-23 but brighter above with orange flank. F: Head and underparts chestnut.

25. TAWNY-TUFTED TOUCANET L-F
Selenidera nattereri 33

Like 108-23 but bill red with several vertical black stripes. F: Underparts chestnut.

26. SPOT-BILLED TOUCANET L-F
Selenidera maculirostris 33

Like 108-23 but lower bill has black patch in center (or whitish with three black spots in e).

Pteroglossus: Head blackish. Rump red. Belly yellow.

27. CURL-CRESTED ARACARI L-F
Pteroglossus beauharnaesii 33

Bill lower pale, upper black. Crown feathers black, curly. Mantle red. Back greenish. Cheeks and throat yellowish. Belly crossed by crimson band.

28. MANY-BANDED ARACARI L-FT
Pteroglossus pluricinctus 41

Bill upper pale, ridge black, lower black. Around eye blue. Back greenish. Throat black. Below yellow, crossed by two blackish bands. Thighs chestnut.

29. IVORY-BILLED ARACARI L-F
Pteroglossus flavirostris 41

Bill ivory white black "teeth" on upper, brown along cutting edge of lower. Head dark brown. Back dull green. Upper breast red, lower breast black. Belly yellow. Includes Brown-mandibled Aracari.

30. BLACK-NECKED ARACARI L-FT
Pteroglossus aracari 40

Very like 109-28 but upper bill all white. Lacks black band across breast.

31. COLLARED ARACARI L-F
Pteroglossus torquatus 37

Bill upper yellow, lower black or pale. Sharp white line around base. Red around eye. Rump red. Below yellow, large black spot on center of breast. Black and red band below breast. Includes Stripe-billed and Pale-mandibled Aracaris.

32. CHESTNUT-EARED ARACARI L-FT
Pteroglossus castanotis 36

Bill upper black and yellow. Ear patch deep chest-nut. Back, wings and tail green. Single red band across belly.

33. GREEN ARACARI L-FT
Pteroglossus viridis 28

Bill upper red with yellowish ridge. Lower black. Back dark green. Throat black. Below yellow, no bands.

34. LETTERED ARACARI L-FT
Pteroglossus inscriptus 28

Bill upper yellowish, ridge and lines along cutting edge black; lower yellowish or black. Back dark green. Throat black, below yellow.

35. RED-NECKED ARACARI L-F
Pteroglossus bitorquatus 28

Bill pale, dusky near end of lower. Mantle, rump and around eye red. Head and throat black with narrow yellow band below. Breast crimson. Belly yellow.

Campephilus: Mostly black. Crest red.
Dryocopus

1. MAGELLANIC WOODPECKER **LM-F**
Campephilus magellanicus 36

Head and long curling crest crimson (f. black). Rest of plumage black with some white on wings.

2. CRIMSON-BELLIED WOODPECKER **LM-F**
Campephilus (Phloeoceastes) haematogaster 33

Above black. Head, rump, breast and belly red. Broad malar white. F: Below lightly barred black.

3 POWERFUL WOODPECKER **MH-F**
Campephilus (Phloeoceastes) pollens 33

Crest red (f. black). Above black. Malar stripes white down to white rump (forming "V"). Below black barred buff.

female

4. CRIMSON-CRESTED WOODPECKER **LMH-FT**
Campephilus (Phloeoceastes) melanoleucos 31

Above black. Crest, head and nape red (f. forehead black, broad malar stripe white). White lines down sides of neck join on back. Throat and breast black. Below barred buffy.

female

5. GUAYAQUIL WOODPECKER **L-FT**
Campephilus (Phloeoceastes) gayaquilensis 31

Much like 110-4 but male with no white at base of bill. F: Like f. 110-4 but browner.

6. ROBUST WOODPECKER **L-F**
Campephilus (Phloeoceastes) robustus 31

Entire head and neck red. Center of back white. Below barred black and white. F: White malar stripe.

7. RED-NECKED WOODPECKER **L-F**
Campephilus (Phloeoceastes) rubricollis 31

Entire head, neck and breast red. Above all black. Belly chestnut. F: White patch below eye.

8. CREAM-BACKED WOODPECKER **L-FT**
Campephilus (Phloeoceastes) leucopogon 29

Body black, center of back buff. Head and neck crimson, spot on ear coverts black and white. F: Center of crown black.

9. LINEATED WOODPECKER **LM-FT**
Dryocopus lineatus 33

Above black. Crown, crest, nape and whisker red (f. forecrown black). Malar stripes white continuing down sides of back but do not join. Below barred buff and black. Is only one of type with throat streaked black and white.

Dryocopus
Colaptes: Usually on or near ground.
Chrysoptilus: Whisker red (f. lacking).

10. BLACK-BODIED WOODPECKER L-FT
Dryocopus schulzi 30

Like 110-9 but all black below with a few dull white bars at sides.

11. HELMETED WOODPECKER LM-F
Dryocopus galeatus 28

Crest, nape and malar red (f. no malar). Ear coverts with fine vertical black lines. Back, wings and tail black. Rump whitish. Below barred black and buff.

12. ANDEAN FLICKER H-O
Colaptes rupicola 33

Crown gray. Back barred black and buff. Rump buff. Whisker red (f. gray). Underparts buff to cinnamon, spotted black on breast.

13. CHILEAN FLICKER L-FT
Colaptes pitius 30

Crown gray. Face buffy white (no whisker). Back brownish barred buffy. Rump white. Throat whitish. Below barred black and white.

14. CAMPO FLICKER L-O
Colaptes campestris 28

Crown and nape black. Back blackish barred white. Throat black. Whisker reddish (f. spotted white). Breast and sides of neck yellow. Belly white barred black. Tail black.

15. FIELD FLICKER L-O
Colaptes campestroides 30

Crown and nape black. Above black barred or scaled white. Throat white. Breast yellow. Belly white scaled or barred black.

16. GREEN-BARRED WOODPECKER L-TOS
Chrysoptilus melanochloros 25

female

Forecrown black. Hindcrown and nape red. Whisker red (f. black, dotted white). Face white. Back barred black and greenish. Throat streaked. Below greenish spotted black. Tail barred black and yellow.

17. BLACK-NECKED WOODPECKER LM-TS
Chrysoptilus atricollis 25

Crown, nape and whisker red (f. only nape red). Above olive barred black. Face white. Throat and breast black. Below yellowish barred black. Tail black, outers barred whitish.

Chrysoptilus: Whisker red (f. lacking).
Piculus: Whisker red (f. lacking).
Celeus: Whisker red (f. lacking).

Leuconerpes

18. GOLDEN-BREASTED WOODPECKER **M-TOS**
Chrysoptilus melanolaimus 25

female

Forecrown black. Hindcrown red. Face white. Whisker red (f. blackish). Throat yellowish white finely streaked. Breast tinged orange. Tail black, barred yellow.

19. CRIMSON-MANTLED WOODPECKER **MH-FT**
Piculus rivolii 25

Crown red (f. black). Above mostly red. Rump yellow barred black. Face whitish. Throat black. Breast black fringed red. Belly yellowish. Tail black.

20. CHESTNUT WOODPECKER **L-FT**
Celeus elegans 25

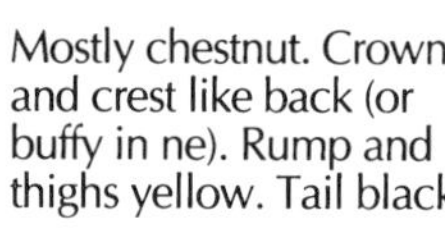

Mostly chestnut. Crown and crest like back (or buffy in ne). Rump and thighs yellow. Tail black.

21. RINGED WOODPECKER **L-FT**
Celeus torquatus 24

Crest and head cinnamon. Above chestnut, more or less barred black. Collar and breast black. Belly buff. Tail chestnut barred black.

22. RUFOUS-HEADED WOODPECKER **L-F**
Celeus spectabilis 25

Head rufous. Line from behind eye to end of crest crimson (f. no crimson). Back buff spotted black. Rump buff. Neck and breast blackish. Below buff spotted black. Wings chestnut. Tail black.

23. WHITE WOODPECKER **LM-TO**
Leuconerpes candidus 24

Head, rump and all underparts white. Line down sides of neck black. Spot on nape and breast and center of belly yellow (f. no yellow).

24. CREAM-COLORED WOODPECKER **L-FT**
Celeus flavus 24

Light yellowish. Wings brown. Tail dusky.

25. CINNAMON WOODPECKER **L-FT**
Celeus loricatus 24

Upperparts chestnut barred black. Throat scaled crimson. Below white strongly barred black.
F: Throat chestnut.

male

female

Celeus: Whisker red (f. lacking).
Piculus: Whisker red (f. lacking).
Melanerpes: No whisker, rump white.

1. SCALE-BREASTED WOODPECKER L-F
Celeus grammicus 21

Very like 112-25 but darker. Rump yellow, unbarred. Below scaled black. Tail black, not barred.

2. BLOND-CRESTED WOODPECKER L-FT
Celeus flavescens 20

Crown and long crest buffy. Back buff barred or spotted black. Rump buffy Throat buffy. Below blackish. Underparts not barred.

3. PALE-CRESTED WOODPECKER L-T
Celeus lugubris 20

Like 113-2 but area around eye dusky. Wings barred chestnut. Underparts brown.

4. WAVED WOODPECKER L-FT
Celeus undatus 20

Crest and head chestnut. Back, wings, tail, rump and underparts all chestnut barred black.

5. WHITE-BROWED WOODPECKER L-F
Piculus aurulentus 20

Crown and nape red f. nape only). Face gray bordered white above and below. Back olive. Throat yellow. Underparts barred gray and white. Tail black.

6. GOLDEN-OLIVE WOODPECKER LM-FTS
Piculus rubiginosus 20

female

Crown dark gray, edged red (f. all gray). Nape red. Face whitish. Back yellowish olive. Rump and underparts barred dusky and yellowish.

7. GOLDEN-GREEN WOODPECKER L-FT
Piculus chrysochloros 20

Like 113-6 but crown all red (f. yellowish), face olive with narrow yellow malar stripe.

8. YELLOW-THROATED WOODPECKER L-F
Piculus flavigula 19

Crown and nape red (f. nape only). Back olive. Face and neck yellow. Throat yellow (red in e). Below white, scalloped olive (or barred in e)

9. WHITE-THROATED WOODPECKER L-F
Piculus leucolaemus 19

Crown and nape red (f. nape only). Back olive. Face yellow. Throat white. Below scalloped or barred olive and buff. F: Whisker white.

10. ACORN WOODPECKER MH-FT
Melanerpes formicivorus 21

Whitish band surrounding black forehead and chin. Eye white. Wing spot white. Above black. Below white, breast streaked black.

Melanerpes
Chrysoptilus
Veniliornus: Crown red. No whisker.

Picoides

11. YELLOW-TUFTED WOODPECKER L-FT
Melanerpes cruentatus 19

female

Black. Crown red. White eyebrow extended to yellow collar. Rump white. Belly red in center. Sides barred black and white. Includes Red-fronted Woodpecker.

12. YELLOW-FRONTED WOODPECKER L-T
Melanerpes flavifrons 18

Forecrown yellow. Nape red (f. no red). Back black. Rump white. Throat yellow. Below red, barred on sides.

13. BLACK-CHEEKED WOODPECKER L-FT
Melanerpes pucherani 18

female

Forehead yellow. Crown red (f. black). Nape red. Above black narrowly barred white. Cheeks black. Throat whitish. Breast olive. Belly barred, red in center.

14. GOLDEN-NAPED WOODPECKER L-FT
Melanerpes chrysauchen 18

Crown red. Nape yellow. Black stripe through eye continued on sides of neck. Center of back white. Throat white.Below buffy gray, barred black on belly.

15. SPOT-BREASTED WOODPECKER L-TS
Chrysoptilus punctigula 19

Forecrown black. Hindcrown, and nape red. Face white. Back yellowish barred black. Throat checkered. Below reddish to yellow, spotted black on breast. Tail outers yellowish barred black.

16. BAR-BELLIED WOODPECKER MH-F
Veniliornis nigriceps 17

Crown and nape red (f. black). Back olive more or less stained red. Underparts barred olive and whitish.

1. CHECKERED WOODPECKER L-TS
Picoides (Dendrocopos) mixtus 16

Crown black, streaked white. Above black prominently spotted white. Small red spot (f. lacking) at side of nape. Long white line back of eye. Underparts white streaked black.

2. STRIPED WOODPECKER LM-TS
Picoides (Dendrocopos) lignarius 15

Crown black streaked white. Back black barred white. Sides of nape red (f. no red). Broad line behind eye. Underparts white streaked black.

Melanerpes
Veniliornis: Crown red. No whisker.

3. WHITE-FRONTED WOODPECKER **LM-TS**
Melanerpes (Trichopicus) cactorum 16

Forecrown and cheeks white. Hindcrown black. Face black Back black with white down center. Throat yellow.

4. RED-CROWNED WOODPECKER **LM-TS**
Melanerpes rubricapillus 16

Crown and nape red (f. nape only). Back, wings and tail barred black and white. Rump white. Face grayish. Below pale gray, red in center of belly.

5. SMOKY-BROWN WOODPECKER **MH-FT**
Veniliornis fumigatus 16

Crown red (f. brown). Uniform brown with no spots. Area around eye and cheeks whitish. Tail black.

6. WHITE-SPOTTED WOODPECKER **LM-FT**
Veniliornis spilogaster 16

Crown brown, streaked red (f. white). Broad white line behind eye.Whisker white. Back barred olive and yellow.Below gray spot ted white. Tail black with pale bars.

7. DOT-FRONTED WOODPECKER **LM-F**
Veniliornis frontalis 16

Like 116-13 but crown dotted white (m. only forehead dotted), back spotted yellowish and tail brown barred buffy.

8. RED-RUMPED WOODPECKER **L-FTS**
Veniliornis kirkii 16

Crown red (f. brown). Nape yellowish. Back golden olive. Wing coverts with yellow spots. Rump and upper tail coverts red.

9. RED-STAINED WOODPECKER **L-FTS**
Veniliornis affinis 16

Very like 115-8 but lacks red rump and tail coverts. Wing coverts with some obscure red stains but no yellow spots. Underparts all barred.

10. GOLDEN-COLLARED WOODPECKER **L-FT**
Veniliornis cassini 14

Like 115-8 but without red rump and with semi-collar yellow.

11. YELLOW-VENTED WOODPECKER **M-F**
Veniliornis dignus 16

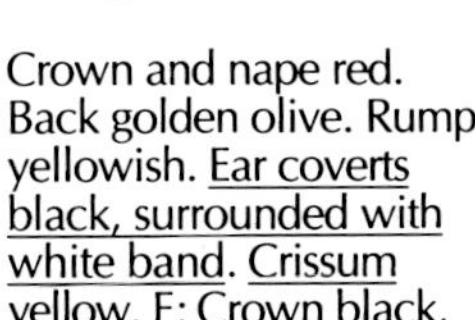

Crown and nape red. Back golden olive. Rump yellowish. Ear coverts black, surrounded with white band. Crissum yellow. F: Crown black, only nape red.

Veniliornis: Crown red. No whisker.
Picumnus: Forecrown black spotted red (f. white). Hindcrown spotted white. Tail black, some white in center and outer edges.

12. YELLOW-EARED WOODPECKER **LM-F**
Veniliornis maculifrons 15

Forecrown brown with pale shaft streaks. Hindcrown red (f. no red). Nape and ear coverts yellow. Back olive. Wing coverts spotted yellow. Below white barred dusky. Tail black barred brownish.

13. LITTLE WOODPECKER **L-TS**
Veniliornis passerinus 14

Forehead gray. Crown and nape red (f. gray). No yellow collar. Back olive yellow. Wing coverts spotted yellow. Below olive barred white. Tail black, more or less barred buff.

male female

14. SCARLET-BACKED WOODPECKER **L-SA**
Veniliornis callonotus 14

Upperparts red. Face and underparts whitish. Tail black, outers white barred dusky. F: Crown and nape black.

15. BLOOD-COLORED WOODPECKER **L-TS**
Veniliornis sanguineus 13

Above red (f. crown brown, spotted whitish). Underparts dark gray barred white.

1. CHESTNUT PICULET **L-TS**
Picumnus cinnamomeus 9

Forehead broadly white. Crown black, spotted yellow. Back chestnut. Below rufous-chestnut. Tail chestnut.

2. RUFOUS-BREASTED PICULET **L-FT**
Picumnus rufiventris 9

female

Back and wings dark olive with rufous collar. Underparts rufous.

3. WHITE-BELLIED PICULET **L-TS**
Picumnus spilogaster 8

Forecrown red. Hindcrown spotted white. Above brown. Below white with a few brown spots or streaks on sides.

PICULETS: TAIL BLACK, CENTRAL AND OUTER FEATHERS EDGED WHITE. F: CROWN BLACK, SPOTTED WHITE

Picumnus: Forecrown black spotted red (f. spotted white). Hindcrown spotted white. Tail black, some white in center and outer edges.

4. MOTTLED PICULET L-F
Picumnus nebulosus 9

Forecrown solid red. Hindcrown dotted white Back buffy brown. Throat whitish. Breast brown. Belly buffy streaked black. F: Crown and nape all dotted white.

5. OLIVACEOUS PICULET L-TS
Picumnus olivaceus 8

Crown spotted orange in front, white behind. Back olive. Throat whitish. Breast light olive brown. Belly yellowish olive, faintly streaked dusky.

6. PLAIN-BREASTED PICULET L-T
Picumnus castelnau 8

Above dusky olive. Crown black dotted red (f. crown all black). Below whitish tinged yellow on belly, no spotting.

7. OCHRACEOUS PICULET L-F
Picumnus limae 8

Above brown. Face and chin whitish. Throat whitish. Below yellowish white, unmarked.

8. GRAYISH PICULET M-TS
Picumnus granadensis 8

Crown black spotted yellow in front and white behind (f. all spotted white). Above brownish gray, scaled all over. Below grayish white.

9. SCALED PICULET LM-FT
Picumnus squamulatus 8

Forecrown black, speckled orange (f. speckled white). Hindcrown black speckled white. Above like 117-10 but more olive brown and lacks whitish spots, but is scaled.

10. ARROWHEAD PICULET L-TS
Picumnus minutissimus 8

Above grayish brown, mantle with a few whitish spots. Underparts whitish scaled black like 117-9.

11. BLACK-DOTTED PICULET L-F
Picumnus nigropunctatus 8

Crown black streaked red. Above greenish yellow olive scaled dusky. Below pale yellow, barred on throat and with round black spots on breast and sides.

PICULETS: TAIL BLACK, CENTRAL AND OUTER FEATHERS EDGED WHITE. F: CROWN BLACK, SPOTTED WHITE.
Picumnus: Forecrown spotted red (f. white). Hindcrown spotted white.

12. OCELLATED PICULET L-F
Picumnus dorbygnianus 8

Above grayish brown, obscurely spotted white. Below white, feathers centered black giving scaly appearance.

13. SPECKLE-CHESTED PICULET LM-F
Picumnus steindachneri 8

Above brownish gray scaled paler. Throat whitish. Breast black spotted white. Belly barred black and white.

14. VARZEA PICULET L-T
Picumnus varzeae 10

Brown. Underparts sparsely dotted white.

15. SPOTTED PICULET L-S
Picumnus pygmaeus 10

Dull brown. Spotted white above and thickly spotted white below.

16. GOLDEN-SPANGLED PICULET LM-FT
Picumnus exilis 8

Above olive barred yellowish and black. Below yellowish barred black.

17. BAR-BREASTED PICULET L-F
Picumnus borbae 8

Above plain olive. Throat whitish. Below yellowish barred black on breast and streaked on belly.

18. ORINOCO PICULET L-SO
Picumnus pumilus 9

Above plain olive. Forecrown black dotted yellow. Hindcrown pale brown spotted buffy. Underparts yellowish, narrowly barred black.

19. GOLD-FRONTED PICULET L-FT
Picumnus aurifrons 7

Above barred yellow and olive. Forecrown spotted orange. Below barred (belly streaked in s).

20. OCHRE-COLLARED PICULET L-F
Picumnus temminckii 8

female

Above buffy brown. Cheeks, sides of neck and collar bright buff. Below white broadly barred black.

21. WHITE-BARRED PICULET LM-TS
Picumnus cirrhatus 8

Forecrown solid red (f. spotted white). Above brownish. Underparts strongly barred black and white.

22. ECUADORIAN PICULET L-SA
Picumnus sclateri 8

Forecrown dotted yellow. Above brownish, faintly barred paler. Below white, throat and breast barred, belly streaked black (all barred in some races).

WOODCREEPERS; BROWN, WINGS AND TAIL RUFOUS. CLIMB TREE TRUNKS.

Nasica

Xiphocolaptes: Heavy bill slightly curved.

Campylorhamphus: Long, thin, sickle-shaped bill.

1. LONG-BILLED WOODCREEPER **L-FT**
Nasica longirostris 31

Bill 2x head, straight. Crown blackish, narrowly streaked. Above chestnut, long eyebrow and streaks on nape white. Throat white. Below light brown, breast boldly streaked white.

2. STRONG-BILLED WOODCREEPER **LMH-F**
Xiphocolaptes promeropirhynchus 28

Like 119-3 but more rufous. Bill grayish. Belly barred black and white.

3. WHITE-THROATED WOODCREEPER **LM-F**
Xiphocolaptes albicollis 25

Bill = head, black. Crown blackish, streaked white. Malar whitish. Back unstreaked. Throat white. Breast streaked.

4. MOUSTACHED WOODCREEPER **L-FT**
Xiphocolaptes falcirostris 25

Very like 119-3 but bill horn color and malar buff. Underparts pale brown finely streaked.

5. CURVE-BILLED SCYTHEBILL **L-F**
Campylorhamphus procurvoides 24

Bill 1-1/2x head, reddish brown. Like 119-7 but much darker and back not streaked except south of the Amazon in Brasil.

6. GREATER SCYTHEBILL **L-FT**
Campylorhamphus pucheranii 27

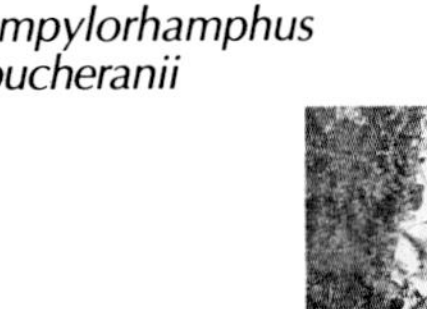

Bill 1-1/2x head, brown. Earthy brown. Crown and mantle faintly streaked Eyebrow and malar strongly white. Rump, wings and tail chestnut. Underparts brown.

7. RED-BILLED SCYTHEBILL **L-FT**
Campylorhamphus trochilirostris 25 (16 in w)

Bill 2x head, reddish. Reddish brown on head, mantle and breast. Throat whitish. Wings and tail rufous.

8. BLACK-BILLED SCYTHEBILL **L-F**
Campylorhamphus falcularius 25

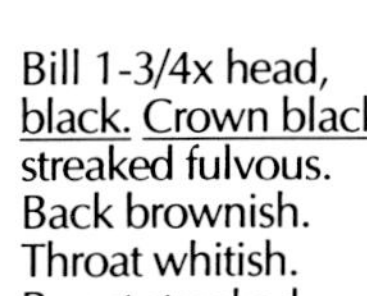

Bill 1-3/4x head, black. Crown black, streaked fulvous. Back brownish. Throat whitish. Breast streaked.

9. BROWN-BILLED SCYTHEBILL **LM-F**
Campylorhamphus pusillus 23

Bill 1-1/4x head, light brown. Like 119-7 but dark olive-brown.

Dendrocolaptes: Strong bill nearly straight.
Xiphorhynchus: Rump, wings and tail chestnut.

10. BLACK-BANDED WOODCREEPER LM-F
Dendrocolaptes picumnus 25

Bill 3/4x head, dusky, tip paler. Crown and mantle streaked. Below brown streaked buff on breast, barred narrowly black on belly.

11. HOFFMANNS' WOODCREEPER L-F
Dendrocolaptes hoffmannsi 25

Bill 3/4x head, black. Brown. Crown reddish, lightly streaked. Back heavily streaked. Throat and breast with inconspicuous buffy hair streaks.

12. PLANALTO WOODCREEPER LM-F
Dendrocolaptes platyrostris 24

Like 119-3 but bill 3/4x head and horn color instead of black. Some races have crown brown instead of blackish.

13. BUFF-THROATED WOODCREEPER L-FTS
Xiphorhynchus guttatus 24

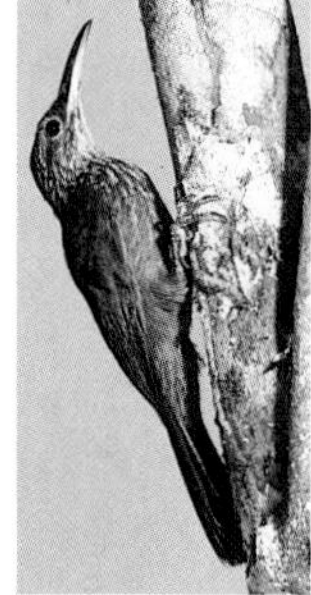

Bill = head, almost straight, Crown black, streaked buff. Back usually not streaked but sometimes is on upper mantle. Throat buffy. Below brown, broadly streaked on breast.

14. DUSKY-BILLED WOODCREEPER L-F
Xiphorhynchus eytoni 25

Like 120-13 but upper back broadly streaked white and streak behind eye white.

15. OCELLATED WOODCREEPER L-F
Xiphorhynchus ocellatus 24

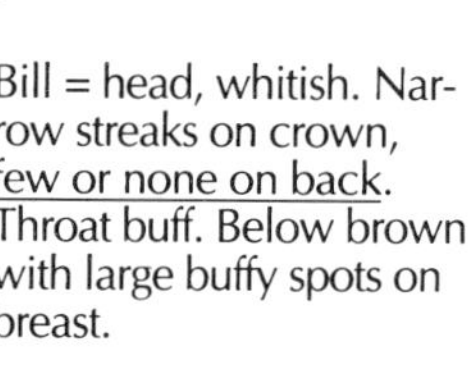

Bill = head, whitish. Narrow streaks on crown, few or none on back. Throat buff. Below brown with large buffy spots on breast.

16. CHESTNUT-RUMPED WOODCREEPER L-FT
Xiphorhynchus pardalotus 23

Bill = head, almost straight, lower pale, upper blackish. Back with long drop-shaped mark

17 BLACK-STRIPED WOODCREEPER L-F
Xiphorhynchus lachrymosus 24

Bill = head. Boldly streaked black and buff on head, back and underparts.

18. ELEGANT WOODCREEPER L-F
Xiphorhynchus elegans 20

Very like 121-19 but back quite prominently spotted buff. Breast with fan-shaped spots. Lower bill dusky.

Xiphorhynchus: Rump, wings and tail chestnut.
Lepidocolaptes: Bill slender, curved, pale.

19. SPIX'S WOODCREEPER L-FT
Xiphorhynchus spixii 20

Bill 3/4x head, lower pale. Above spotted on head. Mantle and underparts with wide, black-edged, buff streaks.

20. STRAIGHT-BILLED WOODCREEPER L-T
Xiphorhynchus picus 20

Bill = head, very straight, whitish. Crown streaked buff. Back not streaked. Throat whitish. Below brown broadly streaked on breast. (Face mostly whitish in n.)

21. ZIMMER'S WOODCREEPER L-F
Xiphorhynchus necopinus 20

Like 121-20 but bill darker. General color less rufous. Back slightly streaked.

22. STRIPED WOODCREEPER L-F
Xiphorhynchus obsoletus 18

Like 121-20 but back prominently streaked buffy.

23. OLIVE-BACKED WOODCREEPER LM-F
Xiphorhynchus triangularis 20

Bill 3/4x head, slightly curved. Crown lightly spotted buff. Back olive brown unstreaked. Eye-ring prominent. Below olive brown conspicuously spotted buff.

24. SPOTTED WOODCREEPER LM-F
Xiphorhynchus erythropgius 20

Like 121-23 but eyebrow prominent buff and crown with only a few buff dots.

25. NARROW-BILLED WOODCREEPER L-TSO
Lepidocolaptes angustirostris 20

Bill = head. Crown dusky lightly streaked pale Above rufous. Broad eyebrow white. Cheeks black. Below whitish more or less streaked dusky.

26. STREAK-HEADED WOODCREEPER L-TSO
Lepidocolaptes souleyetii 19

Bill 3/4x head, upper dusky, lower pale. Crown and nape streaked buff. Throat whitish. Below all strongly streaked with light buff, black-edged streaks.

WOODCREEPERS WITH HEAD STREAKED - IV
WOODCREEPERS WITH HEAD NOT STREAKED - I

Lepidocolaptes: Bill slender, curved, pale.
Xiphocolaptes
Drymornis
Hylexetastes
Dendrocolaptes

27. SPOT-CROWNED WOODCREEPER **MH-FT**
Lepidocolaptes affinis 19

Bill 3/4x head. Crown and nape finely spotted buff. Throat white. Below profusely striped with black-edged white stripes. Cf. 123-10. Separate by range.

28. SCALED WOODCREEPER **L-F**
Lepidocolaptes squamatus 19

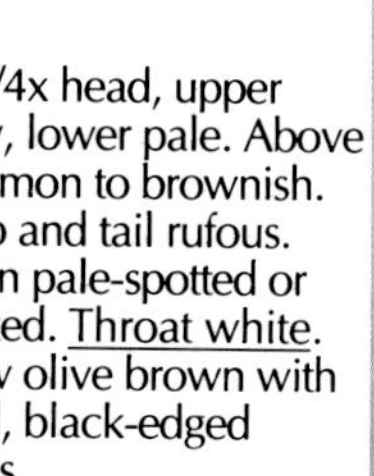

Bill 3/4x head, upper dusky, lower pale. Above cinnamon to brownish. Rump and tail rufous. Crown pale-spotted or streaked. Throat white. Below olive brown with broad, black-edged streaks.

29. LESSER WOODCREEPER **L-FT**
Lepidocolaptes fuscus 18

Bill 3/4x head, upper dusky, lower pale. Crown, nape and mantle brown streaked buff. Dusky line back of eye. Throat buffy. Below brown all streaked dusky.

1. GREAT RUFOUS WOODCREEPER **L-TS**
Xiphocolaptes major 30

Bill = head, heavy. Above uniform bright rufous, crown browner. Throat and breast streaked white. Belly more or less barred dusky.

2. SCIMITAR-BILLED WOODCREEPER **L-S**
Drymornis bridgesii 28

Bill 2x head, thin, curved. Upperparts and face rufous. Long eyebrow and whisker white.Throat white. Below cinnamon streaked dusky.

3. RED-BILLED WOODCREEPER **L-F**
Hylexetastes perrotii 28

Bill = head, heavy, red. Brown, paler below. Face and throat whitish. Rump, wings and tail chestnut. Broad irregular malar stripe whitish.

4. BAR-BELLIED WOODCREEPER **L-F**
Hylexetastes stresemanni 25

Crown and nape red. Back olive tinged red in places. Below barred dark olive and whitish. Tail black. outer feathers barred. F: Crown and nape black.

5. CONCOLOR WOODCREEPER **L-F**
Dendrocolaptes concolor 24

Like 123-6 but no barring. Also like 123-11 but no gray on face.

Dendrocolaptes
Dendrocincla: Rump, wings and tail chestnut
Dendrexetastes
Deconychura
Lepidocolaptes: Bill slender, curved, pale.

6. BARRED WOODCREEPER L-F
Dendrocolaptes certhia 24

Bill = head, dusky (reddish in se). Head, back and underparts narrowly barred black.

7. TYRANNINE WOODCREEPER MH-F
Dendrocincla tyrannina 23

Bill 3/4x head, upper black, lower gray. Uniform dull brown, face and throat lighter brown. Inconspicuous shaft streaks on breast.

8. CINNAMON-THROATED WOODCREEPER L-FT
Dendrexetastes rufigula 21

Bill 3/4x head, heavy. Brown, paler below. A few streaks on breast white, edged black in e.

9. LONG-TAILED WOODCREEPER LM-F
Deconychura longicauda 20

Bill 3/4x head. Brown. Crown streaks not obvious. Rump brown, not rufous. Throat and breast streaks buffy.

10. LINEATED WOODCREEPER L-F
Lepidocolaptes albolineatus 19

Bill 3/4x head. Minute crown dots not obvious. Above uniform reddish brown. Throat whitish. Below olive brown with black-edged buff marks. Cf. 122-27.

11. PLAIN-BROWN WOODCREEPER L-FT
Dendrocincla fuliginosa 19

Bill 3/4x head. Uniform plain brown. Grayish around eye, bordered by faint dusky malar stripe.

12. RUDDY WOODCREEPER L-F
Dendrocincla homochroa 19

Bill 3/4x head. Reddish brown, crown usually noticeably brighter than rest of head.

13. WHITE-CHINNED WOODCREEPER L-FT
Dendrocincla merula 18

Bill 3/4x head. Dark brown. Throat prominent white, sharply contrasting. Eye gray.

FIRST LENGTH FIGURE DOES NOT INCLUDE ELONGATED PART OF TAIL.

Deconychura *Glyphorhynchus* *Schizoeaca:* Tail long, pointed. Webs ragged.
Sittasomus *Schoeniophylax:* Tail long, pointed.

14. SPOT-THROATED WOODCREEPER **L-F**
Deconychura stictolaema 15

Bill 3/4x head. Above brownish rufous. Rump rufous. Throat and breast brown, spotted buff.

15. OLIVACEOUS WOODCREEPER **LM-FT**
Sittasomus griseicapillus 15

Bill 1/2x head, thin. Head, mantle and back grayish brown. Rump, wings and tail rufous. Below grayish brown. Pale band on wing in flight.

16. WEDGE-BILLED WOODCREEPER **L-FT**
Glyphorhynchus spirurus 13

Bill 1/3 head, lower upturned. Above brown becoming rufous on rump and tail. Eyebrow buff. Throat buff. Below dark brown, breast spotted buff. Cinnamon band on wing in flight.

1. CHOTOY SPINETAIL **L-SO**
Schoeniophylax phryganophila 6+4

Crown rufous. Eyebrow white. Above brown streaked black. Patch on throat black. Prominent rufous patch on wing coverts.

2. MOUSE-COLORED THISTLETAIL **H-SO**
Schizoeaca griseomurina 14+2

Very like 124-5 but has no eyebrow. Eye-ring white.

3. EYE-RINGED THISTLETAIL **H-S**
Schizoeaca palpebralis 14+2

Like 124-5 but chestnut brown above. White eye-ring prominent. Chin orange.

4. OCHRE-BROWED THISTLETAIL **H-S**
Schizoeaca coryi 14+2

Like 124-5 but long eyebrow, face and chin rufous (not gray or white).

5. WHITE-CHINNED THISTLETAIL **H-S**
Schizoeaca fuliginosa 14+2

Upperparts rufous brown. Eyebrow grayish. Narrow eye-ring gray. Eye white. Chin white. Below gray. Tail like back.

6. BLACK-THROATED THISTLETAIL **MH-SO**
Schizoeaca harterti 14+2

Like 124-5 but has black throat narrowly streaked white. Below gray.

FIRST LENGTH FIGURE DOES NOT INCLUDE ELONGATED PART OF TAIL.

Schizoeaca: Tail, central feathers elongated, pointed.
Leptasthenura: Tail long, pointed. Bill small, stubby.

7. PUNA THISTLETAIL **H-SO**
Schizoeaca helleri 14+2

Like 124-5 but upperparts chestnut brown and white eye-ring prominent.

8. ARAUCARIA TIT-SPINETAIL **LM-FT**
Leptasthenura setaria 13+4

Crested. Crown black streaked white. Above bright chestnut. Throat white dotted dusky. Below buff. Tail rufous.

9. TAWNY TIT-SPINETAIL **H-TS**
Leptasthenura yanacensis 12+3

Above tawny. Forecrown and rump rufous. Eyebrow buff. Below uniform tawny buff. Tail rufous.

10. ANDEAN TIT-SPINETAIL **H-S**
Leptasthenura andicola 13+2

Crown black streaked rufous. Eyebrow white. Back and breast brown strongly streaked white. Belly dull grayish.

11. STREAKED TIT-SPINETAIL **H-S**
Leptasthenura striata 12+2

Crown black streaked rufous. Back brown streaked buff. Below dull grayish faintly streaked.

12. RUSTY-CROWNED TIT-SPINETAIL **H-TS**
Leptasthenura pileata 12+2

Crown rufous, unstreaked. Back dark brown streaked white. Below grayish streaked white except on belly.

13. WHITE-BROWED TIT-SPINETAIL **H-TS**
Leptasthenura xenothorax 12+2

Crown and mantle rufous. Conspicuous white postocular stripe Back blackish. Throat sharply streaked black and white. Below gray.

14. STRIOLATED TIT-SPINETAIL **LM-TS**
Leptasthenura striolata 12+2

Crown brown streaked black. Narrow eyebrow buffy. Back brown streaked blackish. Below pale buffy.

15. PLAIN-MANTLED TIT-SPINETAIL **LMH-S**
Leptasthenura aegithaloides 14

Crown and nape blackish boldly streaked cinnamon. Lores and short eyebrow white. Back grayish brown. Throat and breast white lightly streaked dusky. Belly buffy. Tail blackish.

16. TUFTED TIT- SPINETAIL **L-TS**
Leptasthenura platensis 12+2

Crested. Crown brown streaked cinnamon. Back plain grayish brown. Throat white spotted black. Below buffy.

17. BROWN-CAPPED TIT-SPINETAIL **MH-S**
Leptasthenura fuliginiceps 12+2

Crown chestnut. Back brown. Throat white. Below pale buffy (grayish in s).Wings and tail rufous.

FURNARIIDS USUALLY ON GROUND - I - EARTHCREEPERS.

Spartanoica
Sylviorthorhynchus

Upucerthia: Bill thin, long, curved.

18. BAY-CAPPED WREN-SPINETAIL **L-OW**
Spartanoica maluroides 11+2

Crown rufous. Above light brown boldly streaked black. Wings blackish, with single buff bar. Below white, breast and flanks tinged brown. Tail chestnut brown, central feathers long and pointed.

19. DES MURS' WIRETAIL **L-FT**
Sylviorthorhynchus desmursii 9+13

Brown, crown tinged reddish. Tail of four thin, wire-like feathers, very long.

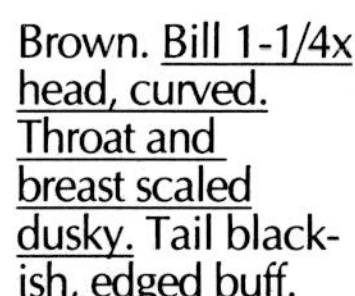

1. SCALE-THROATED EARTHCREEPER **H-O**
Upucerthia dumetaria 21

Brown. Bill 1-1/4x head, curved. Throat and breast scaled dusky. Tail blackish, edged buff.

2. BUFF-BREASTED EARTHCREEPER **H-SO**
Upucerthia validirostris 20

Rather like 126-1 but below uniform buffy and no black in tail

3. WHITE-THROATED EARTHCREEPER **H-SO**
Upucerthia albigula 19

Above dark brown. Eyebrow buff Throat white scaled brown. Below buff. Outer tail feathers cinnamon.

4. STRIATED EARTHCREEPER **H-SO**
Upucerthia serrana 19

Crown dark brown shading to rufous on rump. Throat white. Below streaked dusky. Wings and tail chestnut brown.

5. PLAIN-BREASTED EARTHCREEPER **H-S**
Upucerthia jelskii 18

Upperparts light brown. Underparts whitish, breast faintly streaked dusky.

6. ROCK EARTHCREEPER **H-S**
Upucerthia andaecola 18

Bill only slightly curved. Crown dark brown shading to rufous on rump and tail. Below whitish, flanks brownish. Tail all rufous.

7. STRAIGHT-BILLED EARTHCREEPER **H-S**
Upucerthia ruficauda 18

Bill almost straight. Above brown. Rump cinnamon. Breast lightly streaked rufous, flanks solid rufous. Tail cinnamon with black near outers.

8. CHACO EARTHCREEPER **L-S**
Upucerthia certhioides 16

Above grayish brown. Lores, forehead and face rufous. Throat white. Below grayish. Tail centrals like back, rest rufous.

9. BOLIVIAN EARTHCREEPER **MH-TS**
Upucerthia harterti 15

Crown dark brown. Mantle pale brown shading to rufous on rump. Throat white. Below grayish white Flanks and crissum pale brown.

Eremobius
Chilia
Cinclodes
Clibanornis

10. BAND-TAILED EARTHCREEPER L-SO
Eremobius phoenicurus 16

Bill = head, straight. Upperparts light grayish brown. Lores, eye-stripe, eye-ring and throat white. Below dull white, lightly streaked grayish. Tail chestnut at base, rest black.

11. CRAG CHILIA MH-S
Chilia melanura 19

Bill straight. Crown and mantle light brown. Rump and crissum chestnut. Throat and breast white. Belly pale grayish. Tail black.

12. STOUT-BILLED CINCLODES H-O
Cinclodes excelsior 20

Like 127-19 but bill notably longer, stouter and more curved. Sharp eyebrow whitish.

13. WHITE-BELLIED CINCLODES H-OW
Cinclodes palliatus 19

Like 127-19 but more grayish above and no white eyebrow. Underparts pure white.

14. SEASIDE CINCLODES L-W
Cinclodes nigrofumosus 20

Eyebrow white. Mostly dark brown. Lightly streaked white below. Wings with cinnamon band. Tail black, corners buff. Rocky, coastal habitat.

15. BLACKISH CINCLODES L-OW
Cinclodes antarcticus 20

Bill straight. Uniform dusky brown. No eye-stripe, no wing-band. Coastal.

16. DARK-BELLIED CINCLODES LM-OW
Cinclodes patagonicus 19

Bill slightly curved. Upperparts dark brown Wings with broad buffy band. Below dark gray streaked white. Tail brown, outers tipped buff.

17. GRAY-FLANKED CINCLODES LM-OW
Cinclodes oustaleti 16

Like 127-16 but white at bend of wing, more uniform underparts. Eyebrow and malar stripe white.

18. WHITE-WINGED CINCLODES H-OW
Cinclodes atacamensis 18

Like 127-19 but wing-band white.

19. BAR-WINGED CINCLODES H-O
Cinclodes fuscus 16

Bill thin, slightly curved. Wings with rufous band. Throat whitish. Below brownish. Tail brown, outers rufous.

20. CANEBRAKE GROUND-CREEPER L-TSW
Clibanornis dendrocolaptoides 19

Crown, nape, tail and wings chestnut. Narrow eyebrow whitish. Back brown. Throat white. Below brownish gray, sides and crissum brown.

Furnarius: Usually walking in open.
Sclerurus: Bill thin. Tail black, not tipped.

21. WING-BANDED HORNERO L-SOW
Furnarius figulus 19

Crown brown. Back and tail bright cinnamon. Wide streak back of eye white. Underparts white, tinged buff on breast and sides. Two buff bands show on open wings. Legs dull grayish.

22. RUFOUS HORNERO L-TSO
Furnarius rufus 18

Upperparts and wings uniform rufous brown. Eyebrow faint or lacking. Below white, tinged buff on breast. Tail rufous. Legs dark.

23. PALE-LEGGED HORNERO L-O
Furnarius leucopus 17

Crown and nape brown (or gray in n). Above bright cinnamon rufous. Long eyebrow and throat white. Breast buffy. Legs pinkish. (Includes *F. torridus*).

24. LESSER HORNERO L-SO
Furnarius minor 14

Like brown crowned form of 128-23 but back browner and legs dusky-gray.

25. CRESTED HORNERO L-S
Furnarius cristatus 15

Only hornero with a crest. Above light brown. No eye-brow. Below buffy, throat and center of belly white. Tail rufous.

26. RUFOUS-BREASTED LEAFTOSSER (LEAFSCRAPER) L-F
Sclerurus scansor 18

Above brown. Rump chestnut. Throat white. Breast rufous. Belly dark brown. Tail black.

27. BLACK-TAILED LEAFTOSSER (LEAFSCRAPER) L-F
Sclerurus caudacutus 16

Dark brown. Rump dark dull chestnut. Throat whitish. Below dark brown.

28. GRAY-THROATED LEAFTOSSER (LEAFSCRAPER) L-F
Sclerurus albigularis 16

Like 129-30 but throat gray and broad rufous band on breast.

29. SHORT-BILLED LEAFTOSSER (LEAFSCRAPER) L-F
Sclerurus rufigularis 17

Like 129-30 but bill noticeably shorter.

Sclerurus: Bill thin. Tail black, not tipped.
Lochmias
Geositta: Barren, arid country.

30. TAWNY-THROATED LEAFTOSSER (LEAFSCRAPER) LM-F
Sclerurus mexicanus 15

Above dark brown. Throat and rump rufous. Below dark brown tinged rufous on breast.

31. SCALY-THROATED LEAFTOSSER (LEAFSCRAPER) L-F
Sclerurus guatemalensis 16

Above dark brown, no rufous rump. Throat (and sometimes center of breast) scaled white. Below dark brown.

32. SHARP-TAILED STREAMCREEPER LM-FW
Lochmias nematura 14

Above dark brown. Eyebrow white in se. Below brown boldly spotted white. Tail short, black.

33. SLENDER-BILLED MINER H-O
Geositta tenuirostris 18

Bill = head, narrow, curved. Above sandy brown. Eyebrow buffy. Below whitish, breast mottled brown. Tail blackish, outers cinnamon. Wings with chestnut band.

34. CREAMY-RUMPED MINER H-O
Geositta isabellina 14

Above sandy brown, no band on wings. Rump white. Below dull white. Tail white at base, black on end.

35. RUFOUS-BANDED MINER H-O
Geositta rufipennis 16

Bill 3/4x head. Above grayish brown. Wings with bold rufous band. Below whitish. Tail cinnamon broadly tipped black.

36. COMMON MINER LMH-O
Geositta cunicularia 15

Above grayish brown. Wings with tawny band. Rump buffy. Below whitish, breast streaked dusky Tail buffy, black on end.

37. DARK-WINGED MINER H-O
Geositta saxicolina 15

Above reddish brown. Wings uniform dusky (no paler band). Rump and tail buff, broadly tipped blackish. Throat white, below buff.

38. THICK-BILLED MINER LM-SO
Geositta crassirostris 15

Bill heavy, straight. Brown above. Eyebrow whitish. Wings with chestnut band. Throat whitish. Below pale grayish. Tail brown with broad black band near end.

39. PUNA MINER H-O
Geositta punensis 14

Like 129-35 but paler. Rufous wing patch.

Geositta: Barren, arid country.
Geobates
Coryphistera

Asthenes: Usually has chin spot.
Tail long, feathers pointed.

40. SHORT-BILLED MINER H-OA
Geositta antarctica 14

Bill 1/2x head, straight. Above grayish brown. Below buffy. Breast faintly streaked dusky. Tail black, outers buff.

41. GRAYISH MINER LM-OA
Geositta maritima 13

Bill slender, slightly curved. Above pale sandy gray. Wings uniform gray (no paler band). Below whitish, flanks buffy. Tail blackish, edged buff.

42. COASTAL MINER L-OA
Geositta peruviana 13

Above light grayish brown. Wings with cinnamon-buff band. Tail brown and rusty, edged white.

43. CAMPO MINER L-O
Geobates poecilopterus 12

Above brown. Wings brown with rufous band. Throat white. Below buff streaked dusky on breast. Tail rufous, black near end, quite short.

44. LARK-LIKE BRUSH-RUNNER L-SO
Coryphistera alaudina 15

Conspicuous crest mostly blackish. Above brown streaked dusky. Cheeks white. Ear coverts cinnamon. Below white streaked rufous.

45. LINE-FRONTED CANASTERO H-SO
Asthenes urubambensis 18

Forehead streaked. Above brown. Long eyebrow white. Below whitish streaked dusky. Tail long, all brown.

46. MANY-STRIPED CANASTERO H-SO
Asthenes flammulata 16

Above dark brown streaked white. Crown streaked rufous. Throat white (with rufous throat patch in some races). Below whitish streaked dusky.

47. JUNIN CANASTERO H-O
Asthenes virgata 17

Above dark brown streaked white. Crown streaked rufous. Chin patch cinnamon. Below whitish streaked dusky.

48. SCRIBBLE-TAILED CANASTERO H-SO
Asthenes maculicauda 16

Forecrown chestnut. Above dark brown streaked yellowish buff. No chin patch. Below whitish. Tail brown lined and spotted black.

49. HUDSON'S CANASTERO L-O
Asthenes hudsoni 16

Above brown streaked black. Chin spot yellow. Below buffy somewhat streaked blackish. Tail blackish broadly tipped brown.

50. CORDOBA CANASTERO M-S
Asthenes sclateri 16

Rather like 131-60 with faint streaking on back. No chin spot. Bill normal.

51. BERLEPSCH'S CANASTERO H-SO
Asthenes berlepschi 16

Like 131-60 but rump more rufous and wing coverts edged chestnut.

Asthenes: Usually has chin spot. Tail long, feathers pointed.

52. LESSER CANASTERO **LMH-SO**
Asthenes pyrrholeuca 15

Very like 131-60 but bill not so short and wing coverts more rufous.

53. CHESTNUT CANASTERO **MH-S0A**
Asthenes steinbachi 15

Somewhat like 131-60 but no rufous chin spot and tail brighter chestnut. Below dull gray. Tail brown, outers bright cinnamon.

54. DUSKY-TAILED CANASTERO **LM-S**
Asthenes humicola 15

Above like 131-60 but tail blacker. Short narrow eyebrow white. Shoulders rufous. Throat white, dotted black. Below streaked.

55. CANYON CANASTERO **MH-S**
Asthenes pudibunda 15

Above reddish brown. Below gray Chin patch rufous. A distinctive dark-looking canastero.

56. RUSTY-FRONTED CANASTERO **H-S**
Asthenes ottonis 15

Forehead cinnamon. Prominent eyebrow buff. Above rather dark brown. Wing coverts rufous. Chin patch cinnamon. Below light gray. Long tail mostly rufous.

57. STREAK-THROATED CANASTERO **H-O**
Asthenes humilis 15

Like 131-60 but streaked dusky on throat and breast. Tail mostly brown.

58. AUSTRAL CANASTERO **H-O**
Asthenes anthoides 15

Above brownish heavily streaked black. Wing coverts rufous. Below whitish, usually lightly streaked on breast. Tail outers broadly tipped rufous.

59. CREAMY-BREASTED CANASTERO **MH-SO**
Asthenes dorbignyi 14

Rather like 131-60 but chin spot chestnut. Below whitish, rufous on flanks and crissum.

60. SHORT-BILLED CANASTERO **L-S**
Asthenes baeri 14

Upperparts brown, tinged rufous on rump. Throat rufous. Below whitish. Tail central blackish, outers cinnamon.

61. PATAGONIAN CANASTERO **L-S**
Asthenes patagonica 15

Above light grayish brown. Shoulder rufous. Chin checkered black and white. Below light grayish. Tail short, edged rufous.

62. STREAK-BACKED CANASTERO **H-SO**
Asthenes wyatti 14

Above brown streaked dusky. Narrow eyebrow whitish. Wings and outer tail feathers rufescent.

FURNARIIDS USUALLY IN LOW VEGETATION - 1.

Asthenes: Usually has chin spot.
Tail long, feathers pointed.
Pseudoseisura
Thripadectes
Cichlocolaptes

63. CORDILLERAN CANASTERO **MH-O**
Asthenes modesta 14

Upperparts grayish brown, underparts paler. Throat chestnut. Tail looks mostly rufous.

64. CACTUS CANASTERO **LM-SA**
Asthenes cactorum 13

Like 132-63 but tail looks mostly brown.

1. BROWN CACHOLOTE **L-S**
Pseudoseisura lophotes 24

Conspicuous crest dark brown. Eye light yellow. Above brown, rump and tail cinnamon rufous. Throat rufous, below grayish brown.

2. WHITE-THROATED CACHOLOTE **L-S**
Pseudoseisura gutturalis 23

Rather like 132-1 but duller and grayer. Throat white. Narrow black necklace below throat. Tail brown.

3. RUFOUS CACHOLOTE **L-S**
Pseudoseisura cristata 20

Uniform cinnamon rufous, paler below. Conspicuous crest grayish.

4. BUFF-THROATED TREEHUNTER **H-F**
Thripadectes scrutator 23

Above brown, dusky on crown. Throat buff, feathers edged blackish. Below pale olive brown, faintly spotted buff in center.

5. FLAMMULATED TREEHUNTER **MH-F**
Thripadectes flammulatus 22

Like 133-9 but more boldly streaked on head, neck and underparts.

6. STREAK-CAPPED TREEHUNTER **LM-F**
Thripadectes virgaticeps 20

Bill 1/2x head. Crown and nape blackish, streaked whitish. Back brown, not streaked. Rump and tail rufous. Underparts cinnamon, streaked on throat and breast.

7. PALE-BROWED TREEHUNTER **LM-F**
Cichlocolaptes leucophrys 20

Bill 3/4x head. Above rufous brown, crown and back streaked whitish. Long eyebrow and throat white. Below whitish streaked brown. Tail cinnamon brown.

Thripadectes
Anumbius: Builds large stick nest.
Simoxenops
Phacellodomus

8. BLACK-BILLED TREEHUNTER **M-F**
Thripadectes melanorhynchus 19

Back streaked. Below like 132-6 but throat scaly. Belly unstreaked.

9. STRIPED TREEHUNTER **MH-F**
Thripadectes holostictus 18

Above and underparts streaked buff. Rump, wings and tail rufous, unstreaked.

10. UNIFORM TREEHUNTER **M-F**
Thripadectes ignobilis 17

Bill 1/2x head, thick. Uniform dark chestnut brown, somewhat paler below. Throat and breast obscurely streaked buff. Cf. 133-9

11. FIREWOOD-GATHERER **L-SO**
Anumbius annumbi 19

Bill 3/4x head. Above light brown, lightly streaked dusky. Forehead tinged rufous. Eyebrow white. Throat white surrounded with black spots. Below buffy. Tail outers tipped white.

12. PERUVIAN RECURVEBILL **L-F**
Simoxenops ucayalae 19

Lower bill upcurved. Above rufous brown. Narrow brow buffy. Lores and ear coverts whitish. Rump chestnut. Below cinnamon rufous (Imm. scaled).

13. BOLIVIAN RECURVEBILL **LM-F**
Simoxenops striatus 18

Like 133-12 but mantle streaked buff. Throat rufous. Below brownish.

14. YELLOW-EYED (GREATER) THORNBIRD **L-S**
Phacellodomus ruber 19

Crown, wings and tail rufous. Back brownish. Eye yellow. Below whitish, tinged gray on breast.

15. CHESTNUT-BACKED THORNBIRD **MH-TS**
Phacellodomus dorsalis 19

Crown dull rufous. Back olive brown. Wing coverts and center of back chestnut. Below white, breast mottled rufous. Tail chestnut.

16. FRECKLE-BREASTED THORNBIRD **L-TS**
Phacellodomus striaticollis 18

Crown chestnut. Above brown. Throat white. Breast rufous spotted white. Belly buffy.

Phacellodomus
Limnornis
Limnoctites
Automolus

17. RED-EYED THORNBIRD L-T
Phacellodomus erythrophthalmus 18

Above reddish brown. Eye red. Throat and breast rufous. Belly brown. Tail rufous chestnut.

18. PLAIN (RUFOUS FRONTED) THORNBIRD L-SO
Phacellodomus rufifrons 15

Forecrown rufous (no rufous in nw). Back, wings and tail dull brown. Small eyebrow white. Below whitish.

19. STREAK-FRONTED THORNBIRD H-SO
Phacellodomus striaticeps 12

Forecrown streaked rufous and grayish. Above dull brown. Rump rufous. Below whitish. Tail centrals brown, outers cinnamon, tipped dusky.

20. LITTLE THORNBIRD L-S
Phacellodomus sibilatrix 12

Forehead narrowly chestnut. Crown and back brown. Lesser wing coverts and edge to tail rufous. Small eyebrow gray. Underparts whitish. Cf. 134-18.

21. CURVE-BILLED REED-HAUNTER L-OW
Limnornis curvirostris 17

Bill pale, decurved. Upperparts light brown. Eyebrow and throat white. Below whitish.

22. STRAIGHT-BILLED REED-HAUNTER LM-OW
Limnoctites rectirostris 16

Bill blackish, straight. Above light brown, head grayer. Narrow eyebrow white. Below white.

23. BUFF-THROATED FOLIAGE-GLEANER L-F
Automolus ochrolaemus 18

Above olive brown. Rump and tail rufous. Prominent eye-ring buff. Throat whitish. Below dull brownish.

Automolus
Syndactyla
Philydor

24. CHESTNUT CROWNED FOLIAGE-GLEANER L-FT
Automolus rufipileatus 18

Eye yellow-orange. Crown chestnut. Mostly reddish brown, paler below. Rump and tail chestnut.

25. WHITE-EYED FOLIAGE-GLEANER L-FT
Automolus leucophthalmus 17

Eye white. Upperparts reddish brown. Rump and tail rufous. Lores and throat white. Below buffy becoming light brown on belly.

26. OLIVE-BACKED FOLIAGE-GLEANER L-F
Automolus infuscatus 18

Above brownish olive. Rump and tail rufous. Throat white. Below dull grayish, flanks and crissum browner.

27. WHITE-THROATED FOLIAGE-GLEANER LM-FT
Automolus roraimae 16

Like 135-26 but long white eyebrow sharp and cheeks darker.

28. RUDDY FOLIAGE-GLEANER LM-F
Automolus rubiginosus 18

Dark and unpatterned. Above mostly dark reddish brown. Throat and crissum rufous. Below buffy brown. Birds w of Andes even darker, with black tail.

29. BUFF-BROWED FOLIAGE-GLEANER LM-FT
Syndactyla rufosuperciliata 17

Above olive brown, unstreaked. Prominent eyebrow buff. Throat buff. Below brownish olive streaked buffy. Tail rufous.

30. RUFOUS-TAILED FOLIAGE-GLEANER L-F
Philydor ruficaudatus 16

Above olive brown including rump. Long eyebrow buff. Below pale yellowish buff. Only tail rufous.

31. OCHRE-BREASTED FOLIAGE-GLEANER L-F
Philydor lichtensteini 15

Crown, nape and ear coverts gray. Broad eyebrow ochraceous. Back dull brown. Below buffy ochraceous.

Philydor
Premnoplex: Tail spines protruding.
Premnornis
Phleocryptes
Xenerpestes: Looks like a warbler.

32. CINNAMON-RUMPED FOLIAGE-GLEANER L-F
Philydor pyrrhodes 15

Crown and back rufous olive (rufous brown in w). Wings contrasting blackish. Eyebrow, rump, tail and entire underparts bright cinnamon.

33. RUSSET-MANTLED FOLIAGE-GLEANER L-F
Philydor dimidiatus 15

Like 136-32 but back bright cinnamon brown or light olive brown. Rump and tail dark rufous.

34. RORAIMAN BARBTAIL M-TS
Premnoplex (Roraimia) adusta 14

Crown and nape olive brown. Back, wings and tail dark chestnut. Ear coverts black. Throat white. Below buff streaked blackish.

35. WHITE-THROATED BARBTAIL LM-F
Premnoplex tatei 14

Like 136-36 but throat white. Below streaked (not spotted) white.

36. SPOTTED BARBTAIL M-F
Premnoplex brunnescens 14

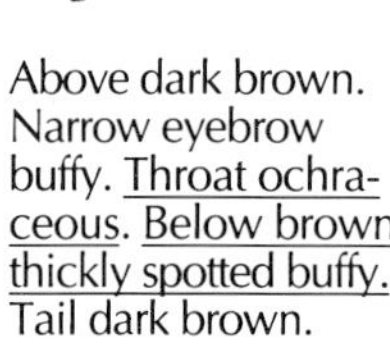

Above dark brown. Narrow eyebrow buffy. Throat ochraceous. Below brown, thickly spotted buffy. Tail dark brown.

37. RUSTY-WINGED BARBTAIL M-F
Premnornis guttuligera 14

Above dark brown. Eyestripe, throat and streaks on nape buff. Below brown, breast with many large buffy spots. Tail rufous.

38. WREN-LIKE RUSHBIRD LMH-OW
Phleocryptes melanops 14

Above blackish, streaked paler. Rump brown. Broad eyebrow whitish. Black eye stripe. Underparts whitish.

39. EQUATORIAL GRAYTAIL L-F
Xenerpestes singularis 10

Forehead rufous. Crown streaked rufous. Eyebrow white. Back olive gray. Below pale yellowish, prominently streaked dusky.

40. DOUBLE-BANDED GRAYTAIL L-F
Xenerpestes minlosi 10

Above dark gray. Narrow eyebrow, lores and two wing-bars whitish. Below creamy whitish. Tail gray.

41. SPECTACLED PRICKLETAIL M-F
Siptornis striaticollis 10

Above reddish brown, wing coverts more chestnut. Short but conspicuous eyebrow white. Below pale grayish. Tail chestnut.

Hylocryptus
Pseudocolaptes
Berlepschia
Philydor
Anabazenops
Automolus
Syndactyla

1. HENNA-HOODED FOLIAGE-GLEANER **M-FT**
Hylocryptus erythrocephalus 20

Head, neck, throat, wings and tail bright rufous. Back olive-brown. Below grayish olive.

2. CHESTNUT-CAPPED FOLIAGE-GLEANER **L-F**
Hylocryptus rectirostris 19

Upperparts plain reddish brown. Crown, wings and tail rufous. Below light buffy brown.

3. STREAKED TUFTEDCHEEK **MH-F**
Pseudocolaptes boissonneautii 19

Above brown streaked buff. Rump and tail bright rufous. Throat and broad semi-collar white. Below white scaled cinnamon. Includes Buffy Tuftedcheeks.

4. POINT-TAILED PALMCREEPER **L-T**
Berlepschia rikeri 19

Woodcreeper-like. Head, mantle and all underparts black finely streaked white. Back, wings and tail bright rufous chestnut.

5. BUFF-FRONTED FOLIAGE-GLEANER **LM-F**
Philydor rufus 17

Forehead ochraceous. Crown, nape and eyestripe grayish. Above olive brown. Below buff. Wings and tail rufous.

6. WHITE-COLLARED FOLIAGE-GLEANER **LM-F**
Anabazenops fuscus 17

Above brown. Long narrow eyebrow white. Collar and throat white. Below buffy brown. Tail rufous.

7. CRESTED FOLIAGE-GLEANER **L-F**
Automolus dorsalis 17

Like 135-26 but upperparts dark reddish brown and has conspicous buff eye-stripe.

8. BROWN-RUMPED FOLIAGE-GLEANER **L-F**
Automolus melanopezus 17

Above reddish brown. Throat cinnamon. Below buffy brown. Tail (but not rump) rufous.

9. RUFOUS-NECKED FOLIAGE-GLEANER **M-F**
Automolus ruficollis 16

Above bright rufescent brown. Eyebrow and sides of neck rufous. Below brownish, breast streaked buff. Tail rufous.

10. GUTTULATED FOLIAGE-GLEANER **LM-F**
Syndactyla guttulata 17

Very like 138-11 but crown unstreaked and buff eyebrow more prominent. Lower bill distinctly upcurved. Much more broadly streaked below than 138-11.

Syndactyla
Philydor
Anabacerthia

11. LINEATED FOLIAGE-GLEANER **M-F**
Syndactyla subalaris 16

Above brown narrowly streaked buff, most prominently on hind neck. (Crown unstreaked in n).Throat plain buff. Below sharply streaked. Wings and tail rufous-brown.

12. NEBLINA FOLIAGE-GLEANER **M-F**
Philydor hylobius 16

Very like 138-14 but generally darker.

13. CHESTNUT-WINGED FOLIAGE-GLEANER **L-F**
Philydor erythropterus 16

Above olive brown, wings and tail contrasting rufous Long narrow eyebrow buff. Throat yellowish. Below dull ochraceous.

14. BLACK-CAPPED FOLIAGE-GLEANER **LM-F**
Philydor atricapillus 15

Crown, stripe behind eye and malar stripe blackish. Broad eye-ring white. Eyebrow ochraceous. Above cinnamon-brown. Underparts ochraceous.

15. WHITE-BROWED FOLIAGE-GLEANER **LM-F**
Anabacerthia amaurotis 16

Above brown. Prominent broad eyebrow white. Throat white. Below brown, streaked or spotted white on breast. Tail bright cinnamon.

16. RUFOUS-RUMPED FOLIAGE-GLEANER **L-F**
Philydor erythrocercus 15

Upperparts olive-brown. Long eyebrow buff. Wings like back (gray in w). Rump and tail rufous. Underparts buffy.

17. MONTANE FOLIAGE-GLEANER **M-FT**
Anabacerthia striaticollis 15

Upperparts brown. Prominent eye-ring and narrow stripe behind eye white. Throat whitish. Below pale brownish, virtually unstreaked. Rump cinnamon.

18. SPECTACLED (SCALY-THROATED) FOLIAGE-GLEANER **LM-F**
Anabacerthia variegaticeps 15

Like 138-17 but crown dusky and spectacles cinnamon.

Hyloctistes
Ancistrops
Thripophaga
Megaxenops
Margarornis

19. STRIPED WOODHAUNTER L-F
Hyloctistes subulatus 16

Above brown, crown narrowly streaked. Back streaked (mostly lacking w of Andes). Throat buffy. Below with blurry buff streaks. Wings brown. Tail rufous. Cf. 138-11.

20. CHESTNUT-WINGED HOOKBIILL L-F
Ancistrops strigilatus 17

Bill heavy, hooked. Above brown sharply streaked buffy, contrasting with bright chestnut wings. Below yellowish buff faintly streaked olive. Tail rufous.

21. RUSSET-MANTLED SOFTTAIL H-TS
Thripophaga berlepschi 16

Crown light olive-brown. Upperparts and tail cinnamon-rufous. Rump olivaceous. Throat and breast cinnamon. Belly light olive brown. Tail chestnut.

22. STRIATED SOFTTAIL L-FT
Thripophaga macroura 17

Crown chestnut and back reddish brown, both narrowly pale streaked. Throat buff. Below brown broadly streaked whitish. Long tail bright cinnamon.

23. PLAIN SOFTTAIL L-FT
Thripophaga fusciceps 17

Above olive brown. Wings and tail rufous. Eyebrow pale. Below light brown.

24. ORINOCO SOFTTAIL L-FT
Thripophaga cherriei 15

Above olive-brown. Wings more rufous. Throat bright orange. Face, neck and underparts olive-brown streaked buff. Tail rufous chestnut.

25. GREAT XENOPS L-TS
Megaxenops parnaguae 15

Bill very heavy, lower much upturned. Mostly bright cinnamon rufous, paler below. Throat and sides of neck white.

26. PEARLED TREERUNNER MH-F
Margarornis squamiger 14

Crown brown, back chestnut. Eyebrow and throat creamy white. Below brown thickly spotted white. Tail chestnut.

27. FULVOUS-DOTTED TREERUNNER M-F
Margaronis stellatus 14

Upperparts chestnut brown. Throat white bordered below by blackish spots. Below chestnut. Tail chestnut.

Pygarrhichas
Xenops: Wing band cinnamon.
Heliobletus
Metopothrix
Aphrastura

28. WHITE-THROATED TREERUNNER **LM-FT**
Pygarrhichas albogularis 12

Bill 3/4x head, slender, slightly upturned. Upperparts and belly dark brown. Throat and breast white. Tail bright rufous, spines protruding. Climbs on trunks and branches.

29. STREAKED XENOPS **LM-FTS**
Xenops rutilans 12

Bill = 1/2 head, lower sharply upturned.Above brown, head and back narrowly streaked buff. Rump rufous. Malar stripe white. Below brown conspicuously streaked white. Cf. 140-31.

30. PLAIN XENOPS **L-FT**
Xenops minutus 11

Bill = 1/2x head, lower upturned. Above brown, not streaked. Narrow eyebrow buffy. Prominent malar white. Throat white. Below brown. Tail rufous, black near sides.

31. RUFOUS-TAILED XENOPS **L-FT**
Xenops milleri 10

Like 140-29 but bill only slightly upturned, has no white malar stripe and has more streaking on back and less streaking below. Tail all rufous.

32. SLENDER-BILLED XENOPS **L-FT**
Xenops tenuirostris 10

Very like 140-29 but bill practically straight. More streaking on back. Malar stripe white.

33. SHARP-BILLED XENOPS (TREE-HUNTER) **LM-FT**
Heliobletus contaminatus 11

Bill = 1/3x head, straight Above brown, crown and nape streaked whitish. Long eyebrow and partial collar whitish. Throat white. Below pale brown broadly streaked white. Tail rufous.

34. ORANGE-FRONTED PLUSHCROWN **L-FT**
Metopothrix aurantiacus 10

Forehead orange. Throat yellow. Above light olive-brown. Below grayish tinged yellow on breast. Legs orange.

35. THORN-TAILED RAYADITO **LM-FT**
Aphrastura spinicauda 8+1

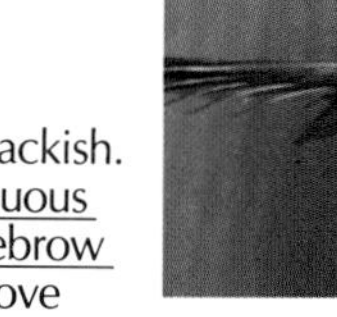

Head blackish. Conspicuous long eyebrow buff. Above brown,rump rufous. Below white. Tail black and rufous with protruding spines.

REDDISH BROWN CROWN INCLUDED IN THIS GROUP.

Synallaxis
Certhiaxis

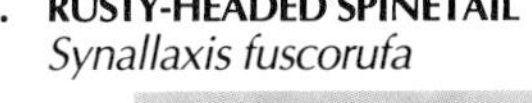

1. RUSTY-HEADED SPINETAIL **M-FT**
Synallaxis fuscorufa 16

Mostly rufous, back contrasting grayish. Belly buff.

2. RUFOUS SPINETAIL **MH-FT**
Synallaxis unirufa 16

Uniform rufous. Lores black. Chin blackish in some races. Cf. 143-10.

3. CABANIS' SPINETAIL **LM-TS**
Synallaxis cabanisi 15

Above brown Face gray. Throat feathers dusky with pale tips. Underparts light grayish olive. Tail all dark rufous chestnut.

4. CHICLI SPINETAIL **LM-TS**
Synallaxis spixi 15

Face and eyebrow light gray. Back and tail olive brown. Wing coverts prominent rufous. Center of belly white. Throat and breast gray.

5. RUFOUS-CAPPED SPINETAIL **M-FT**
Synallaxis ruficapilla 15

Prominent eye-stripe buffy. Throat gray. Tail rather short, rufous.

6. YELLOW-CHINNED (-THROATED) SPINETAIL **L-SW**
Certhiaxis cinnamomea 14

Upperparts all rufous. Forehead gray. Eyebrow whitish. Dusky line through eye. Below very white.

7. RED-AND-WHITE SPINETAIL **L-SW**
Certhiaxis mustelina 14

Very like 141-6 but bill larger and forehead not gray.

Cranioleuca

8. STREAK-CAPPED SPINETAIL **MH-FT**
Cranioleuca hellmayri 14

Crown chestnut, streaked black. Back olive brown. Eye-stripe white. Below grayish.

9. MARCAPATA SPINETAIL **H-F**
Cranioleuca marcapatae 14

Upperparts rufous, sides of crown blackish. Short eyebrow whitish. Face grayish. Below whitish.

10. TEPUI SPINETAIL **M-FT**
Cranioleuca demissa 14

Crown, wings and tail all rufous except back olive brown. Eyebrow and underparts grayish.

11. RUSTY-BACKED SPINETAIL **L-SW**
Cranioleuca vulpina 14

Upperparts, wings and tail all bright rufous. Below grayish.

12. ASH-BROWED SPINETAIL **M-F**
Cranioleuca curtata 14

Forehead dull rufous olive. Crown chestnut (not streaked). Back olive brown. Wings and tail rufous. Faint streaks on breast. Eyebrow and underparts grayish brown.

13. SCALED SPINETAIL **L-F**
Cranioleuca muelleri 14

Crown rufous brown. Above olive brown, feathers scaled blackish. Throat whitish. Below brownish olive.

14. RED-FACED SPINETAIL **LM-FT**
Cranioleuca erythrops 13

Crown and face rufous. Back olive-brown. Underparts grayish. Wings and tail rufous.

15. LINE-CHEEKED SPINETAIL **MH-TS**
Cranioleuca antisiensis 13

Crown, wings and tail rufous Back olive brown or gray. Bold eyebrow white. Below whitish, belly browner. Wings and tail rufous.

16. SPECKLED SPINETAIL **L-F**
Cranioleuca gutturata 13

Above olive-brown. Eye-stripe buff. Face and underparts buff, speckled dusky. Small chin spot yellowish.

Synallaxis

1. **AZARA'S SPINETAIL** MH-TS
Synallaxis azarae 16

Forecrown and back brown. Hindcrown, nape, wings and long tail rufous. Face and breast gray. Throat and belly white.

2. **BUFF-BROWED SPINETAIL** M-FT
Synallaxis superciliosa 16

Like 141-5 but forecrown olive and below whitish.

3. **SILVERY-THROATED SPINETAIL** H-TS
Synallaxis subpudica 16

Very like 141-4 but forecrown olive and below gray.

4. **PALE-BREASTED SPINETAIL** LM-SO
Synallaxis albescens 16

Forehead brownish gray. Wing coverts rufous Below whitish to pale gray. Tail olive-brown.

5. **SLATY SPINETAIL** L-TS
Synallaxis brachyura 15

Forecrown, face, back and underparts dark gray except throat whitish. Tail long (short w of Andes) grayish brown.

6. **DUSKY SPINETAIL** L-S
Synallaxis moesta 15

Very like 143-5 but tail dark chestnut. Throat dusky.

7. **DARK-BREASTED SPINETAIL** L-TS
Synallaxis albigularis 15

Very like 143-5 but throat more prominently white. Breast sometimes much darker.

8. **SOOTY-FRONTED SPINETAIL** L-S
Synallaxis frontalis 15

Forehead and back olive brown. Variable eyebrow and eye-ring. Rear crown and long tail chestnut. Underparts grayish.

9. **CINEREOUS-BREASTED SPINETAIL** L-TS
Synallaxis hypospodia 15

Like 141-4 but forehead brownish gray and underparts much darker gray.

10. **RUDDY SPINETAIL** L-FT
Synallaxis rutilans 14

Mostly dark rufous (back browner in some races). Throat black. Rump gray. Tail black.

11. **GRAY-BROWED SPINETAIL** L-FT
Synallaxis poliophrys 13

Rather like 143-8 but has definite whitish eyebrow. Tail short. Now considered a subspecies of 143-8.

Synallaxis *Siptornopsis*
Cranioleuca *Oreophylax*

12. CHESTNUT-THROATED SPINETAIL **L-FT**
Synallaxis cherriei 13

Like brown back forms of 143-10 but throat dull chestnut (not black).

13. PALLID SPINETAIL **LM-FT**
Cranioleuca pallida 13

Forehead whitish spotted black. Above dull light reddish brown Long eyebrow white. Underparts whitish.

1. GREAT SPINETAIL **MH-TS**
Siptornopsis hypochondriacus 16

Above light brown. Eyebrow white.Wing coverts rufous. Below white,breast boldly streaked dusky.

2. ITATIAIA SPINETAIL **MH-TS**
Oreophylax moreirae 16

Upperparts, wings and tail brown, somewhat darker on crown and tinged rufous on tail. Throat ochraceous. Below whitish. Tail very long.

3. CREAMY-CRESTED SPINETAIL **H-TS**
Cranioleuca albicapilla 15

Forehead whitish. Crown cinnamon-buff. Back olive-brown. Short eyebrow white. Below whitish. Wings and tail rufous.

4. LIGHT-CROWNED SPINETAIL **MH-F**
Cranioleuca albiceps 14

Crown and nape whitish. Face black. Above rufous. Underparts gray.

5. CRESTED SPINETAIL **LM-FT**
Cranioleuca subcristata 14

Crown dull olive-brown streaked blackish. Back olive-brown. No eyebrow. Throat whitish. Below gray-ish brown. Wings and tail rufous.

6. STRIPE-CROWNED SPINETAIL **LMH-S**
Cranioleuca pyrrhophia 13

Crown strikingly streaked buff and black. Eye-stripe white. Back brown. Below white. Wing coverts and tail rufous.

7. GRAY-HEADED SPINETAIL **L-TS**
Cranioleuca semicinerea 13

Head and neck grayish. Above uniform rufous chestnut. Below pale grayish.

Cranioleuca
Gyalophylax
Synallaxis
Poecilurus

8. SULPHUR-BEARDED SPINETAIL **L-SW**
Cranioleuca sulphurifera 14

Upperparts light brown. Eyebrow and cheeks dull cinnamon. Underparts whitish, small yellow spot on throat. Tail rufous edged.

9. OLIVE SPINETAIL **LM-FT**
Cranioleuca obsoleta 12

Above olive brown Eyebrow and underparts dingy buff. Wing coverts and tail rufous.

10. RED-SHOULDERED SPINETAIL **L-S**
Gyalophylax hellmayri 15

Above light brownish gray. Large area on wing coverts bright rufous. Throat patch dull black. Below light grayish.Tail dusky.

11. WHITE-BELLIED SPINETAIL **L-T**
Synallaxis propinqua 15

Above brownish gray. Wing coverts and tail rufous. Below gray, center of belly white.

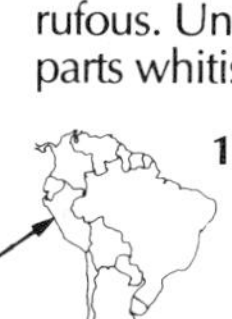

12. PLAIN-CROWNED SPINETAIL **L-T**
Synallaxis gujanensis 14

Crown and nape grayish brown. Above olive-brown. Wings and tail bright rufous. Underparts whitish or grayish.

13. RUSSET-BELLIED SPINETAIL **MH-T**
Synallaxis zimmeri 14

Crown gray becoming rufous on rump. Throat grayish. Below bright cinnamon-rufous.

14. WHITE-WHISKERED SPINETAIL **L-SO**
Poecilurus candei 14

Crown and nape gray. Back and wings bright rufous. Cheeks black. Large throat patch white bordered below by black patch. Breast rufous. Belly white. Tail rufous tipped black.

15. HOARY-THROATED SPINETAIL **L-SO**
Poecilurus kollari 14

Like 145-14 but cheeks gray bordered below by rufous. Throat blackish and tail not tipped.

Poecilurus
Synallaxis

16. OCHRE-CHEEKED SPINETAIL L-TS
Poecilurus scutatus 13

Like 145-12 but crown brown (not gray) and back grayish brown (not olive brown).

17. WHITE-BROWED SPINETAIL MH-F
Hellmayrea (Synallaxis) gularis 12

Upperparts, wings and tail brown. Eyebrow white. Throat white. Looks and acts more like a wren then a spinetail. Tail short.

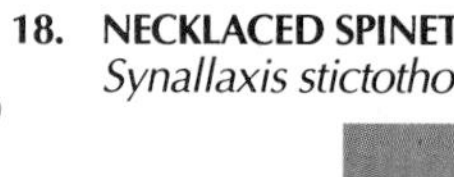

18. NECKLACED SPINETAIL L-S
Synallaxis stictothorax 11

Forehead streaked black and white. Eyebrow white. Above brownish. Underparts white, breast conspicuously streaked dusky. Rump and wing coverts rufous.

19. BLACK-FACED (BLACKISH-HEADED) SPINETAIL L-T
Synallaxis tithys 14

Forecrown and face black. Upperparts olive brown. Wing coverts cinnamon. Throat blackish. Below light gray.Tail dusky.

20. GRAY-BELLIED SPINETAIL L-F
Synallaxis cinerascens 13

Upperparts uniform olivaceous brown. Wings and tail chestnut. Throat black dotted white. Below uniform gray.

21. STRIPE-BREASTED SPINETAIL LM-FT
Synallaxis cinnamomea 14

Above brown, wings more rufous. Eyebrow buffy. Throat white, streaked black. Breast cinnamon conspicuously streaked buffy. Tail brown.

ANTSHRIKES HAVE HEAVY, HOOKED BILL.

Batara	*Hypoedaleus*
Mackenziaena	*Taraba*
Frederickena	*Cymbilaimus*

1. GIANT ANTSHRIKE LM-F
Batara cinerea 32

female

Crest black. Above black finely barred white. Underparts gray. F: Crest chestnut. Above barred black and rufous. Underparts pale brown.

2. LARGE-TAILED ANTSHRIKE LM-FT
Mackenziaena leachii 24

female

Bill unusually small. Black, thickly spotted white except on throat, breast and tail. F: Crown chestnut. Above, underparts and tail black thickly spotted buffy or whitish.

3. TUFTED ANTSHRIKE LM-T
Mackenziaena severa 22

Crested. Dark gray. Crown, cheeks and throat black. F: Crown rufous. Above black banded rufous. Below buff banded black.

4. BLACK-THROATED ANTSHRIKE L-F
Frederickena viridis 21

Crested. Dark gray. Crown, cheeks, throat and breast black. F: Above rufous. Underparts and tail banded black and pale gray.

5. UNDULATED ANTSHRIKE L-F
Frederickena unduligera 21

Black waved white except throat all black. F: Crown chestnut. Back brown, barred black. Crown chestnut. Rump and tail black barred gray.

6. SPOT-BACKED ANTSHRIKE LM-F
Hypoedaleus guttatus 19

Above black, spotted white. Below white. Tail black, barred white. F: Buff instead of white.

7. GREAT ANTSHRIKE L-TS
Taraba major 19

female

Eye red. Above black. Wings barred white. Underparts white. F: Upperparts uniform rufous.

8. FASCIATED ANTSHRIKE L-FT
Cymbilaimus lineatus 18

female

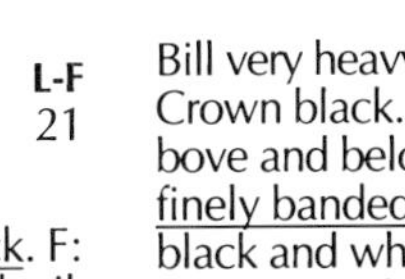

Bill very heavy. Crown black. Above and below finely banded black and white. F: Crown rufous. Above black banded buff. Below buff finely (sometimes faintly) barred black.

Sakesphorus: Conspicuous crest.
Biatas
Thamnophilus

9. COLLARED ANTSHRIKE L-SA
Sakesphorus bernardi 17

Very like 148-13 but with semi-concealed white dorsal patch.

10. BAND-TAILED ANTSHRIKE L-F
Sakesphorus melanothorax 17

No crest. Black. Wing coverts and tail broadly tipped white. F: Rufous. Face, throat and breast black. Belly brownish.

11. GLOSSY ANTSHRIKE L-SWT
Sakesphorus luctuosus 17

All black except small white patch on wing coverts and tips of tail. Prominent shaggy crest black (f. chestnut).

female

12. SILVERY-CHEEKED ANTSHRIKE L-S
Sakesphorus cristatus 15

Very like 148-13 but tail brown, barred white (f. buff).

13. BLACK-CRESTED ANTSHRIKE L-SO
Sakesphorus canadensis 14

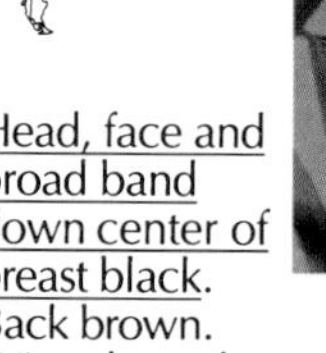

Head, face and broad band down center of breast black. Back brown. Wings barred and spotted white. Below white. Tail black tipped and edged white. F: Crest rufous Face speckled. Below whitish lightly streaked dusky.

female

14. BLACK-BACKED ANTSHRIKE L-A
Sakesphorus melanonotus 13

Above black. Below black, sides white. Tail black tipped white. F: Crest black. Above brown. Below buffy. Tail chestnut.

15. WHITE-BEARDED ANTSHRIKE LM-F
Biatas nigropectus 17

Crown and breast black. Collar and throat white. Back reddish brown. Below brown. F: Crown rufous.

16. RUFOUS-CAPPED ANTSHRIKE LM-TS
Thamnophilus ruficapillus 16

female

Crown rufous Above reddish brown. Below whitish lightly barred black (barring sometimes missing).
F: Back olive brown, less barring.

Thamnophilus

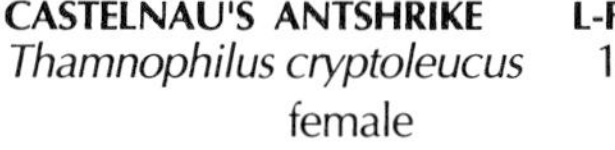

17. CASTELNAU'S ANTSHRIKE L-FT
Thamnophilus cryptoleucus 16

female

Shiny black. Wing coverts boldly edged white. F: No white shows on closed wing.

18. BARRED ANTSHRIKE L-TSO
Thamnophilus doliatus 15

Shaggy crest. Eye yellow. Crown black All barred black and white. F: Above rufous. Face streaked black and white. Throat whitish, below buffy.

female

19. BAR-CRESTED ANTSHRIKE LM-TS
Thamnophilus multistriatus 15

M (right): Very like m. 149-18.
F (left: Very like f. 149-20.

20. LINED ANTSHRIKE L-TS
Thamnophilus palliatus 15

Like m. Barred Antshrike but black and white lines are narrower. F: Very like f. 149-19.

21. BLACKISH-GRAY ANTSHRIKE L-F
Thamnophilus nigrocinereus 15

female

Above black (back gray in some races). Wing coverts narrowly edged white. Underparts gray. Tail black tipped white. F: Above brown. Underparts cinnamon rufous.

22. BLACK ANTSHRIKE L-TS
Thamnophilus nigriceps 14

female

Black. F: Above rufous brown. Head and underparts black streaked buff. Belly and crissum brown.

23. WHITE-SHOULDERED ANTSHRIKE L-F
Thamnophilus aethiops 14

Appears all blackish. White spots on wing coverts usually not obvious. F: Above uniform chestnut. No wing spots. Below paler chestnut.

Thamnophilus

24. UNIFORM ANTSHRIKE M-F
Thamnophilus unicolor 14

Uniform slaty gray. Eye pale gray. F: Rufous brown, brighter on crown. Face gray.

male

female

25. STREAK-BACKED ANTSHRIKE LM-FT
Thamnophilus insignis 14

Like150-28 but back streaked whitish. Underparts gray. F: Forehead black dotted white. Crown fhestnut. Otherwise like m., thus very different from f. 150-28.

26. VARIABLE ANTSHRIKE LM-TS
Thamnophilus caerulescens 14

M (right): Crown black. Back gray spotted black. Underparts vary from whitish to cinnamon to black. F (left): Crown gray to rufous. Throat and breast grayish. Belly buffy.

27. AMAZONIAN ANTSHRIKE L-FT
Thamnophilus amazonicus 14

female

Male like 150-28 but black cap missing on some. F: Head rufous. Back gray. Underparts rufous.

28. SLATY ANTSHRIKE L-F
Thamnophilus punctatus 14

Crown black. Back gray or blackish Wings barred and spotted white. Face gray, speckled white. Below gray. F: Above reddish brown Throat grayish. Below pale brownish (whitish with breast olive in sw).

female

29. BLACK-CAPPED ANTSHRIKE L-F
Thamnophilus schistaceus 13

Eye red. Uniform gray with black cap. F: Crown rufous. Back and face grayish. Underparts ochraceous.

female

Thamnophilus
Megastictus
Pygiptila
Thamnistes
Xenornis
Clytoctantes

30. UPLAND ANTSHRIKE M-F
Thamnophilus aroyae 13

Above dark gray, below lighter. Wing coverts black with large white spots. F: Above rufous. Face gray. Below olive brown.

31. RUFOUS-WINGED ANTSHRIKE L-S
Thamnophilus torquatus 13

Crown black. Back grayish. Wings rufous. Below whitish. Breast and tail black barred white. F: Crown and tail rufous, unbarred below.

32. MOUSE-COLORED ANTSHRIKE L-S
Thamnophilus murinus 13

Light gray. Bill "plump". Wings brownish. Small tips to wing coverts buffy. Tail tipped white. F: Crown rufous. Back reddish brown. Wing coverts tipped like male.

female

33. PEARLY ANTSHRIKE L-T
Megastictus margaritatus 13

Above blue-gray, no dorsal patch. Wings and rump with large round white (f. buff) spots. Below pale gray, whitish on throat and center of belly.

34. SPOT-WINGED ANTSHRIKE L-T
Pygiptila stellaris 13

Crown and nape black. Back gray mixed black. Wings gray with small white dots. Underparts uniform pale gray. F: Forehead and underparts ochraceous. Back and tail gray Wings broadly edged rufous.

35. RUSSET ANTSHRIKE LM-T
Thamnistes anabatinus 14

Bill heavy. Crown, wings and tail reddish brown. Back brown. Eyebrow, throat and breast buffy.

36. SPECKLED ANTSHRIKE L-F
Xenornis setifrons 15

Upperparts dusky brown with short tawny streaks. Two wing-bars cinnamon. Face and underparts dark gray. F: No gray on head. Below light brown mottled whitish.

37. RECURVE-BILLED BUSHBIRD L-F
Clytoctantes alixi 16

Bill as in 152-38 but larger. Lores, throat and breast black, rest of plumage dark gray. F: Forehead, face and underparts chestnut. Wings and tail dusky.

Neoctantes
Thamnomanes: Bill thinner, less hooked.

38. BLACK BUSHBIRD L-F
Neoctantes niger 15

female

All deep black. Bill narrow, Lower much upturned. F: Like m. but breast chestnut.

39. WESTERN ANTSHRIKE L-F
Thamnomanes occidentalis 16

Slaty black. Dorsal patch concealed. Wing coverts with bars of small white dots. F: Crown chestnut. Above brown. Eyebrow, face amd underparts slaty gray, faintly streaked whitish.

40. CINEREOUS ANTSHRIKE L-F
Thamnomanes caesius 15

All slate-gray (throat mottled white s of Amazon). No white on wings or tail. F: Above brownish. Throat whitish. Breast olive. Belly rufous.

male

female

41. BLUISH-SLATE ANTSHRIKE L-F
Thamnomanes schistogynus 14

Very like 152-40 but tinged more bluish. Throat mottled white. F: Mostly blue-gray but with contrasting rufous belly.

42. SATURNINE ANTSHRIKE L-F
Thamnomanes saturninus 12

Very like (152-44) but black throat patch much larger. Obvious white dorsal patch. F: Clear white throat. Underparts ochraceous.

43. PLUMBEOUS ANTSHRIKE LM-F
Thamnomanes plumbeus 13

Dark gray. Shoulder and spots on wing coverts white. Throat and breast blackish. F: Above brownish, tinged rufous on crown. Below gray streaked white (no streaks in Brazil).

female

44. DUSKY-THROATED ANTSHRIKE L-F
Thamnomanes ardesiacus 12

Uniform gray, usually with black throat patch. F: Upperparts grayish brown. Throat whitish. Below dull ochraceous, shaded olive on breast.

female

STOCKY, LONG-LEGGED, SHORT TAIL, TERRESTRIAL.

Grallaria
Chamaeza

Formicarius: Tail usually held erect.

1. GIANT ANTPITTA MH-F
Grallaria gigantea 24

Above olivaceous brown. Forehead rufous. Throat white. Underparts deep orange-rufous with narrow wavy black bars.

2. GREAT ANTPITTA M-F
Grallaria excelsa 24

Crown and nape gray. Above brown. Throat white, not margined black. Below tawny with bold wavy black bars.

3. UNDULATED ANTPITTA MH-F
Grallaria squamigera 21

Upperparts grayish olive. Throat white. Whiskers black. Below buff with coarse wavy black barring.

4. CHESTNUT-CROWNED ANTPITTA M-T
Grallaria ruficapilla 18

Head and nape all rufous. Back, wings and tail olive-brown Throat white. Below white streaked dusky.

5. STRIATED ANTTHRUSH L-F
Chamaeza nobilis 21

Very like 153-6 but crown darker, back more rufous and no pale tips on tail. Eye stripe, cheeks and throat white.

6. SHORT-TAILED ANTTHRUSH LM-FS
Chamaeza campanisona 19

Upperparts uniform brown. Streak back of eye white. Below white streaked dusky. Tail brown, blackish bar near end and pale-tipped.

7. RUFOUS-TAILED ANTTHRUSH LM-F
Chamaeza ruficauda 19

Very like 153-6 but more rufescent above and tail is not pale-tipped. Below more heavily streaked black.

8. BARRED ANTTHRUSH MH-F
Chamaeza mollissima 18

Upperparts uniform brown. Lines back of eye and below ear barred black and white. Underparts narrowly barred black and whitish.

9. BLACK-FACED ANTTHRUSH L-FT
Formicarius analis 17

Upperparts brownish. Throat black. Below grayish. Crissum chestnut. Tail black, held erect.

Formicarius: Tail usually held erect.
Grallaria

10. RUFOUS-BREASTED ANTTHRUSH LM-F
Formicarius rufipectus 18

Like 153-9 but breast bright rufous contrasting with black throat.

11. RUFOUS-CAPPED ANTTHRUSH L-F
Formicarius colma 17

Crown and nape bright rufous (forehead black in upper Amazon). Above olive. Face, throat and breast black. Belly gray. Tail black. F: Lores and throat white spotted black.

12. BLACK-HEADED ANTTHRUSH LM-FT
Formicarius nigricapillus 15

Head, throat and breast dull black. Back and wings dark olive-brown. Rump dark chestnut. Below pale gray. Crissum chestnut.

13. CHESTNUT-NAPED ANTPITTA MH-F
Grallaria nuchalis 19

Crown and nape bright chestnut. Above rufous brown. Face and throat dusky. Below uniform slaty gray.

14. WHITE-THROATED ANTPITTA M-F
Grallaria albigula 19

Crown and nape bright chestnut. Back olive brown. Below mostly white. Breast and sides pale gray.

15. VARIEGATED ANTPITTA L-F
Grallaria varia 18

Above brown, nape gray, scaled black. Throat brown, whisker and patch below white. Breast brown streaked whitish. Belly buff.

16. PLAIN-BACKED ANTPITTA M-F
Grallaria haplonota 18

Upperparts plain brown. Throat white, whisker blackish. Below brownish.

17. RUFOUS-FACED ANTPITTA M-F
Grallaria erythrotis 18

Above olive-brown. Face rufous. Below white, breast streaked rufous.

18. SCALED ANTPITTA LM-F
Grallaria guatimalensis 17

Gray crown and brown back scaled black. Throat brown, whiskers buff. Throat-bar white. Breast brown faintly streaked whitish. Belly buff.

19. TACHIRA ANTPITTA M-F
Grallaria chthonia 17

Above olive scaled black. Whisker whitish. Throat brown with white patch below. Breast brownish mottled buffy. Belly bright ochraceous.

Grallaria
Pittasoma
Hylopezus

20. OCHRE-STRIPED ANTPITTA L-F
Grallaria dignissima 17

Above reddish brown. Throat orange-rufous. Below white striped orange-rufous. Long black and white plumes on flanks.

21. ELUSIVE ANTPITTA L-F
Grallaria eludens 17

Above brown. Throat white. Breast buffy.

22. SANTA MARTA ANTPITTA M-F
Grallaria bangsi 17

Above olive-brown. Throat ochraceous. Below white heavily streaked olive on breast.

23. STRIPE-HEADED ANTPITTA H-T
Grallaria andicola 17

Above brown (streaked buffy in s). Eye-ring white. Below whitish streaked black.

24. BICOLORED ANTPITTA MH-F
Grallaria rufocinerea 17

Upperparts, face and throat rufous brown. Below iron gray.

25. BAY-BACKED ANTPITTA M-FT
Grallaria hypoleuca 17

Upperparts chestnut brown. Below whitish, yellow or rufous, sides always chestnut brown.

26. BLACK-CROWNED ANTPITTA L-F
Pittasoma michleri 17

Like 155-27 but crown and nape black. Boldly scalloped below.

27. RUFOUS-CROWNED ANTPITTA L-F
Pittasoma rufopileatum 16

Crown rufous. Long broad eye-stripe black. Above olive broadly streaked black. Underparts orange rufous (barred black in s).

28. TAWNY ANTPITTA MH-TS
Grallaria quitensis 15

Above brownish olive. Eye-ring and lores buffy white. Below buffy mixed with white.

29. GRAY-NAPED ANTPITTA M-F
Grallaria griseonucha 15

Like 156-32 but nape gray and underparts bright rufous.

30. SPOTTED ANTPITTA L-F
Hylopezus macularius 14

Like 156-34 but back unstreaked and flanks plain brown

31. FULVOUS-BELLIED ANTPITTA L-F
Hylopezus fulviventris 14

Like 156-34 but olive gray above and wings unspotted.

Grallaria
Hylopezus
Myrmothera

Grallaricula

32. RUFOUS ANTPITTA MH-FTO
Grallaria rufula 13

Uniform rufous chestnut.

33. BROWN-BANDED ANTPITTA H-F
Grallaria milleri 13

Uniform dark brown except lores, throat and center of belly whitish.

34. STREAK-CHESTED ANTPITTA L-F
Hylopezus perspicillatus 13

Crown gray. Back olive streaked buff. Wing coverts with buff dots. Conspicuous eye-ring buff. Below white, streaked black on breast and sides.

35. SPECKLE-BREASTED ANTPITTA L-FT
Hylopezus ochroleucus 13

Upperparts plain brownish olive. Below speckled, white in center of belly (or speckled only on sides).

36. AMAZONIAN ANTPITTA L-FT
Hylopezus berlepschi 13

Upperparts olive. Below white, breast and sides tinged buff (or streaked black in w). No eye-ring.

37. THRUSH-LIKE ANTPITTA L-F
Myrmothera campanisona 13

Olive brown above with small white loral spot. White below with variable amount of dusky streaking.

38. BROWN-BREASTED ANTPITTA M-F
Myrmothera simplex 13

Upperparts chestnut brown. Throat white sharply outlined. Breast and sides plain gray or brown. Belly white.

39. CRESCENT-FACED ANTPITTA H-FT
Grallaricula lineifrons 12

Head black with prominent white crescent before eye. Above golden olive. Below whitish broadly streaked brown

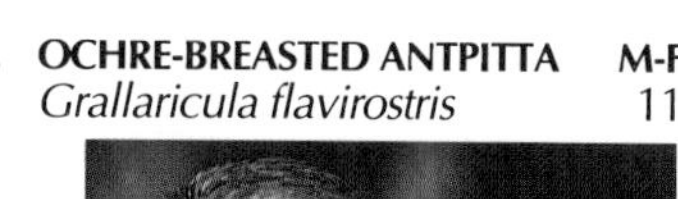

40. OCHRE-BREASTED ANTPITTA M-F
Grallaricula flavirostris 11

Upperparts brown. Broad loral spot and eye-ring buff. Below plain, (streaked dusky in some races).

41. RUSTY-BREASTED ANTPITTA M-F
Grallaricula ferrugineipectus 11

Very like 157-42 but crown olive brown like back, less white below and legs flesh-color (not gray).

Grallaricula
Myrmeciza
Phaenostictus

42. SLATE-CROWNED ANTPITTA M-F
Grallaricula nana 11

Crown dark gray. Above dark brown. Below rufous. White patch below throat in some races. Center of belly white. Legs gray.

43. SCALLOP-BREASTED ANTPITTA M-F
Grallaricula loricata 11

Crown and nape chestnut. Lores and eye-ring yellow. Back, wings and tail brown. Throat buff. Whisker dusky.Below white, breast boldly scalloped black.

44. PERUVIAN ANTPITTA M-F
Grallaricula peruviana 11

Upperparts brownish. Lower bill dusky. Below white, breast boldly scalloped black.

45. HOODED ANTPITTA M-F
Grallaricula cucullata 11

Bill yellow. Head rufous. Above brown. Below grayish with white crescent on breast.

1. GOELDI'S ANTBIRD L-TSW
Myrmeciza goeldii 18

Like 157-4 but has large white dorsal patch (usually partly visible). F: Above bright rufous. Wings and tail brown. Cheeks and throat white. Below bright cinnamon.

2. OCELLATED ANTBIRD L-F
Phaenostictus mcleannani 18

Crown grayish brown. Collar rufous. Back blackish, scaled buff. Bare skin around eye bright blue. Throat black. Below rufous spotted black.

3. WHITE-SHOULDERED ANTBIRD L-FT
Myrmeciza melanoceps 17

Black, but shoulder shows more or less white. Skin around eye blue. Tail extends about 2.5cm beyond wings. F: Rufous except head and throat black. Cf. 157-5.

4. IMMACULATE ANTBIRD LM-F
Myrmeciza immaculata 17

female

Deep black. Skin around eye blue. Small white patch at bend of wing (often hidden). Tail extends about 5cm beyond wings. F: Underparts dull brownish mixed with gray.

5. SOOTY ANTBIRD L-F
Myrmeciza fortis 16

Very like 157-4 but duller black. Sometimes shows white edge to wing. F: Like f. 157-4 but face and underparts gray.

Myrmeciza
Cercomacra
Pyriglena: Bill small.
Phlegopsis

6. PLUMBEOUS ANTBIRD L-F
Myrmeciza hyperythra 16

Male (left): Uniform dark gray. Wings black with conspicuous small white spots. Orbital skin whitish or bluish. F (right): Below uniform bright rufous.

7. MATO GROSSO ANTBIRD L-TS
Cercomacra melanaria 17

female

Black. Shoulders white (often not visible). Wing coverts tipped white. F: Above ashy gray. Below pale gray, whiter on throat and belly.

8. WHITE-BACKED FIRE-EYE LM-FT
Pyriglena leuconota 17

Glossy black with large white dorsal patch often visible. Eye bright red. F: Above brown, dorsal patch usually visible. Below olive,brown or black. Tail black. Variable

female

9. WHITE-SHOULDERED FIRE-EYE L-FT
Pyriglena leucoptera 16

Bill 1/2x head. Eye red. Glossy black with narrow white wing-bars. F. Like f. 158-8 but no white dorsal patch. Tail black.

female

10. BLACK-SPOTTED BARE-EYE L-FT
Phlegopsis nigromaculata 16

Head, neck and breast black. Occipital skin red. Back and wings brown with large black spots. Belly brown.Tail rufous.

11. REDDISH-WINGED BARE-EYE L-F
Phlegopsis erythroptera 15

Black. Back and rump scaled white. Orbital skin red. Wings with large chestnut patch. F: Above brown. Wings blackish with three rufous bars. Below rufous. Tail blackish.

Cercomacra

12. RIO DE JANEIRO ANTBIRD L-TS
Cercomacra brasiliana 15

Like 159-15 but much paler gray. F: Like f. 159-15 but wing coverts not tipped.

13. BANANAL ANTBIRD L-T
Cercomacra ferdinandi 15

Black. Wing coverts edged white. Tail narrowly tipped white. F: Grayish black. Throat and breast with distinct but narrow white streaks.

14. RIO BRANCO ANTBIRD L-FT
Cercomacra carbonaria 15

Like 159-18 but tail longer. F: Above dark gray. Wing coverts tipped white. Throat white, speckled gray. Below buffy.

15. DUSKY ANTBIRD LM-FT
Cercomacra tyrannina 14

female

Uniform gray, wing coverts tipped white. Tail blackish tipped white. F: Above olive-brown. Underparts bright ochraceous becoming grayish at rear. Cf. 159-16.

16. GRAY ANTBIRD L-FT
Cercomacra cinerascens 14

Like 159-15 but white tips on wing coverts smaller or lacking entirely. Tail broadly tipped white. F: Olive brown above. Below dull ochraceous.

17. BLACK ANTBIRD L-F
Cercomacra serva 14

Blackish. Blacker on throat and breast. Wing coverts edged white. F: Above olive-brown. Brow and face buffy.

18. JET ANTBIRD L-T
Cercomacra nigricans 14

female

Black. White shoulder patch sometimes visible. Wing coverts tipped white. Tail broadly tipped white. F: Slaty, finely streaked white on throat and breast.

Cercomacra
Gymnocichla
Gymnopithys
Rhegmatorhina

19. BLACKISH ANTBIRD L-FT
Cercomacra nigrescens 14

Blackish
Bend of wing whitish (sometimes hidden). Wing coverts very narrowly edged white.
F: Forecrown rufous. Above olive-brown. Below rufous. Tail olive-brown.

female

20. BARE-CROWNED ANTBIRD L-T
Gymnocichla nudiceps 15

Black. Cap and face are bright blue. Wings with three narrow whitish bars.
F: Above brown. Bare skin around eye blue. Three obscure rufous wing-bars. Below bright rufous.

female

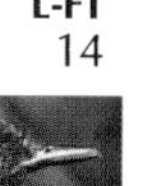

21. WHITE-THROATED ANTBIRD L-F
Gymnopithys salvini 15

Gray. Brow and throat white. Tail black, barred white. F: Mostly chestnut brown. Crown blackish. Tail chestnut barred black.

female

22. LUNULATED ANTBIRD L-F
Gymnopithys lunulata 15

Like 160-21 but tail all black.
F: Brown, feathers of back fringed buffy. Below more olive brown. Tail with some white barring.

23. HAIRY-CRESTED ANTBIRD L-F
Rhegmatorhina melanosticta 14

female

Crown and crest pale gray. Eye-ring whitish. Face and throat black. Above brown (f. with large black, buff-fringed spots).

Rhegmatorhina
Percnostola
Myrmorchilus

Myrmornis

24. HARLEQUIN ANTBIRD **L-F**
Rhegmatorhina berlepschi 14

Mostly buffy brown barred black. Crown and breast chestnut. Face black. F: Above brown, barred black. Crown and breast chestnut.

25. CHESTNUT-CRESTED ANTBIRD **L-F**
Rhegmatorhina cristata 14

Crown, nape and back chestnut. Wings and tail brown. Bare skin around eye light blue or whitish. Face and throat black. Below rufous chestnut.
F: Few large black spots on mantle.

26. WHITE-BREASTED ANTBIRD **L-F**
Rhegmatorhina hoffmannsi 14

Lores, crown and crest deep black. Above olive-brown. Cheeks, throat and breast white. F: Like f. 161-25 but has contrasting white throat and breast.

27. BARE-EYED ANTBIRD **L-F**
Rhegmatorhina gymnops 14

Large bare area around eye pale blue-green. Crested. Head black. Above brown. Below black.

28. CAURA ANTBIRD **L-F**
Percnostola caurensis 16

Male and female very like m. and f. 162-4 but much larger. Dark gray. Prominent white spots on wing coverts. F: Reddish brown, wing spots cinnamon.

29. STRIPE-BACKED ANTBIRD **L-TS**
Myrmorchilus strigilatus 15

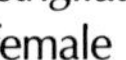

female

Above rufous broadly streaked black. Wing coverts black, broadly tipped white. Eyebrow white. Throat and breast black. Below whitish. Tail centrals chestnut, rest black. F: Underparts white, breast streaked black.

30. WING-BANDED ANTBIRD **L-F**
Myrmornis torquata 14

Above chestnut. Wings blackish, crossed by three buff bars. Cheeks speckled black and white. Throat and breast black. Below gray. Tail short, rufous.

1. BLACK-HEADED ANTBIRD **L-F**
Percnostola rufifrons 14

Leaden gray. Eye red. Crown and throat black. Wing coverts black with three white wing-bars. Tail blackish without white tips. F: Three wing-bars and all underparts buff or rufous.

male

female

Percnostola
Sclateria
Myrmoborus

2. WHITE-LINED ANTBIRD L-FT
Percnostola lophotes 14

Like 161-1 but darker gray. F: Crown cinnamon rufous. Above brown, wings spotted cinnamon. Face and most of underparts gray, white in center.

3. SLATE-COLORED ANTBIRD L-F
Percnostola schistacea 14

Very like 162-4 but more uniform gray, not paler below. F: Face and underparts bright rufous.

4. SPOT-WINGED ANTBIRD L-FT
Percnostola leucostigma 14

M: (right) Gray, paler below. F: (left) Head gray. Back brown. Wings with prominent large cinnamon spots.

5. SILVERED ANTBIRD L-FTW
Sclateria naevia 14

Above lead gray Wings dotted white. Below whitish usually marked gray. Legs pink. F: Above brown, sides rufous.

6. ASH-BREASTED ANTBIRD L-F
Myrmoborus lugubris 14

Forehead pale gray. Face and throat black. Above gray. Below white. F: Above rufous. Face black like m. in w.

7. WHITE-BROWED ANTBIRD L-T
Myrmoborus leucophrys 12

Forecrown and long broad eyebrow white. Face and throat black. Rest of plumage gray. F: Forecrown cinnamon. Wing coverts tipped buffy. Below white.

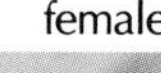
female

8. BLACK-FACED ANTBIRD L-F
Myrmoborus myotherinus 11

Gray. Forehead white. Three white wing-bars. F: Above brown. Throat white. Below cinnamon.

female

Myrmoborus
Myrmeciza

9. BLACK-TAILED ANTBIRD L-F
Myrmoborus melanurus 11

female

Slaty gray. Head, neck and tail black. Wings black, margined white. F: Above brown. Below white, breast brownish.

10. SQUAMATE ANTBIRD L-F
Myrmeciza squamosa 14

Above brown, mixed black on back.Brow white. Face and tbroat black. Wing-bars white. Below white, scalloped black. F: Face black only through eye. Below white.

female

11. WHITE-BELLIED ANTBIRD L-TS
Myrmeciza longipes 40

Upperparts bright rufous. Broad brow gray. Throat and breast black (f. cinnamon). Belly white.

12. WHITE-BIBBED ANTBIRD L-F
Myrmeciza loricata 14

Upperparts brown. Prominent eyebrow white (f. buff). Face and throat black. Below white speckled black on breast.

female

13. CHESTNUT-BACKED ANTBIRD L-FT
Myrmeciza exsul 13

Head blackish gray. Orbital skin blue. Above brown, small white spots on wings. Below dark gray (f. rufous).

female

Myrmeciza

14. FERRUGINOUS-BACKED ANTBIRD L-FT
Myrmeciza ferruginea 13

female

Upperparts chestnut. Wing coverts black barred cinnamon. Face throat and breast black, bordered in back by a white line. F: Throat white.

15. SCALLOPED ANTBIRD L-F
Myrmeciza ruficauda 13

Like 163-10 but wing coverts fringed cinnamon, not white. Mantle scaled, (not plain).

16. DULL-MANTLED ANTBIRD LM-F
Myrmeciza laemosticta 13

Head and neck dark gray. Above brown, small white spots on wing. Throat black. Below dark gray. F: Throat sharply checkered black and white.

17. BLACK-THROATED ANTBIRD L-FT
Myrmeciza atrothorax 13

female

Upperparts dark brown. Wings black dotted white. Throat and breast black Belly gray F: Above olive brown. Face gray. Throat white. Breast and sides rufous. Center of belly white.

18. GRAY-HEADED ANTBIRD M-F
Myrmeciza griseiceps 13

Head and neck gray. Back brown Wings black spotted white. Throat and breast black (f. gray). Tail dark gray tipped white.

19. SPOT-BREASTED ANTBIRD L-FT
Myrmeciza stictothorax 13

Upperparts brown. Dorsal patch white. Rump blackish. Wings dotted white. Throat black. Breast black streaked white. Belly gray. F: Like 164-17.

20. GRAY-BELLIED ANTBIRD L-F
Myrmeciza pelzelni 12

Above rufous brown, wings with large buff spots. Lores and face mixed gray and white. Throat and breast black. Belly gray. F: Breast white scaled dusky. Flanks chestnut.

21. YAPACANA ANTBIRD L-FT
Myrmeciza disjuncta 12

Above mostly blackish gray. Wing coverts tipped white (f. buff). Lores and face gray. Chin white. Below ochraceous. Tail black.

22. CHESTNUT-TAILED ANTBIRD L-F
Myrmeciza hemimelaena 11

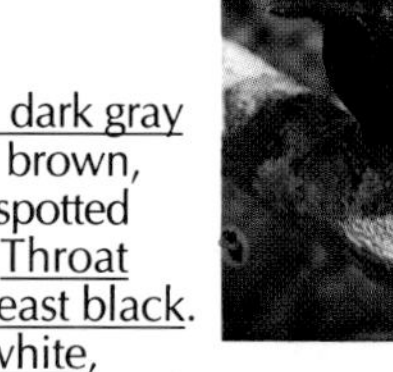

Crown dark gray Above brown, wings spotted white. Throat and breast black. Belly white, sides rufous. Tail chestnut. F: Brow white. Wings spotted buff. Throat and breast cinnamon. Below white.

Gymnopithys
Drymophila

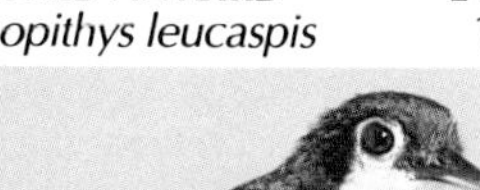

23. BICOLORED ANTBIRD L-FT
Gymnopithys leucaspis 13

Above reddish brown or dark brown. Cheeks black. Orbital skin blue in some races. Below white, sides black or brown.

24. RUFOUS-THROATED ANTBIRD L-FT
Gymnopithys rufigula 13

Forehead black. Above olive-brown. Skin around eye blue. Cheeks and throat rufous. Below buff, sides brown.

25. LONG-TAILED ANTBIRD M-FT
Drymophila caudata 14

Above streaked buff and black. Rump and belly rufous. Breast streaked white and dusky. Flanks cinnamon.

26. STRIATED ANTBIRD L-F
Drymophila devillei 13

Very like 165-25 but smaller.

27. FERRUGINOUS ANTBIRD LM-FT
Drymophila ferruginea 13

Crown black Long eyebrow white. Back brown. Rump chestnut. Below rufous.

28. RUFOUS-TAILED ANTBIRD M-FT
Drymophila genei 13

Crown black. Brow white. Back grayish finely streaked white. Rump and tail rufous. Below white spotted black. F: Above rufous.

29. DUSKY-TAILED ANTBIRD LM-FT
Drymophila malura 13

Head, neck, throat and breast streaked black and whitish. Back and belly gray. Tail long. F: Brownish.

30. SCALED ANTBIRD L-FT
Drymophila squamata 11

Above black, back spotted white. Dorsal patch white, concealed. Below white spotted black. Tail black, barred white. F: Above brown with large round fulvous spots on lower back.

Drymophila
Herpsilochmus

31. OCHRE-RUMPED ANTBIRD **LM-FT**
Drymophila ochropyga 12

Crown black. Brow white. Back mixed gray and black. Rump rufous. Throat and breast white streaked black. Belly rufous.

1. LARGE-BILLED ANTWREN **L-ST**
Herpsilochmus longirostris 12

female

Crown black. Long eyebrow white. Back gray. Wings black, spotted white. Breast whitish with pale gray spots. Belly gray. Tail black broadly tipped white. F: Head and nape rufous. Below cinnamon, becoming white or gray on belly.

2. RORAIMAN ANTWREN **M-Ft**
Herpsilochmus roraimae 12

Like 166-1 but tail longer. F: Crown spotted white.

3. BLACK-CAPPED ANTWREN **L-TS**
Herpsilochmus pileatus 12

Like 166-1 but back mixed gray and black. Tail outers mostly white.

4. PECTORAL ANTWREN **L-SA**
Herpsilochmus pectoralis 12

Like 166-1 but has black crescent on breast. F: Rump tipped white.

5. YELLOW-BREASTED ANTWREN **LM-FT**
Herpsilochmus axillaris 11

Crown and nape black, spotted white. Long eyebrow yellow. Back olive gray. Underparts yellow. F: Crown dull rufous.

6. TODD'S ANTWREN **L-F**
Herpsilochmus stictocephalus 11

Like 166-1 but tail spotted white. F: Crown spotted white, otherwise like male.

7. SPOT-TAILED ANTWREN **L-F**
Herpsilochmus sticturus 10

Rather like 166-1 but tail black with large white spots on central feathers. F: Like f. 166-1 but crown streaked.

8. SPOT-BACKED ANTWREN **L-F**
Herpsilochmus dorsimaculatus 11

Rather like 166-1 but back prominently streaked black and white. F: Forehead spotted deep buff.

9. RUFOUS-WINGED ANTWREN **LM-FT**
Herpsilochmus rufimarginatus 11

Like 166-1 but large rufous patch on wing and underparts pale yellowish. F: Crown chestnut.

Formicivora
Hylophylax: Tail short.

10. RUSTY-BACKED ANTWREN **L-TSO**
Formicivora rufa 13

Upperparts brown. Long eyebrow white. Below black, sides whitish. F: Underparts all streaked black and white.

female

11. WHITE-FRINGED ANTWREN **L-TS**
Formicivora grisea 12

Above grayish brown. Long eyebrow white. Below black surrounded by white fringe. F: Varies from white to cinnamon below. Breast more or less freckled brown.

female

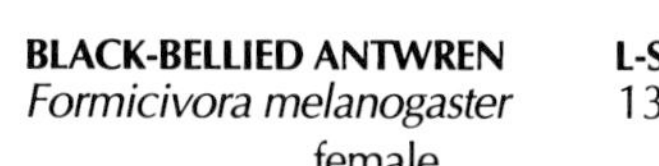

12. BLACK-BELLIED ANTWREN **L-S**
Formicivora melanogaster 13

female

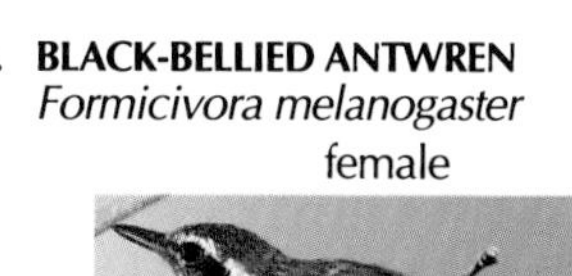

Upperparts dark slaty brown. Long eyebrow white. Below black, long silky gray feathers at sides. Wings and tail like 167-11. Underparts whitish.

13. SERRA ANTWREN (ANTBIRD) **L-SO**
Formicivora serrana 13

Upperparts dark reddish brown. Below black. Sides of breast and flanks smoky gray. F: Throat white, below buff.

female

14. NARROW-BILLED ANTWREN **LM-T**
Formicivora iheringi 12

Like 171-49 but feathers of throat edged white, of breast edged gray. F: Like f. 171-49 but rump cinnamon.

15. SCALE-BACKED ANTBIRD **L-F**
Hylophylax poecilonota 12

Gray (throat black in some races). Lower back and wings black scaled white. Tail black with white spots and tips. F: Head and throat rufous. Below cinnamon (or gray in some races).

female

Hylophylax
Sipia
Pithys
Dysithamnus

16. SPOTTED ANTBIRD L-F
Hylophylax naevioides 10

Head dark gray. Back and wing-bars chestnut. Throat black (f. lacking). Below white with band of black spots across breast.

17. SPOT-BACKED ANTBIRD L-F
Hylophylax naevia 10

Head gray. Above blackish spotted buff. Rump not spotted. Throat black. Below white with band of black spots across breast. F: Browner. Breast buffy.

female

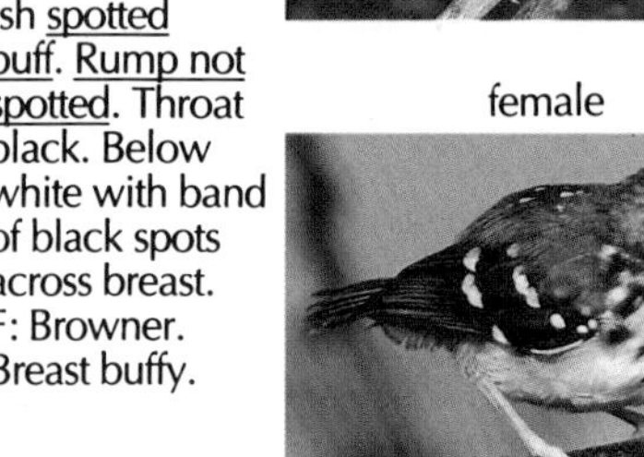

18. DOT-BACKED ANTBIRD L-F
Hylophylax punctulata 10

Very like 168-16 but rump spotted white. F: Like f. 168-17.

19. ESMERALDAS ANTBIRD LM-F
Sipia rosenbergi 12

Leaden gray. Eye red. Wings black spotted white. F: Throat (only) spotted white.

20. STUB-TAILED ANTBIRD L-F
Sipia berlepschi 12

female

Black. No white spots on wing. Tail short. F: Blackish. Throat and breast dotted white.

21. WHITE-PLUMED ANTBIRD L-F
Pithys albifrons 12

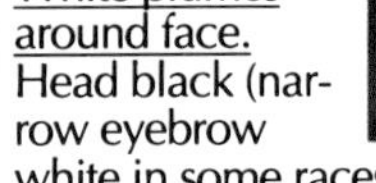

White plumes around face. Head black (narrow eyebrow white in some races). Back and wings gray. Collar, all underparts, rump and tail chestnut.

22. SPOT-BREASTED ANTVIREO LM-F
Dysithamnus stictothorax 12

Crown gray (f. rufous). Area behind eye speckled black and white. Below whitish. Breast spotted gray.

female

Dysithamnus
Hypocnemoides
Dichrozona
Myrmochanes

23. RUFOUS-BACKED ANTVIREO LM-F
Dysithamnus xanthopterus 11

Head gray, face speckled white. Lower back and wings bright rufous chestnut. Below grayish. Tail black and rufous. F: Above rufous. Below pale olive.

24. PLAIN ANTVIREO LM-FT
Dysithamnus mentalis 11

Above gray. Distinctive black cheek patch. Throat white or grayish. Belly usually yellowish. F: Crown rufous. Above olive to brownish.

female

25. SPOT-CROWNED ANTVIREO L-F
Dysithamnus puncticeps 11

Crown black spotted gray. Eye pale. Above gray. Wings spotted white. Below white streaked dusky on breast.

female

26. BLACK-CHINNED ANTBIRD L-FTW
Hypocnemoides melanopogon 11

Gray, paler on belly. Throat patch black. Wing coverts black, conspicuously margined white. Tail narrowly tipped white. F: Light gray. Below white, mottled on breast.

female

27. BAND-TAILED ANTBIRD L-FT
Hypocnemoides maculicauda 11

Very like 169-26 but white tips to tail larger and has large white dorsal patch.

28. BANDED ANTBIRD L-F
Dichrozona cincta 11

Bill slender. Brown. White band on rump. Wings barred buff. Below white, breast spotted black.

29. BLACK-AND-WHITE ANTBIRD L-S
Myrmochanes hemileucus 11

Above black, white in center of back. Rump gray. Underparts white. F: Lores white.

Myrmotherula
Terenura

30. CHECKER-THROATED ANTWREN **L-FT**
Myrmotherula fulviventris 11

Above grayish brown. Throat more or less checkered black. Eye pale.

31. WHITE-EYED ANTWREN **L-F**
Myrmotherula leucophthalma 11

Very like 170-30 but breast purer gray.

32. RUFOUS-TAILED ANTWREN **L-F**
Myrmotherula erythrura 11

Back, rump and tail rufous. Wing coverts spotted. Throat whitish, often spotted black. Below gray (f. buff).

33. BLACK-HOODED ANTWREN **LM-F**
Myrmotherula erythronotos 11

Hood black. Back chestnut. Sides white, belly dark gray. Wing coverts spotted white. F: Mostly olive brown above, back chestnut. Below light buffy brown, sides white.

34. PLAIN-WINGED ANTWREN **M-F**
Myrmotherula behni 11

Dark gray (f. brown). Throat black (f. white). Wings plain. Tail not tipped.

35. LEADEN ANTWREN **L-T**
Myrmotherula assimillis 11

Light gray, paler below. Wing coverts tipped white (f. buff). F: Throat white, below buffy.

36. RUFOUS-RUMPED ANTWREN **LM-F**
Terenura callinota 10

Crown and nape black. Wings broadly barred yellowish. Back olive, rump rufous. F: Crown brownish olive.

37. CHESTNUT-SHOULDERED ANTWREN **L-F**
Terenura humeralis 10

Like 170-36 but shoulders chestnut (not yellow) and belly gray (not yellow).

38. YELLOW-RUMPED ANTWREN **M-F**
Terenura sharpei 10

Like 170-36 but rump yellow (not rufous).

39. ORNATE ANTWREN **L-F**
Myrmotherula ornata 9

Above gray. Back and rump chestnut gray. Wing coverts black spotted white. Throat black (except in s).F: Above like m. Throat black checkered white (lacking in e). Below buffy.

40. ASH-WINGED ANTWREN **L-F**
Terenura spodioptila 10

Crown black. Narrow white eyestripe. Back and rump bright chestnut. Otherwise gray above, wings with two bold white bars. Below whitish. F: Crown, throat and breast brownish.

Terenura
Myrmotherula
Hypocnemis

41. STREAK-CAPPED ANTWREN L-F
Terenura maculata 10

Like 170-36 but crown and face black streaked white and breast white lightly streaked dusky.

42. STRIPE-CHESTED ANTWREN L-T
Myrmotherula longicauda 10

Very like 171-48 but underparts much less streaked and tail broadly tipped. F: Like f. 171-48.

43. CHERRIE'S ANTWREN L-T
Myrmotherula cherriei 10

Very like 171-48 but breast and belly heavily streaked black. F: Like f. 171-48 but breast and belly broadly streaked black.

44. BROWN-BELLIED ANTWREN L-F
Myrmotherula gutturalis 10

Above reddish brown, wing coverts spotted white. Throat checkered black and white. Breast grayish. Belly brown.

45. YELLOW-BROWED ANTBIRD L-F
Hypocnemis hypoxantha 10

Like 171-47 but back not streaked and eyebrow yellow (not white).

46. STAR-THROATED ANTWREN LM-F
Myrmotherula gularis 9

Upperparts and crissum reddish brown, shoulders white. Wing coverts black dotted white. Throat and upper breast black spotted white. Below gray.

47. WARBLING ANTBIRD L-T
Hypocnemis cantator 10

Crown and back streaked black and white (f. back brown). Eyebrow white. Below whitish or yellow, more or less streaked black. Sides rufous.

48. STREAKED ANTWREN L-TW
Myrmotherula surinamensis 9

Streaked black and white above and below. Tail black narrowly tipped white. F: Head and breast rufous. Throat and below whitish mostly unstreaked.

female

49. WHITE-FLANKED ANTWREN L-FT
Myrmotherula axillaris 9

Dark grayish. Wings spotted white. Long white flank plumes usually seen. Tail tipped white. F: Above gray to reddish brown. Wings spotted rufous. Below buff. Tail brown.

female

Microrhopias
Myrmotherula

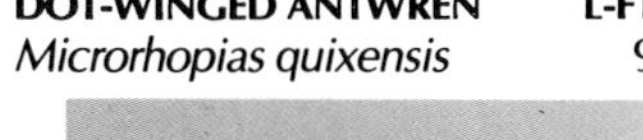

50. DOT-WINGED ANTWREN L-FT
Microrhopias quixensis 9

Black. Large dorsal patch white. Wings conspiucuously spotted white. Tail tipped white. F: Underparts chestnut (throat or belly black in w).

female

51. ASHY ANTWREN L-F
Myrmotherula grisea 9

Uniform slaty gray (wing coverts unmarked). F: Above olive-brown. Below bright rufous brown. Tail tinged rufous.

52. STIPPLE-THROATED ANTWREN L-F
Myrmotherula haematonota 9

Head brown. Back chestnut (or upperparts all slaty gray in w). Wing coverts black tipped white. Throat black checkered white. Breast gray. Belly rufous. F: Mostly brown.

53. LONG-WINGED ANTWREN L-F
Myrmotherula longipennis 10

Gray. Throat black. Tail tipped white. F: Above brown. Eye-ring, throat and breast buff. Belly white in center.

54. SLATY ANTWREN LM-F
Myrmotherula schisticolor 9

Dark gray, throat and breast black. Wings with small white spots. Tail narrowly fringed white. F: Above grayish brown. No marks on wings. Underparts ochraceous.

male

female

55. BAND-TAILED ANTWREN L-F
Myrmotherula urosticta 9

Gray. Wing coverts black with large white tips. Tail feathers with large ends white except central pair. F: Below buffy, throat whitish.

56. UNICOLORED ANTWREN L-F
Myrmotherula unicolor 9

Dark gray. Throat blackish. Wing coverts unmarked. F: Above brown. Wing coverts unmarked. Throat whitish. Below pale olive buff.

57. GRAY ANTWREN L-F
Myrmotherula menetriesii 9

female

Light gray (throat more or less black in w). Wing coverts have black bar and white tip. Tail short. F: Above gray. Below light rufous.

Myrmotherula

58. RIO SUNO ANTWREN L-F
Myrmotherula sunensis 8

Like 172-54 but tail shorter. Wing spots very small. Tail not tipped white. F: Above grayish olive. Below olivaceous, paler on throat.

59. SALVADORI'S ANTWREN L-F
Myrmotherula minor 9

Like 172-54 but tail with black bar near end and white tips. F: Above pale olive, crown gray. Throat whitish, below buff.

60. IHERING'S ANTWREN L-F
Myrmotherula iheringi 9

Rather like 172-54 but bill larger and tail lacks white tips. F: Above pale gray. Wing coverts black with large buff spots. Below pale buff.

61. KLAGES' ANTWREN L-FT
Myrmotherula klagesi 8

Very like 171-48 but has no white concealed patch on back. F: Above streaked buff, streaked black on breast.

62. RUFOUS-BELLIED ANTWREN L-F
Myrmotherula guttata 8

Gray. Rump brown. Wing coverts and tail conspicuously tipped cinnamon. Belly rufous. F: Back olive-brown.

63. PLAIN-THROATED ANTWREN L-F
Myrmotherula hauxwelli 8

Gray, paler below. Wing and tail coverts black tipped white. F: Above olive brown. Below cinnamon-rufous. Wing and tail coverts tipped buff.

64. PYGMY ANTWREN L-FT
Myrmotherula brachyura 8

Quite like 171-48 but underparts not streaked.

65. SHORT-BILLED ANTWREN LM-F
Myrmotherula obscura 8

Quite like 171-48 but less streaked above, rump blackish and underparts all pale yellow. F: Throat and breast ochraceous. Cf. 173-64.

66. SCLATER'S ANTWREN L-F
Myrmotherula sclateri 8

Quite like 171-48 but above black streaked yellow. Wing-bars white. Rump gray. Underparts yellow. F: Below pale yellow narrowly streaked black. Cf. 173-64.

67. YELLOW-THROATED ANTWREN L-FT
Myrmotherula ambigua 8

Quite like 171-48 but crown and face black streaked white (f. tawny). Back streaked yellow. Underparts all pale yellow. Cf. 173-64.

Conopophaga: Long white eye-stripe, sometimes tufted in males.

1. BLACK-BELLIED GNATEATER **L-F**
Conopophaga melanogaster 13

Head black. Back, wings and tail chestnut. Underparts black. F: Above brown. Eye-stripe gray. Throat white. Below pale gray, belly white.

2. BLACK-CHEEKED GNATEATER **LM-F**
Conopophaga melanops 12

Crown bright orange. Back brownish. Face black. Throat and belly white. Breast gray. Tuft white (lacking in this specimen). F: Lacks black on face. Below ferruginous.

female

3. ASH-THROATED GNATEATER **L-F**
Conopophaga peruviana 12

Crown dark brown. Back gray. Wings dark brown, coverts spotted white. Throat whitish. Breast gray (f. reddish). Belly white.

4. SLATY GNATEATER **LM-F**
Conopophaga ardesiaca 12

Upperparts, wings and tail dark olive brown. Forehead gray. Below uniform gray. F: Above reddish brown, forehead rufous.

5. CHESTNUT-BELTED GNATEATER **LM-F**
Conopophaga aurita 12

Upperparts brown. Face and throat black. Breast rufous. Belly white in center. F: Throat whitish.

6. HOODED GNATEATER **L-F**
Conopophaga roberti 12

Head, throat and breast black. Above rufous. Below gray. Belly white in center. F: Crown rufous. Below pale gray.

7. CHESTNUT-CROWNED GNATEATER **LM-F**
Conopophaga casteneiceps 12

Forecrown bright orange-rufous. Hindcrown chestnut. Above dark olive-brown. Below gray. F: Breast rufous. Belly whitish.

8. RUFOUS GNATEATER **L-F**
Conopophaga lineata 11

Upperparts, wings and tail uniform brown. Eyebrow gray. Throat and breast rufous. Belly white. F: Tuft gray.

Pteroptochos
Rhinocrypta
Actropternis
Scelorchilus
Liosceles
Merulaxis
Teledromas

1. CHESTNUT-THROATED HUET-HUET **M-F**
Pteroptochos castaneus 21

Above blackish, rump barred black and buff. Eyebrow and underparts rufous, barred black on belly.

2. BLACK-THROATED HUET-HUET **LM-F**
Pteroptochos tarnii 21

Forecrown chestnut. Head, neck and throat blackish. Rump chestnut. Breast and below chestnut, barred black on belly.

3. MOUSTACHED TURCA **LM-S**
Pteroptochos megapodius 19

Above smoky brown. Narrow eyebrow and broad whiskers white. Throat brown. Breast rufous brown. Belly whitish barred rufous and dusky.

4. CRESTED GALLITO **L-SA**
Rhinocrypta lanceolata 19

Head and crest rufous. Above gray. Tail blackish. Throat and breast pale gray, sides bright chestnut. Belly white.

5. OCELLATED TAPACULO **H-F**
Acropternis orthonyx 18

Face and throat bright rufous. Back, wings and underparts blackish profusely spotted white. Rump and vent plain rufous. Tail blackish.

6. WHITE-THROATED TAPACULO **LM-S**
Scelorchilus albicollis 18

Above rufous brown, wings and tail rufous. Eyebrow and throat whitish. Below buffy white with irregular dark brown bars.

7. CHUCAO TAPACULO **L-F**
Scelorchilus rubecula 17

Above dark brown. Eye-stripe , throat and upper breast rufous. Lower breast black barred white. Belly dark gray.

8. RUSTY-BELTED TAPACULO **L-F**
Liosceles thoracicus 18

Upperparts rufous brown. Narrow eyebrow white. Sides of neck and of breast gray. Throat and breast white, breast crossed by rufous band. Belly black, barred white and rufous. Eye yellow.

9. STRESEMANN'S BRISTLEFRONT **L-F**
Merulaxis stresemanni 20

Blackish. Long, pointed, bushy plumes in front of eyes. Lower back, flanks and belly dark olive brown F: Dark brown above, bright rufous below.

10. SLATY BRISTLEFRONT **M-F**
Merulaxis ater 18

Blackish. Long, pointed, bushy plumes in front of eyes. Lower back, flanks and belly dark olive-brown. F: Brown above. Cinnamon brown below.

11. SANDY GALLITO **LM-SO**
Teledromas fuscus 16

Above pale brown. Eyebrow whitish. Below whitish tinged cinnamon. Tail blackish, outermost feathers tipped white.

Melanopareia
Scytalopus: Tail cocked, usually quite short.
Psilorhamphus
Eugralla
Myornis

12. MARANON CRESCENT-CHEST L-SA
Melanopareia maranonica 14

Head all black with long buffy eyebrow. Back brown. Wing feathers edged white. Throat white. Breast and tail black. Belly rufous. Tail long, pointed.

13. OLIVE-CROWNED CRESCENT-CHEST L-S
Melanopareia maximiliani 14

Upperparts olive-brown. Eyebrow and throat buffy. Face and pectoral band black. Below chestnut.

14. COLLARED CRESCENT-CHEST L-S
Melanopareia torquata 12

Upperparts brown. Collar rufous. Eyebrow white. Face black. Below buffy with black band across breast.

15. ELEGANT CRESCENT-CHEST L-SA
Melanopareia elegans 12

Head all black except long eyebrow white. Above olive. Throat whitish. Black band across breast. Below buff.

16. LARGE-FOOTED TAPACULO M-F
Scytalopus macropus 14

Dark ashy gray. Rump, flanks and crissum brown barred black. Feet very large.

17. UNICOLORED TAPACULO MH-F
Scytalopus unicolor 12

Uniform slaty gray. Imm: Above dark brown. Below buffy. No bars.

18. SPOTTED BAMBOO-WREN L-F
Psilorhamphus guttatus 12

Wren-like. Above mostly gray, dotted white. Rump and belly rufous. Below whitish dotted black. Tail long, brown, tipped white.

19. OCHRE-FLANKED TAPACULO LM-F
Eugralla paradoxa 12

Bill blackish, lower yellowish. Slaty gray, paler below. Rump and flanks rufous, barred dusky.

20. ASH-COLORED TAPACULO H-F
Myornis senilis 13

Uniform ashy gray, paler below. Tail rather long. F: Rearparts edged brown.

21. RUFOUS-VENTED TAPACULO LMH-F
Scytalopus femoralis 12

Above blackish becoming dark brown on rump. Below gray, belly and flanks brown barred black. Has white crown spot in e. Tail fairly long.

22. PALE-THROATED TAPACULO LMH-F
Scytalopus panamensis 12

Like 176-21 but eyebrow white in ne and tail shorter. Throat pale gray.

Scytalopus: Tail cocked, usually quite short.
Cephalopterus
Pyroderus
Gymnoderus
Haematoderus
Querula

23. BROWN-RUMPED TAPACULO **MH-F**
Scytalopus latebricola 11

Ashy gray. Rump and flanks rusty, mostly barred dusky.

24. BRASILIA TAPACULO **L-T**
Syctalopus novacapitalis 12

Above slaty blue-gray. Throat and breast pale gray. Rump and flanks rusty, barred dusky.

25. WHITE-BREASTED TAPACULO **L-F**
Scytalopus indigoticus 12

Above slaty blue-black. Throat and center of underparts white. Flanks brown barred dusky. F: Above dark brown.

26. WHITE-BROWED TAPACULO **MH-FT**
Scytalopus superciliaris 10

Mostly brownish. Eyebrow and throat white or pale grayish. Crissum and flanks barred brown and black.

27. ANDEAN TAPACULO **MH-FT**
Scytalopus magellanicus 10

Very variable from dark gray (in s) to pale gray (in n). Rump and flanks more rufous in n races.

28. MOUSE-COLORED TAPACULO **M-F**
Scytalopus speluncae 10

Much like 176-21. Blackish gray. F: Dark brown, barred dusky below.

1. AMAZONIAN UMBRELLABIRD **LM-F**
Cephalopterus ornatus 43

Black. Tall, upstanding umbrella-shaped crest. Flat hanging wattle at base of neck. F: Has smaller crest and wattle.

2. LONG-WATTLED UMBRELLABIRD **LM-F**
Cephalopterus penduliger 43

Black. Upstanding umbrella-like crest. Hanging wattle cylindrical, up to 18" long, hanging from lower throat, feathered all around. F: Has smaller crest, much shorter wattle.

3. RED-RUFFED FRUITCROW **LM-F**
Pyroderus scutatus 35

Upperparts glossy black. Throat and breast orange reddish. Belly mostly brown (chestnut in w).

4. BARE-NECKED FRUITCROW **L-FT**
Gymnoderus foetidus 35

Black. Neck sparsely feathered, skin blue to whitish. Wings silvery gray. F: Grayish. Wings slaty like back.

5. CRIMSON FRUITCROW **L-F**
Haematoderus militaris 35

All red (including bill) except wings and tail blackish brown. F: Head red. Above dark brown. Below pinkish red.

6. PURPLE-THROATED FRUITCROW **L-F**
Querula purpurata 26

Glossy black. Throat patch red (f. black). Bill slate blue.

Perissocephalus
Lipaugus
Chirocylla
Rupicola

7. CAPUCHINBIRD L-F
Perissocephalus tricolor 33

Crown and face bare, gray. Above and below chestnut rufous. Wings dark brown. Tail black.

8. DUSKY PIHA MH-F
Lipaugus fuscocinereus 26

All ashy gray, lighter below. Crissum whitish. Tail noticeably long. Very like 178-9.

9. SCREAMING PIHA L-F
Lipaugus vociferans 24

All grayish, lighter below. Has loud explosive three-note call.

10. CINNAMON-VENTED PIHA LM-F
Lipaugus lanioides 24

Like 178-9 but more brownish on back, wings and tail. Throat and breast grayish with white streaks.

11. SCIMITAR-WINGED PIHA M-F
Chirocylla uropygialis 24

Above dark gray. Rump and sides chestnut. Below paler gray.

12. GRAY-TAILED PIHA L-F
Lipaugus subalaris 21

Above bright olive green, semi-concealed crest black. Some yellow on shoulders. Below grayish. Tail pale gray. Cf. 178-13

13. OLIVACEOUS PIHA M-F
Lipaugus cryptolophus 21

Wings and tail olive green, semi-concealed crest black. Some yellow on shoulder. Below yellowish-olive becoming yellow on belly.

14. RUFOUS PIHA L-F
Lipaugus unirufus 21

Very like 203-44 but wings somewhat more uniform and underparts with more white.

15. ROSE-COLLARED PIHA LM-F
Lipaugus streptophorus 19

Above dark gray. Below pale gray with pink band across lower throat, forming collar on hindneck. Crissum purplish. F: Lacks pink collar. Crissum rufous.

16. GUIANAN COCK-OF-THE-ROCK LM-F
Rupicola rupicola 26

Like 179-17 but wings brownish with no gray. F: Like f. 179-17 but dark olive brown.

Rupicola *Procnias* *Tijuca* *Carpodectes* *Phibalura* *Ampelion* *Phoenicircus*

17. ANDEAN COCK-OF-THE-ROCK **LM-F**
Rupicola peruviana 26

Prominent red crest. Body mostly crimson, wings and tail black. Inner wing coverts gray. F: Cinnamon brown. Crest small.

male

female

18. WHITE BELLBIRD **L-F**
Procnias alba 25

White. Long, thin wattle hanging from forehead. F: Above olive green. Below yellowish, heavily streaked olive.

19. BARE-THROATED BELLBIRD **LM-F**
Procnias nudicollis 24

White. Bare skin around eye and on throat greenish with black bristles. F: Head black. Above olive green. Below yellowish.

20. BEARDED BELLBIRD **LM-F**
Procnias averano 23

Head brown. Back and tail white. Wings black. Throat covered with black wattles. Below white. F: Above olive. Below streaked. No wattles.

21. BLACK-AND-GOLD COTINGA **M-F**
Tijuca atra 26

Black. Bill orange. Yellow patch on wings. F: Dull green, yellowish on belly.

22. WHITE COTINGA **L-F**
Carpodectes hopkei 22

All white except small black spot at end of wing. Central tail feathers black. F: Above grayish brown. Underparts whitish.

23. SWALLOW-TAILED COTINGA **LM-FT**
Phibalura flavirostris 21

Crown black (f. olive). Concealed crest red. Back olive, barred black. Throat yellow. Breast white, barred black. Below light yellow, spotted black. Tail long, black, deeply forked.

24. CHESTNUT-CRESTED COTINGA **M-F**
Ampelion rufaxilla 20

Forecrown black. Crest chestnut. Back and breast olive gray. Throat and collar rufous. Belly yellow striped dusky.

25. BLACK-NECKED RED-COTINGA **L-F**
Phoenicircus nigricollis 20

Bright red. Back, sides of head, throat, wings and tip of tail black (f. olive brown). F: Belly dull red.

26. GUIANAN RED-COTINGA **L-F**
Phoenicircus carnifex 18

Crown and rump crimson. Face, back and wings blackish. Throat and breast reddish black. Belly red. Tail red tipped blackish. F: Mostly olive brown. Crown, tail and belly dull red.

Ampelion
Doliornis
Zaratornis
Cotinga
Xipholena
Conioptilon

27. RED-CRESTED COTINGA **MH-T**
Ampelion rubrocristatus 18

Dark gray. Crest dark red. Lower back white, streaked black. Belly gray mixed white. Tail gray with broad white band near end.

28. BAY-VENTED COTINGA **H-F**
Doliornis sclateri 19

Crown and nape black. Face, throat and mantle gray. Breast and belly brown. Crissum pale brownish red.

29. WHITE-CHEEKED COTINGA **H-T**
Zaratornis stresemanni 18

Crown black. Cheeks white. Back streaked black and buff. Throat and breast grayish brown, below streaked cinnamon and black.

30. SPANGLED COTINGA **L-FT**
Cotinga cayana 19

Shining blue spotted black on back. Throat red. Wings and tail black. F: Brown, scaled white.

31. PURPLE-BREASTED COTINGA **L-F**
Cotinga cotinga 18

Upperparts and belly shining blue. Wings and tail black. Throat and breast reddish purple. F: Brown, scaled white.

32. BANDED COTINGA **L-F**
Cotinga maculata 18

Upperparts shining purplish blue Wings and tail black. Below reddish purple with blue band across breast. F: Brown, scaled white.

33. BLUE COTINGA **L-FT**
Cotinga nattererii 18

Shining blue, throat and belly purple. Wings and tail black. F: Like f. 180-34 but darker.

34. PLUM-THROATED COTINGA **L-F**
Cotinga maynana 18

female

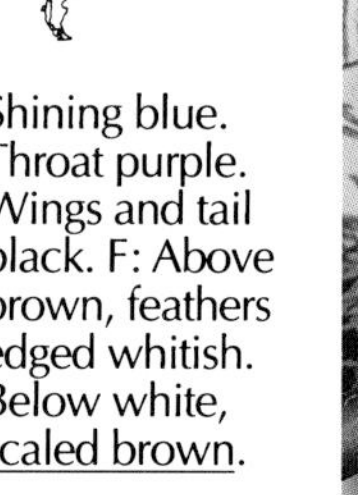

Shining blue. Throat purple. Wings and tail black. F: Above brown, feathers edged whitish. Below white, scaled brown.

35. WHITE-TAILED COTINGA **L-FT**
Xipholena lamellipennis 18

Deep blackish purple. Wings and tail white. F: Brownish.

36. WHITE-WINGED COTINGA **L-F**
Xipholena atropurpurea 18

Dark purple. Wings white. Eye white. Tail brownish purple. F: Brownish.

37. POMPADOUR COTINGA **L-F**
Xipholena punicea 18

Shining reddish purple, including tail. Eye white. Wings white, wing coverts purple, fringed. F: Gray. Wings broadly edged white. Tail blackish.

38. BLACK-FACED COTINGA **L-F**
Conioptilon mcilhennyi 18

Head black. Back gray. Wings and tail black. Below pale gray.

Porphyrolaema
Laniisoma
Tityra
Carpornis
Pipreola

39. PURPLE-THROATED COTINGA **L-F**
Porphyrolaema porphyrolaema 16

Upperparts black, scaled white on back. Throat purple. Below white. F: Upperparts brown scaled whitish. Throat cinnamon rufous. Below buff narrowly barred black.

40. SHRIKE-LIKE COTINGA **L-F**
Laniisoma elegans 16

Crown and nape black (f. greenish). Back, wings and tail olive green. Underparts yellow, barred black on sides.

41. MASKED TITYRA **LM-FT**
Tityra semifasciata 21

White. Mask black. Face and base of bill red. Wings black. Tail black broadly tipped white. F: Above brownish.

male

female

42. BLACK-TAILED TITYRA **L-FT**
Tityra cayana 19

Pale silvery gray. Bill red tipped black. Cap, wings and entire tail black. F: Crown brownish.

43. BLACK-CROWNED TITYRA **L-FT**
Tityra inquisitor 17

Cap and bill black. Tail mostly black. F: Cheeks rufous. Mantle dark brown.

44. HOODED BERRYEATER **M-F**
Carpornis cucullatus 21

Hood and breast black (f. greenish). Back brown.

45. BLACK-HEADED BERRYEATER **L-F**
Carpornis melanocephalus 18

Hood black (f. greenish). Collar breast and belly yellow.

46. BARRED FRUITEATER **MH-F**
Pipreola arcuata 20

Hood and breast black (f. no black). Above olive green. Large yellow spots on wings. Below yellow closely barred black.

47. GREEN-AND-BLACK FRUITEATER **MH-F**
Pipreola riefferii 18

Hood and breast black, bordered by narrow yellow line. F: All grass green, streaked yellow on belly. Eye-ring yellow. Tail green.

male

female

Pipreola
Ampelioides
Platypsaris

48. BAND-TAILED FRUITEATER MH-F
Pipreola intermedia 18

Like 181-47 but tail with black bar near end and narrow white tip. F: Like f. 181-47 but crown and back tinged bluish and tail tipped white.

49. SCALED FRUITEATER M-F
Ampelioides tschudii 18

Cap and nape glossy black (f. green). Lores white. Back black, scaled green. Throat and collar whitish, spotted black.

50. ORANGE-BREASTED FRUITEATER M-F
Pipreola jucunda 17

Above like 181-47 but lacks yellow collar and white tips on wing. Breast orange surrounded by black. F: Uniformily streaked green and yellow below.

51. MASKED FRUITEATER M-F
Pipreola pulchra 17

Rather like 181-47 but hood dark green. Above bright green. Breast orange narrowly surrounded by black. Belly light yellow. F: Throat yellow.

52. RED-BANDED FRUITEATER M-F
Pipreola whitelyi 17

Upperparts dull greenish gray. Forehead, eyebrow and semi-collar dull orange. Breast band red. Throat and belly gray. F: Below yellow, boldly streaked black.

53. BLACK-CHESTED FRUITEATER M-F
Pipreola lubomirskii 16

Hood and breast glossy black (f. green). Back, wings and tail green. No white on wings. Below yellow in center.

54. GOLDEN-BREASTED FRUITEATER M-F
Pipreola aureopectus 16

Upperparts, wings and tail bright green. Throat and breast yellow extending in semi-collar. Belly yellow (f. streaked green on all underparts).

male

female

55. SCARLET-BREASTED FRUITEATER M-F
Pipreola frontalis 15

Like 182-54 but forehead and bill black. Throat yellow and red. Breast red. F: Like f. 182-54.

56. HANDSOME FRUITEATER M-F
Pipreola formosa 15

Like 182-54 but large white tips on inner wing feathers. F: Like f. 182-54.

57. CRESTED BECARD L-FT
Platypsaris rufus 17

female

Cap glossy black, crested. Back, wings and tail grayish black, concealed dorsal patch white. Underparts brownish or gray. F: Crown dark gray. Back, wings and tail rufous. Underparts buffy.

Platypsaris
Pachyramphus

58. PINK-THROATED BECARD L-FT
Platypsaris minor 15

Male (left) black. Below dark gray with pink patch on throat. F: Cap and mantle gray. Rump and tail rufous. Underparts buff.

59. ONE-COLORED BECARD L-FT
Platypsaris homochrous 14

Crown dark gray. Back gray. Wings blackish. Below light gray. Tail black. F: Like f. 182-57 but crown rufous. Cf. f. 184-65.

60. GREEN-BACKED BECARD L-FTS
Pachyramphus viridis 13

Crown black. Lores white. Above uniform olive green. Underparts white with broad breast band yellowish. F: Cap grayish. Wing coverts chestnut.

male

female

61. WHITE-WINGED BECARD LM-TS
Pachyramphus polychopterus 14

In e: Cap and mantle black. Collar, rump and underparts gray. Much white in wings. In w: Black, wing coverts broadly edged white. Tail in both forms black broadly tipped white. F: Crown, nape and back olive brown. Below pale yellowish. Wing-bars, tip and sides of tail buff.

female

e form

w form

62. GLOSSY-BACKED BECARD L-F
Pachyramphus surinamus 13

Above black. Below white. Tail black, outers tipped white. F: Crown dark brown. Back gray. Wings black, coverts broadly edged chestnut. Rump and underparts white.

63. SLATY BECARD L-FT
Pachyramphus spodiurus 13

Above blackish with narrow white edging on wing coverts and flight feathers. Below gray. Tail dark gray. F: Like 184-65.

Pachyramphus

64. CHESTNUT-CROWNED BECARD LM-FT
Pachyramphus castaneus 13

Crown dark chestnut. Broad eyebrow gray joining at back of head. Back, wing coverts and tail rufous. Below buff, whitish in center.

65. CINNAMON BECARD L-FT
Pachyramphus cinnamomeus 13

Upperparts wings and tail cinnamon. Primaries blackish. Whitish line above dusky lores, like females of several becards but line more definite.

66. BLACK-AND-WHITE BECARD LM-FT
Pachyramphus albogriseus 13

female

Male like e form of 183-61 but back plain gray (not black). F: Crown chestnut, margined black. Eye-brow white. Throat white. Below yellow.

67. BLACK-CAPPED BECARD L-FT
Pachyramphus marginatus 13

Crown and nape shiny black (f. rufous). Back mixed gray and black. Rump gray. Lores, face and underparts pale gray. Wing coverts broadly edged white.

68. BARRED BECARD M-FT
Pachyramphus versicolor 12

Crown and back glossy black. Rump and tail gray. Wings black, coverts profusely tipped forming white patch. Sides of head and throat greenish yellow. Below dull white finely barred dusky. F: Crown dark gray. Wings with prominent rufous patch. Underparts yellowish.

female

69. CINEREOUS BECARD L-T
Pachyramphus rufus 12

Cap and nape shiny black. Forehead and lores white. Back light gray. Wings and tail blackish, feathers edged white. Underparts and sides of neck white. F: Very like f. 184-65 but white stripe above lores less prominent.

Xenopsaris
Pipreola
Iodopleura: In treetops

Calyptura

70. WHITE-NAPED XENOPSARIS L-S
Xenopsaris albinucha 12

female

Crown and nape deep black (f. brownish). Back gray. Wings and tail dull brown. Wing coverts edged white. Underparts white.

71. FIERY-THROATED FRUITEATER L-F
Pipreola chlorolepidota 11

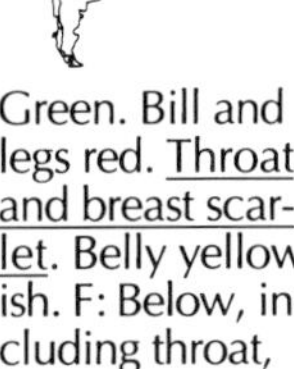

Green. Bill and legs red. Throat and breast scarlet. Belly yellowish. F: Below, including throat, barred green and yellow.

female

72. WHITE-BROWED PURPLETUFT L-FT
Iodopleura isabellae 10

Above blackish. Rump band white. Eye-stripe and lores white. Underparts white, sides barred dusky with purple patch (f. lacks purple).

73. DUSKY PURPLETUFT L-FT
Iodopleura fusca 9

Above black, rump white. Below brown, center of belly white, purple patch on sides. F: Patch on sides white instead of purple.

74. BUFF-THROATED PURPLETUFT L-FT
Iodopleura pipra 8

Above gray. Throat and upper breast buff. Belly white barred gray. Purple on sides. F: Sides white.

75. KINGLET CALYPTURA LM-F
Calyptura cristata 7

Crown scarlet bordered by broad black stripes. Greenish above, rump yellow. Wing coverts tipped white forming two bars. Below yellow. Tail very short.

(SMALL PLAIN MANAKINS ARE ON PAGES 192-194)

Schiffornis   *Antilophia*
Sapayoa   *Chiroxiphia*

1. THRUSH-LIKE MANAKIN — LM-F
Schiffornis turdinus — 16

Variable. Upperparts dull reddish brown, olive brown brow. Wings and tail sometimes more rufous than back. Underparts brownish or olivaceous or grayish. F: Like m.

2. GREENISH MANAKIN — LM-F
Schiffornis virescens — 15

Uniform dull olive. Wings and tail more reddish. Bill small. Whitish around eye. Rather like dull olive races of 186-1. F: Like m.

3. BROAD-BILLED MANAKIN — L-F
Sapayoa aenigma — 14

Bill flat and wide. Oily olive-green. Crown stripe yellow. Below somewhat paler and yellower. F: Lacks crown stripe, otherwise like m.

4. GREATER MANAKIN — L-F
Schiffornis major — 15

Mostly uniform cinnamon rufous (head and throat gray in n). Wings blackish. Breast and belly paler. Rump and tail bright cinnamon. F: Like m.

5. HELMETED MANAKIN — L-FT
Antilophia galeata — 14

Black. Projecting frontal crest, crown and nape crimson. F: Dull olive green. Paler and grayer below.

male — female

6. BLUE (SWALLOW-TAILED) MANAKIN — LM-FT
Chiroxiphia caudata — 13+2

Above blue. Crown red. Face, throat, nape and wings black. Below blue. Tail extended centrals blue, outers black. F: Green. Imm m: Green with red forecrown.

male — female

Chiroxiphia
Heterocercus
Xenopipo

Chloropipi

7. LANCE-TAILED MANAKIN L-TS
Chiroxiphia lanceolata 11+2

Black. Crown red. Back blue. Central tail feathers extended. Legs orange. F: Olive green. Tail centrals extended like m. Imm very like imm 187-8.

female

8. BLUE-BACKED MANAKIN LM-FT
Chiroxiphia pareola 12

Deep black. Crown red (yellow crown patch in ne Brasil). Back blue. Tail square. F. at 194-11. Imm. m: Tail square like m, no extension. Greenish or bluish. Crown red

imm. m

9. YELLOW-CROWNED MANAKIN L-FT
Heterocercus flavivertex 13

Upperparts green, crown stripe yellow. Throat white. Below chestnut to cinnamon. F: Crown and face all olive. Throat grayish, rest like m. but much duller.

10. FLAME-CROWNED MANAKIN L-FT
Heterocercus linteatus 13

Like 187-9 but head black with red spot in center of crown. F: Like f. l87-9.

11. ORANGE-CROWNED MANAKIN L-FT
Heterocercus aurantiivertex 13

Crown green, central stripe orange. Above bright green. Throat white. Below all cinnamon.

12. BLACK MANAKIN L-FT
Xenopipo atronitens 13

Uniform black. Wings and fairly long tail browner. F: At 194-16.

13. OLIVE MANAKIN M-F
Chloropipo uniformis 13

Uniform olive. Throat grayish. Belly paler. Bill and legs dusky. F: Like m.

Chloropipo
Neopelma: Crown streak yellow.
Piprites
Ilicura

14. YELLOW-HEADED MANAKIN M-F
Chloropipo flavicapilla 12

Crest and nape yellow. Eye bright light orange. Back olive yellow. Below yellowish. F: Like m. except crown olive yellow like back.

15. JET MANAKIN LM-F
Chloropipo unicolor 12

Black. Bill bluish. Feathers at sides of breast white. F: Like m. but dark green, tinged gray on throat and belly.

16. PALE-BELLIED TYRANT-MANAKIN L-TS
Neopelma pallescens 13

Above uniform olive. Crown streak yellow. Throat whitish streaked gray. Breast gray. Belly white. F: Like m.

17. WIED'S TYRANT-MANAKIN LM-F
Neopelma aurifrons 12

Like 188-16 but belly yellowish. F: Like m.

18. SULPHUR-BELLIED TYRANT-MANAKIN L-FT
Neopelma sulphureiventer 12

Very like 188-16 but belly clearer yellow. F: Like m.

19. SAFFRON-CRESTED TYRANT-MANAKIN L-F
Neopelma chrysocephalum 12

Like 188-16 but yellow crown patch much larger. Eye orange. F: Like m.

20. BLACK-CAPPED MANAKIN LM-F
Piprites pileatus 11

Cap black. Back maroon chestnut. Wings edged yellow. Throat, breast and sides light cinnamon. Belly pale yellow in center. F: Like m.

21. PIN-TAILED MANAKIN LM-FT
Ilicura militaris 11+2

Forecrown and rump red. Back black. Eye bright yellow. Wings pale brown. Throat, neck and underparts whitish. Tail black, centrals elongated. F: Above olive. Below whitish. Neck gray. Tail like m. but shorter.

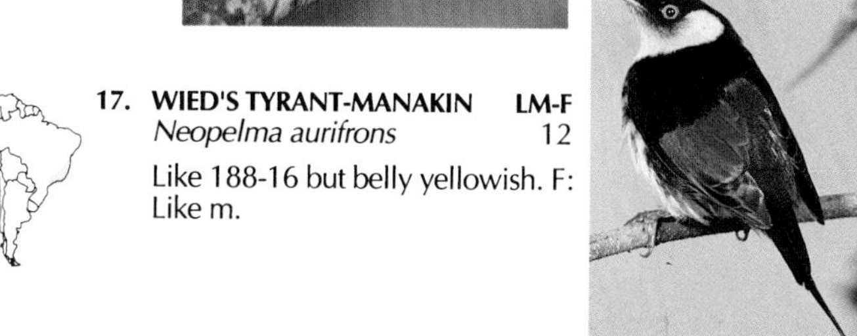

male

female

Pipra: Mostly olive above, yellowish below.
Piprites
Teleonema
Manacus
Masius
Allocotopterus

22. SCARLET-HORNED MANAKIN **LM-F**
Pipra cornuta 11

Glossy blue black. Entire head and two-pronged crest red. Thighs red. F: Above olive. Below grayish olive. Thighs yellowish.

23. WING-BARRED MANAKIN **LM-F**
Piprites chloris 11

Above olive green, nape gray. Prominent eye-ring whitish. Lores and throat yellow. Breast grayish. Belly bright yellow or gray. F: Like m.

24. WIRE-TAILED MANAKIN **L-F**
Teleonema filicauda 10+3

Crown and nape red. Back black. Face and underparts yellow. Tail black ending in long hair-like filaments.

25. GOLDEN-COLLARED MANAKIN **L-T**
Manacus vitellinus 10

Crown, upper back, wings and tail black. Rump olive. Collar, throat and breast bright yellow. Belly yellowish olive. Legs orange.

26. GOLDEN-WINGED MANAKIN **M-FT**
Masius chrysopterus 10

Black. Crest yellow, curving forward. Nape orange. Breast spot yellow. Legs orange. Wings show much yellow in flight.
F: Olive green. Crest small. Throat and belly yellowish.

27. CLUB-WINGED MANAKIN **L-FT**
Allocotopterus deliciosus 9

Crown red. Nape, back, throat and breast brown. Wings black, some white showing. Bend of wing yellow. Belly blackish. F: At 193-6.

Corapipo
Manacus
Machaeropterus
Neopipo

28. WHITE-RUFFED MANAKIN LM-F
Corapipo leucorrhoa 9

All glossy black except collar, throat and sides of neck white. Crissum whitish. F: At 194-15.

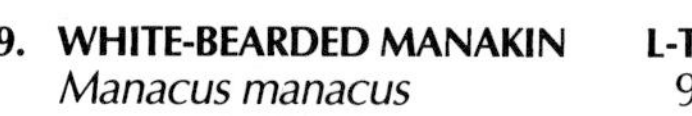

29. WHITE-BEARDED MANAKIN L-T
Manacus manacus 9

Crown, back, wings and tail black. Rump gray. Collar white. Below all white. Legs orange. F: At 192-3.

30. WHITE-THROATED MANAKIN L-F
Corapipo gutturalis 8

Like 190-28 but white throat feathers extend down in point to upper breast. F: At 194-12.

31. STRIPED MANAKIN L-F
Machaeropterus regulus 8

Crown and nape red. Back, face and wings olive green. Below striped white and pinkish. F: At 193-5.

32. FIERY-CAPPED MANAKIN L-F
Machaeropterus pyrocephalus 8

Crown and nape yellow, central stripe red. Back rosy chestnut. Below whitish lightly streaked pink. F: At 192-1.

33. CINNAMON MANAKIN L-F
Neopipo cinnamomea 8

Very like 232-41. Head and back gray, semi-concealed crown stripe yellow (f. rufous). Rump, wings and tail mostly rufous. Cinnamon buffy below.

Pipra: Mostly olive, yellowish below.

34. GOLDEN-HEADED MANAKIN L-F 9
Pipra erythrocephala

Glossy blue-black. Cap golden yellow. Thighs red. Legs pinkish. F: At 192-2.

35. BAND-TAILED MANAKIN L-FT 10
Pipra fasciicauda

Eye white. Forehead and throat yellow. Crown and nape red. Back and wings black. White wing-band shows in flight. Below red or yellow. Tail black with white band at base. F: At 193-4.

36. RED-HEADED MANAKIN L-F 10
Pipra rubrocapilla

Like 191-40 but thighs red. Eye brownish.

37. ROUND-TAILED MANAKIN LM-F 10
Pipra chloromeros

Cap, nape and face red. Underwing coverts black. Thighs yellow. Tail short.

38. RED-CAPPED MANAKIN L-F 10
Pipra mentalis

All glossy black except head and nape red. Thighs yellow. Eye white. F: At 193-7.

39. CRIMSON-HOODED MANAKIN L-FT 10
Pipra aureola

Eye white. Crown, nape, breast and center of belly red. Flanks black. Forehead and throat yellow. Back, wings and tail black. F: At 194-13.

40. WHITE-CROWNED MANAKIN LM-FT 9
Pipra pipra

Glossy black. Crown and nape white. Eye orange. Legs black. F: At 194-14.

41. SNOW-CAPPED MANAKIN L-F 8
Pipra nattereri

Crown, nape and rump white (f. greenish). Back, throat and breast dull green. Below yellow. F: Upperparts all green.

ARRANGED BY LEG COLOR - 1. (FLESH COLOR) .

Pipra: Mostly olive above, yellowish below. *Manacus*
Machaeropterus

42. WHITE-FRONTED MANAKIN L-T
Pipra serena 9

Black. Forehead white. Rump bright blue. Patch in center of breast yellowish. Belly yellow. F: At 195-18.

43. BLUE-RUMPED MANAKIN L-F
Pipra isidorei 8

Black. Top of head white. Rump blue. F: Head yellowish, rest greenish.

44. CERULEAN-CAPPED MANAKIN L-F
Pipra coeruleocapilla 9

Black. Crown light blue. Rump blue. F: Greenish.

45. BLUE-CROWNED MANAKIN L-F
Pipra coronata 8

Black (some races partly greenish or grayish). Crown blue. F: At 195-17.

46. OPAL-CROWNED MANAKIN L-F
Pipra iris 9

Grass green. Crown silvery. F: Like m. but crown green;.

1. FIERY-CAPPED MANAKIN L-F
Machaeropterus pyrocephalus 8
female

F: Above bright olive. Throat grayish, Below yellowish, faintly streaked. Legs flesh color.

2. GOLDEN-HEADED MANAKIN L-FT
Pipra erythrocephala 9
female

F: Upperparts, throat and breast olive. Belly pale yellowish. Eye gray. Eye-ring prominent. Legs medium flesh color.

3. WHITE-BEARDED MANAKIN L-T
Manacus manacus 9
female

F: Olive green, throat grayiah. Belly whitish. Legs orange flesh color.

ARRANGED BY LEG COLOR - 2. (DARK FLESH COLOR).

Pipra: Mostly olive above, yellowish below. *Tyranneutes* *Allocotopterus*
Machaeropterus *Chloropipo*

4. BAND-TAILED MANAKIN L-FT
Pipra fasciicauda 10

female

F: Olive green, paler and yellower below. Undewing coverts white. Legs dark flesh color.

5. STRIPED MANAKIN L-F
Machaeropterus regulus 8

female

F: Upperparts bright olive. Throat grayish. Below often very plain or streaked. Legs dark flesh.

6. CLUB-WINGED MANAKIN L-FT
Allocotopterus deliciosus 9

female

F: Olive green. Throat white bordered by chestnut. Belly yellow in center. Legs gray flesh color.

7. RED-CAPPED MANAKIN L-FT
Pipra mentalis 10

female

F: Eye brown. Olive green paler below. Underwing coverts yellow. Legs gray flesh color.

8. DWARF TYRANT-MANAKIN L-F
Tyranneutes stolzmanni 8

Olive green. No crown patch. Eye straw color or whitish. Legs gray flesh color. F: Like m.

9. TINY TYRANT-MANAKIN L-F
Tyranneutes virescens 7

Tiny. Eye gray. Uppertarts, wing and tail uniform dull olive with semi-concealed crown stripe yellow. Below yellowish white. Like 193-8. Legs gray flesh color.

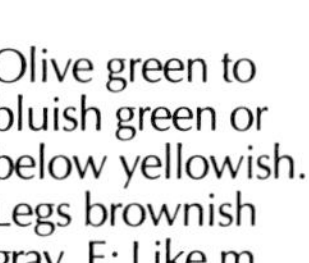

10. GREEN MANAKIN L-F
Chloropipo holochlora 11

Olive green to bluish green or below yellowish. Legs brownish gray. F: Like m.

ARRANGED BY LEG COLOR - 3. (GRAY TO BLACK FLESH COLOR).

Chiroxiphia
Corapipo
Pipra: Mostly olive above, yellowish below.
Xenopipo

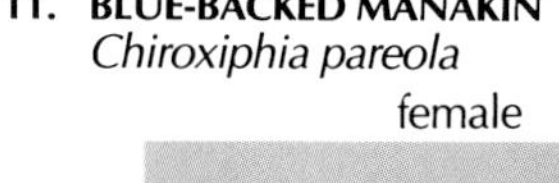

11. BLUE-BACKED MANAKIN L-T
Chiroxiphia pareola 9

female

F: Above pale green. Below paler. Center of belly pale yellowish. Legs grayish flesh color.

12. WHITE-THROATED MANAKIN L-F
Corapipo gutturalis 8

female

F: Above bright olive. Below white, light band across breast. Legs blackish flesh color.

13. CRIMSON-HOODED MANAKIN L-FT
Pipra aureola 10

female

F: Olive green, paler and yellower below. Underwing coverts white. Legs blackish flesh color.

14. WHITE-CROWNED MANAKIN LM-F
Pipra pipra 9

female

F: Crown and nape blue gray. Eye red. Legs blackish flesh color.

15. WHITE-RUFFED MANAKIN LM-F
Corapipo leucorrhoa 9

female

F: Above bright olive. Throat gray. Breast and sides yellowish. Legs blackish.

16. BLACK MANAKIN L-FT
Xenopipo atronitens 13

female

F: Above dark olive green. Head tinged grayish. Paler and yellower below. Legs black.

Pipra: Mostly olive above, yellowish below.
Agriornis: Throat white, streaked black.
Neoxolmis
Muscisaxicola: Below whitish unless noted. Tail black, edged white.

17. BLUE-CROWNED MANAKIN L-F
Pipra coronata 8

female

F: Upperparts grass green to bluish green. Throat dull yellowish gray, breast dull green. Below pale yellow. Legs black.

18. WHITE-FRONTED MANAKIN L-F
Pipra serena 9

female

F: Forecrown blue. Above grass green to bluish green. Throat whitish. Below yellow. Legs deep black.

1. GREAT SHRIKE-TYRANT LM-SO
Agriornis livida 26

Like 195-3 but above dark brown. Throat white conspicuously streaked black. Below light brown, belly tinged cinnamon. No eyebrow. Tail black, edged white.

2. WHITE-TAILED SHRIKE-TYRANT H-SO
Agriornis albicauda 25

Lower bill pale. Above dark brown. Narrow eyebrow buff. Below brown. Tail outers all white.

3. GRAY-BELLIED SHRIKE-TYRANT LM-S
Agriornis microptera 24

Short eyebrow white. Above brown. Below light grayish. Tail black, edged white.

4. BLACK-BILLED SHRIKE-TYRANT H-O
Agriornis montana 22

Bill black. Above dark brown. Short eyebrow buff. Below dull brown. Tail black, outers all white or half white.

5. CHOCOLATE-VENTED TYRANT LM-O
Neoxolmis rufiventris 21

Above gray. Face black. Much white in wings shows in flight. Throat and breast pale gray. Belly rufous. Tail black, edged white.

6. WHITE-FRONTED GROUND-TYRANT H-O
Muscisaxicola albifrons 21

Above gray-brown. Forehead and streak before eye white. Lores dusky. Below whitish.

7. OCHRE-NAPED GROUND-TYRANT MH-O
Muscisaxicola flavinucha 19

Forehead broadly white. Prominent eyebrow and cheeks whitish. Conspicuous patch on nape buffy yellow. Back dull mouse-gray. Below whitish.

Muscisaxicola: Below whitish unless noted. Tail black, edged white.
Machetornis

8. BLACK-FRONTED GROUND-TYRANT **H-O**
Muscisaxicola frontalis 17

Forehead and center of crown black. Lores white. Above gray brown. Below whitish. Tail mostly black.

9. WHITE-BROWED GROUND-TYRANT **H-O**
Muscisaxicola albilora 17

Long narrow eyebrow white. Above brownish gray. Patch on hindcrown rufous (usually not prominent). Below whitish.

10. CINNAMON-BELLIED GROUND-TYRANT **MH-O**
Muscisaxicola capistrata 17

Above gray-brown. Forehead and face black. Crown and nape chestnut. Throat whitish, breast grayer. Belly cinnamon.

11. PLAIN-CAPPED GROUND-TYRANT **H-O**
Muscisaxicola alpina 16

Upperparts grayish (tinged brownish in n). Eyebrow white. Lores dusky.

12. RUFOUS-NAPED GROUND-TYRANT **H-O**
Muscisaxicola rufivertex 15

Crown chestnut. Above pale gray. Short narrow eyebrow white.

13. PUNA GROUND-TYRANT **H-O**
Muscisaxicola juninensis 15

Forecrown grayish. Hindcrown dull rufous. Back dark brown.

14. DARK-FACED GROUND-TYRANT **LMH-O**
Muscisaxicola macloviana 14

Crown dark reddish brown. Face blackish. Above brownish.

15. SPOT-BILLED GROUND-TYRANT **LMH-O**
Muscisaxicola maculirostris 14

Bill black, lower yellow at base. Short eyebrow whitish. Upperparts light brown.

16. LITTLE GROUND-TYRANT **L-OW**
Muscisaxicola fluviatilis 13

Upperparts grayish brown. Throat and breast pale buff.

17. CATTLE TYRANT **M-TO**
Machetornis rixosus 18

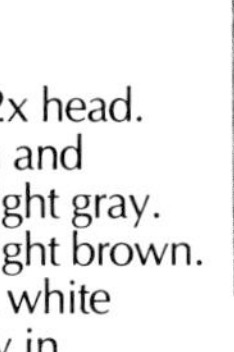

Bill 1/2x head. Crown and nape light gray. Back light brown. Throat white (yellow in Colombia and Venezuela). Underparts yellow. Tail pale-edged. Legs long.

Hirundinea
Sayornis
Lessonia
Fluvicola
Serpophaga
Muscioralla

18. CLIFF FLYCATCHER L-TO
Hirundinea ferruginea 17

Upperparts dark brown. Face freckled. Underparts bright chestnut. Often around buildings.

19. BLACK PHOEBE LMH-W
Sayornis nigricans 17

Blackish. White shows on wing coverts, center of belly and edge of tail. Bobs tail. Usually around rocky streams.

20. RUFOUS-BACKED NEGRITO LMH-OW
Lessonia rufa 12

Black, back and wing coverts rufous. F: Grayish instead of black.

21. PIED WATER-TYRANT L-W
Fluvicola pica 13

Forecrown, face, neck and underparts white. Hindcrown, nape, back and wings black. Tail black (f. tipped white).

22. WING-BARRED WATER-TYRANT L-W
Fluvicola (pica) albiventris 13

Forecrown, face neck and underparts white. Hindcrown, nape, back and wings black. Wings have white bars. Tail black.

23. TORRENT TYRANNULET M-W
Serpophaga cinerea 11

Head, wings and tail black. Some races have definite wingbars. Back light gray. Below whitish. Usually along rocky streams. Bobs tail.

24. SHORT-TAILED FIELD-TYRANT L-SA
Muscigralla brevicauda 10

Above brownish gray. Eye-stripe yellow. Wing-bars whitish. Rump chestnut. Underparts whitish. Tail black, very short. Legs long.

Myiotheretes
Muscipipra
Xolmis

1. STREAK-THROATED BUSH-TYRANT **H-TS**
Myiotheretes striaticollis 21

Above brown. Lores buffy. Throat white streaked black. Below cinnamon. Flight feathers and outer tail feathers mostly cinnamon (very conspicuous in flight).

2. RED-RUMPED BUSH-TYRANT **H-SO**
Myiotheretes erythropygius 21

Crown gray. Above dark gray, rump rufous. Wings blackish with white patch. Forehead and throat whitish. Breast gray. Belly rufous. Outer tail feathers rufous, tipped dusky.

3. SHEAR-TAILED GRAY-TYRANT **LM-TS**
Muscipipra vetula 21

Dark gray. Wings and tail black. Tail long, conspicuously forked. F: Below whitish.

4. GRAY MONJITA **LM-O**
Xolmis cinerea 21

Above gray. Forehead and short eyebrow white. Wings black with large white patch conspicuous in flight. Throat and belly white. Breast gray.

5. RUFOUS-WEBBED TYRANT **MH-S0**
Xolmis rufipennis 20

Mostly dark gray, paler on throat. Belly white. Wings and tail with rufous showing in flight.

6. BLACK-CROWNED MONJITA **L-SO**
Xolmis coronata 19

Crown black, surrounded by white. Back gray. Wings blackish with white stripe conspicuous in flight. Below white. Tail black, tipped white.

7. WHITE-RUMPED MONJITA **L-S**
Xolmis velata 19

Above gray. Forehead and eyebrow white. Rump and underparts white. Tail black, white at base. Wings black with white stripe obvious in flight.

8. BLACK-AND-WHITE MONJITA **L-SW**
Xolmis dominicana 19

female

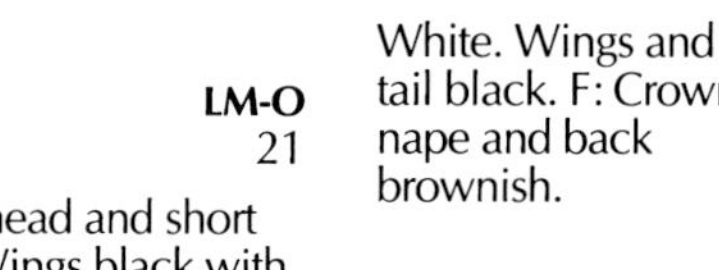

White. Wings and tail black. F: Crown, nape and back brownish.

9. MOUSE-BROWN MONJITA **L-SO**
Xolmis murina 18

Above grayish brown. Wings blackish, feathers edged white. Throat white streaked dusky. Breast grayish brown. Belly white.

10. RUSTY-BACKED MONJITA **L-SO**
Xolmis rubetra 18

Above rufous brown. Broad eyebrow white. Wings blackish.Below white, streaked black on breast and sides of neck.

Xolmis
Tyrannus: Crown stripe orange. Eye stripe dusky. Tail slightly forked.
Tyrannopsis

11. WHITE MONJITA L-SO
Xolmis irupero 17

White. Primaries black. Tail white with black band at end.

12. TROPICAL KINGBIRD LMH-TSO
Tyrannus melancholicus 21

Head gray, Back and breast olive gray. Throat whitish. Below yellow, washed olive on breast.

13. GRAY KINGBIRD L-O
*Tyrannus dominicensis** 20

Above ashy gray. Underparts white, shaded gray on breast.

14. SNOWY-THROATED KINGBIRD L-TS
Tyrannus niveigularis 19

Very like 199-12 but throat whiter and more extensive

15. WHITE-THROATED KINGBIRD L-TSO
Tyrannus albogularis 18

Crown and nape light gray, Throat white. Below yellow.

16. EASTERN KINGBIRD L-O
*Tyrannus tyrannus** 18

Crown and face black. No eye stripe. Above dark gray. Underparts white. Tail inconspicuously tipped white.

17. SULPHURY FLYCATCHER L-TS
Tyrannopsis sulphurea 17

Crown, nape and face dark gray. Indistinct eyebrow whitish. Back olive brown. Wing feathers edged rufous. Throat extensively white, faint streaks on breast. Below yellow. Tail square.

18. DUSKY-CHESTED FLYCATCHER L-FT
Tyrannopsis luteiventris 14

Like 199-17 but head dark brown (not gray). Concealed crest orange (f. lacking). Throat white, streaked dusky. Belly yellow. Tail square.

Pitangus
Megarhynchus
Myiozetetes

Conopias: Long broad eyebrows encircle crown. No rufous in wings or tail.

19. GREAT KISKADEE L-TSO
Pitangus sulphuratus 20

Bill heavy but not broad. Crown black, yellow crest usually shows. Above brown with much rufous on rump, wings and tail. Throat white. Below yellow. Usual call: three loud notes.

20. BOAT-BILLED FLYCATCHER LM-FT
Megarhynchus pitangua 20

Very like 200-19 but bill broad and flat, top edge curved. Crown patch seldom shows. Little rufous in wings -- on feather edges only. Call: one or two sustained notes.

21. LESSER KISKADEE L-SOW
Pitangus lictor 18

Very like 200-19 but bill more slender. Faint rufous edgings on wings and tail. Call soft.

22. RUSTY-MARGINED FLYCATCHER L-TSW
Myiozetetes cayanensis 16

Bill short and stubby.Crown and face dusky, crest yellow. Long, broad eyebrow white. Above dark brown. Wing feathers strongly edged rufous. Throat white. Below yellow. Usual call: a long drawn "peeeee".

23. SOCIAL FLYCATCHER L-TSO
Myiozetetes similis 16

Very like 200-22 but crown stripe red (not yellow) and wings feathers without rufous edges. Most common call. "Kree-yoo".

24. GRAY-CAPPED FLYCATCHER L-TS
Myiozetetes granadensis 16

Crown and nape pale gray. Forehead white. No eyebrow . Back olive. Wing and tail feathers edged yellow. Throat whitish. Below bright yellow.

25. WHITE-BEARDED FLYCATCHER L-SO
Myiozetetes inornatus 15

Very like 200-22 but no rufous edges on wings. Crown black with no patch. Above dark brown. Throat white. Below yellow.

26. LEMON-BROWED FLYCATCHER M-FT
Conopias cinchoneti 16

Crown and face olive. Above dark olive-green, wings and tail browner. Long broad eyebrow yellow. Below all bright yellow.

Conopias: Long, broad eyebrows encircle crown. No rufous in wings or tail.
Myiodynastes
Attila

27. WHITE-RINGED FLYCATCHER L-FT
Conopias parva 15

Very like 200-23 but eyebrow extends narrowly across forehead and completely around back of crown. Underparts yellow (throat white in w).

28. THREE-STRIPED FLYCATCHER LM-FT
Conopias trivirgata 14

Like 200-23 but crown and face black, no crown patch and eyebrow does not go across forehead.

29. BAIRD'S FLYCATCHER L-SA
Myiodynastes bairdi 21

Forehead and lores black. Above olive brown, rump rufous. Eyebrow broadly edged rufous. Throat white, streaked gray. Below pale yellow.

30. STREAKED FLYCATCHER L-TO
Myiodynastes maculatus 20

Bill black, lower pale at base. Forehead, eyebrow, malar and throat white. Back dark brown streaked buff. Underparts white, heavily streaked black except on throat and crissum.

31. SULPHUR-BELLIED FLYCATCHER LM-T
*Myiodynastes luteiventris** 20

Very like 201-30 but bill all black, wing-bars white and underparts tinged yellowish.

32. GOLDEN-CROWNED FLYCATCHER MH-FT
Myiodynastes chrysocephalus 20

Crown and face dusky, crest yellow. Malar and narrow eyebrow white. Back olive. Chin white. Below yellow, streaked olive on breast. Wings and tail dusky, feathers edged rufous.

33. GRAY-HOODED ATTILA L-F
Attila rufus 21

Hood gray. Above rufous. Rump, underparts and tail cinnamon.

34. WHITE-EYED (DULL-CAPPED) ATTILA L-F
Attila bolivianus 19

Eye whitish. crown and nape dull brown gradually becoming cinnamon on rump and tail. Below cinnamon rufous.

Attila
Pseudattila
Rhytipterna
Laniocera

35. BRIGHT-RUMPED ATTILA LM-F
Attila spadiceus 18

Varies from olivaceous to plain rufous. Told in all races by wing-bars and contrasting bright yellow rump. Breast streaked.

36. OCHRACEOUS ATTILA L-F
Attila torridus 19

Rather like 202-37 but larger and paler. Wing coverts black with two cinnamon bars.

37. CINNAMON ATTILA L-TW
Attila cinnamomeus 18

Bill black. Above bright chestnut brown, lighter on rump. No wing-bars. Below cinnamon brown, belly lighter.

38. CITRON-BELLIED ATTILA L-F
Attila citriniventris 17

Hood gray faintly streaked dusky. Back brown becoming cinnamon on rump. Throat and breast olive to brown. Belly yellowish in center.

39. RUFOUS-TAILED ATTILA LM-F
Pseudattila phoenicurus 18

Like 202-37 but crown and face slaty, contrasting with rufous back.

40. GRAYISH MOURNER L-F
Rhytipterna simplex 21

Mostly uniform gray with greenish cast, paler below.

41. PALE-BELLIED MOURNER L-TS
Rhytipterna immunda 20

Above grayish brown. Wings with two narrow whitish wing-bars and feathers edged rufous.

42. CINEREOUS MOURNER L-F
Laniocera hypopyrrha 20

Above gray, wings more brownish with two rows of cinnamon spots. Below paler gray. Crissum rufous. Tail tipped cinnamon.

43. SPECKLED MOURNER L-F
Laniocera rufescens 18

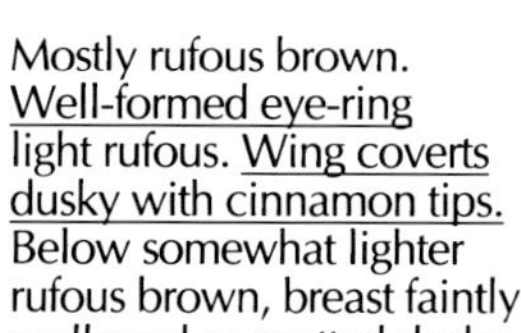

Mostly rufous brown. Well-formed eye-ring light rufous. Wing coverts dusky with cinnamon tips. Below somewhat lighter rufous brown, breast faintly scalloped or spotted dusky.

Rhytipterna
Pyrope
Myiarchus: Sometimes has black mixed in crown.

44. RUFOUS MOURNER LM-F
Rhytipterna holerythra 18

Uniform rufous, paler below. Lower bill pale at base. Cf. 178-14.

45. FIRE-EYED DIUCON LM-T
Pyrope pyrope 20

Eye red. Above gray. Wings blackish. Throat and belly whitish. Breast and tail gray.

46. GREAT-CRESTED FLYCATCHER LM-FT
*Myiarchus crinitus** 19

Very like 203-47 but throat not paler than breast. Tail with much rufous -- appears all rufous below.

47. BROWN-CRESTED FLYCATCHER L-S
Myiarchus tyrannulus 18

Upperparts brownish olive, crown browner. Some rufous in wing. Inner webs of tail feathers rufous.

48. PALE-EDGED FLYCATCHER M-FT
Myiarchus cephalotes 18

Like 203-49 but wing-bars wider and more conspicuous. Outer tail feathers edged whitish.

49. SHORT-CRESTED FLYCATCHER L-TS
Myiarchus ferox 18

Above dull dark olive. No rufous in wings or tail of adult. Underparts very like 203-47.

50. APICAL FLYCATCHER LM-S
Myiarchus apicalis 18

Like 203-49 but darker and tail broadly tipped whitish.

51. SOOTY-CROWNED FLYCATCHER L-TS
Myiarchus phaeocephalus 18

Crown blackish. Above gray becoming olive on rump. Forehead and lores ashy gray. Tail tipped pale grayish.

52. SWAINSON'S FLYCATCHER L-TS
*Myiarchus swainsoni** 18

Very like 203-49 but lower bill reddish brown (not black). No rufous in wings or tail of adult. Rather pale over all.

ELAENIAS: USUALLY A WHITE CROWN PATCH AND WING-BARS

Myiarchus
Myiotheretes

Elaenia

53. RUFOUS FLYCATCHER L-SA
Myiarchus semirufus 17

Upperparts and face dark brown. Rump rufous. Wing edging and tail rufous. Throat and breast dark gray.

54. DUSKY-CAPPED FLYCATCHER LM-FT
Myiarchus tuberculifer 16

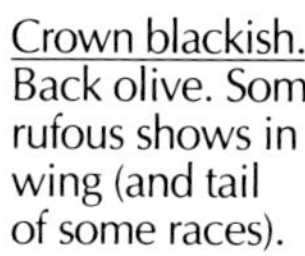

Crown blackish. Back olive. Some rufous shows in wing (and tail of some races).

55. SMOKY BUSH-TYRANT MH-F
Myiotheretes fumigatus 18

Dark smoky brown. Eyebrow whitish. Faint wing-bars clay color. Wing edges rufous. Throat streaked white.

56. SANTA MARTA BUSH-TYRANT H-FT
Myiotheretes pernix 18

Above brown. Wings darker brown, feathers edged rufous. Throat white, streaked black. Breast and belly rufous. Tail dusky, edged rufous.

57. RUFOUS-BELLIED BUSH-TYRANT H-FT
Myiotheretes fuscorufus 18

Above brown. Wings dusky with two rufous bars. Throat buffy white, not streaked. Below cinnamon. Tail blackish, feathers edged cinnamon.

58. BROWNISH ELAENIA L-SW
Elaenia pelzelni 18

Above dull dark brown. Two wing-bars narrow, whitish. Throat pale grayish. Breast and sides pale brown. Belly white.

59. GREAT ELAENIA M-T
Elaenia dayi 18

A large dark elaenia. Crown blackish without white. Back dark brown. Two wing-bars broad, conspicuous, whitish. Below grayish becoming yellowish on belly.

60. HIGHLAND ELAENIA LM-FT
Elaenia obscura 18

Upperparts uniform dark dull olive. No crown patch. Two conspicuous white wing-bars. Below uniform yellowish.

61. MOTTLE-BACKED ELAENIA L-FT
Elaenia gigas 17

Rather like 204-60 but has conspicuous white crest and feathers of back mottled brown and white.

62. LARGE ELAENIA L-FTS
Elaenia spectabilis 16

Very like 207-2 but larger and has three wide whitish wing-bars. Little white shows in crest.

Gubernetes
Empidonomus
Contopus
Sirystes
Cnipodectes
Casiornis

63. STREAMER-TAILED TYRANT L-T
Gubernetes yetapa 18+16

Above pale gray streaked dusky. Eyebrow, throat and belly white. Neck and breast band chestnut. Breast gray. Tail blackish, much elongated.

64. VARIEGATED FLYCATCHER L-T
Empidonomus varius 17

Like 212-39 but wing covert feathers edged white, back mottled and tail with prominent rufous edges.

65. GREATER PEWEE MH-FT
Contopus fumigatus 17

All gray, lighter below. Prominent crest. (Throat and center of belly whitish in some races).

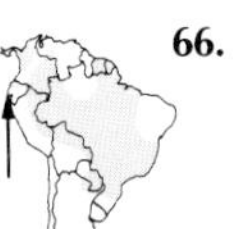

66. SIRYSTES L-FT
Sirystes sibilator 17

Cap and nape blackish. Back grayish, much white on wings. Rump white in some races. Underparts whitish. Tail black (tipped white w of Andes).

67. OLIVE-SIDED FLYCATCHER LM-TS
*Contopus (Nuttallornis) borealis** 17

Upperparts brownish olive except white tufts on sides of rump (often not visible). Throat and narrow line down center of breast white, sides brownish and streaked. Tail blackish.

68. BROWNISH FLYCATCHER L-FT
Cnipodectes subbrunneus 17

Eye orangish. Above dull, dark brown. Throat grayish. Breast brown. Belly grayish white.

69. CROWNED SLATY-FLYCATCHER L-TS
Empidonomus aurantioatrocristatus 17

Cap black, concealed crest yellow. Above brownish gray. Underparts pure gray.

70. RUFOUS CASIORNIS L-TS
Casiornis rufa 16

Upperparts chestnut rufous. Throat and breast cinnamon. Belly yellowish white.

Casiornis
Onychorhynchus
Knipolegus

71. ASH-THROATED CASIORNIS **L-TS**
Casiornis fusca 16

Like 205-70 but back browner in contrast to rufous cap and rump. Throat gray.

72. ROYAL FLYCATCHER **L-F**
Onychorhynchus coronatus 16

Large crest reddish (f. yellow) but seldom seen. Folded crest gives "hammerhead" look. Above brown, wing coverts spotted buff. Throat whitish. Below brownish. Rump and tail cinnamon.

73. CRESTED (BLACK-) TYRANT **L-SO**
Knipolegus lophotes 18

All glossy blue-black. Conspicuously crested. Bill black. Prominent white band in wings in flight. F: Like m. but smaller.

74. VELVETY (BLACK-) TYRANT **LM-SO**
Knipolegus nigerrimus 17

Very like 206-73 but crest shorter and bill bluish. F: Throat cinnamon, streaked black.

75. RIVERSIDE TYRANT **L-W**
Knipolegus orenocensis 15

Crown, lores and wings blackish. Bill pale blue. Eye reddish brown. F: Like m. but more brownish gray (or below buffy in e Brazil), (or above brown buffy streaked gray in Peru and w Brazil.

76. RUFOUS-TAILED TYRANT **MH-TS**
Knipolegus poecilurus 15

Eye red. Above grayish. Wings black, broad wing-bars buffy. Throat buffy. Breast obscurely streaked gray. Belly pale brown. Tail inner webs rufous (tail all dark gray in some races).

ELAENIAS: USUALLY A WHITE CROWN PATCH AND WING-BARS.

Knipolegus
Elaenia

77. WHITE-WINGED (BLACK-) TYRANT **MH-TS**
Knipolegus aterrimus 16

Dull black. Bill whitish or light blue. White band across primaries. F: Grayish brown. Rump rufous. Wings with two whitish wing-bars.

78. BLUE-BILLED (BLACK-) TYRANT **LMH-FT**
Knipolegus cyanirostris 15

All black. Bill blue. Eye red. F: Crown dull rufous. Back dark brown. Rump rufous. underparts whitish, heavily streaked black.

female

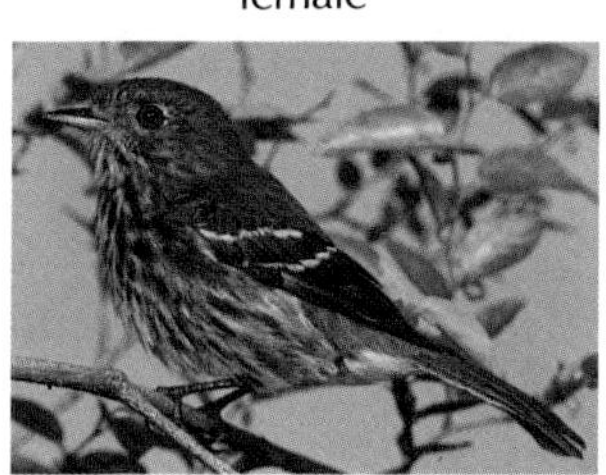

79. PLUMBEOUS TYRANT **LM-F**
Knipolegus cabanisi 15

Slaty gray, lighter below. Wings and tail blackish. F: Above grayish brown, rump rufous. Wing-bars and underparts whitish.

1. SLATY ELAENIA **LM-F**
Elaenia strepera 15

Mostly slaty gray. Semi-concealed white crown patch. Wings with two narrow, inconspicuous gray (f. rufous) bars.

2. YELLOW-BELLIED ELAENIA **LM-TSO**
Elaenia flavogaster 15

Upperparts grayish olive. Wing-bars whitish. Throat white. Breast grayish. Belly pale yellow. Crest usually raised showing white in center.

3. WHITE-CRESTED ELAENIA **MH-S**
Elaenia albiceps 14

Above dark olive. Wing-bars whitish. Prominent eye-ring whitish. Throat and breast grayish. Belly white in center.

4. SMALL-BILLED ELAENIA **LM-TS**
Elaenia parvirostris 15

Like 207-3 but crest shorter and white eye-ring more prominent. Below grayish. Bill not obviously smaller.

5. OLIVACEOUS ELAENIA **L-FT**
Elaenia mesoleuca 15

Above olive. Wing-bars narrow. Below rather dark olive grayish, paler and yellower on belly.

Elaenia
Myiopagis

6. RUFOUS-CROWNED ELAENIA L-TS
Elaenia ruficeps 15

Above dark brown. Crown patch rufous. Below pale yellow with blurry gray streaking on breast. Wing-bars conspicuous, pale gray.

7. SIERRAN ELAENIA M-T
Elaenia pallatangae 15

Concealed crown patch white. Two broad conspicuous wing-bars white. Underparts mostly yellow -- more yellow than other elaenias.

8. LESSER ELAENIA LM-SO
Elaenia chiriquensis 14

Very like 208-9 but has white crown patch. Above brownish gray. Throat white. Breast pale gray.

9. PLAIN-CRESTED ELAENIA L-SO
Elaenia cristata 13

Upperparts grayish No crown patch.Conspicuous white wing-bars. Breast pale gray. Belly pale yellow

10. MOUNTAIN ELAENIA MH-TS
Elaenia frantzii 13

Rather like 208-9 with no crown patch and not as gray above.

11. PACIFIC ELAENIA L-T
Myiopagis subplacens 15

Crown grayish brown with semi-concealed bright yellow patch. Broad eyebrow grizzled whitish curling around darker ear coverts. Throat and breast pale gray streaked whitish. Belly pale yellow.

12. GREENISH ELAENIA L-TS
Myiopagis viridicata 13

Above olive green. Crown patch yellow. Short eyebrow. Wing feathers edged yellow but no distinct wing-bars. Breast gray. Belly yellow.

13. FOREST ELAENIA L-FT
Myiopagis gaimardii 12

Like 208-12 but has prominent yellowish white wing-bars and usually concealed crown stripe.

14. YELLOW-CROWNED ELAENIA L-TW
Myiopagis flavivertex 12

Above dull olive green. Semi-concealed bright yellow crown patch. Wings and tail brownish. Wing-bars yellowish. Throat whitish. Breast pale grayish. Belly pale yellow.

It is the Collaborator's opinion that the illustration at #9 is the Lesser Elaenia (#8).

Myiopagis
Phaeotriccus
Yetapa
Muscivora
Alectrurus
Suiriri
Sublegatus

15. GRAY ELAENIA L-FT
Myiopagis caniceps 12

Above blue-gray. Concealed crown patch white. Wings black with two bold white bars. Below white, breast tinged gray. F: Crown patch and underparts yellow.

16. HUDSON'S (BLACK-) TYRANT L-S
Phaeotriccus hudsoni 14

Glossy black. Bill black. Wings with white band showing in flight. F: Above grayish brown, rump rufous. Two whitish wing-bars. Below light buffy. Tail cinnamon buff, black band near end. Cf. 209-17.

17. AMAZONIAN (BLACK-) TYRANT L-FT
Phaeotriccus poecilocercus 12

female

Glossy black. Bill black (not blue). F: Above olive brown, rump and tail mostly rufous. Two buffy wing-bars. Below whitish streaked dark brown on breast.

18. STRANGE-TAILED TYRANT L-SO
Yetapa risora 14+16

Above black, rump gray. Wing coverts white. Below white with broad black breast band. Tail black, central feathers wider and much elongated. F: Above brown. Tail like m. but shorter.

19. FORK-TAILED FLYCATCHER L-SO
Muscivora tyrannus 14+13

Cap black, concealed crown patch yellow. Back gray. Underparts white. Tail black, edged white, outer feathers much elongated. F: like m.

20. COCK-TAILED TYRANT L-SO
Alectrurus tricolor 13+6

Above black, rump gray. Forehead, eyebrow and underparts white, partial breast band black. Wing coverts whitish. Tail outers broad, elongated. F: Above brown, tail normal.

21. SUIRIRI FLYCATCHER L-S
Suiriri suiriri 14

Above gray. Prominent wide wing-bars white. Throat white. Breast light grayish. Belly pale yellow. Tail black, tipped or edged white.

22. SCRUB FLYCATCHER L-TS
Sublegatus modestus 13

Bill 1/3x head, black. Above brownish gray. Line through eye white. Quite like 207-2 but no white crown patch.

Rhynchocyclus
Ramphotrigon
Satrapa

23. FULVOUS-BREASTED FLATBILL LM-F
Rhynchocyclus fulvipectus 15

Bill very broad and flat. Above olive. Breast fulvous. Belly yellow, lightly streaked buff.

24. EYE-RINGED FLATBILL L-F
Rhynchocyclus brevirostris 15

Above olive green. Prominent narrow eye-ring white. Throat and breast greenish yellowish. Wing coverts edged rufous.

25. OLIVACEOUS FLATBILL L-FT
Rhynchocyclus olivaceus 15

Like 210-24 but throat and breast grayish olive (not greenish).Wing coverts not edged rufous.

26. DUSKY-TAILED FLATBILL L-FT
Ramphotrigon fuscicauda 14

Like 210-27 but underparts mostly dull yellow and tail blackish (not rufous).

27. RUFOUS-TAILED FLATBILL L-F
Ramphotrigon ruficauda 14

Upperparts dark olive. Eye-ring white. Below olive streaked whitish. Tail and closed wing bright rufous.

28. LARGE-HEADED FLATBILL L-F
Ramphotrigon megacephala 13

Crown dark brown. Narrow eyebrow white. Two cinnamon wing-bars. Below yellowish, breast washed brownish.

29. YELLOW-BROWED TYRANT LM-TO
Satrapa icterophrys 15

Upperparts olive, paler on rump. Long, broad eyebrow yellow. Eye stripe dusky. Underparts bright yellow.

Ochthoeca

30. BROWN-BACKED CHAT-TYRANT **H-S**
Ochthoeca fumicolor 14

Above brown. Broad eyebrow buffy. Wing-bars rufous. Throat grayish. Below cinnamon. Tail dark brown.

31. D'ORBIGNY'S CHAT-TYRANT **H-TS**
Ochthoeca oenanthoides 15

Like 211-30 but grayish brown above, forehead and long, broad eyebrow white.

32. WHITE-BROWED CHAT-TYRANT **LMH-TS**
Ochthoeca leucophrys 13

Above greenish brown. Forehead and long, broad eyebrow white. Two broad rufous wing-bars (lacking in n). Throat and breast pale gray. Belly white.

33. SLATY-BACKED CHAT-TYRANT **MH-F**
Ochthoeca cinnamomeiventris 12

Slaty black. Short white eyebrow. Breast and belly dark chestnut (below all slaty in ne).

34. RUFOUS-BREASTED CHAT-TYRANT **MH-T**
Ochthoeca rufipectoralis 13

Above dark brown. Rufous wing-bars (lacking in se). Prominent long white eyebrow. Throat grayish. Breast rufous. Belly white.

35. CROWNED CHAT-TYRANT **H-T**
Ochthoeca frontalis 12

Upperparts and face dark brown. Eyebrow yellow becoming white at rear. Wing-bars lacking in n (rufous in s). Underparts ashy gray.

36. GOLDEN-BROWED CHAT-TYRANT **MH-T**
Ochthoeca pulchella 12

Very like s form of 211-35 but back and rump more reddish brown, belly whiter.

37. YELLOW-BELLIED CHAT-TYRANT **MH-F**
Ochthoeca diadema 11

Crown blackish. Forehead and long eyebrow yellow. Back brownish. Rufous wing-bars (lacking in some races). Throat yellowish. Breast olive. Belly bright yellow.

Ochthoeca
Legatus
Contopus
Empidonax

38. PIURA CHAT-TYRANT M-S
Ochthoeca piurae 11

Above dark brown. Forehead and long broad eyebrow white. Two bright rufous wing-bars. Throat and breast light gray. Belly white.

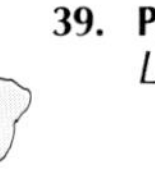

39. PIRATIC FLYCATCHER L-T
Legatus leucophaius 14

Bill 1/3x head. Crown brown. Crest yellow. Eyebrow whitish. Face brownish. Throat white. Breast whitish streaked dusky. Belly yellow. No rufous in wings or tail. Cf. 205-64.

40. WOOD PEWEE LMH-FT
*Contopus virens** 14

Very like 212-41 but lores gray (not white) and when perched wings reach more than halfway down tail. Call: "pee-wee" or "pee-a-wee".

41. TROPICAL PEWEE LM-T
Contopus cinereus 13

Crown dark gray. Back brownish gray. Lores whitish. Throat whitish. Breast grayish. Belly pale yellowish. Wings relatively short, reaching less than halfway down tail. Call: an upward inflected "see-rip". Cf. 212-40.

42. BLACKISH PEWEE L-FT
Contopus nigrescens 12

Uniform dark gray. No wing-bars in adult but immatures have two whitish bars.

43. TRAILL'S FLYCATCHER L-TS
*Empidonax traillii** 13

Very like 212-44 but slightly more brownish olive.

44. ACADIAN FLYCATCHER LM-T
*Empidonax virescens** 13

Eye-ring buffy. Above olive green. Wing-bars and throat white. Breast grayish. Belly pale yellow.

45. EULER'S FLYCATCHER L-FT
Empidonax euleri 13

Above brown. Wing-bars cinnamon. Narrow eye-ring white. Throat whitish. Breast brownish. Belly pale yellow.

46. GRAY-BREASTED FLYCATCHER L-T
Empidonax griseipectus 12

Above olive gray, grayer on crown. Prominent incomplete white eye-ring. Wing-bars white. Throat whitish. Breast pale gray, contrasting with white belly.

Cnemotriccus
Tolmomyias: Bill broad and flat.
Pyrocephalus
Mionectes

47. FUSCOUS FLYCATCHER L-TSO
Cnemotriccus fuscatus 14

Upperparts brown. Eyebrow and throat white. Breast grayish. Belly white or pale yellow. Wing-bars buffy to whitish.

48. YELLOW-OLIVE FLYCATCHER LM-T
Tolmomyias sulphurescens 14

Bill upper black, lower all pale. Crown or head vary much in amount of gray. Wing feathers edged yellowish, usually not forming definite wing-bars. Throat grayish or yellow. Below all pale yellow.

49. YELLOW-MARGINED FLYCATCHER LM-F
Tolmomyias assimilis 13

Very like 213-48 but often shows small white speculum on wing. Also crown deeper gray than gray-capped form of 213-48.

50. GRAY-CROWNED FLYCATCHER L-FT
Tolmomyias poliocephalus 12

Very like gray crowned forms of 213-48 but gray usually darker and more extensive.

51. YELLOW-BREASTED FLYCATCHER L-T
Tolmomyias flaviventris 12

Can be separated from others of genus by no gray on crown and generally more extensive and brighter yellow. Lores yellow.

52. VERMILION FLYCATCHER LMH-SO
Pyrocephalus rubinus 14

Crown and underparts crimson. Eye stripe, back, wings and tail sooty brown. F: Above ashy brown. Throat white. Breast white streaked dusky. Belly pinkish or yellowish.

female

53. STREAK-NECKED FLYCATCHER M-F
Mionectes striaticollis 14

Very like 214-54 but head all gray and belly more extensively yellow, and usually at higher elevations.

Mionectes
Stigmatura
Colonia
Hymenops
Pipromorpha

54. OLIVE-STRIPED FLYCATCHER LM-FT
Mionectes olivaceus 14

Above olive green. Wing-bars buffy (lacking in some races). Small white spot back of eye. Throat and breast olive heavily streaked whitish. Belly yellow in center.

55. GREATER WAGTAIL-TYRANT L-S
Stigmatura budytoides 14

Above grayish olive. Single broad wing-bar white. Long eyebrow and underparts pale yellow. Tail long, with large white ends. Bobs tail.

56. LESSER WAGTAIL-TYRANT L-SW
Stigmatura napensis 13

Very like 214-55 but back browner, and tail shorter.

57. LONG-TAILED TYRANT L-T
Colonia colonus 12+15

Black. (Center of back white in w.) Cap whitish. Rump white. Tail centrals very thin, much elongated.

58. SPECTACLED TYRANT L-SWO
Hymenops perspicillata 13

Black. Bill and conspicuous wattle around eye yellow. F: Above dark brown, feathers edged lighter. Wing coverts dark brown, pale-tipped. Below buff, streaked dusky on breast. Open wings show much white.

male

female

59. GRAY-HOODED FLYCATCHER LM-FT
Pipromorpha rufiventris 13

Entire head and throat gray, contrasting with olive back and ochraceous breast and belly. Wings and tail brownish.

60. OCHRE-BELLIED FLYCATCHER L-FT
Pipromorpha oleaginea 12

Above olive green. Below ochraceous tinged olive on throat. Wing-bars faint, buffy.

Pipromorpha	*Fluvicola*
Xanthomyias	*Ochthornis*
Myiotheretes	*Tumbezia*

61. McCONNELL'S FLYCATCHER **L-F**
Pipromorpha macconnelli 12

Very like 214-60 but no wing-bars. Mouth lining black.

62. GREENISH TYRANNULET **LM-F**
Xanthomyias virescens 12

Upperparts olive green. Two bold wing-bars and wing edging yellowish. Eyebrow and eye-ring white. Throat whitish. Breast olive, mottled yellow. Belly yellow.

63. SCLATER'S TYRANNULET **M-F**
Xanthomyias sclateri 12

Olive green above. Bold wing-bars and edging yellowish. Forehead grayish, lores and eye-ring white. Throat and breast grayish white, mottled yellow. Belly whitish mottled yellow. Carried as Olrog's Tyrannulet in BSA.

64. REISER'S TYRANNULET **LM-F**
Xanthomyias reiseri 11

Above yellowish green. Wing-bars yellowish. Forehead grayish, lores and eye-ring white. Throat whitish. Breast olive, mottled yellow. Belly yellow. Cf. 215-62.

65. JELSKI'S BUSH-TYRANT **L-S**
Myiotheretes signatus 13

Above dark olive gray. Throat and center of belly yellowish. Breast olive gray, paler than back. Tail dusky, feathers edged rufous brown. Considered in 207-79 (*Knipolegus cabanisi*) by some.

66. MASKED WATER-TYRANT **L-W**
Fluvicola nengeta 13

Head white, long eye stripe dusky. Back pale gray. Rump white. Underparts white. Wings blackish. Tail white with broad black band near end.

67. DRAB WATER-TYRANT **L-W**
Ochthornis littoralis 12

Pale sandy brown, paler below and on rump. Eyebrow white. Eye stripe, wings and tail dusky.

68. TUMBES TYRANT **L-SA**
Tumbezia salvini 12

Forehead, broad eyebrow and underparts yellow. Crown, face and back dusky gray. Wings black with two conspicuous white bars (one often concealed). Tail black, edged and tipped white.

Myiobius: Semi-concealed crown patch yellow (f. often lacking).
Phylloscartes

69. TAWNY-BREASTED FLYCATCHER M-F
Myiobius villosus 13

Above dark olive. Rump pale yellow. Throat grayish. Breast dark ochraceous. Belly yellow. Tail black.

70. BLACK-TAILED FLYCATCHER L-T
Myiobius atricaudus 12

Above brownish olive. Large rump patch yellow. Breast light brownish. Belly yellow. Tail long, black. Cf. 216-69.

71. SULPHUR-RUMPED FLYCATCHER L-F
Myiobius barbatus 12

Very like 216-70 but breast olive. F: No crown patch.

72. BLACK-FRONTED TYRANNULET M-F
Phylloscartes nigrifrons 13

Forehead black. Crown grayish, above drab olive. Short whitish eyebrow, face mottled light gray and blackish. Two broad yellowish wing-bars. Below pale grayish, whiter on belly.

73. SERRA DO MAR TYRANNULET M-FT
Phylloscartes difficilis 12

Above olive green, wing and tail feathers edged yellowish. Prominent eye-ring white. Throat whitish. Breast gray. Belly white.

74. RUFOUS-BROWED TYRANNULET M-F
Phylloscartes superciliaris 12

Crown grayish. Forehead and eyebrow rufous. Back olive green. Wing-bars yellowish. Cheeks white surrounded by dusky line. White below, tinged gray on breast and yellow on belly.

75. MOTTLE-CHEEKED TYRANNULET M-FT
Phylloscartes ventralis 12

Above olive. Lores dusky. Bold double wing-bars pale yellow. Throat grayish yellow. Below dull yellow, flecked with olive on breast. Long tail often "half-cocked".

76. OLIVE-GREEN TYRANNULET L-F
Phylloscartes virescens 12

Above dull olive. Wing-bars yellow. Eye-ring yellow. Lores and throat grayish. Below pale yellow mottled olive on breast.

Mecocerculus
Colorhamphus
Corythopis
Leptopogon

77. WHITE-THROATED TYRANNULET **MH-T**
Mecocerculus leucophrys 13

Above brown or olive brown or dark reddish brown. Short eyebrow white. Wings dusky with two prominent whitish or rufous bars. Throat contrastingly white. Breast grayish. Belly yellowish. Tail rather long.

78. PATAGONIAN TYRANT **LM-FT**
Colorhamphus parvirostris 13

Bill very small. Cheek patch black. Dark grayish brown above. Wing-bars cinnamon. Below dark gray becoming yellowish on belly.

79. RINGED ANTPIPIT **L-F**
Corythopis torquata 13

Above, wings and tail dark olive brown. Crown blackish (f. brown). Face dark gray. Below white with broad, irregular black breast band. Underwing coverts gray. Walks when on ground.

80. SOUTHERN ANTPIPIT **L-F**
Corythopis delalandi 13

Very like 217-79 but above lighter, tinged olive. Underwing coverts white.

81. SLATY-CAPPED FLYCATCHER **M-FT**
Leptopogon superciliaris 13

Crown dark gray. Face and eyebrow marbled black and white. Ear patch black. Above olive green. Wing-bars whitish. Throat and breast pale gray. Belly pale yellow.

82. RUFOUS-BREASTED FLYCATCHER **M-F**
Leptopogon rufipectus 12

Crown gray. Lores and area around eye rufous. Back olive green. Wings dusky with two buffy bars. Throat and breast rufous. Belly pale yellow.

83. INCA FLYCATCHER **M-F**
Leptopogon taczanowskii 12

Crown olive. Lores and around eye gray. Back olive green. Wings dusky, bars ochraceous. Throat gray. Breast pale rufous. Belly yellow.

84. SEPIA-CAPPED FLYCATCHER **L-FT**
Leptopogon amaurocephalus 12

Cap brownish. No eyebrow. Ear patch. Broad wing-bars cinnamon. Belly pale yellow. Cf. 217-81.

Mitrephanes
Myiophobus

1. TUFTED FLYCATCHER **M-FT**
Mitrephanes phaeocercus 12

Pointed crest brownish. Above dull olive. Throat and breast buffy. Belly pale yellow. Grayish wing-bars in s.

2. OCHRACEOUS-BREASTED FLYCATCHER **M-F**
Myiophobus ochraceiventris 12

Above dark brownish olive. Two light buffy wing-bars. Throat and breast light ochraceous. Belly bright yellow.

3. OLIVE-CHESTED FLYCATCHER **L-TS**
Myiophobus cryptoxanthus 12

Semi-concealed crown patch yellow. Above dark brown. Double buffy wing-bars. Throat white. Breast brownish. Belly pale yellow streaked brownish on sides.

4. ORANGE-BANDED FLYCATCHER **M-F**
Myiophobus lintoni 11

Like 219-8 but upperparts much darker and browner. Below more greenish yellow.

5. BRAN-COLORED FLYCATCHER **LM-TS**
Myiophobus fasciatus 11

Above reddish brown (grayish in some races). Concealed crown patch yellow. Wing-bars cinnamon. Below whitish or pale yellow heavily (or lightly) streaked brownish.

6. FLAVESCENT FLYCATCHER **M-F**
Myiophobus flavicans 11

Incomplete eye-ring yellowish. Above olive brown. Two wing-bars ochraceous (one often covered). Below light yellow shaded olive on breast.

7. ORANGE-CRESTED FLYCATCHER **L-F**
Myiophobus phoenicomitra 11

Above like 218-6 but darker and greener and breast band olive. Belly yellow.

Myiophobus
Aphanotriccus
Anairetes

Serpophaga: Mostly gray.

8. HANDSOME FLYCATCHER M-F
Myiophobus pulcher 11

Cap gray. Above, wings and tail olive brown to dull olive. Wing-bars cinnamon. Throat and breast yellowish orange. Belly light yellow. Tail brownish.

9. RORAIMAN FLYCATCHER LM-F
Myiophobus roraimae 11

Above olive to reddish brown. Two conspicuous cinnamon wing-bars. Below pale yellow, breast and sides tinged olive.

10. BLACK-BILLED FLYCATCHER L-F
Aphanotriccus audax 12

Above olive green, tinged grayish on crown. Eye-ring and line above lores white. Wings brownish, two wing-bars pale buffy. Throat whitish. Broad olive breast band. Below pale yellow.

11. ASH-BREASTED TIT-TYRANT H-S
Anairetes alpinus 12

Mostly dark gray. Long crest black. Wings black, double bars white. Belly white. Tail tipped white.

12. PIED-CRESTED TIT-TYRANT H-S
Anairetes reguloides 11

Long recurved crest black. Hind-crown white. Back black streaked white. Wing-bars white. Below white heavily streaked black on breast. Upper bill black, lower yellow.

13. TUFTED TIT-TYRANT MH-S
Anairetes parulus 10

Crown and long recurved crest black. Eye white. Back olive. Wings black with two narrow white bars. Below pale yellow, streaked black on breast.

14. YELLOW-BILLED TIT-TYRANT H-S
Anairetes flavirostris 10

Quite like 219-13 but base of lower bill yellow. Below whitish coarsely streaked black on throat and breast. Belly pale yellow.

15. SOOTY TYRANNULET L-SW
Serpophaga nigricans 12

Semi-concealed crown patch white. Above dark gray, below paler gray. Wings blackish with two pale gray bars. Tail black.

16. BANANAL TYRANNULET L-TS
Serpophaga araguayae 11

Quite like 227-4 but has wing-bars.

Serpophaga
Mecocerculus
Phaeomyias
Inezia

17. WHITE-CRESTED TYRANNULET LM-TS
Serpophaga subcristata 10

Crown gray with concealed white crest. Back greenish gray. Wings dusky, two bars yellowish white. Throat white. Breast gray. Belly pale yellow. Now includes White-bellied Tyrannulet and Gray-crowned Tyrannulet.

18. WHITE-TAILED TYRANNULET MH-F
Mecocerculus poecilocercus 10

Crown gray. Back olive green. Rump pale yellow. Eyebrow white. Wing-bars pale yellowish. Throat and breast pale gray. Belly pale yellowish. Tail gray with some white on inner webs.

19. BUFF-BANDED TYRANNULET M-F
Mecocerculus hellmayri 10

Above olive green. Two wing-bars buff. Eyebrow white. Below pale grayish becoming pale yellow on belly. Tail brownish.

20. RUFOUS-WINGED TYRANNULET M-FT
Mecocerculus calopterus 10

Crown gray. Broad eyebrow white. Eye stripe black. Back olive gray. Conspicuous rufous patch on wings. Breast pale gray. Belly pale yellow.

21. SULPHUR-BELLIED TYRANNULET M-F
Mecocerculus minor 10

Crown gray. Back olive. Wings gray with two broad cinnamon bars. Eyebrow white. Below bright yellow, paler on throat, shaded olive on breast.

22. WHITE-BANDED TYRANNULET MH-F
Mecocerculus stictopterus 11

Crown gray. Above olive to olive brown. Long, broad eyebrow white. White wing-bars well marked. Throat and breast pale grayish. Belly white.

23. MOUSE-COLORED TYRANNULET L-OS
Phaeomyias murina 10

Above dull brownish (or grayish brown). Wings darker, bars buffy. Eye stripe and throat whitish. Breast washed gray. Belly whitish.

24. GRAY-AND-WHITE TYRANNULET L-SA
Phaeomyias leucospodia 11

Like 220-23 but darker and has semi-concealed white crown patch.

25. PLAIN TYRANNULET LM-S
Inezia inornata 10

Like 220-17 but shows no white in crest.

Inezia
Pogonotriccus: Eyebrow curls around black ear patch.
Euscarthmus

26. PALE-TIPPED TYRANNULET L-SW
Inezia subflava 11

Upperparts brownish olive. Wing-bars whitish. Lores and eye-ring white. Below dull yellow. Tail like back, tipped and edged whitish (ochraceous in e).

27. SLENDER-BILLED TYRANNULET L-SA
Inezia tenuirostris 9

Very like 223-42 but crown same color as back and not as much crested. Wing-bars whiter.

28. MARBLE-FACED BRISTLE-TYRANT M-F
Pogonotriccus ophthalmicus 11

Crown gray. Face freckled black and white. Back olive green. Two narrow olive yellow wing-bars. Breast olive. Belly yellow.

29. YELLOW-BELLIED BRISTLE-TYRANT LM-F
Pogonotriccus flaviventris 11

Crown gray. Back olive. Lores, eye-brow and eye-ring rufous. Ear coverts dull buff surrounded by black line. Wing-bars conspicuous, yellow. Underparts bright yellow.

30. ECUADORIAN BRISTLE-TYRANT M-F
Pogonotriccus gualaquizae 10

Like 221-28 but ear coverts mostly pale yellowish surrounded by a dark line. Eye-ring and streak through eye white.

31. VARIEGATED BRISTLE-TYRANT M-F
Pogonotriccus poecilotis 10

Crown and nape dark gray. Face freckled. Back olive green. Wings with two very broad yellowish bars. Underparts yellowish.

32. SPECTACLED BRISTLE-TYRANT M-F
Pogonotriccus orbitalis 10

Crown gray. Conspicuous eye-ring white. Ear coverts yellowish. Back dull olive. Wing-bars yellowish. Below yellow.

33. VENEZUELAN BRISTLE-TYRANT M-F
Pogonotriccus venezuelanus 10

Very like 221-28 but lower bill pale and wing-bars yellowish. Below yellow.

34. RUFOUS-SIDED PYGMY-TYRANT L-S
Euscarthmus rufomarginatus 11

Above brown. Wings with two ochraceous bars. Throat white, below pale yellow, deep ochraceous on sides and crissum.

Tyranniscus
Oreotriccus

35. TAWNY-RUMPED TYRANNULET MH-F
Tyranniscus uropygialis 11

Crown dark brown. Eyebrow white. Back brown, rump tawny. Wings black with two buffy bars. Throat and breast pale grayish, below pale yellowish.

36. BLACK-CAPPED TYRANNULET MH-FT
Tyranniscus nigrocapillus 11

Crown black (or dark brown). Back olive green. Wings blackish. Eyebrow, wing-bars and throat whitish. Below yellow.

37. SLENDER-FOOTED TYRANNULET LM-F
Tyranniscus gracilipes 11

Bill 1/4x head. Crown dark gray. Eye white. Back olive. Wings and tail dusky with two yellow wing-bars and edging. Below yellowish, clear pale yellow on belly.

38. ASHY-HEADED TYRANNULET M-F
Tyranniscus cinereiceps 10

Crown blue-gray. Forehead and face grizzled white. Back greenish olive. Black spot on ear coverts. Wings black, bars buffy. Throat and breast greenish yellow. Belly bright yellow.

39. PLUMBEOUS-CROWNED TYRANNULET M-F
Oreotriccus plumbeiceps 11

Crown gray. Eyebrow white. Spot on ear coverts black bordered with whitish. Back olive green. Wings blackish with two yellow bars. Throat whitish, below yellow, washed olive on breast and sides.

40. GRAY-CAPPED TYRANNULET M-FT
Oreotriccus griseocapillus 11

Head grayish brown. Eye-ring and lores pale gray. Back olive green. Two wing-bars and broad wing-edging yellow. Below grayish white, greenish yellow on sides.

The identity of #39 is uncertain. It is the Collaborator's opinion that this bird is actually an Ashy-headed Tyrannulet (#38).

Capsiempis
Camptostoma
Acrochordopus
Phyllomyias
Tyrannulus
Pseudocolopteryx

41. YELLOW TYRANNULET L-FTS
Capsiempis flaveola 10

Above yellowish olive. Eyebrow yellow. Wing-bars and throat yellowish white. Below bright yellow, tinged dusky on breast.

42. SOUTHERN BEARDLESS TYRANNULET LM-TSO
Camptostoma obsoletum 9

Small peaked crest and above grayish to brownish. Eyestripe white. Wing-bars pale grayish. Underparts pale yellowish tinged olive on breast.

43. ROUGH-LEGGED TYRANNULET LM-F
Acrochordopus burmeisteri 11

Lower bill pale reddish. Crown dark gray (olive in se part of range). Forehead, eyebrow and around eye whitish. Back olive. Wings blackish with two broad yellow wing-bars and edging. Below yellow, throat and breast tinged olive.

44. PLANALTO TYRANNULET LM-FT
Phyllomyias fasciatus 10

Head gray. Short white eye-stripe. Above light olive, wing-bars whitish. Throat whitish. Breast yellowish tinged gray. Belly pale yellow.

45. YELLOW-CROWNED TYRANNULET L-TS
Tyrannulus elatus 9

Broad crown stripe yellow bordered black. Back dull olive. Face gray. Throat whitish. Breast olive yellow. Belly dull yellow.

46. WARBLING DORADITO L-SW
Pseudocolopteryx flaviventris 10

Upperparts, wings and tail dull brown. Cheeks blackish. Wing-bars buffy. Underparts yellow.

47. SUBTROPICAL DORADITO M-S
Pseudocolopteryx acutipennis 9

Like 223-46 but olive green above and underparts bright yellow.

Pseudocolopteryx
Entotriccus
Idioptilon

48. CRESTED DORADITO **L-SW**
Pseudocolopteryx sclateri 10

Prominent crest of black, yellow-edged feathers. Back dull olive mottled dusky. Two grayish wing-bars. Underparts bright yellow.

49. DINELLI'S DORADITO **LM-S**
Pseudocolopteryx dinellianus 9

Rather like 223-46 but above dull greenish and with three pale yellowish wing-bars.

50. CINEREOUS TYRANT **L-S**
Entotriccus striaticeps 11

Hood and breast blackish. Eye red. Back and belly gray. Wing-bars whitish. Tail blackish, feathers edged rufous. F: Head brown. Below white streaked brown.

female

51. YUNGAS TODY-TYRANT **LM-FT**
Idioptilon spodiops 10

Above olive green. Wings dusky with two olive wing-bars. Throat and breast grayish olive, streaked whitish. Belly yellowish.

52. PEARLY-VENTED TODY-TYRANT **L-TS**
Idioptilon margaritaceiventer 10

Eye bright yellow. Above olive (dull brown in n). Two wing-bars whitish. Shoulder yellow. Below white streaked gray on throat and breast.

53. WHITE-EYED TODY-TYRANT **L-F**
Idioptilon zosterops 10

Above olive green. Two yellowish wing-bars. Eye-ring and lores white. Throat and breast whitish, streaked gray.

54. ZIMMER'S TODY-TYRANT **L-F**
Idioptilon aenigma 9

Above dark olive green. Two broad yellowish wing-bars. Throat whitish, sharply streaked dusky. Breast and sides yellowish streaked dusky. Center of belly yellowish white.

55. KAEMPFER'S TODY-TYRANT **LM-S**
Idioptilon kaempferi 9

Above brownish. Two broad buff wing-bars. Below buffy, yellower on belly. Included in 229-24 in BSA but differs by presence of wing-bars.

Poecilotriccus
Snethlagea
Lophotriccus
Atalotriccus
Phylloscartes
Polystictus
Todirostrum: Bill long, narrow, flat.

56. RUFOUS-CROWNED TODY-TYRANT M-T
Poecilotriccus ruficeps 9

Crown bright rufous. Back bright olive green. Cheeks buff. Throat white. Dusky bar across breast. Belly bright yellow.

57. SNETHLAGE'S TODY-TYRANT L-F
Snethlagea minor 9

Above dull olive. Eye white. No white eye-ring or lores. Wing-bars whitish. Throat and breast pale yellowish lightly streaked olive. Belly yellowish.

58. DOUBLE-BANDED PYGMY-TYRANT L-FT
Lophotriccus vitiosus 10

Crest feathers tipped gray or yellow. Back olive green. Wing-bars whitish. Underparts whitish, streaked gray on throat and breast.

59. SCALE-CRESTED PYGMY-TYRANT LM-F
Lophotriccus pileatus 10

Crest black, feathers tipped chestnut. Back olive green. Underparts whitish, streaked gray.

60. PALE-EYED PYGMY-TYRANT L-S
Atalotriccus pilaris 8

Eye white. Above olive green (crown gray in e). Face buff. Below whitish, obscurely streaked dusky.

61. CHAPMAN'S TYRANNULET M-F
Phylloscartes chapmani 11

Above olive green. Eye-ring and long eyebrow whitish. Face mottled pale yellow and grayish. Two broad wing-bars and wing edging ochraceous buff. Below pale greenish yellow, clearest on belly.

62. GRAY-BACKED TACHURI LM-SO
Polystictus superciliaris 9

Head gray, eyebrow white. Back brownish gray. Faint pale gray wing-bars. Underparts cinnamon, center of belly white.

63. BEARDED TACHURI LMH-O
Polystictus pectoralis 9

Crown gray streaked white. Eye stripe white. Above brown. Two wing-bars buffy. Throat gray mottled white. Below white in center, sides cinnamon.

64. SLATE-HEADED TODY-FLYCATCHER L-S
Todirostrum sylvia 10

Crown and nape dark gray. Lores white. Back olive. Wings black, two broad wing-bars yellow. Throat white. Breast pale gray. Belly yellow.

Todirostrum: Bill long, narrow, flat.
Ornithion
Oncostoma

65. RUDDY TODY-FLYCATCHER **M-F**
Todirostrum russatum 10

Crown and nape dark gray. Forehead, face, throat and breast rufous. Back dark olive. Two wing-bars rufous. Belly gray.

66. OCHRE-FACED TODY-FLYCATCHER **LM-FT**
Todirostrum plumbeiceps 9

Crown dark gray. Back olive. Wings with two yellowish bars. Face and throat cinnamon with dusky ear patch. Below gray, center of belly white.

67. BLACK-HEADED TODY-FLYCATCHER **L-FT**
Todirostrum nigriceps 9

Cap, nape and face glossy black. Back olive yellow. Prominent wing-bars yellow. Throat white. Below yellow.

68. YELLOW-LORED (GRAY-HEADED) TODY-FLYCATCHER **L-TS**
Todirostrum poliocephalum 9

Crown gray. Forecrown and large loral patch yellow. Back yellowish green. Wings black with yellow bars. Below bright yellow.

69. GOLDEN-WINGED TODY-FLYCATCHER **L-T**
Todirostrum calopterum 9

Cap and nape black. Back olive. Shoulder chestnut bordered below by single broad yellow band. Throat white. Below all bright yellow. Tail black.

70. SMOKY-FRONTED TODY-FLYCATCHER **L-S**
Todirostrum fumifrons 9

Forehead grayish. Around eye buffy white. Crown and back olive green. Wings blackish with two prominent yellowish white bars. Throat white. Below yellow.

71. WHITE-LORED TYRANNULET **L-FT**
Ornithion inerme 8

Sharp, narrow eyebrow white. Back olive. Two wing-bars of distinct white spots. Throat whitish. Below greenish yellow, clear yellow on belly.

72. SOUTHERN BENTBILL **L-FT**
Oncostoma olivaceum 8

Upper bill much decurved, appears too heavy for such a small bird. Above uniform olive. Below yellow with grayish wash on throat and breast.

Myiornis	*Pyrrhomyias*	*Serpophaga*
Myiophobus	*Uromyias*	*Tyranniscus*

73. EARED PYGMY-TYRANT **L-T**
Myiornis auricularis 8

Above olive green. Crown tinged brownish. Conspicuous ear patch black (gray in w). Wing-bars yellowish. Throat white, streaked black. Below yellow.

1. UNADORNED FLYCATCHER **MH-FT**
Myiophobus inornatus 11

Like 218-6 but upperparts more brownish and olive of breast streaked pale yellow. Wing-bars faint or absent.

2. CINNAMON FLYCATCHER **M-FT**
Pyrrhomyias cinnamomea 12

Above cinnamon or brownish olive with indefinite collar. Rump and prominent wing patch cinnamon. Underparts cinnamon, becoming lighter on belly. Form in ne all chestnut.

form in s

form in ne

3. AGILE TIT-TYRANT **MH-F**
Uromyias agilis 12

Long crest black bordered by thin whitish line on each side. Back brown streaked dusky. Below light yellow strongly streaked dark brown on throat and breast. Tail long, dark brown.

4. RIVER TYRANNULET **L-OW**
Serpophaga hypoleuca 11

Above grayish brown. No wing-bars. Crown blackish. Underparts whitish. Tail dark brown edged whitish.

5. BOLIVIAN TYRANNULET **M-F**
Tyranniscus bolivianus 11

Bill black. Above uniform dark olive green. Wings dusky edged yellow. Below pale yellow, tinged gray on breast, brightest on belly.

6. RED-BILLED TYRANNULET **LM-F**
Tyranniscus cinereicapillus 11

Lower bill reddish. Crown grayish olive. Back olive green. Wings dusky, coverts edged yellow. Below bright yellow.

7. PALTRY TYRANNULET **LMH-FT**
Tyranniscus villissimus 11

Like 228-8 but lores dusky. Eyebrow and eye-ring white (not golden).

Tyranniscus	*Euscarthmus*	*Ceratotriccus*
Pogonotriccus	*Leptotriccus*	*Platyrinchus:* Bill very broad and flat, Tail short.
Culicivora	*Phyllomyias*	

8. GOLDEN-FACED TYRANNULET **LM-FT**
Tyranniscus viridiflavus 11

Forehead and lores yellow. Crown and back grayish olive. No wing-bars but each wing feather sharply edged yellow. Chin yellowish. Below light gray or yellowish. Cf. 227-7.

9. SOUTHERN BRISTLE-TYRANT **LM-F**
Pogonotriccus eximius 10

Forehead, large eye-ring and eye stripe white. Crown gray. Above bright olive green. Wings and tail edged yellow. Below bright yellow.

10. SHARP-TAILED TYRANT **L-O**
Culicivora caudacuta 11

Above brown streaked black. Crown blackish, lores and eyebrow white. Below pale brownish. Tail narrow and pointed.

11. TAWNY-CROWNED PYGMY-TYRANT **L-S**
Euscarthmus meloryphus 10

Above brown. Wing-bars faint (strong in n). Face buff. Concealed crown rufous. Below whitish, sides gray.

12. BAY-RINGED TYRANNULET **LM-F**
Leptotriccus sylviolus 11

Lores and eye-ring chestnut. Upperparts bright yellowish green. Wing and tail feathers edged olive. Below whitish, throat and sides washed with greenish yellow.

13. SOOTY-HEADED TYRANNULET **L-T**
Phyllomyias griseiceps 10

Crest, crown and nape blackish. Short eyebrow white. Eyestripe dusky. Above olive. Throat whitish. Below yellow, tinged olive on breast.

14. FORK-TAILED PYGMY-TYRANT **LM-F**
Ceratotriccus furcatus 9

Hood rufous. Back olive green. Breast gray. Belly white. Tail much-forked, outer feathers curving outward.

15. RUSSET-WINGED SPADEBILL **L-F**
Platyrinchus leucoryphus 11

Above dull olive. Large crown streak white. Lores and prominent eye-ring white. Much rufous in wing.

16. WHITE-CRESTED SPADEBILL **L-F**
Platyrinchus platyrhynchos 10

Head and face gray, broad crest white. Above olive brown. Throat white. Below buffy brown.

Platyrinchus: Bill broad and flat. Tail short.
Idioptilon

17. WHITE-THROATED SPADEBILL **LM-F**
Platyrinchus mystaceus 9

Crown patch yellow (m. only). Eye-ring white. Above brown. Throat and belly whitish. Breast brownish.

18. GOLDEN-CROWNED SPADEBILL **L-F**
Platyrinchus coronatus 8

Broad crown golden, edged black. Above greenish olive. Below light yellow, breast washed brownish.

19. CINNAMON-CRESTED SPADEBILL **L-F**
Platyrinchus saturatus 9

Like 229-17 but crown patch cinnamon and face plain.

20. YELLOW-THROATED SPADEBILL **M-F**
Platyrinchus flavigularis 9

Crown reddish brown, patch white. Face brown, throat yellow. Breast olive. Belly pale yellow.

21. BUFF-THROATED TODY-TYRANT **LM-FT**
Idioptilon rufigulare 10

Like 229-22 but only faint streaks on breast, and belly white.

22. STRIPE-NECKED TODY-TYRANT **L-FT**
Idioptilon striaticolle 10

Upperparts olive green. Eye-ring and lores white. Throat and breast prominently streaked dusky. Belly bright yellow.

23. EYE-RINGED TODY-TYRANT **LM-F**
Idioptilon orbitatum 10

Eye-ring white. Above olive. Inner wing feathers edged white showing as a stripe. Throat whitish. Breast brownish. Belly yellow.

24. BUFF-BREASTED TODY-TYRANT **LM-S**
Idioptilon mirandae 9

Above olive. Lores and eye-ring buffy. Face and underparts bright brownish buff. Includes 224-55 in BSA.

25. BLACK-THROATED TODY-TYRANT **MH-FT**
Idioptilon granadense 9

Prominent white patch in front of eye. Above olive green. Bend of wing yellow. Throat black. Breast gray. Belly white.

Idioptilon
Hemitriccus
Pseudotriccus
Lophotriccus

26. HANGNEST TODY-TYRANT M-FT
Idioptilon nidipendulum 9

Above uniform olive green, bend of wing yellow. Throat and breast pale gray lightly streaked whitish. Belly whitish.

27. BROWN-BREASTED PYGMY-TYRANT M-F
Hemitriccus obsoletus 11

Upperparts olive brown. Large buff patch in front of eye. Below brown, sometimes lightly flecked whitish. Belly white in center. Flanks and crissum yellowish.

28. FLAMMULATED PYGMY-TYRANT L-F
Hemitriccus flammulatus 11

Like 230-27 but lores gray and throat and breast streaked white.

29. DRAB-BREASTED PYGMY-TYRANT L-F
Hemitriccus diops 11

Like 230-27 but conspicuous preocular spot white. Below gray. Center of belly white.

30. BRONZE-OLIVE PYGMY-TYRANT M-F
Pseudotriccus pelzelni 11

Upperparts uniform dark brownish olive. Below yellowish tinged brownish on breast and sides. West race: darker, browner, crown slaty.

31. RUFOUS-HEADED PYGMY-TYRANT MH-F
Pseudotriccus ruficeps 11

Hood, rump, wings and tail rufous. Back dark olive. Breast and sides olive. Belly yellowish.

32. HAZEL-FRONTED PYGMY-TYRANT M-F
Pseudotriccus simplex 9

Like 230-30 but forehead, sides of head and edges of wing and tail feathers brown. Center of belly bright yellow.

33. LONG-CRESTED PYGMY-TYRANT L-F
Lophotriccus eulophotes 10

Like 225-58 but has conspicuous buffy eye-ring and no wing-bars.

Colopteryx	*Tachuris*
Taeniotriccus	*Phylloscartes*
Arundinicola	*Myiotriccus*

34. HELMETED PYGMY-TYRANT L-FT
Colopteryx galeatus 9

Very like 225-58 but lacks wing-bars.

35. BLACK-CHESTED TYRANT L-F
Taeniotriccus andrei 11

Forehead, face and throat chestnut. Above black (f. olive). Conspicuous yellow patch on wings. Breast black. Belly grayish.

36. WHITE-HEADED MARSH-TYRANT L-W
Arundinicola leucocephala 11

Black. Hood white. F: Above pale grayish, wings and tail darker. Fore-crown, face and underparts white.

female

37. MANY-COLORED RUSH-TYRANT LMH-W
Tachuris rubrigastra 11

Crown black, central stripe red. Long brow yellowish. Face deep blue. Back green. Single wing-bar white. Below yellow or white. Crissum orange. Tail black, outers white.

38. OUSTALET'S TYRANNULET LM-F
Phylloscartes oustaleti 11

Conspicuous eye-ring yellow. Cheeks black, bordered behind by bright yellow ear patch. Above olive green. Below yellow tinged olive. Tail olive.

39. SAO PAULO TYRANNULET LM-F
Phylloscartes paulistus 10

Forehead and eyebrow yellowish. Above light olive green. Cheeks dusky. Below uniform deep yellow.

40. ORNATE FLYCATCHER LM-T
Myiotriccus ornatus 11

Crown black, yellow in center. Prominent white patch in front of eye. Back olive. Rump yellow. Throat gray. Belly yellow. Tail black, cinnamon at base.

Terenotriccus
Todirostrum: Bill long, narrow, flat.
Ornithion
Myiornis

41. RUDDY-TAILED FLYCATCHER L-F
Terenotriccus erythrurus 10

Bill 1/3x head. Head gray becoming cinnamon on rump. Face whitish gray. Throat buffy. Below cinnamon. Tail bright rufous Cf. 190-32.

42. SPOTTED TODY-FLYCATCHER L-TS
Todirostrum maculatum 10

Eye pale. Crown grayish (or blackish). Back olive green. Throat white. Below yellow. All spotted black except on belly.

43. RUSTY-FRONTED TODY-FLYCATCHER L-S
Todirostrum latirostre 10

Above greenish olive, darker on crown. Lores and face ochraceous. Throat and belly whitish. Wing feathers, sometimes forming bars.

44. BLACK-AND-WHITE TODY-FLYCATCHER L-F
Todirostrum capitale 9

Upperparts black. Lores and eye-ring white. Bend of wing yellow. Underparts white (black breast band in w Brasil). F: Above olive. Crown chestnut. Breast gray.

45. COMMON TODY-FLYCATCHER L-TSO
Todirostrum cinereum 9

Eye pale. Crown blackish. Back gray or olive. Throat yellow (white in some races). Underparts bright yellow. Tail rather long, tipped white.

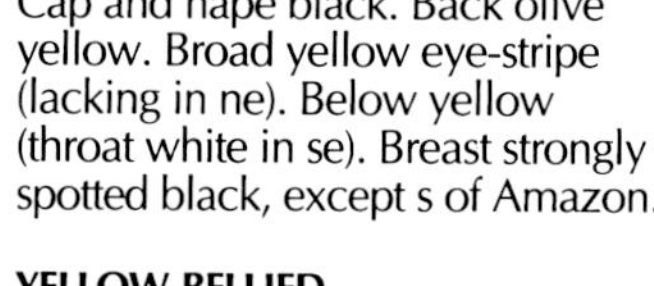

46. PAINTED TODY-FLYCATCHER L-F
Todirostrum chrysocrotaphum 9

Cap and nape black. Back olive yellow. Broad yellow eye-stripe (lacking in ne). Below yellow (throat white in se). Breast strongly spotted black, except s of Amazon.

47. YELLOW-BELLIED TYRANNULET L-FT
Ornithion semiflavum 8

Crown brown. Above brownish olive. Prominent eyebrow white. Underparts bright yellow, tinged olive on breast.

48. SHORT-TAILED PYGMY-TYRANT L-FT
Myiornis ecaudatus 7

Conspicuous white line above lores. Eye-ring white. Crown blackish. Back bright olive green. Below whitish. Tail very short.

Cyanocorax

1. VIOLACEOUS JAY L-T
Cyanocorax violaceus 35

Violet blue. Head, throat and breast black. Hindcrown whitish.

2. AZURE JAY L-F
Cyanocorax caeruleus 33

Bright blue. Head, throat and breast black.

3. AZURE-NAPED JAY L-FT
Cyanocorax heilprini 32

Grayish blue. Forecrown, face and throat black. Nape bluish white. Tail tipped white.

4. PLUSH-CRESTED JAY L-T
Cyanocorax chrysops 32

Crest, head, face, throat and breast black. Spot above eye silvery blue. Malar stripe deep blue. Nape whitish, becoming dark blue on back and wings. Breast and belly whitish. Tail dark blue broadly tipped creamy white.

5. WHITE-NAPED JAY L-TS
Cyanocorax cyanopogon 32

Like 233-4 but uncrested. Nape and mantle bluish white. Belly and broad tips of tail pure white.

6. BLACK-CHESTED JAY L-FT
Cyanocorax affinis 31

Head, throat and breast black. Whisker and spots above and below eye bright blue. Above violet brown. Belly white.

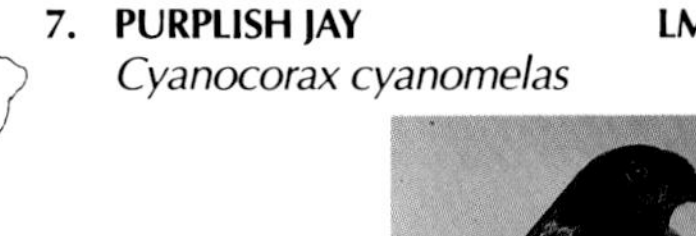

7. PURPLISH JAY LM-T
Cyanocorax cyanomelas 30

Dull violet. Hood and breast black.

8. CAYENNE JAY L-FT
Cyanocorax cayanus 30

Forecrown, face, throat and breast black. Spots around eye white. Back dull violet. Nape, rump and belly white. Tail black, broadly tipped white.

9. WHITE-TAILED JAY L-SA
Cyanocorax mystacalis 30

Head, throat and breast black. Small spots around eye and malar stripe white. Mantle and belly white. Tail centrals blue, rest white.

IMMATURE THRUSHES ARE OFTEN SPOTTED ON UNDERPARTS.

Cyanocorax
Cyanolyca

Turdus: Most juveniles spotted like 235-9.

10. CURL-CRESTED JAY L-S
Cyanocorax cristatellus 28

Crest, head, throat and breast black. Mantle brownish. Back and wings blue. Belly and outer half of tail white.

11. GREEN JAY M-T
Cyanocorax yncas 26

Frontal crest and face blue. Crown and nape blue or yellow. Back and wings green. Throat and breast black. Belly yellow. Tail green, outer feathers yellow.

12. COLLARED JAY MH-F
Cyanolyca viridicyana 28

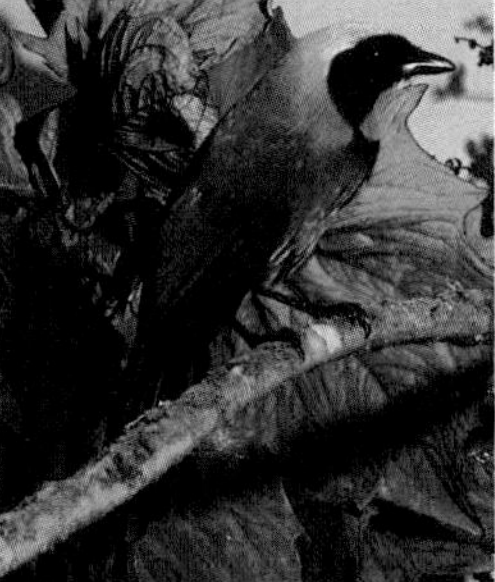

Purplish blue. Forehead and face black. Narrow band across breast black (white in s).

13. TURQUOISE JAY MH-F
Cyanolyca turcosa 27

Like 234-12 but crown and throat much paler blue and breast band narrower.

14. BEAUTIFUL JAY LM-F
Cyanolyca pulchra 23

Forehead and face black. Crown, nape and throat bluish white. Back, wings and below all purplish blue.

1. GREAT THRUSH MH-TS
Turdus fuscater 30

Identify by large size. Varies from blackish to light brown, underparts paler. Eye-ring, bill and legs orange yellow. F: Throat streaked.

2. CHIGUANCO THRUSH LMH-TS
Turdus chiguanco 23

Grayish brown, paler below. Throat vaguely streaked whitish. Bill and legs yellow.

3. GLOSSY-BLACK THRUSH MH-FT
Turdus serranus 23

Uniform glossy black (f. brown). Eye dark. Eye-ring, bill and legs yellow-orange. Cf. 237-24.

4. RUFOUS-BELLIED THRUSH LM-TS
Turdus rufiventris 23

Upperparts olive brown. Throat white, streaked brown. Breast grayish. Belly and crissum rufous.

Turdus: Most juveniles spotted like 235-9.

5. AUSTRAL THRUSH LM-TS
Turdus falcklandii 23

Cap, face and nape blackish. Above olive brown. Throat white, sharply streaked black. Below buffy. Tail blackish. Bill and legs yellow.

6. CHESTNUT-BELLIED THRUSH M-FT
Turdus fulviventris 21

Head and throat black. Above dark gray. Belly rufous.

7. PLUMBEOUS-BACKED THRUSH L-FT
Turdus reevei 27

Eye bluish white. Bill dusky, tipped yellow. Upperparts blue-gray. Throat white, sharply streaked black. Below grayish.

8. PALE-BREASTED THRUSH LM-TSO
Turdus leucomelas 22

Head gray. Back brownish. Ear coverts streaked white. Throat white streaked brown. Below pale brownish or grayish, center of belly white.

9. CREAMY-BELLIED THRUSH L-TS
Turdus amaurochalinus 22

adult

Bill yellow tipped black (f. all black). Upperparts, wings and tail dark olive brown. Lores dusky. Throat white, streaked dusky. Patch at base of throat white.

juvenile

10. BLACK-BILLED THRUSH L-TS
Turdus ignobilis 22

Bill black. Lores dusky. Above grayish brown. Throat streaked (white crescent below in some races). Breast grayish brown. Belly whitish. Cf. 235-9.

11. CLAY-COLORED THRUSH L-TS
Turdus grayi 22

Bill yellow olive. Above dull olive brown. Underparts uniform pale sandy brown except throat faintly streaked dusky and center of belly buffy.

Turdus: Most juveniles spotted like 235-9.

12. BARE-EYED THRUSH L-TS
Turdus nudigenis 21

Above olive brown. Large bare eye-ring yellow (except in w Ecuador). Throat streaked. Below light brown, belly and crissum whitish.

13. UNICOLORED THRUSH L-FT
Turdus haplochrous 21

Rather like 236-12 but browner throughout. Crissum brownish olive instead of whitish.

14. WHITE-NECKED THRUSH LM-FT
Turdus albicollis 22

Above rich dark brown. Throat white conspicuously streaked dark brown. Lower throat pure white. Breast varies grayish or brownish. Center of belly white.

15. LAWRENCE'S THRUSH L-F
Turdus lawrencii 21

Bill yellow, tip black. Eye-ring yellow. Upperparts dark smoky brown. Throat streaked. Below light smoky brown, belly white in center.

16. BLACK-HOODED THRUSH LM-FT
Turdus olivater 21

Bill yellow. Hood and breast black (f. no black). Above olive brown. Underparts light brown. Legs yellowish.

female

17. SLATY THRUSH M-F
Turdus nigriceps 21

Upperparts, wings and tail black or dark gray (f. brown). Throat white sharply streaked black. Below gray, belly white in center. Bill and legs yellow.

18. PALE-VENTED THRUSH LM-F
Turdus obsoletus 20

Like 237-19 but less rufescent above. Bill black. Crissum pure white.

Turdus: Most juveniles spotted like 235-9.
Entomodestes
Platycichla
Myadestes

19. COCOA THRUSH L-FT
Turdus fumigatus 21

Upperparts, wings and tail light reddish brown (most rufescent thrush). Throat whitish, streaked brown. Below cinnamon brown. Center of belly white. Cf. 236-18.

20. MARANON THRUSH M-T
Turdus maranonicus 20

Bill blackish. Above brown. Underparts white profusely spotted dark brown.

21. WHITE-EARED SOLITAIRE M-F
Entomodestes leucotis 21

Crown and nape black (f. brown). Broad streak below eye white. Back chestnut. Wings black with white patch seen in flight. Below glossy black. Tail black, outers broadly tipped white.

22. BLACK SOLITAIRE M-F
Entomodestes coracinus 20

All black except cheek patch, shoulders and part of outer tail feathers white. Bill black above, orange below.

23. YELLOW-LEGGED THRUSH LM-FT
Platycichla flavipes 20

Bill orange-yellow. Hood, wings, tail and breast black. Back gray. F: Brown.

24. PALE-EYED THRUSH M-F
Platycichla leucops 20

Glossy blue-black. Eye white. No eye-ring. Legs yellow. F: Brown, belly pale gray. Eye dark. Prominent eye-ring yellow. Bill blackish. Legs yellowish brown.

male

female

25. RUFOUS-BROWN SOLITAIRE M-F
Myadestes leucogenys 19

Upperparts, wings and tail reddish brown. Throat and breast more rufous. Belly pale grayish. Crissum orange (buff in se).

Myadestes
Catharus

26. ANDEAN SOLITAIRE **M-FT**
Myadestes ralloides 16

Bill short and wide. Nape and back rufous brown. Forehead, face and underparts all leaden gray (head like back in some races). Tail brown, white on inner web of outer feathers.

27. SLATY-BACKED NIGHTINGALE-THRUSH **M-F**
Catharus fuscater 16

Eye white. Eye-ring orange. Above dark gray Below paler gray. Crissum and center of belly white. Bill and legs orange.

28. ORANGE-BILLED NIGHTINGALE-THRUSH **LM-T**
Catharus aurantiirostris 15

Upperparts brown (crown grayish in e). Below gray, throat and center of belly white. Eye-ring, bill and legs orange.

29. SPOTTED NIGHTINGALE-THRUSH **LM-F**
Catharus dryas 16

Top and sides of head black. Eye-ring, bill and legs orange. Back, wings and tail dark gray. Underparts yellow, throat and breast spotted dusky.

30. VEERY **LM-FT**
*Catharus fuscescens** 16

Upperparts, wings and tail uniform reddish brown. Lores whitish. Throat whitish. Breast buff, lightly spotted brown. Belly and crissum white.

31. SWAINSON'S THRUSH **LM-T**
*Catharus ustulatus** 16

Upperparts uniform brownish olive. Prominent eye-ring and face buffy. Throat and breast whitish spotted dusky. Belly white. Cf. 238-30.

32. GRAY-CHEEKED THRUSH **LM-FT**
*Catharus minimus** 15

Very like 238-31 but upperparts olive brown, lores and cheeks gray and spots on breast darker and more prominent.

Mimus
Donacobius

1. LONG-TAILED MOCKINGBIRD **L-SA**
Mimus longicaudatus 27

Above grayish. Wing-bars white. Eye-stripe and whiskers black. Throat and belly white. Breast scalloped gray.

2. CHILEAN MOCKINGBIRD **LM-S**
Mimus thenca 26

Upperparts dull brown. Eye stripe blackish. Wings and whiskers dusky. Wing-bars, broad eyebrow and throat white. Below brownish gray.

3. BROWN-BACKED MOCKINGBIRD **H-S**
Mimus dorsalis 26

Above brown becoming rufous on rump. Wings black with white patch. Underparts white. Tail centrals black, outers white.

4. TROPICAL MOCKINGBIRD **LM-SOA**
Mimus gilvus 24

Above pale gray. Dusky patch below eye. Underparts whitish. Tail black graduated with broad white tips which show prominently in flight.

5. CHALK-BROWED MOCKINGBIRD **LM-SO**
Mimus saturninus 23

Above dark brown. Eye-stripe black. Underparts whitish. Tail dark brown, outers broadly tipped white.

6. PATAGONIAN MOCKINGBIRD **LM-S**
Mimus patagonicus 21

Upperparts plain brownish gray. Wings black with two white bars. Throat white. Breast brownish. Belly white.

7. WHITE-BANDED MOCKINGBIRD **L-S**
Mimus triuris 22

Like 239-4 but rump brown.

8. BLACK-CAPPED MOCKING-THRUSH **L-SW**
Donacobius atricapillus 18

Cap and mantle black. Eye yellow. Rump cinnamon. Speculum white. Underparts buffy, more or less barred black on sides. Tail black, broadly tipped white.

Campylorhynchus
Cinnycerthia

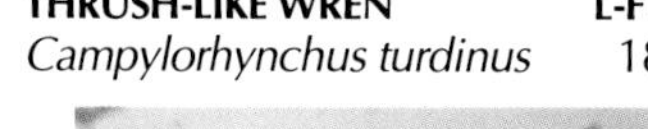

1. THRUSH-LIKE WREN L-FT
Campylorhynchus turdinus 18

Above dull grayish brown. Eyebrow and throat white. Below white more or less spotted dark brown. Crissum spotted.

2. WHITE-HEADED WREN L-FT
Campylorhynchus albobrunneus 18

Hood white. Back and tail dark brown. Underparts white (mixed dusky in s).

3. BAND-BACKED WREN L-FT
Campylorhynchus zonatus 18

Collar rufescent-tinged. Above barred black and white. Breast and belly cinnamon buff. Tail outer feathers barred.

4. FASCIATED WREN L-SA
Campylorhynchus fasciatus 18

Quite like 240-5 but upperparts banded instead of striped.

5. STRIPE-BACKED WREN L-TS
Campylorhynchus nuchalis 18

Crown grayish mottled black. Back striped black and white. Below white spotted black.

6. BICOLORED WREN L-SO
Campylorhynchus griseus 18

Crown and eye-stripe blackish. Underparts and long broad eye-brow white. Above rufous brown. Wings not barred. Tail blackish, some white at near end.

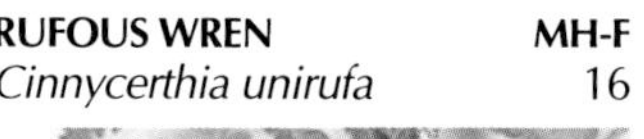

7. RUFOUS WREN MH-F
Cinnycerthia unirufa 16

Uniform rufous chestnut. Faint barring on wings and tail. Imm: Forecrown and cheeks whitish.

immature

Cinnycerthia
Thryothorus: Long, narrow eyebrow white. Cheeks white, streaked dusky.

8. SEPIA-BROWN WREN **MH-FT**
Cinnycerthia peruana 15

Reddish brown (some white on forehead in some races). Wings and tail narrowly barred black.

12. RUFOUS-AND-WHITE WREN **LM-S**
Thryothorus rufalbus 14

Upperparts rufous. Wings and tail barred black. Prominent long eyebrow white. Underparts white.

9. PLAIN-TAILED WREN **MH-F**
Thryothorus euophrys 15

Crown grayish brown. Malar white. Above rufous. Wings and tail unbarred. Throat white. Breast spotted. Belly buff.

13. NICEFORO'S WREN **L-T**
Thryothorus nicefori 14

Like 241-12 but crown and upper back olive brown contrasting with rufous lower back and rump.

10. MOUSTACHED WREN **LM-T**
Thryothorus genibarbis 15

Crown and nape gray to brownish gray. Back brown. Wings not barred. Malar stripe and throat white. Prominent whisker black. Below buffy. Tail barred (all rufous in ne).

14. SUPERCILIATED WREN **L-SA**
Thryothorus superciliaris 14

Crown dark brown. Back reddish brown. Wings and tail barred. Eyebrow broad, white, narrow eye-stripe black. Cheeks white, unstreaked. Crissum rufous.

11. CORAYA WREN **L-FT**
Thryothorus coraya 13

Crown and nape dark grayish. Back chestnut. Wings not barred. Face blackish with little or no white streaking. Throat white. Below grayish. Tail barred.

15. BUFF-BREASTED WREN **L-T**
Thryothorus leucotis 13

Bill 2/3x head. Above brown becoming rufous on rump. Wings and tail barred black. Eyebrow and throat white. Breast buff. Belly rufous.

Thryothorus

16. FAWN-BREASTED WREN L-TS
Thryothorus guarayanus 13

Very like 241-15 but back darker, grayer, less reddish and cheeks more strongly streaked.

17. LONG-BILLED WREN L-TS
Thryothorus longirostris 14

Very like 241-15 but bill much longer (bill = head instead of bill 2/3x head).

18. SOOTY-HEADED WREN L-FT
Thryothorus spadix 14

Crown dark gray. Face and throat black. Above and below chestnut, belly gray in center. Tail broadly barred black.

19. BLACK-BELLIED WREN L-T
Thryothorus fasciatoventris 14

Upperparts rufous. Eyebrow, throat and breast white. Wings faintly barred. Belly black, narrowly barred white. Tail barred.

20. RUFOUS-BREASTED WREN LM-TS
Thryothorus rutilus 13

Above rufous brown. Wings not barred. Throat checkered black and white. Breast and sides rufous (spotted in n). Belly white.

21. SPOT-BREASTED WREN LM-TS
Thryothorus maculipectus 13

Above olive brown to reddish brown. Wings not barred. Eyebrow and eye-ring white. Underparts white all scaled and spotted black.

22. BAY WREN L-T
Thryothorus nigricapillus 13

Crown, nape and sides of neck black. Back bright chestnut. Wings and tail barred. Prominent ear patch white. Breast white, belly rufous, both barred black.

23. GRAY WREN L-T
Thryothorus griseus 12

Above light grayish brown. Eyebrow dull white. Below smoky gray, darker on flanks. Tail very short, gray, barred black.

24. STRIPE-THROATED WREN L-FT
Thryothorus leucopogon (thoracicus) 11

Upperparts brown. Long narrow eyebrow white. Wings and tail barred black. Throat streaked black and white. Below brownish.

Cyphorhinus *Troglodytes*
Odontorchilus
Cistothorus: Back strongly streaked.

25. CHESTNUT-BREASTED WREN M-F
Cyphorhinus thoracicus 13

Upperparts dark brown. Wings not barred. Throat and breast rufous. Belly dark brown. Tail black, not barred.

26. MUSICIAN WREN L-F
Cyphorhinus arada 12

Head and throat rufous. Collar of white and black stripes (lacking in form w of Andes). Back brown. Wings and tail barred black. Below chestnut, more or less white on belly.

27. SONG WREN L-F
Cyphorhinus phaeocephalus (arada) 12

Bare blue skin around eye. Back and belly dark brown. Wings and tail barred black. Throat and breast rufous. Considered a race of 243-26 in BSA.

28. TOOTH-BILLED WREN L-F
Odontorchilus cinereus 11

Above mouse-gray, crown tinged dark brown. Eyebrow buffy. Below whitish. Tail grayish, banded black.

29. GRAY-MANTLED WREN M-F
Odontorchilus branickii 11

Above bluish slaty gray. Crown brownish. Face streaked white. Underparts white. Tail long, barred black and gray.

30. APOLINAR'S MARSH-WREN H-OW
Cistothorus apolinari 11

Crown brown. Back black streaked buff, rump barred. Short eyebrow gray. Underparts grayish. Tail rufous barred black. In marsh.

31. GRASS WREN LMH-O
Cistothorus platensis 10

Very like 243-30 but eyebrow buffy.

32. PARAMO WREN H-O
Cistothorus meridae 10

Very like 243-30 but eyebrow broad, white and longer, and back streaking extends to tail.

33. HOUSE WREN LMH-TS
Troglodytes aedon 10

Above grayish brown to reddish brown. Wings and tail barred dusky. Eye-stripe whitish. Below dull whitish. Crissum barred or plain.

Troglodytes
Microcerculus
Henicorhina: Tail quite short.

34. TEPUI WREN **M-FT**
Troglodytes rufulus 10

Upperparts rufous. Wings and tail faintly barred black. Eyebrow pale chestnut. Below rufescent or grayish white.

35. MOUNTAIN WREN **MH-FT**
Troglodytes solstitialis 9

Like redder forms of 243-33 but smaller and has conspicuous broad whitish or buffy eyebrow.

36. NIGHTINGALE WREN **LM-F**
Microcerculus marginatus 10

Bill rather long. Above dark wood brown. Wings and tail not barred. Below varies from mostly scaled brown to breast all white. Tail very short.

37. WHITE-BREASTED WOOD-WREN **LM-FT**
Henicorhina leucosticta 10

Crown and eyestripe black. Long eyebrow white. Above rufous brown. Wings and tail barred black. Throat and breast pure white. Belly brown.

38. GRAY-BREASTED WOOD-WREN **MH-FT**
Henicorhina leucophrys 10

Above rufous brown. Wings and tail faintly barred. Long eyebrow whitish. Throat and breast gray. Belly brown.

39. WING-BANDED WREN **L-F**
Microcerculus bambla 10

Upperparts dark reddish brown. Wings with single broad white bar. Throat and breast gray. Belly reddish brown.

40. FLUTIST WREN **M-F**
Microcerculus ustulatus 9

Upperparts uniform chestnut brown. No eyebrow. Below brown tinged gray on throat and becoming barred on belly.

Phytotoma
Oxyruncus
Eremophila

Anthus: Walks (not hops) on open grassy areas. Outer tail feathers white.

1. RUFOUS-TAILED PLANTCUTTER LM-TS
Phytotoma rara 18

Crown chestnut. Back olive brown heavily streaked black. Wings black, prominent patch white. Face black. Eye red. Whisker white. Underparts deep rufous. Tail dusky with chestnut patch. F: Sparrow-like. Underparts buff streaked black on breast.

female

2. WHITE-TIPPED PLANTCUTTER LMH-S
Phytotoma rutila 18

Like 245-1 but back gray streaked black. F: Like f. 245-1 but below white, all streaked black.

3. PERUVIAN PLANTCUTTER L-TS
Phytotoma raimondii 17

Like 245-1 but back gray spotted black. Wings with double wing-bar. F: Like f. 245-1 but back brown streaked white.

4. SHARPBILL LM-F
Oxyruncus cristatus 16

Bill 1/2x head, sharply pointed. Back olive green. Face speckled. Underparts whitish or pale yellow, all spotted black.

5. HORNED LARK H-O
Eremophila alpestris 14

Prominent forehead and eyebrow white. Lores and stripe below eye black. Above brownish, streaked black. Throat yellowish. Breast band black. Below white. Terrestrial. Walks, not hops.

6. CORRENDERA PIPIT LMH-O
Anthus correndera 14

Like 246-11 but above boldly striped black and cinnamon, one conspicuous long white stripe on each side of back.

7. YELLOWISH PIPIT L-O
Anthus lutescens 13

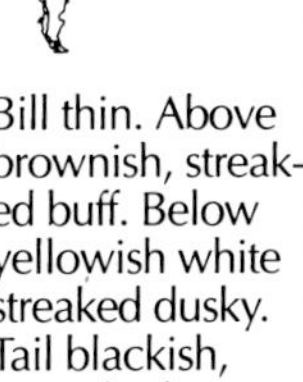

Bill thin. Above brownish, streaked buff. Below yellowish white streaked dusky. Tail blackish, outer feathers show white in flight. Terrestrial. Walks.

Anthus: Walks (not hops) on open grassy areas. Outer tail feathers white.
Ramphocaenus *Polioptila*
Microbates

8. SHORT-BILLED PIPIT H-O
Anthus furcatus 14

Like 245-7 but breast buff, heavily streaked dusky, sharply demarcated from white belly.

9. OCHRE-BREASTED PIPIT L-O
Anthus nattereri 14

Rather like 245-7 but very yellow appearance, especialy on face and breast.

10. PARAMO PIPIT H-O
Anthus bogotensis 14

Rather like 245-7 but has rufous brown shoulders and buffy brown underparts. Little streaking below.

11. HELLMAYR'S PIPIT MH-O
Anthus hellmayri 14

Like 245-7 but outer tail feathers buffy. Below buffy. Legs pinkish.

12. CHACO PIPIT L-O
Anthus chacoensis 13

Much like 245-7 but streaks on back whiter and underparts more buffy instead of yellowish.

13. LONG-BILLED GNATWREN L-T
Ramphocaenus melanurus 12

Bill 1-1/4x head, slender. Upperparts light brown. Face cinnamon. Definite eye-ring white. Back brown. Below whitish. Tail black, edged white.

14. COLLARED GNATWREN L-F
Microbates collaris 10

Bill = head. Upperparts olive brown. Eyebrow white. Below white with broad black band across breast.

15. TAWNY-FACED (HALF-COLLARED) GNATWREN L-F
Microbates cinereiventris 10

Upperparts olive brown. Face cinnamon rufous with dusky eyestripe. Throat white. Narrow whisker black. Below grayish. Tail short.

16. MASKED GNATCATCHER L-S
Polioptila dumicola 11

Above blue-gray. Face and forehead black. Malar stripe white. Underparts grayish or whitish. F: Little or no black on face.

Polioptila *Smaragdolanius*
Cyclarhis

17. TROPICAL GNATCATCHER **L-FTS**
Polioptila plumbea 11

Cap black. (Face white in w.) Back blue gray. Underparts white. Tail centrals black, outers white. F: Like m. but has no black on head.

female

18. CREAM-BELLIED GNATCATCHER **L-FT**
Polioptila lactea 10

Crown black. Above gray. Below creamy white.

19. GUIANAN GNATCATCHER **L-FT**
Polioptila guianensis 9

Dark gray. Narrow eye-ring, chin, belly and crissum white. F: Paler gray. Eyebrow white. Below paler and more white than m. Tail of both like 247-17.

20. SLATE-THROATED GNATCATCHER **L-FT**
Polioptila schistaceigula 9

Like 247-17 but upperparts, throat and breast all dark slaty. Belly white.

1. RUFOUS-BROWED PEPPERSHRIKE **LM-FT**
Cyclarhis gujanensis 14

Bill heavy, strongly hooded, pale brown Variable but all races have broad rufous eyebrow. Crown and cheeks gray. Back yellowish olive. Below yellowish, white in center.

2. BLACK-BILLED PEPPERSHRIKE **M-TS**
Cyclarhis nigrirostris 14

Bill heavy, black. Narrow eyebrow chestnut. Above olive green. Below gray, sides of breast olive yellow.

3. SLATY-CAPPED SHRIKE-VIREO **LM-F**
Smaragdolanius leucotis 13

Crown and nape black. Broad eyebrow yellow. Spot below eye yellow (also white spot in e). Cheeks dark gray. Back, wings and tail olive green. Underparts bright yellow.

Smaragdolanius
Vireo
Hylophilus

4. GREEN SHRIKE-VIREO L-F
Smaragdolanius pulchellus 13

Crown blue. Long narrow eyebrow and spot below eye yellow. Back, wings and tail green. Underparts yellowish.

5. YELLOW-THROATED VIREO LM-FT
*Vireo flavifrons** 13

Crown and face olive green. Spectacles bright yellow. Wings blackish, two wing-bars white. Rump gray. Throat yellow. Below white.

6. RED-EYED VIREO LMH-TS
Vireo olivaceus 12

Eye red or brown. Crown and nape gray. Prominent white eyebrow outlined by black. Above olive green. Below whitish. Crissum yellow.

7. BLACK-WHISKERED VIREO LM-TSO
*Vireo altiloquus** 13

Very like 248-6 but has narrow black whiskers.

8. BROWN-CAPPED VIREO LMH-T
Vireo leucophrys (gilvus) 11

Very like 248-6 but crown and nape dark brownish and underparts yellowish.

9. RUFOUS-CROWNED GREENLET LM-F
Hylophilus poicilotis 12

Crown bright rufous. Back wings and tail yellowish olive green. Ear coverts dusky. Below grayish, sides yellowish.

10. RUFOUS-NAPED GREENLET M-F
Hylophilus semibrunneus 12

Crown and nape rufous. Face whitish. Back olive green. Underparts whitish, sides of breast cinnamon.

11. TAWNY-CROWNED GREENLET L-F
Hylophilus ochraceiceps 10

Forecrown rufous. Eye pale. Back and wings olive. Throat whitish. Below grayish faintly streaked yellow. Crissum yellowish.

12. GOLDEN-FRONTED GREENLET L-TS
Hylophilus aurantiifrons 10

Forehead dull yellow. Crown brown. Above olive. Throat whitish. Below buffy yellowish.

Hylophilus

13. LEMON-CHESTED GREENLET L-TS
Hylophilus thoracicus 11

Crown and nape gray. Eye pale. Back, wings and tail yellowish olive. Throat grayish. Breast lemon yellow. Belly grayish.

14. GRAY-CHESTED GREENLET L-FT
Hylophilus semicinereus 10

Like 249-13 but crown olive gray. Breast gray tinged olive yellow only at sides.

15. ASHY-HEADED GREENLET L-TS
Hylophilus pectoralis 10

Hood gray. Back and wings yellowish olive green. Throat and belly white. Breast lemon yellow.

16. TEPUI GREENLET M-FT
Hylophilus sclateri 11

Like 249-15 but crown and wings gray, contrasting strongly with olive green back. Breast and sides yellowish.

17. BROWN-HEADED GREENLET L-F
Hylophilus brunneiceps 11

Crown and nape dull brown. Brownish olive above. Dull grayish below, tinged buff on breast. (Belly yellowish s of the Amazon).

18. DUSKY-CAPPED GREENLET L-F
Hylophilus hypoxanthus 10

Cap brownish. Back olive brown becoming olive green on rump and tail. Throat whitish. Below bright olive yellow, tinged buff on breast.

19. OLIVACEOUS GREENLET M-TS
Hylophilus olivaceus 12

Above dull olive, more yellowish on forehead. Below yellowish olive, yellower on belly.

20. SCRUB GREENLET L-TS
Hylophilus flavipes 11

Upperparts dull olive green. Throat whitish. Breast buffy. Belly pale yellow. Legs flesh color. Eye pale (imm. dark).

21. BUFF-CHEEKED (-CHESTED) GREENLET L-F
Hylophilus muscicapinus 11

Eye dark. Forehead, face and breast bright buff. Rear crown gray. Above olive green. Below whitish.

22. LESSER GREENLET L-FT
Hylophilus minor 9

Upperparts bright yellowish olive green. Eye-ring white. Below white. Sides of body and undertail coverts lemon yellow.

Oreomanes
Conirostrum: Bill short, cone-shaped, pointed.

1. GIANT CONEBILL H-T
Oreomanes fraseri 16

Upperparts light gray. Eyebrow and underparts chestnut. Broad streak from below eye to ear coverts white. Bill long for a conebill.

2. BLUE-BACKED CONEBILL MH-FT
Conirostrum sitticolor 12

Hood, upper breast, wings and tail black. (Eyebrow blue in some races). Back bright blue. Breast and belly cinnamon rufous.

3. RUFOUS-BROWED CONEBILL H-TS
Conirostrum rufum 12

Upperparts dark gray. Wings and tail slaty black, inner wing feathers lined whitish. Face and all underparts rufous.

4. CINEREOUS CONEBILL LMH-TS
Conirostrum cinereum 11

Crown blackish. Above grayish or brownish. Forehead and broad eyebrow white. Wings blackish, single wing-bar and speculum white.

5. WHITE-BROWED CONEBILL H-FT
Conirostrum ferrugineiventre 12

Crown black. Broad eyebrow and patch on shoulder white. Back and sides of head gray. Chin white, rest of underparts bright rufous.

6. CAPPED CONEBILL MH-FT
Conirostrum albifrons 13

Dark blue with white crown (crown bluish in n). Bobs tail constantly. F: Yellowish green, bluer on crown.

7. CHESTNUT-VENTED CONEBILL L-TS
Conirostrum speciosum 11

Upperparts dark blue-gray. Below paler gray. Crissum chestnut. F: Above greenish, tinged blue on crown and yellow on wings and tail.

8. WHITE-EARED CONEBILL L-TS
Conirostrum leucogenys 9

Crown and nape black. Cheeks white. Back dark blue-gray. Rump white. Below light blue-gray. Crissum chestnut. F: Cheeks and underparts buffy.

9. BICOLORED CONEBILL L-TSW
Conirostrum bicolor 9

Upperparts blue-gray (imm. brownish). Underparts grayish buff. Legs pale flesh.

10. PEARLY-BREASTED CONEBILL L-FT
Conirostrum margaritae 9

Very like 250-9 but paler above and pure gray below.

FLOWER-PIERCERS HAVE A DISTINCTIVE UPCURVED BILL, STRONGLY HOOKED AT TIP.

Diglossa

11. GREATER FLOWER-PIERCER **M-FT**
Diglossa major 17

Mostly bluish slate. Facial mask black. Crissum chestnut.

12. GLOSSY FLOWER-PIERCER **H-TS**
Diglossa lafresnayii 14

Glossy black, shoulders blue-gray.

13. CARBONATED FLOWER-PIERCER **H-TS**
Diglossa carbonaria 13

Variable but mostly black. Shoulder patch or rump gray, below or crissum chestnut in some. Includes Black Flower-Piercer (*D. humeralis* by some). Like 251-12.

female

14. MASKED FLOWER-PIERCER **MH-FT**
Diglossa cyanea 14

Dark purplish blue. Forehead, face and throat black. Eye red.

15. SCALED FLOWER-PIERCER **M-FT**
Diglossa duidae 13

Above blackish. Face black. Underparts slaty, feathers scaled gray Crissum scaled white.

16. RUSTY (SLATY) FLOWER-PIERCER **M-TS**
Diglossa sittoides (baritula) 12

Above bluish gray. Forehead and face blackish. Underparts cinnamon. F: Upperparts olive brown. Underparts pale dull buffy brown.

female

Diglossa
Cyanerpes: Bill curved.

17. BLUISH FLOWER-PIERCER **MH-F**
Diglossa caerulescens 12

Uniform dull blue or bluish gray. Area around eye blackish. Bill and legs blackish. Bill less upturned than most flower-piercers.

18. WHITE-SIDED FLOWER-PIERCER **MH-T**
Diglossa albilatera 13

Upperparts slaty gray. Below lighter. Patch at sides of breast white. F: Olive brown above. Underparts brownish.

female

19. VENEZUELAN FLOWER-PIERCER **M-FT**
Diglossa venezuelensis 14

Like 252-18 but deeper black. F: Head yellowish olive.

20. DEEP-BLUE FLOWER-PIERCER **M-F**
Diglossa glauca 11

Very like 252-21 but duller and darker. Eye orange. Lores and forehead black.

21. INDIGO FLOWER-PIERCER **M-F**
Diglossa indigotica 11

Eye red. Shining bluish purple. Lores black. Below bright purple.

22. RED-LEGGED HONEYCREEPER **L-FT**
Cyanerpes cyaneus 12

Bill=head. Crown shining light blue. Eye-stripe, back, wings and tail black. Rest of body purple-blue. Legs red. F: Like f. 252-23 but pale eyebrow prominent and legs reddish.

23. PURPLE HONEYCREEPER **L-FTS**
Cyanerpes caeruleus 11

Bill=head. Purple. Eye-stripe, throat, wings and tail black. Legs yellow. F: Green, face tawny. Whiskers blue. Breast green streaked yellowish. Belly and legs yellow.

female

Cyanerpes
Chlorophanes
Iridophanes
Dacnis: Bill short, straight, conical, sharp pointed.

24. SHORT-BILLED HONEYCREEPER **L-FT**
Cyanerpes nitidus 10

Very like 252-23 but bill only 1/2x head and legs pinkish.

25. SHINING HONEYCREEPER **L-FT**
Cyanerpes lucidus 11

Very like 252-23 but face light blue and black throat patch smaller. F: Breast streaked blue.

26. GREEN HONEYCREEPER **LM-FT**
Chlorophanes spiza 13

All shining green except cap and sides of neck black. Bill 3/4x head, straight, upper black, lower yellow. F: No black on head. Grass green, yellowish green below.

female

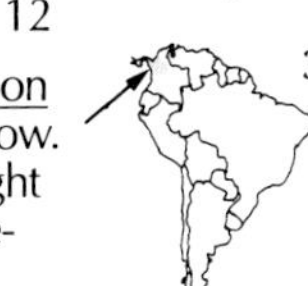

27. GOLDEN-COLLARED HONEYCREEPER **M-FT**
Iridophanes pulcherrima 12

Hood and mantle black. Collar on nape golden yellow. Rump yellow. Shoulders bright blue. Below light green. F: No black. Above olive-green.

28. BLUE DACNIS **L-FTS**
Dacnis cayana 11

Blue. Eye-stripe, wings, tail, throat and center of back black. Legs reddish. F: Green, head blue. Throat gray.

female

29. SCARLET-THIGHED DACNIS **L-FT**
Dacnis venusta 11

Crown, back, sides of head and patch on shoulder blue. Forehead, area around eye, throat, sides of back and underparts black. Thighs red. F: Above greenish blue. Below including thighs, buffy. Tail mostly black.

female

30. VIRIDIAN DACNIS **L-FT**
Dacnis viguieri 11

Eye pale. Shining blue green, rump more bluish. Wing coverts bright green. Lores, upper back, primaries and tail black. F: Lacks black on back. Below yellowish green.

ICTERIDS HAVE LONG, CONICAL, SHARP-POINTED BILL.

OROPENDOLAS: OUTER TAIL FEATHERS BRIGHT YELLOW.

Dacnis *Xenodacnis* *Coereba* *Gymnostinops*

31. YELLOW-BELLIED DACNIS **L-FT**
Dacnis flaviventer 11

Crown bluish green. Forehead, sides of head, back, wings, tail and throat black. Eye red. Whisker, shoulder, rump and underparts golden yellow. F: Above dull green. Below buffy.

32. BLACK-FACED DACNIS **L-FT**
Dacnis lineata 12

Crown light blue. Forehead, face, back, wings and tail black. Below blue. Rump and belly white (yellow in w). F: Brownish. Below pale greenish.

33. SCARLET-BREASTED DACNIS **L-FT**
Dacnis berlepschi 11

Hood and upper breast dark blue. Back and wing coverts dark blue, streaked silver blue. Breast red. Belly yellowish. F: Brown with band across breast washed orange-red.

34. BLACK-LEGGED DACNIS **L-FT**
Dacnis nigripes 10

Very like 253-28 but less black on back and throat. F: Quite like f. 253-29. Above brownish. Below pale.

35. WHITE-BELLIED DACNIS **L-F**
Dacnis albiventris 10

Shiny purple blue. Forehead, face, wings and tail black. Center of underparts white. F: Greenish. Belly yellow in center.

36. TIT-LIKE DACNIS **H-TS**
Xenodacnis parina 12

Bright blue. Bill small. F: Head light blue (only face and forecrown in n). Above brown. Wing coverts and rump blue. Below dull rufous. Belly yellow in center.

37. BANANAQUIT **LMH-TSO**
Coereba flaveola 10

Bill short, curved. Prominent long eyebrow white. Above black or dark gray. Speculum white. Rump yellow. Throat gray. Below yellow.

1. OLIVE OROPENDOLA **L-FT**
Gymnostinops yuracares m 51
f 40

Foreparts bright olive yellow. Back, wings, belly and crissum chestnut. Bill black tipped orange. Bare cheeks pink.

2. BLACK OROPENDOLA **L-FT**
Gymnostinops guatimozinus m 42
f 38

Head, nape, mantle and underparts black. Cheeks bare, bluish. Bill black, tipped yellow. Back, rump and crissum chestnut. Cf. 255-3.

Gymnostinops: Tail yellow, centrals black.
Psarocolius: Tail yellow, centrals black. Undertail all yellow.
Clypicterus
Zarhynchus
Ocyalus
Scaphidura

3. CHESTNUT-MANTLED OROPENDOLA **L-FT**
Gymnostinops cassini 42

Upperparts and wings bright chestnut. Bare cheeks blue. Underparts black, flanks chestnut.

4. PARA OROPENDOLA **L-FT**
Gymnostinops bifasciatus 42

Upperparts, wings, breast and belly chestnut. Head, neck and throat blackish. Bare cheeks pink.

5. CRESTED OROPENDOLA **LM-FT**
Psarocolius decumanus m 38 f 30

Bill ivory white. Mostly black. Eye blue. Rump and crissum chestnut.

6. GREEN OROPENDOLA **L-FT**
Psarocolius viridis m 38 f 32

Olive green. Bill green,tipped red. Rump, flanks, thighs and crissum dark chestnut.

7. RUSSET-BACKED OROPENDOLA **LM-FT**
Psarocolius angustifrons m 38 f 31

Above dull chestnut, forehead more or less yellow. Underparts olive brown. Bill yellow or blackish.

8. DUSKY-GREEN OROPENDOLA **M-FT**
Psarocolius atrovirens m 36 f 32

Mostly dark olive green. Bill pale greenish yellow. Rump and belly chestnut. Tail as in 255-9 but tipped olive.

9. CASQUED OROPENDOLA **L-F**
Clypicterus oseryi m 33 f 29

Mainly chestnut. Rounded frontal shield and bill whitish. Eye blue. Throat and breast bright olive yellow. Tail yellow, centrals and outermost olive.

10. CHESTNUT-HEADED OROPENDOLA **L-FT**
Zarhynchus wagleri m 30 f 23

Bill whitish to pale greenish yellow. Eye blue. Head and neck chestnut. Back, wings and belly black. Rump and sides of body chestnut. Tail yellow, central black.

11. BAND-TAILED OROPENDOLA **L-FT**
Ocyalus latirostris m 29 f 20

Crown and mantle chestnut. Back, wings and underparts black. Outer tail feathers bright yellow broadly tipped black. Bill black, tipped yellow.

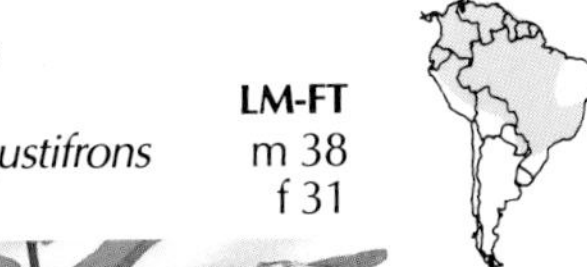

12. GIANT COWBIRD **LM-TS**
Scaphidura oryzivora m 33 f 25

Shiny purple. Eye red. Feathers of neck elongated forming a ruff, giving bird a small-headed appearance.

Cassidix	*Quiscalus*
Hypopyrrhus	*Lampropsar*
Macroagelaius	*Cacicus*

13. GREAT-TAILED GRACKLE **L-OW**
Cassidix mexicanus m 36
f 28

Shiny black, tinged violet. Eye yellow. Wings and tail greenish black. Tail very long, wedge-shaped. F: Above brownish. Eyebrow and underparts lighter buffy brown.

14. RED-BELLIED GRACKLE **M-FT**
Hypopyrrhus pyrohypogaster m 27
f 23

Bill 3/4x head. Black. Belly and crissum red. Eye white.

15. MOUNTAIN GRACKLE **H-F**
Macroagelaius subalaris 26

Bill 3/4x head. Silky blue-black. Semi-concealed chestnut tufts under wings.

16. GOLDEN-TUFTED GRACKLE **M-F**
Macroagelaius imthurni m 25
f 22

Black. Bill = head. Semi-concealed golden tufts under wing.

17. CARIB GRACKLE **L-OW**
Quiscalus lugubris m 23
f 21

female

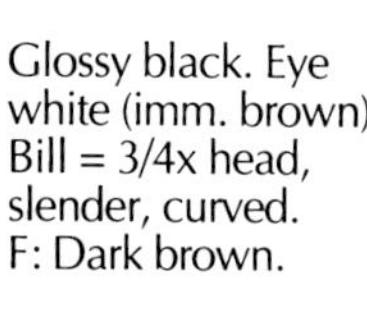

Glossy black. Eye white (imm. brown). Bill = 3/4x head, slender, curved. F: Dark brown.

18. VELVET-FRONTED GRACKLE **L-SW**
Lampropsar tanagrinus m 19
f 17

Bill 3/4x head. Like 261-59 but much less glossy.

19. YELLOW-RUMPED CACIQUE **L-FT**
Cacicus cela m 25
f 21

Glossy black. Inner wing coverts, rump, upper and lower tail coverts bright yellow. Tail centrals black, rest yellow broadly tipped black.

20. SCARLET-RUMPED CACIQUE **LM-F**
Cacicus uropygialis m 25
f 22

Glossy blue-black. Eye blue. Rump red (sometimes mostly concealed).

21. RED-RUMPED CACIQUE **L-FT**
Cacicus haemorrhous m 26
f 23

Like 256-20 but rump patch larger, intense scarlet. Eye blue.

22. MOUNTAIN CACIQUE **MH-F**
Cacicus leucorhamphus m 26
f 21

Very like 256-19 but tail all black, only rump and wing coverts yellow (no yellow on wings in s). Eye blue.

Cacicus
Gymnomystax
Curaeus
Gnorimopsar
Oreopsar
Agelaius

23. SOLITARY BLACK CACIQUE L-TS
Cacicus solitarius m 25 f 23

All black except bill yellowish white. Eye brown.

24. SELVA CACIQUE L-F
Cacicus koepckeae 21

All black but rump yellow. Bill gray with pale tip.

25. GOLDEN-WINGED CACIQUE LM-FT
Cacicus chrysopterus 19

All black but rump and wing coverts yellow. Bill gray with white tip.

26. YELLOW-BILLED CACIQUE LMH-TS
Cacicus holosericeus m 23 f 19

All black. Eye pale yellow. Bill yellowish white.

27. ECUADORIAN BLACK CACIQUE L-FT
Cacicus sclateri m 18 f 17

Black. Like 257-26 but bill bluish tipped whitish. Eye blue.

28. ORIOLE BLACKBIRD L-SO
Gymnomystax mexicanus 27

Golden yellow. Back, wings and tail black. Skin around eye bare, black.

29. AUSTRAL BLACKBIRD LM-TSO
Curaeus curaeus 25

Glossy black. Bill black.

30. FORBES' BLACKBIRD L-O
Curaeus forbesi m 22 f 20

Black. Bill black. Head feathers glossy.

31. CHOPI BLACKBIRD L-SO
Gnorimopsar chopi 23

Glossy blue-black. Bill stout with distinct grooves on lower bill. Eye dark.

32. BOLIVIAN BLACKBIRD H-S
Oreopsar bolivianus 21

Dull brownish black, wings browner. Bill short, black. Eye dark.

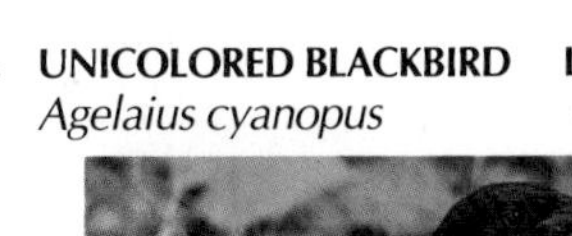

33. UNICOLORED BLACKBIRD L-OW
Agelaius cyanopus 21

Glossy black. F: Above streaked chestnut and black. Below yellow streaked gray.

female

Dives
Amblyramphus
Leistes
Agelaius

34. SCRUB BLACKBIRD **L-SA**
Dives warszewiczi 21

All glossy black including bill. (Birds in s are 6cm larger).

35. SCARLET-HEADED BLACKBIRD **L-OW**
Amblyramphus holosericeus 22

Black. Hood, breast and thighs scarlet.

36. PALE-EYED BLACKBIRD **L-OW**
Agelaius xanthophthalmus 21

Black. Eye pale orange.

37. YELLOW-WINGED BLACKBIRD **LM-OW**
Agelaius thilius 18

All black or brownish except shoulder patch yellow. F: Blackish streaked brown. Eyebrow whitish. Shoulder patch like m.

female

38. CHESTNUT-CAPPED BLACKBIRD **L-OW**
Agelaius ruficapillus 17

All glossy black except crown, throat and breast chestnut. F: Streaked black and brown. Throat light olive.

39. YELLOW-HOODED BLACKBIRD **LMH-OW**
Agelaius icterocephalus 17

Hood and breast bright light yellow. Rest of plumage black. F: Crown and nape yellowish. Back olive streaked black. Eyebrow and throat bright yellow. Below yellowish to olive on belly.

female

40. WHITE-BROWED BLACKBIRD **L-O**
Leistes superciliaris 17

Very like 259-42 but male has long buffy white eye-stripe.

Xanthopsar
Leistes
Icterus

41. SAFFRON-COWLED BLACKBIRD **L-W**
Xanthopsar flavus 20

Male (left): Back, wings and tail black. Head, rump and underparts bright yellow. Female (right): Upperparts brown, shoulder and rump yellow.

42. RED-BREASTED BLACKBIRD **L-O**
Leistes militaris 17

Upperparts black feathers edged brown. Throat and breast red. F: Upperparts dark brown streaked sandy brown. Crown-stripe and eyebrow buffy. Below buffy, some red stains on breast.

female

43. TROUPIAL **L-TSW**
Icterus icterus 21

Hood and breast black. (Crown orange in s). Wings black with prominent white patch. Back, shoulders and underparts orange.

44. YELLOW-TAILED ORIOLE **L-TSW**
Icterus mesomelas 21

Mostly bright yellow. Face, throat, breast and back black. Wings black with large yellow patch on coverts. Tail yellow, central feathers black.

45. YELLOW-BACKED ORIOLE **LMH-TS**
Icterus chrysater 20

Golden yellow. Forehead, face, throat, breast, wings and tail black.

46. YELLOW ORIOLE **L-SO**
Icterus nigrogularis 20

Lemon yellow. Lores, throat and breast black. Wings black with more or less white-tipped coverts.

47. EPAULET ORIOLE **L-FT**
Icterus cayanensis 19

Deep black. Large shoulder patch chestnut, tawny or yellow.

Icterus
Pseudoleistes
Sturnella

48. MORICHE ORIOLE **L-FT**
Icterus chrysocephalus 19

Black. Hind-crown, shoulder, rump, thighs and crissum yellow.

49. WHITE-EDGED ORIOLE **L-SA**
Icterus graceannae 18

Face, throat and breast black, Crown, nape, rump, belly and sides rich yellow. Wings black, shoulder yellow. Inner wing feathers edged white.

50. NORTHERN (BALTIMORE) ORIOLE **LMH-T**
*Icterus galbula** 17

Hood and mantle black. Wings black with white wing-bars. Rump and underparts orange. Tail centrals black, rest yellow. F: Replaced by brown.

51. ORCHARD ORIOLE **LM-S**
*Icterius spurius** 16

Head and mantle black. Back and underparts chestnut. Wings and tail black, edged white. F; Below yellowish.

52. ORANGE-CROWNED ORIOLE **L-T**
Icterus auricapillus 17

Forehead, face, throat and breast black. Crown and nape orange. Rump and below yellow.

53. YELLOW-RUMPED MARSHBIRD **L-OW**
Pseudoleistes guirahuro 22

Much like 260-53 but rump and flanks yellow and yellow wing coverts more extensive.

54. BROWN-AND-YELLOW MARSHBIRD **L-OW**
Pseudoleistes virescens 21

Brown. Wing coverts more or less yellow. Belly yellow.

55. LONG-TAILED MEADOWLARK **L-O**
Sturnella loyca 23

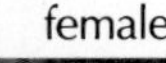

female

Upperparts and belly blackish, feathers scaled brown. Eyebrow red before eye, white behind eye. Throat and breast bright red, thighs dark. F: Above black scaled brown. Eyebrow white. Throat white. Below gray streaked black. Belly pinkish.

Sturnella
Molothrus
Dolichonyx

56. EASTERN MEADOWLARK **LMH-O**
Sturnella magna 22

Chunky with slender bill and short tail. Above brown streaked black and buff. Below yellow with broad, U-shaped black band on breast. Outer tail feathers conspicuously white in flight.

57. PERUVIAN (RED-BREASTED) MEADOWLARK **L-O**
Sturnella bellicosa 19

Very like 260-54 but bill shorter and more slender and thighs white. F: Lacks white throat.

58. PAMPAS (LESSER RED-BREASTED) MEADOWLARK **L-O**
Sturnella defilippi 19

Like 260-54 but bill shorter and more slender and thighs black. F: Lacks white throat.

59. BAY-WINGED COWBIRD **L-SO**
Molothrus badius 18

Upperparts grayish brown. Below paler and grayer. Wings rufous. Tail blackish.

60. SHINY COWBIRD **LM-SO**
Molothrus bonariensis 19

Shiny black with shining purplish gloss. F: Dull grayish brown, paler below. Wings and tail brown. Faint eyebrow.

female

61. SCREAMING COWBIRD **L-SO**
Molothrus rufoaxillaris 15

Like 261-59 but less shiny and has small chestnut spot on shoulder (hard to see). F: Like m.

62. BOBOLINK **L-SO**
*Dolichonyx oryzivorus** 13

nb plumage

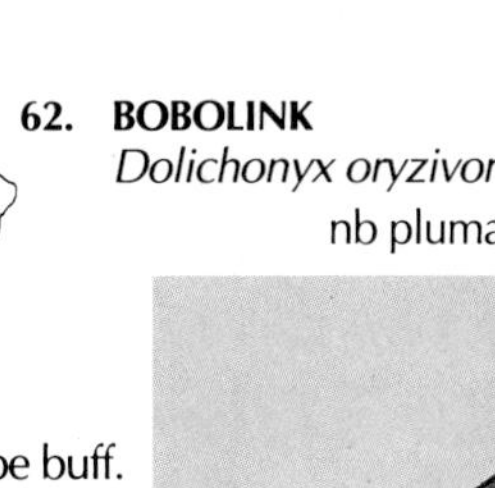

Black, nape buff. Rump and shoulders white. Female and winter m. rather sparrow-like. Above streaked brown, buff and black. Eyebrow, crown-stripe and underparts buff. Brown streaks on sides.

MOST WARBLERS SHOWN IN WINTER PLUMAGE.

Mniotilta *Protomotaria*
Vermivora *Dendroica*

1. BLACK-AND-WHITE WARBLER **LM-FT**
*Mniotilta varia** 11

Streaked black and white. Cheeks and throat black. F: Less streaked. Cheeks gray. Throat white. Little streaking below.

female

2. TENNESSEE WARBLER **LM-TS**
*Vermivora peregrina** 10

female or imm.

A very plain-looking warbler. Crown gray. Lores and eyebrow white. Above olive green. Faint wing-bar. Below whitish. Female and Imm: Yellower below, no gray on crown.

3. PROTHONOTARY WARBLER **L-TSW**
*Protonotaria citrea** 12

female

Hood and underparts yellow. F: Crown, back and wings grayish.

4. GOLDEN-WINGED WARBLER **LM-FT**
*Vermivora chrysoptera** 11

Forecrown and wing coverts yellow. Face and throat black. F: Duller.

5. BLACKPOLL WARBLER **LM-T**
*Dendroica striata** 12

female

Cap all black. Cheeks white. Rest streaked, black and white. F: Face grayish white. Cf. 262-1.

6. CERULEAN WARBLER **LM-T**
*Dendroica cerulea** 11

Above grayish blue. Below white with dusky breast bar. F: Above greenish. Eyebrow white.

7. BLACKBURNIAN WARBLER **LMH-FT**
*Dendroica fusca** 12

nb male

Eyebrow and throat orange. Eye stripe black. Single white wing-bar. F: Above brown. Two bars on wings.

Dendroica
Seiurus
Oporornis

8. BAY-BREASTED WARBLER **LM-FT**
*Dendroica castanea** 12

nb plumage

Forehead and face black (f and nb no black). Cheeks, wingbars and belly white. Sides chestnut. Back streaked. Nb resembles nb 262-1.

9. OVENBIRD **LM-T**
*Seiurus aurocapillus** 13

Crown stripe rufous bordered by black. Above olive brown. Eyering white. No eyebrow. Below white. Whisker and conspicuous spots on breast black. Often walks on ground.

10. NORTHERN WATERTHRUSH **LM-TSW**
*Seiurus noveboracensis** 13

Above dark ashy brown. Long eyebrow whitish. Throat whitish, finely streaked black. Breast yellowish white, heavily streaked black. Usually walks on ground. Teeters.

11. LOUISIANA WATERTHRUSH **LM-TW**
*Seiurus motacilla** 13

Very like 263-10 but throat unstreaked.

12. KENTUCKY WARBLER **LM-FT**
*Oporornis (Geothlypis) formosus** 12

Above, wings and tail dull olive. Forecrown and stripe below eye black. Spectacles and underparts bright yellow.

13. CONNECTICUT WARBLER **L-TS**
*Oporornis (Geothlypis) agilis** 13

Hood and breast gray. Prominent complete eye-ring white in all plumages. Nb f. lacks hood. Walks, (not hops).

14. MOURNING WARBLER **LM-TS**
*Oporornis (Geothlypis) philadelphia** 12

Head gray. Back, wings and tail dull olive. Partial eye-ring white. Breast band black. Belly yellow. F: Upperparts olive. Underparts yellow. Very like nb 263-13 but white eye-ring not complete. Hops, (not walks).

Wilsonia	*Dendroica*	*Granatellus*
Setophaga	*Geothlypis*	*Myioborus:* Tail black, outer feathers white.

15. CANADA WARBLER LM-FT
*Wilsonia canadensis** 12

Forecrown, back,wings and tail light gray, crown spotted black. Eye-ring white. Band of black spots across breast. F: Faint breast band of pale gray spots.

16. AMERICAN REDSTART LM-T
*Setophaga ruticilla** 11

Black. Patch on wings, sides of breast and outer tail feathers orange. Belly white. F: Gray. Orange patches replaced by yellow.

female

1. YELLOW WARBLER LM-TSW
Dendroica petechia 12

Usually appears yellow or yellowish all over with breast streaked chestnut but very variable with chestnut on crown or face or throat. F: Little or no chestnut.

2. OLIVE-CROWNED YELLOWTHROAT L-S
Geothlypis semiflava 13

Back, wings and tail olive green. Large black patch on forecrown, face and sides of neck. F: Very like f. 264-3 but forecrown yellowish olive.

3. MASKED YELLOWTHROAT L-S
Geothlypis aequinoctialis 13

Crown gray. Small mask through eye and forehead black (f. lacking). Above olive green. Underparts bright yellow.

4. ROSE-BREASTED CHAT L-FT
Granatellus pelzelni 12

Head black. Eye-streak white. Above bluish slate. Throat white outlined by black line. Below rosy red. F: Upperparts slaty blue. Underparts rosy pink.

5. SLATE-THROATED WHITESTART (REDSTART) LM-FT
Myioborus miniatus 12

Crown chestnut. Above and face slaty. Throat blackish. Breast and belly bright yellow. Tail black edged white.

Myioborus: Tail black, outer feathers white.
Basileuterus: Striped crown and yellow underparts.

6. GOLDEN-FRONTED WHITESTART (REDSTART) **MH-FT**
Myioborus ornatus 12

Forecrown and face yellow (cheeks white in some races). Above dark gray. Underparts yellow.

7. SPECTACLED WHITESTART (REDSTART) **MH-FT**
Myioborus melanocephalus 13

Crown chestnut or black. Face black with yellow spectacles. Back slaty gray. Underparts bright yellow.

8. WHITE-FRONTED WHITESTART (REDSTART) **MH-FT**
Myioborus albifrons 13

Forehead and face white. Crown black with rufous patch in center. Back dark gray. Below bright yellow.

9. YELLOW-CROWNED WHITESTART (REDSTART) **MH-FT**
Myioborus flavivertex 13

Center of crown yellow. Lores and underparts yellow. Face black. Above olive green.

10. WHITE-FACED WHITESTART (REDSTART) **MH-FT**
Myioborus albifacies 13

Crown and nape black. Face and neck white. Back brownish gray. Underparts bright yellow.

11. BROWN-CAPPED WHITESTART (REDSTART) **M-FT**
Myioborus brunniceps 12

Crown chestnut. Eyebrow and eye-ring white. Above olive. Below bright yellow. Crissum white.

12. YELLOW-FACED WHITESTART (REDSTART) **M-FT**
Myioborus pariae 12

Forehead and eye-ring yellow. Crown chestnut. Eyebrow and back grayish. Below bright yellow, crissum white.

13. SAFFRON-BREASTED WHITESTART (REDSTART) **M-FT**
Myioborus cardonai 12

Crown, lores and below eye black. Eye-ring and chin white. Back dark gray. Underparts orange yellow.

14. RUSSET-CROWNED WARBLER **MH-FT**
Basileuterus coronatus 14

Crown stripe rufous. Face and broad eyebrow gray. Eye stripe black. Back, wings and tail olive. Throat grayish white. Cf. 267-28.

Basileuterus: Striped crown and yellow underparts.

15. WHITE-STRIPED WARBLER L-TS
Basileuterus leucophrys 15

Like 266-24 but black crown stripes fainter and white eyebrow broad. Back olive. Underparts white.

16. GRAY-AND-GOLD WARBLER L-TSA
Basileuterus fraseri 14

Crown yellow or orange, bordered by black stripes. Above gray. White streak or spot over lores.

17. SANTA MARTA WARBLER H-FT
Basileuterus basilicus 14

Rather like 266-23 but face not black and belly more yellow. Center of throat white. Back, wings and tail olive green.

18. FLAVESCENT WARBLER L-TS
Basileuterus flaveolus 13

Upperparts, wings and tail olive green. Bill dark. Yellow eyebrow. Legs pale yellowish.

19. PALE-LEGGED WARBLER MH-FT
Basileuterus signatus 13

Like 266-18 but duller above and legs yellowish flesh.

20. TWO-BANDED WARBLER LM-F
Basileuterus bivittatus 13

Very like 267-27 but eyebrow yellow olive.

21. CITRINE WARBLER MH-FT
Basileuterus luteoviridis 13

Very like 266-18 but eyebrow yellow and shorter. Below dull yellow (brighter in s).

22. BLACK-CRESTED WARBLER H-T
Basileuterus nigrocristatus 13

Broad crown stripe black. Back, wings and tail olive green.

23. THREE-STRIPED WARBLER LM-FT
Basileuterus tristriatus 13

Back, wings and tail dull olive. Three broad whitish stripes on crown and brows. Face black.

24. WHITE-BROWED WARBLER LM-FT
Basileuterus leucoblepharus 13

Crown striped gray in center, bordered by black. Narrow eye-ring and brows white. Back olive. Below whitish, grayish on sides. Undertail coverts yellowish.

Basileuterus: Striped crown and yellow underparts.
Parula

25. GRAY-THROATED WARBLER M-FT
Basileuterus cinereicollis 13

Crown, face, throat and breast gray. Partly concealed crown stripe yellow. Back, wings and tail dark olive. Belly yellow.

26. GRAY-HEADED WARBLER M-FT
Basileuterus griseiceps 13

Head gray, lores white. Above yellowish olive.

27. GOLDEN-BELLIED WARBLER L-F
Basileuterus chrysogaster 12

Crown stripe orange bordered by broad black lines. Back dark olive. No eye stripe.

28. GOLDEN-CROWNED WARBLER LM-FT
Basileuterus culicivorus 12

Crown yellow or orange bordered by broad black stripes. Eyebrow white. Eye-stripe black. Above olive to gray. Cf. 265-14.

29. THREE-BANDED WARBLER M-FT
Basileuterus trifasciatus 12

Head and face gray. Eye-stripe and two broad stripes at sides of crown black. Above grayish olive. Throat and breast grayish white.

30. WHITE-BELLIED WARBLER L-T
Basileuterus hypoleucus 12

Crown rufous, two broad black stripes at sides of crown. Lores and long eyebrow white. Back,wings and tail olive gray. Underparts white clouded gray.

31. RUFOUS-CAPPED WARBLER L-TS
Basileuterus rufifrons 11

Crown and ear coverts chestnut. Long eyebrow white. Back, wings and tail olive green.

32. RIVER WARBLER L-FTW
Basileuterus rivularis 11

Above and wings olive. Face buff with black eye stripe. Rump and tail cinnamon buff. (Base of tail buff in w.) Underparts whitish.

33. TROPICAL PARULA LM-FTS
Parula pitiayumi 10

Above bluish, yellowish patch on back.Wing-bars white. Eye patch black. Underparts yellow

Cissopis
Sericossypha
Buthraupis

Anisognathus: Black face and cheeks.

1. MAGPIE TANAGER LM-FT
Cissopis leveriana 25

Eye yellow. Hood and breast black. Back and belly white. Wings and tail black, feathers edged white.

2. WHITE-CAPPED TANAGER MH-F
Sericossypha albocristata 23

Glossy blue-black. Cap snow white. Throat and upper breast scarlet.

3. SCARLET-THROATED TANAGER L-TS
Sericossypha loricata 21

Glossy blue-black. Throat and center of upper breast scarlet (f. all black).

4. HOODED MOUNTAIN-TANAGER MH-F
Buthraupis montana 20

Hood black. Back shining purplish blue. Underparts golden yellow with blue band at vent.

5. MASKED MOUNTAIN-TANAGER H-T
Buthraupis wetmorei 20

Above mostly yellowish green, rump brighter. Mask and throat black bordered by bright yellow. Wings black, coverts blue. Below bright yellow.

6. BLACK-CHESTED MOUNTAIN-TANAGER H-FT
Buthraupis eximia 20

Crown and nape blue. Back mossy green (rump blue in ne). Shoulders blue. Face, throat and breast black. Below golden yellow.

7. BLACK-CHINNED MOUNTAIN-TANAGER LM-FT
Anisognathus notabilis 19

Like 269-11 but chin black and rear crown yellow. Back olive.

8. SCARLET-BELLIED MOUNTAIN-TANAGER H-TS
Anisognathus igniventris 18

Black. Patch on ear coverts red. Shoulders and rump shining blue. Belly and crissum red (black in n).

9. SANTA MARTA (BLACK-CHEEKED) MOUNTAIN-TANAGER MH-FT
Anisognathus melanogenys 18

Crown and nape bright blue. Back, wings and tail dull bluish. Small yellow spot below eye. Underparts golden yellow.

Anisognathus: Black face and cheeks. *Ramphocelus*
Dubusia
Chlorornis

10. LACRIMOSE MOUNTAIN-TANAGER **MH-FT**
Anisognathus lacrymosus 17

Back black. Rump bluish. Cheeks with two yellow spots. Wings and tail blackish, feathers edged blue. Underparts orange-yellow to orange.

11. BLUE-WINGED MOUNTAIN-TANAGER **M-FT**
Anisognathus flavinucha 17

Back olive. Rump blue in s. Crown and underparts yellow. Wings mostly blue. Tail black, feathers edged blue.

12. BUFF-BREASTED MOUNTAIN-TANAGER **H-FTS**
Dubusia taeniata 18

Crown, face and throat black. Long eyebrow blue. Back blue. Wings and tail black, feathers edged blue. Breast buffy. Below yellow.

13. GRASS-GREEN TANAGER **MH-FT**
Chlorornis riefferii 19

Bright grass green. Face, crissum and center of belly chestnut. Bill and legs red.

14. FLAME-RUMPED TANAGER **LM-TS**
Ramphocelus flammigerus 18

Black. Bill light blue. Lower back and rump bright red. F: Above dark brown. Breast and rump orange. Belly yellow.

female

Ramphocelus
Orthogonys
Rhodinocichla
Wetmorethraupis
Stephanophorus
Habia

15. YELLOW-RUMPED TANAGER **LM-TS**
Ramphocelus icteronotus 18

Black. Bill light blue. Lower back and rump bright yellow. Tail blackish. F: Crown and back brownish, rump yellow. Underparts yellow.

female

16. OLIVE-GREEN TANAGER **L-F**
Orthogonys chloricterus 19

Bill rather slender. Upperparts, wings and tail dark olive green. Underparts olive yellow.

17. ROSY (ROSE-BREASTED) THRUSH-TANAGER **L-TS**
Rhodinocichla rosea 19

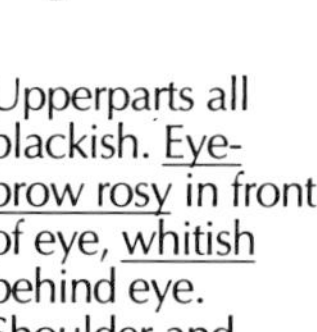

Upperparts all blackish. Eyebrow rosy in front of eye, whitish behind eye. Shoulder and underparts bright rosy. Usually on ground. F: Rosy replaced by cinnamon.

18. ORANGE-THROATED TANAGER **L-F**
Wetmorethraupis sterrhopteron 18

Above velvety black. Wing coverts shining blue. Throat and breast bright orange. Below bright yellow.

19. DIADEMED TANAGER **LM-FT**
Stephanophorus diadematus 18

Shining purplish blue. Forecrown, face and throat black. Rear crown white. Mid-crown red.

20. SOOTY ANT-TANAGER **L-FT**
Habia gutturalis 18

Mostly slaty gray. Throat and conspicuous bushy crest scarlet. Sides of head black. F: Throat pinkish white.

21. CRESTED ANT-TANAGER **M-FT**
Habia cristata 17

Quite like a cardinal with long pointed crest scarlet. Above brick red, browner on wings. Head, neck, throat and breast scarlet, brightest on throat. Lower underparts grayish tinged crimson.

22. RED-CROWNED ANT-TANAGER **L-FT**
Habia rubica 17

female

Very like 271-23 but throat not extensively red. F: Has concealed yellow crown stripe.

Habia
Ramphocelus
Lanio

23. RED-THROATED ANT-TANAGER L-T
Habia fuscicauda 17

Above mostly dull reddish. Throat extensively bright red. F: Very like f. 270-22 but throat contrasting yellow and no crown stripe.

24. BRAZILIAN TANAGER L-TS
Ramphocelus bresilius 17

Scarlet. Somewhat darker on mantle. Base of lower bill silvery. Wings and tail black. F: Hood brown. Wings and tail brownish black. Rump and underparts dull red.

female

25. MASKED CRIMSON TANAGER L-FTW
Ramphocelus nigrogularis 17

Upper bill blackish, lower silvery. All crimson except upper back, wings, tail, mask and center of belly black.

26. SILVER-BEAKED TANAGER L-TSO
Ramphocelus carbo 16

Above blackish red to velvety black. Base of lower bill silvery. Throat and breast dark crimson. Wings and tail black. F: Brownish with rufous tinge, paler below.

female

27. BLACK-BELLIED TANAGER L-TS
Ramphocelus melanogaster 16

Like 271-26 but rump crimson and black line down center of belly. F: Like f. 271-26 but forehead bright red.

28. CRIMSON-BACKED TANAGER L-TS
Ramphocelus dimidiatus 16

Like 271-26 but center of underparts extensively black.

29. WHITE-WINGED SHRIKE-TANAGER L-F
Lanio versicolor 17

immature

Hood black. Forecrown yellow. Above ochraceous, rump yellow. Wing coverts largely white. Below yellow. F: Mostly rufous brown.

Lanio
Piranga
Thraupis

30. FULVOUS SHRIKE-TANAGER **L-F**
Lanio fulvus 16

Mostly yellowish. Hood, wings and tail black. White spots on shoulder. Breast dull chestnut. F: Mostly rufous brown.

31. RED-HOODED TANAGER **MH-F**
Piranga rubriceps 18

Hood and breast scarlet. Back olive yellow. Rump yellow. Wings black, coverts bright yellow. Underpartsbright yellow.

32. HEPATIC TANAGER **LM-TSO**
Piranga flava 17

Dark red to orange. Large grayish cheek patch. Bill has conspicuous notch on upper cutting edge. F: Above olive yellow. Below brighter yellow. Cf. 272-34.

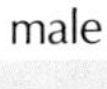

male

female

33. SUMMER TANAGER **LMH-T**
*Piranga rubra** 16

Rosy red. Bill yellowish, without notch. (Cf. 272-32) F: Like f. 272-32.

34. SCARLET TANAGER **LM-FT**
*Piranga olivacea** 17

Scarlet. Wings and tail black. Nb plumage: Olive above, yellow below. F. nb: Like f. 272-32 but lighter and yellower.

35. AZURE-SHOULDERED TANAGER **LM-FT**
Thraupis cyanoptera 17

Much like 272-36 but back bluer and head darker and bluer than back (instead of paler).

36. BLUE-GRAY TANAGER **LM-TO**
Thraupis episcopus 16

Body all pale blue or bluish gray, paler on head and somewhat darker on back. Wings and tail dark blue. Shoulder blue (or white e of Andes). Cf. 272-37

37. SAYACA TANAGER **LM-TSA**
Thraupis sayaca 16

Very like 272-36 but duller. Wings blue-gray instead of blue. Form in n has grayer head, whiter belly.

38. PALM TANAGER **LM-TSO**
Thraupis palmarum 16

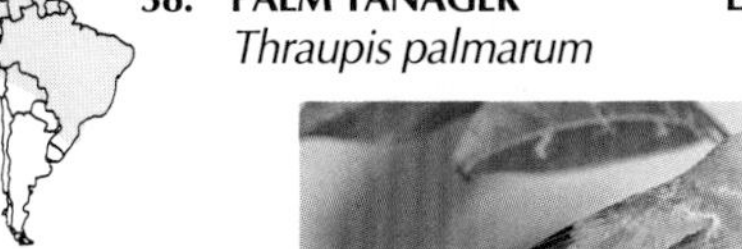

Grayish olive, sometimes glossed blue or violet, (especially underparts). Wings bicolored, grayish olive with black primaries. Whitish speculum sometimes shows.

Thraupis
Mitrospingus
Orchesticus
Eucometis

39. BLUE-CAPPED TANAGER **MH-FTS**
Thraupis cyanocephala 17

Crown and nape bright blue. Lores black. Back, wings and tail yellowish olive. Underparts gray (or blue in Venezuela). Thighs bright yellow.

40. BLUE-AND-YELLOW TANAGER **MH-TSO**
Thraupis bonariensis 16

Male (left): Hood blue, lores black. Back blackish. Rump and underparts orange-yellow. Wings and tail black, feathers edged blue. Female (right): Above olive. Underparts buffy.

41. GOLDEN-CHEVRONED TANAGER **LM-FT**
Thraupis ornata 17

Head and underparts violet blue, bluer on crown. Mantle dull dark blue becoming dull dark olive on rump. Wing coverts edged bright yellow. F: Duller and grayer.

42. DUSKY-FACED TANAGER **L-FT**
Mitrospingus cassinii 17

Eye white. Face, back and tail blackish. Crown and nape olive yellow. Throat gray. Below olive yellow.

43. OLIVE-BACKED TANAGER **LM-F**
Mitrospingus oleagineus 18

Like 273-42 but head and back olive yellow. Below yellow.

44. BROWN TANAGER **LM-F**
Orchesticus abeillei 17

Bill black. Above brown.Wings and tail more rufous brown. Below ochraceous.

45. GRAY-HEADED TANAGER **L-TS**
Eucometis penicillata 17

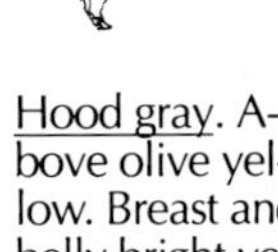

Hood gray. Above olive yellow. Breast and belly bright yellow.

Recent research indicates that #44 is actually an Olive-green Tanager (p.270 #16).

Conothraupis *Calochaetes*
Schistochlamys *Neothraupis*
Urothraupis *Bangsia*

46. BLACK-AND-WHITE TANAGER L-S
Conothraupis speculigera 17

Glossy blue-black. Rump gray. Wing speculum and belly white. F: Above olive. Below light yellow lightly streaked olive on breast.

47. BLACK-FACED TANAGER L-TSO
Schistochlamys melanopis 16

Gray, paler below. Bill short and stubby. Forecrown, face, throat and breast black. Imm: Olive green, paler below. Center of belly yellowish

immature

48. CINNAMON TANAGER LM-TS
Schistochlamys ruficapillus 15

Bill short and stubby. Mask black. Upperparts gray. Neck, throat, breast and crissum cinnamon. Belly white.

49. BLACK-BACKED BUSH-TANAGER H-TS
Urothraupis stolzmanni 15

Upperparts black. Extensive throat white. Below gray mottled white.

50. VERMILION TANAGER LM-FT
Calochaetes coccineus 16

Brilliant scarlet. Small mask, throat, wings and tail black.

51. WHITE-BANDED TANAGER L-S
Neothraupis fasciata 15

Upperparts bluish gray. Wing coverts black with single broad white bar. Face black. Below whitish.

52. BLACK-AND-GOLD TANAGER M-F
Bangsia melanochlamys 15

Mainly black. Shoulders and rump blue. Breast orange yellow. Broad yellow stripe to lower belly.

53. GOLDEN-CHESTED TANAGER LM-F
Bangsia rothschildi 15

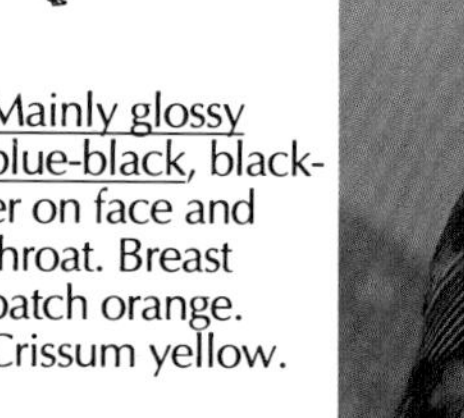

Mainly glossy blue-black, blacker on face and throat. Breast patch orange. Crissum yellow.

Bangsia
Dubusia
Cyanicterus
Heterospingus
Creurgops
Trichothraupis

54. MOSS-BACKED TANAGER LM-FT
Bangsia edwardsi 15

Above mostly moss green. Crown and nape black, face blue. Below yellowish green, breast patch yellow.

55. GOLD-RINGED TANAGER LM-F
Bangsia aureocincta 15

Like 275-54 but with yellow ring back of eye, encircling ear coverts.

56. CHESTNUT-BELLIED MOUNTAIN-TANAGER H-FT
Dubusia castaneoventris 15

Above blue, silvery on crown. Face and whisker black. Below chestnut.

57. BLUE-BACKED TANAGER L-F
Cyanicterus cyanicterus 15

Upperparts and throat bright blue. Breast and belly bright yellow. Thighs black. F: Above greenish blue.

58. SCARLET-BROWED TANAGER L-F
Heterospingus xanthopygius 15

Black. Eye stripe scarlet behind eye. Shoulders and rump yellow. F: Mostly gray. Large rump patch yellow.

59. RUFOUS-CRESTED TANAGER M-F
Creurgops verticalis 15

Above bluish gray. Crown patch and entire underparts cinnamon rufous. F: Lacks crown patch.

60. SLATY TANAGER M-F
Creurgops dentata 14

Slaty gray. Crown chestnut bordered black. F: No chestnut. Eyebrow, eye-ring and throat whitish. Below rufous.

61. BLACK-GOGGLED TANAGER LM-FT
Trichothraupis melanopus 15

Forehead and face black. Yellow crown stripe. Back olive gray. Wings and tail black. Underparts buff. F: No black or yellow.

Tersina
Iridosornis
Chlorothraupis

1. SWALLOW-TANAGER LM-FT
Tersina viridis 15

Greenish blue. Bill wide and flat. Face and throat black. Flanks barred dusky.
F: Grass green. Lacks black on face and throat.

2. GOLDEN-CROWNED TANAGER H-FT
Iridosornis rufivertex 15

Hood black with yellow crown patch. Rest of plumage shining purple-blue.

3. PURPLISH-MANTLED TANAGER M-F
Iridosornis porphyrocephala 15

Purplish blue. Wings and tail black broadly edged blue. Throat bright yellow. Center of belly buff. Crissum chestnut.

4. YELLOW-SCARFED TANAGER MH-FT
Iridosornis reinhardti 15

Like 276-2 but head all black and broad golden yellow band extends across nape to ear coverts.

5. YELLOW-THROATED TANAGER M-F
Iridosornis analis 14

Like 276-3. Lower breast and below all tawny buff.

6. GOLDEN-COLLARED TANAGER H-FT
Iridosornis jelskii 14

Back, wings and tail blue. Forehead, face and throat black. Crown and broad collar golden yellow. Above blue. Breast and belly dull chestnut.

7. OCHRE-BREASTED TANAGER L-FT
Chlorothraupis stolzmanni 15

Face, upperparts, and tail brownish olive. Throat grayish buffy. Center of breast and belly ochraceous buff.

8. LEMON-SPECTACLED (-BROWED) TANAGER L-F
Chlorothraupis olivacea 15

Dark olive. Prominent yellow lores and eye-ring. Throat and center of belly yellowish.

9. CARMIOL'S TANAGER L-F
Chlorothraupis carmioli 15

Like 276-8 but lacks bright yellow lores and eye-ring.

Tachyphonus: Black. Usually some white on shoulder.

10. FLAME-CRESTED TANAGER L-FT
Tachyphonus cristatus 15

Black. Crest red. Rump and throat buff. White patch sometimes shows at shoulder. F: Above all brownish. Narrow eye-ring buffy. Throat whitish. Below ochraceous.

female

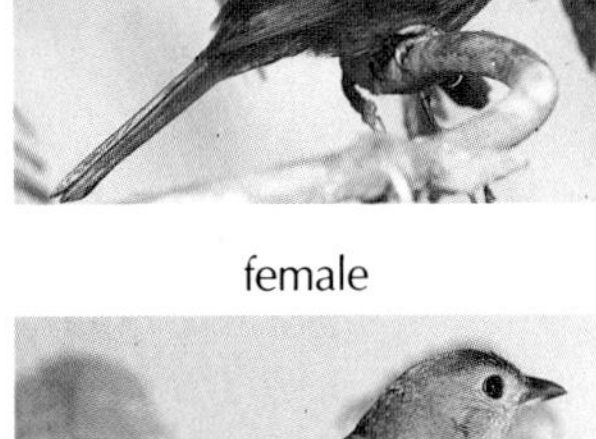

11. RED-SHOULDERED TANAGER L-SO
Tachyphonus phoenicius 15

Glossy black. Small shoulder spot red, usually not visible in field. Wing coverts may show a little white. F: Hood gray. Above brownish gray. Below whitish tinged grayish on breast. Tail blackish.

female

12. WHITE-LINED TANAGER L-TS
Tachyphonus rufus 15

female

Normally appears all black with small white line showing at shoulder. Sometimes no white shows at rest but white shoulders prominent in flight. F: Upperparts, wings and tail uniform rufous brown. Below slightly lighter rufous brown.

13. RUBY-CROWNED TANAGER LM-FT
Tachyphonus coronatus 15

female

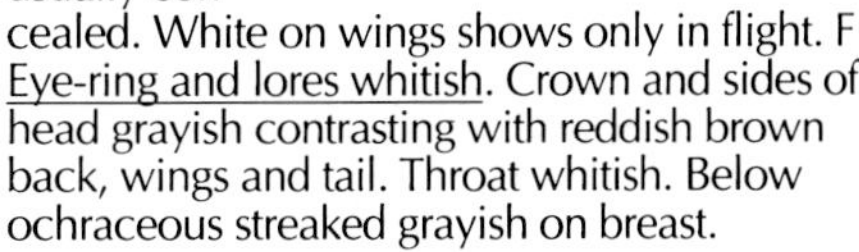

Glossy blue black. Stripe on crown red, usually concealed. White on wings shows only in flight. F: Eye-ring and lores whitish. Crown and sides of head grayish contrasting with reddish brown back, wings and tail. Throat whitish. Below ochraceous streaked grayish on breast.

14. YELLOW-CRESTED TANAGER L-FT
Tachyphonus rufiventer 14

Above black, throat and rump buff. Crest yellow. Face, neck, sides and narrow breast band black. Underparts chestnut. F: Above dull lemon color. Face grayish. Throat white. Below ochraceous.

Tachyphonus: Black. Usually some white on shoulder.
Hemispingus
Cnemoscopus

15. FULVOUS-CRESTED TANAGER L-F
Tachyphonus surinamus 14

Glossy black, shoulder white. Crown stripe fulvous. Rump pale ochraceous. F: Head gray. with yellow spectacles. Back olive. Underparts buffy.

female

16. TAWNY-CRESTED TANAGER L-F
Tachyphonus delatrii 14

Black with large orange crest. F:All dark brown.

female

17. GRAY-CAPPED HEMISPINGUS MH-FT
Hemispingus reyi 14

Cap gray. Above olive. Below yellow, more olive on sides and vent.

18. BLACK-CAPPED HEMISPINGUS MH-FT
Hemispingus atropileus 15

Crown and face black. Long eyebrow white. Above olive green. Underparts dull oily olive yellow.

19. GRAY-HOODED BUSH-TANAGER H-F
Cnemoscopus rubrirostris 15

Bill pink. Hood gray. Back, wings and tail olive. Belly bright yellow.

20. SUPERCILIARIED HEMISPINGUS MH-F
Hemispingus superciliaris 14

Upperparts, wings and tail olive green. Eyebrow whitish. Below yellow, tinged olive on sides.

21. OLEAGINOUS HEMISPINGUS MH-F
Hemispingus frontalis 14

Above olive with long, narrow, yellowish eye-brow. Underparts dull yellowish olive.

Hemispingus
Chlorospingus

22. BLACK-EARED HEMISPINGUS M-FT
Hemispingus melanotis 14

Variable. Above gray, rump olive, wings and tail browner. Face black. Below cinnamon to buff. Rather like 280-40 but no blue.

23. SLATY-BACKED HEMISPINGUS H-FT
Hemispingus goeringi 14

Head black, long eyebrow white. Above slaty gray. Below rufous, flanks grayish brown.

24. DRAB HEMISPINGUS H-F
Hemispingus xanthophthalmus 14

Like gray-backed form of 278-20 but no eyebrow. Eye yellow (not brown). Below grayish white.

25. BLACK-HEADED HEMISPINGUS H-FT
Hemispingus verticalis 13

Hood black with pale crown stripe. Eye pale. Back gray, wings and tail blackish. Below gray. Belly white.

26. THREE-STRIPED HEMISPINGUS H-F
Hemispingus trifasciatus 13

Crown stripe and long eyebrow buffy white. Above olive brown. Face black. Underparts ochraceous tawny.

29. YELLOW-GREEN BUSH-TANAGER LM-FT
Chorospingus flavovirens 13

Crown and face dark gray. Forecrown blackish. Back olive green. Underparts yellowish.

28. YELLOW-THROATED BUSH-TANAGER LM-F
Chlorospingus flavigularis 13

Upperparts yellowish olive. Lores gray. Throat yellow (Only sides of throat yellow w of Andes). Below gray.

29. COMMON BUSH-TANAGER MH-TS
Chlorospingus ophthalmicus 13

Crown, nape and face blackish (white back of eye in some). Throat white more or less speckled blackish. Breast yellow. Belly whitish.

30. YELLOW-WHISKERED (SHORT-BILLED) BUSH-TANAGER M-F
Chlorospingus parvirostris 14

Very like 279-28 but lores olive. Yellow mostly on sides of throat.

31. ASH-THROATED BUSH-TANAGER M-FT
Chlorospingus canigularis 13

Crown gray, throat unspotted. Above olive green. Breast yellow. Belly whitish.

Chlorospingus
Thlypopsis
Lamprospiza
Pipraeidea
Tangara

32. DUSKY-BELLIED BUSH-TANAGER **LM-FT**
Chlorospingus semifuscus 13

Eye yellow. Hood and underparts gray. Back, wings and tail dark olive.

33. ORANGE-HEADED TANAGER **L-TS**
Thlypopsis sordida 13

Above gray. Hood orange, yellower on throat. Breast light gray. Crissum and center of belly white.

34. FULVOUS-HEADED TANAGER **M-T**
Thlypopsis fulviceps 13

Like 280-33 but hood more rufous and darker gray above and below.

35. BUFF-BELLIED TANAGER **M-T**
Thlypopsis inornata 13

Like 280-33 but crown orange rufous and underparts cinnamon buff.

36. RUFOUS-CHESTED TANAGER **M-FT**
Thlypopsis ornata 13

Hood and underparts orange rufous, center of belly white. Upperparts, wings and tail gray.

37. BROWN-FLANKED TANAGER **H-TS**
Thlypopsis pectoralis 12

Head, throat and breast orange rufous. Back, wings and tail gray. Center of belly white, flanks grayish brown.

38. RUST-AND-YELLOW TANAGER **MH-FT**
Thlypopsis ruficeps 12

Head orange rufous. Back,wings and tail olive green. Below bright yellow, olive at sides.

39. RED-BILLED PIED TANAGER **L-F**
Lamprospiza melanoleuca 15

Bill red. Upperparts, wings and tail blue-black. Throat black. Below white. F: Blue-gray nape and back.

40. FAWN-BREASTED TANAGER **LM-FT**
Pipraeidea melanonota 14

Upperparts bright light blue, back and wings darker blue. Forehead and mask black. Underparts buff.

41. GRAY-AND-GOLD TANAGER **L-F**
Tangara palmeri 14

Forehead and mask black. Upperparts pale grayish. Wings and tail black. Below whitish, with fringe of black spots across breast.

Tangara

42. OPAL-CROWNED TANAGER L-FT
Tangara callophrys 14

Forecrown, eyebrow and rump silvery whitish. Back, wings and tail black. Underparts shining purple. Crissum black.

43. OPAL-RUMPED TANAGER L-FT
Tangara velia 14

Very like 281-42 but no silvery whitish on head or belly. Crissum chestnut.

44. PARADISE TANAGER L-FT
Tangara chilensis 14

Crown and face yellowish green. Back and tail black. Rump red. Underparts brilliant blue, black in center.

45. SEVEN-COLORED TANAGER L-FT
Tangara fastuosa 14

Forehead and chin black. Rest of head shining turquoise blue. Mantle, lower throat and upper breast black. Lower breast turquoise blue. Belly violet blue. Lesser wing coverts turquoise blue. Greater coverts violet blue. Tail black.

46. GREEN-HEADED TANAGER LM-FT
Tangara seledon 14

Head and mantle green. Throat black. Rump orange. Below shining blue. Tail black, edged green.

47. GILT-EDGED TANAGER M-F
Tangara cyanoventris 14

Crown and face yellow. Forehead and throat black. Above streaked black and gold. Below shining blue. Wings and tail black, feathers edged green.

48. BRASSY-BREASTED TANAGER M-F
Tangara desmaresti 14

Green. Prominent breast patch ochre yellow. Above streaked black and green.

49. BLUE-WHISKERED TANAGER L-T
Tangara johannae 13

Crown green. Forehead, face and throat black. Short blue whisker streak. Throat edged below with blue. Breast greenish yellow. Rump yellow. Belly green.

Tangara

50. GREEN-AND-GOLD TANAGER **L-FT**
Tangara schrankii 13

Crown, rump and breast yellow. Face black with small green crescent before eye (hard to see in field). Back streaked black and green.

51. EMERALD TANAGER **L-F**
Tangara florida 13

Crown, rump and belly yellow. Ear patch black. Back streaked green and black. Face and underparts green. F: Crown green.

52. GOLDEN TANAGER **LM-F**
Tangara arthus 13

Variable. Orange-yellow, prominent ear patch black. Back streaked black and gold. Rump yellow. Chin black. Underparts yellow. (Breast chestnut in some races).

53. GOLDEN-EARED TANAGER **M-FT**
Tangara chrysotis 13

Mostly green. Crown and nape black. Eyebrow shining yellow. Eye patch coppery. Back streaked black and green. Breast and sides green. Belly chestnut.

54. FLAME-FACED TANAGER **M-FT**
Tangara parzudakii 13

Face flame-red. Crown and neck yellow. Large shoulder patch white. Back black. Underparts whitish.

55. RUFOUS-CHEEKED TANAGER **M-FT**
Tangara rufigenis 13

Crown and rump glistening blue-green. Back dark green. Wings and tail black. Cheeks and throat rufous. Breast silvery green to blue. Center of belly and crissum cinnamon buff.

56. SCRUB TANAGER **LM-S**
Tangara vitriolina 13

Crown rufous. Face black. Above silvery green, wings often bluer. Below greenish or grayish. Belly and undertail coverts buff.

Tangara
Cypsnagra
Tachyphonus

57. BURNISHED-BUFF TANAGER L-TSO
Tangara cayana 13

form in n

form in s

Form in n: Like 282-56 but back and underparts straw color (not green or gray) and crown not rufous (only tinged rufous). Throat often bluish.
Form in s: Upperparts straw color, crown tinged rufous. Face neck and center of underparts deep black. Wings blue.

58. CHESTNUT-BACKED TANAGER LM-FT
Tangara preciosa 14

female

Crown, nape and mantle bright coppery chestnut (f.crown and nape only). Underparts silvery bluish green (f. pale silvery green

59. BLACK-BACKED TANAGER L-FT
Tangara peruviana 13

Like 283-58 but center of back black.

60. BLUE-AND-BLACK TANAGER H-FT
Tangara vassorii 13

Uniform shining purplish blue (nape patch yellow in s). Wings, and tail black.

61. WHITE-RUMPED TANAGER L-S
Cypsnagra hirundinacea 14

Above black. Wing coverts and large area on rump white. Throat deep buff, becoming paler on breast and white on belly.

62. WHITE-SHOULDERED TANAGER LM-FT
Tachyphonus luctuosus 12

female

Glossy black except large white patch on shoulder. F: Hood gray, throat paler. Above yellowish green. Breast and below bright yellow.

Tangara

63. SPECKLED TANAGER M-F
Tangara guttata 13

Above yellowish green spotted black. Face yellow. Below white, speckled on sides. Cf. 287-9.

64. SILVER-THROATED TANAGER LM-FT
Tangara icterocephala 12

Cap yellow. Back striped yellow and black. Wings and tail black. Rump yellow. Throat silvery white. Below yellow.

65. SAFFRON-CROWNED TANAGER M-FT
Tangara xanthocephala 12

Crown and neck yellow. Face black. Back striped bluish and black. Rump and breast blue. Belly buff.

66. SILVERY TANAGER M-FT
Tangara viridicollis 12

Crown and nape black. Back shining silvery. Wings and tail black, edged blue. Below mostly black. F: Crown brown. Breast dull silvery green. Belly gray.

67. MASKED TANAGER L-FT
Tangara nigrocincta 12

Hood pale silvery blue. Mask, back and breast black. Rump blue. Belly white.

68. GOLDEN-HOODED TANAGER L-TS
Tangara larvata (nigrocincta) 12

Hood yellow, mask black. Above black. Large shoulder patch and rump blue.

69. GOLDEN-NAPED TANAGER M-FT
Tangara ruficervix 12

Mainly turquoise blue, more purplish in Peru. Crown blackish, hindcrown golden or orange. Center of belly buff.

70. BLUE-NECKED TANAGER LM-TS
Tangara cyanicollis 12

Hood blue. Lores black. Back black. Wing coverts blue to gold. Rump blue. Breast and belly black.

Tangara
Piranga

71. TURQUOISE TANAGER L-FT
Tangara mexicana 12

Appears mostly black above with blue rump and shoulders. Fore-crown, face and breast purplish blue. Below yellow.

72. BAY-HEADED TANAGER LM-FT
Tangara gyrola 13

Hood reddish chestnut. Body blue or green with more or less yellow on shoulders or neck.

73. RUFOUS-WINGED TANAGER L-FT
Tangara lavinia 12

Like 285-72 but with prominent rufous patch on wings. F: Duller but usually with some rufous on head and wings.

74. METALLIC-GREEN TANAGER M-FT
Tangara labradorides 13

Mostly shining silver green or bluish. Broad eyestripe straw color. Hindcrown, face. wings and tail black.Crissum buff.

75. BERYL-SPANGLED TANAGER M-FT
Tangara nigroviridis 12

Forehead, face and back black. Crown and rump silvery blue. Mantle and underparts spotted black and silvery blue.

76. BLACK-CAPPED TANAGER M-FTS
Tangara heinei 13

Cap and nape black (f. grayish green). Cheeks shining green. Below glistening green, scaled black on breast. Belly grayish.

77. RUFOUS-THROATED TANAGER LM-FT
Tangara rufigula 12

Cap, cheeks and nape black. Back, wings and tail scaled yellowish. Throat rufous. Below white, spotted black.

78. WHITE-WINGED TANAGER LM-FT
Piranga leucoptera 13

Red. Lores, wings and tail black, wings with bold white wing-bars. F: Olive above. Yellow below. Wings grayish black with two bold white bars. Tail grayish black.

Tangara *Nemosia*
Hemithraupis *Chlorochrysa*

79. RED-NECKED TANAGER LM-F
Tangara cyanocephala 12

Broad collar crimson. Crown blue. Eye-ring lighter blue. Underparts green. Wings and tail black edged green.

1. YELLOW-BACKED TANAGER L-FT
Hemithraupis flavicollis 12

Cap, back, wings and tail black. Rump extensively yellow. Speculum white. Throat yellow or white. Below whitish. Crissum yellow. F: Dull olive green, yellow below.

2. GUIRA TANAGER LM-FT
Hemithraupis guira 12

Above yellowish green. Rump and breast ochraceous. Face and throat black. Eyebrow yellow. Crissum and center of belly yellow. F: Dull olive green, yellow below.

3. RUFOUS-HEADED TANAGER LM-FT
Hemithraupis ruficapilla 12

Hood orange rufous, ear patch yellow. Back, wings and tail olive green. Rump and breast ochraceous. Belly whitish. F: Above olive green. Crissum yellow.

4. HOODED TANAGER L-TS
Nemosia pileata 12

Above, wings and tail blue-gray. Head and neck black (f. lacking). Lores white. Eye yellow. Underparts white.

5. ORANGE-EARED TANAGER M-F
Chlorochrysa calliparaea 12

Upperparts shining green with yellow spot on crown. Rump orange. Orange tufts on ear coverts. Throat black. Breast and belly shining blue.

6. GLISTENING-GREEN TANAGER M-F
Chlorochrysa phoenicotis 12

Shining green. Small spot back of ear coverts gray and red.

7. MULTICOLORED TANAGER LM-F
Chlorochrysa nitidissima 12

Hood and back yellow. Nape green. Patch below ear coverts black. Belly glistening blue in center, sides green. F: Lacks yellow back.

Tangara
Erythrothlypis

8. YELLOW-BELLIED TANAGER L-FT
Tangara xanthogastra 12

Upperparts, throat and breast green spotted black. Rump green. Center of belly bright yellow. Tail black edged green. Cf. 284-63.

9. SPOTTED TANAGER L-F
Tangara punctata 11

All scaled green and black except belly white. No yellow on face. Cf. 284-63.

10. DOTTED TANAGER L-FT
Tangara varia 10

Body all green. Very sparsely spotted black. Wings and tail light blue.

11. BLUE-BROWED TANAGER M-FT
Tangara cyanotis 12

Above mostly black (dark blue in s). Long, broad eyebrow, wing coverts, rump, throat and breast sky blue. Belly and crissum buff.

12. PLAIN-COLORED TANAGER L-T
Tangara inornata 12

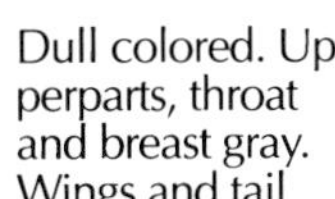

Dull colored. Upperparts, throat and breast gray. Wings and tail black. Wing coverts bright blue (sometimes hard to see). Belly white.

13. GREEN-THROATED TANAGER M-FT
Tangara argyrofenges 12

Crown, wings and tail black. Back straw color. Cheeks and throat silvery green. Below black.

14. BLACK-HEADED TANAGER LM-F
Tangara cyanoptera 12

Hood black. Back and underparts greenish yellow. Wings and tail black, feathers edged blue. F: Mostly greenish. Has no black.

15. SCARLET-AND-WHITE TANAGER L-F
Erythrothlypis salmoni 12

Hood and breast flame scarlet. Back red. Wings brownish red. Belly red in center. Sides white. F: Above uniform bronzy olive. Below whitish.

female

EUPHONIAS GROUPED BY AMOUNT OF YELLOW IN CROWN.

Pyrrhocoma *Chlorophonia*
Pseudodacnis *Euphonia*

16. CHESTNUT-HEADED TANAGER LM-FT
Pyrrhocoma ruficeps 12

Hood chestnut, forehead and lores black. Rest of plumage dark gray, lighter on belly. F: Olive. Head cinnamon. Cf. 280-33.

17. TURQUOISE DACNIS-TANAGER M-F
Pseudodacnis hartlaubi 11

Eye yellow. Crown and rump blue. Nape, back, wings and tail black. Throat black. Below blue.

18. BLUE-NAPED CHLOROPHONIA LMH-FT
Chlorophonia cyanea 11

Head, throat and breast bright grass green. Narrow eye-ring, upper back and rump bright blue. Belly golden yellow. F: No blue on rump. Underparts duller yellow.

19. YELLOW-COLLARED CHLOROPHONIA L-F
Chlorophonia flavirostris 10

female

Bright grass green. Eye-ring yellow. Broad collar yellow. Rump and belly yellow. F: No collar. Below yellowish.

20. CHESTNUT-BREASTED CHLOROPHONIA MH-F
Chlorophonia pyrrhophrys 11

Crown and nape blue bordered black. Back and wings green. Rump yellow. Throat green. Below yellow with central stripe chestnut (f. lacks chestnut).

EUPHONIAS - GROUP I.
(Crown nearly or all yellow)

1. THICK-BILLED EUPHONIA LM-T
Euphonia laniirostris 12

Slightly thicker bill hard to see in field. Yellow forecrown reaches past eye. Above blue black. Underparts all bright yellow. F: Olive above. Olive yellow below. Center of belly clear yellow.

female

2. ORANGE-BELLIED EUPHONIA LM-FT
Euphonia xanthogaster 11

Forecrown to past eye yellow. Upperparts, face and throat black. Below orange. F: Above olive. Forehead yellowish. Nape and underparts grayish.

Euphonia

3. TAWNY-CAPPED EUPHONIA L-T
Euphonia anneae 11

Like 288-2 but entire crown rufous chestnut. F: Forecrown rufous.

4. ORANGE-CROWNED EUPHONIA L-TS
Euphonia saturata 10

Entire crown and nape orange yellow. Above black. Throat and breast black. Below orange. F: Bright yellowish olive.

5. TRINIDAD EUPHONIA L-FTS
Euphonia trinitatis 9

Like 288-2 but yellow crown extends only slightly beyond eye. Throat black. Crissum yellow.

EUPHONIAS GROUP 2.
(Crown about half yellow)

6. GREEN-THROATED EUPHONIA L-FT
Euphonia chalybea 11

Upperparts shiny bronze green. Yellow forecrown reaches only to eye. Chin black. Below bright yellow.

7. VIOLACEOUS EUPHONIA L-T
Euphonia violacea 10

Yellow forecrown reaches only to eye. Large white spots on two outer tail feathers.

female

8. PURPLE-THROATED EUPHONIA L-TS
Euphonia chlorotica 10

Very like 288-2 but with forecrown only to eye yellow. F: Bright olive green above, forehead dull yellowish.

9. FULVOUS-VENTED EUPHONIA L-T
Euphonia fulvicrissa 9

Yellow forecrown reaches slightly past eye. Throat black. Below yellow. Crissum tawny in m and f.

10. WHITE-VENTED EUPHONIA L-FT
Euphonia minuta 9

Yellow forehead reaches only to eye. Throat black. Belly and crissum white.

11. FINSCH'S EUPHONIA LM-TS
Euphonia finschi 9

Like 288-2 but belly and crissum fulvous (not white).

12. VELVET-FRONTED EUPHONIA L-TS
Euphonia concinna 9

Like 288-2 but forehead black with small yellow patch on forecrown.

13. BRONZE-GREEN EUPHONIA M-FT
Euphonia mesochrysa 9

Bronzy green. Forehead yellow. Belly and crissum yellow. Below more olive (f. gray).

Euphonia

EUPHONIAS GROUP 3.
(Crown with no yellow)

14. BLUE-HOODED EUPHONIA M-T
Euphonia musica 11

female

Crown and nape blue. Forehead, face, throat and back black. Below and rump yellow. F: Olive green. Forehead rufous. Crown like m.

15. CHESTNUT-BELLIED EUPHONIA L-FT
Euphonia pectoralis 11

Upperparts, throat and breast blue-black, patch at sides of breast yellow. Belly dark chestnut. F: Above olive green. Below olive yellow on sides, gray in center.

female

16. WHITE-LORED (GOLDEN-BELLIED) EUPHONIA L-TS
Euphonia chrysopasta 11

female

Above olive. Large spot before eye whitish (both m and f). Below yellow (f. whitish).

17. RUFOUS-BELLIED EUPHONIA L-FT
Euphonia rufiventris 10

No yellow on head. Upperparts, throat and breast steel blue. Below orange rufous. No white in tail. F: Olive, nape gray. Crissum rufous.

18. GOLDEN-SIDED EUPHONIA L-FT
Euphonia cayannensis 10

All steel blue except patch at sides of breast orange yellow. F: Above olive. Below gray in center, olive yellow on sides. Vent gray.

19. PLUMBEOUS EUPHONIA L-FT
Euphonia plumbea 9

Upperparts, sides of head, throat and breast glossy grayish blue. Belly rich yellow. F: Crown and nape gray (no yellow). Above olive. Throat pale gray. Below yellow.

Saltator: Bill heavy. Throat white.

1. RUFOUS-BELLIED SALTATOR **H-S**
Saltator rufiventris 21

Upperparts, throat and breast gray. Wings and tail dusky. Broad eyebrow white. Belly rufous.

2. BLACK-COWLED SALTATOR **M-TS**
Saltator nigriceps 20

Gray. Bill red. Head black. Center of belly buff. Outer tail feathers tipped white.

3. BUFF-THROATED SALTATOR **L-FT**
Saltator maximus 19

Upperparts, wings and tail bright olive green. Short eyebrow white. Throat and crissum buff. Whisker black.

4. BLACK-WINGED SALTATOR **M-FT**
Saltator atripennis 19

Crown black (gray in w). Back olive. Wings black. Face black. Ear patch and long eyebrow white.Throat white. Below light gray.

5. GREEN-WINGED SALTATOR **LM-TS**
Saltator similis 19

Very like 291-6 but crown and mantle olive and edges of wings bright green. Range mostly different.

6. GRAYISH SALTATOR **L-TSA**
Saltator coerulescens 19

Nondescript. Dull gray to dark gray above. Medium eyebrow white. Throat white. Whiskers black. Below grayish.

7. GOLDEN-BILLED SALTATOR **MH-TS**
Saltator aurantiirostris 18

imm. male

Bill yellow. Above gray. Face black. Throat and long eye stripe white. Broad breast band black. Below buffy. Tail black tipped white.

8. MASKED SALTATOR **MH-F**
Saltator cinctus 19

Above dark gray. Mask and whiskers black. Breast white with black band below. Sides gray. Belly and crissum white.

9. BLACK-THROATED SALTATOR **L-S**
Saltator atricollis 19

Bill orange. Above brown. Lores, cheeks and throat black. Ear coverts and sides of neck gray. Breast and belly white, flanks buffy. Tail dusky.

Saltator
Periporphyrus
Pitylus: Bill bright red.

Pheucticus: Bill very heavy.

10. THICK-BILLED SALTATOR LM-TS
Saltator maxillosus 18

Like 291-6 but bill stubby. Long eyebrow white. Throat buff (not white).

11. STREAKED SALTATOR LM-TS
Saltator albicollis 18

Above olive, rump and tail grayer. Short eyebrow white. Below white streaked gray (unstreaked race in s).

12. ORINOCAN SALTATOR L-TS
Saltator orenocensis 16

Upperparts gray. Long white eyebrow conspicuous. White spot at base of lower bill. Face and neck black. Throat white. Below buffy.

13. RED-AND-BLACK GROSBEAK L-F
Periporphyrus erythromelas 19

Crimson (f. olive). Hood and breast black.

14. BLACK-THROATED GROSBEAK L-F
Pitylus fuliginosus 18

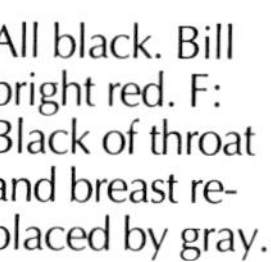

All black. Bill bright red. F: Black of throat and breast replaced by gray.

15. SLATE-COLORED GROSBEAK L-F
Pitylus grossus 17

Bill bright red. Dark gray, wings blacker. Throat white surrounded by black. Below gray.

16. BLACK-BACKED GROSBEAK MH-TS
Pheucticus aureoventris 19

Hood black. Back black but varies in yellow on rump. Wings black with large white patches. Belly yellow. Tail black, outers broadly tipped white. F: Browner. Eyebrow yellow and below mottled black in some.

Pheucticus: Bill very heavy.
Caryothraustes: Bill heavy.
Cyanocompsa: Bill very heavy.
Cyanoloxia

17. ROSE-BREASTED GROSBEAK **LM-T**
Pheucticus ludovicianus 19

Black. Large white patches on wings. Breast red. Below white. F: Brown, streaked black. Crown stripe and long eyebrow white. Below buffy, heavily streaked dusky. Nb male: Rather like f. but breast reddish.

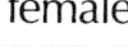

nb male

female

20. YELLOW-SHOULDERED GROSBEAK **L-FT**
Caryothraustes humeralis 15

Like 293-19 but crown gray and broad eye stripe black.

21 BLUE-BLACK GROSBEAK **L-F**
Cyanocompsa cyanoides 15

Dark blue. F: Uniform reddish brown.

male

female

18. YELLOW GROSBEAK **LMH-TSA**
Pheucticus chrysopeplus 18

Yellow. Back more or less streaked dusky. Wings black with large white patches. Underparts bright yellow. Tail black broadly edged white.

19. YELLOW-GREEN GROSBEAK **L-FT**
Caryothraustes canadensis 16

Upperparts yellow. Face and throat black. Below yellowish.

22. ULTRAMARINE GROSBEAK **LM-ST**
Cyanocompsa cyanea 14

Very like 293-21 but bill shorter and more curved. F: Pale brown.

23. INDIGO GROSBEAK **L-S**
Cyanoloxia glaucocaerulea 14

Bill small and stubby for a grosbeak. Bright light blue. Wings and tail black edged blue. F: Above dark brown, lighter brown below.

male

female

Embernagra
Atlapetes

24. GREAT PAMPA-FINCH **LM-SO**
Embernagra platensis 19

Bill orange, ridge black. Upperparts olive. Below grayish. Belly white in center.

25. PALE- (BUFF-) THROATED PAMPA-FINCH **L-O**
Embernagra longicauda 19

Like 294-24 but eyebrow, throat and spot below eye whitish.

26. BLACK-HEADED BRUSH-FINCH **LM-FT**
Atlapetes atricapillus 18

Cap, face and nape deep black. Back and wings olive green. Underparts white, sides gray. Tail black.

27. TRICOLORED BRUSH-FINCH **M-FT**
Atlapetes tricolor 16

Like 295-38 but crown and nape brownish gold (and has no speculum in n).

28. RUFOUS-EARED BRUSH-FINCH **H-T**
Atlapetes rufigenis 17

Cap and nape bright rufous. Lores, throat and sides of neck white. Whisker black. Back, wings and tail grayish. Underparts whitish, clouded gray on breast.

29. CHESTNUT-CAPPED BRUSH-FINCH **M-FT**
Atlapetes brunneinucha 17

Forecrown black with three small white spots. Crown and nape chestnut. Face black. Back and wings olive green. Throat and center of underparts white. Narrow black breast band (lacking in w).

30. STRIPE-HEADED BRUSH-FINCH **MH-FT**
Atlapetes torquatus 17

Crown black with three gray stripes. Back and wings olive. Face black. Underparts white (with black breast band e of Andes). Cf. 300-9.

31. WHITE-RIMMED BRUSH-FINCH **M-F**
Atlapetes leucopis 17

Dark bird. Crown and nape chestnut. Face black. Eye-ring and short eye stripe white. Above black. Throat gray. Below dark olive green.

Atlapetes

32. SLATY BRUSH-FINCH MH-FT
Atlapetes schistaceus 17

Crown and nape rufous. Face black. Above slate gray (with conspicuous speculum in w). Throat white. Whisker black. Below gray, white in center.

33. YELLOW-THROATED BRUSH-FINCH M-TS
Atlapetes gutturalis 17

Cap black, central streak white. Above gray. Throat bright yellow. Below whitish.

34. MOUSTACHED BRUSH-FINCH M-F
Atlapetes albofrenatus 16

Crown and nape chestnut. Forehead, face and neck black. Malar white. Narrow whisker black. Back olive. Throat white. Below bright yellow. Sides and crissum olive.

35. PALE-NAPED BRUSH-FINCH MH-TS
Atlapetes pallidinucha 16

Forecrown cinnamon. Hindcrown and nape white. Face black. Above dusky gray. Underparts dull yellow.

36. RUSTY-BELLIED BRUSH-FINCH MH-T
Atlapetes nationi 16

Cap dark brown with forecrown and eyebrow grayish. Back, wings and tail grayish brown. Eye-ring and throat white. Breast gray. Belly cinnamon.

37. SANTA MARTA BRUSH-FINCH M-FTS
Atlapetes melanocephalus 16

Head black, conspicuous cheek patch gray. Above dark gray. Underparts bright yellow.

38. RUFOUS-NAPED BRUSH-FINCH M-TS
Atlapetes rufinucha 16

Variable. Crown and nape chestnut. Above gray to black (with prominent speculum in n). Underparts yellow.

39. TEPUI BRUSH-FINCH M-TS
Atlapetes personatus 16

Varies from head rufous to hood, nape and breast rufous. Below yellow. Back dark gray.

Atlapetes

40. BAY-CROWNED BRUSH-FINCH M-TS
Atlapetes seebohmi 16

Like 295-32 but lacking white lores or wing speculum. Side of neck white in s.

41. WHITE-HEADED BRUSH-FINCH LM-TS
Atlapetes albiceps 15

Forecrown, face and throat white. Hindcrown black. Back brown. Speculum white. Breast gray. Belly buffy.

42. PALE-HEADED BRUSH-FINCH LM-SA
Atlapetes pallidiceps 15

Head whitish, eye-stripe pale brown. Above light brownish. Conspicuous white speculum. Below white, sides gray.

43. DUSKY-HEADED BRUSH-FINCH M-TS
Atlapetes fusco-olivaceus 16

Above dark olive green. Head brownish black. Distinct dusky whisker. Below yellow, mottled olive on sides. Tail blackish.

44. OLIVE-HEADED BRUSH-FINCH M-TS
Atlapetes flaviceps 16

Head and nape yellowish olive. Eye-ring, lores and underparts yellow.

45. OCHRE-BREASTEED BRUSH-FINCH MH-TS
Atlapetes semirufus 15

Hood, nape and underparts orange rufous. Center of belly yellow. Back, wings and tail olive.

46. FULVOUS-HEADED BRUSH-FINCH M-T
Atlapetes fulviceps 15

Head and whisker rufous chestnut. Loral spot and underparts yellow. Back, wings and tail olive.

47. WHITE-WINGED BRUSH-FINCH MH-TS
Atlapetes leucopterus 15

Crown rufous. Back, wings and tail gray. Narrow black whisker. Conspicuous wing speculum white. Face black. Underparts white, sides gray. In s Ecuador and Peru, forecrown and face white.

Atlapetes
Gubernatrix
Cardinalis
Paroaria
Phrygilus

48. YELLOW-STRIPED BRUSH-FINCH M-TS
Atlapetes citrinellus 15

Above brownish olive. Conspicuous eyebrow and underparts yellow. Face and whisker black.

49. YELLOW CARDINAL L-S
Gubernatrix cristata 19

Long pointed crest and throat black. Broad eyebrow and whisker bright yellow (f. white). Wings brown, bars yellow.

50. VERMILION CARDINAL L-SA
Cardinalis phoeniceus 18

All red. Long upright crest. F: Upperparts brown with small red crest. Underparts ochraceous buff.

51. RED-CRESTED CARDINAL L-SO
Paroaria coronata 17

Long crest, hood and throat extending to a point on breast scarlet. Back gray. Below white. Tail black.

52. RED-COWLED CARDINAL L-S
Paroaria dominicana 17

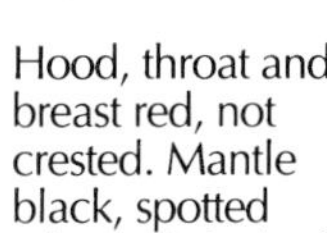

Hood, throat and breast red, not crested. Mantle black, spotted white. Flight feathers edged white.

53. RED-CAPPED CARDINAL L-SW
Paroaria gularis 16

Hood crimson (with broad black eye-stripe in n). Back black. Throat red or black. Below white.

54. CRIMSON-FRONTED CARDINAL L-SW
Paroaria baeri 17

Very like 297-53 form with black eye-stripe, but hindcrown black and black band on breast.

55. YELLOW-BILLED CARDINAL L-SW
Paroaria capitata 17

Bill and legs completely brownish pink (upper bill not black). White collar nearly complete. Cf. 297-53.

56. WHITE-THROATED SIERRA-FINCH H-O
Phrygilus erythronotus 16

Quite like 299-67 but lacks white on wings or eye-ring and crissum is pinkish.

57. RED-BACKED SIERRA-FINCH H-O
Phrygilus dorsalis 15

Very like 299-67 but back rufous brown. Belly all white instead of white only in center.

Phrygilus
Emberizoides
Oreothraupis
Compsospiza
Idiopsar

58. GRAY-HOODED SIERRA-FINCH MH-O
Phrygilus gayi 16

Hood dark gray. Above yellowish green, rump yellower. Below bright greenish yellow. F: No definite hood. Back olivaceous. Below paler, more greenish

female

59. BLACK-HOODED SIERRA-FINCH H-SO
Phrygilis atriceps 15

Hood, wings and tail deep black. Back bright brown. Belly yellow. F: No black hood. Back pale brown.

60. MOURNING SIERRA-FINCH H-SO
Phrygilus fructiceti 16

Slate gray streaked black. Double wing-bar white. Bill orange. Throat and breast black. Below gray. F: Below dirty white, streaked dusky on throat and breast.

61. WEDGE-TAILED GRASS-FINCH L-O
Emberizoides herbicola 15+3

Tail extended, pointed. Upperparts brown streaked black. Lores and eye-ring white. Below whitish.

62. TANAGER-FINCH M-F
Oreothraupis arremonops 18

Cap black with three prominent broad whitish stripes. Back, wings, breast and sides rufous. Center of belly gray.

63. TUCUMAN MOUNTAIN-FINCH H-S
Compsospiza baeri 16

Gray. Forecrown, eyebrow, malar stripe and throat rufous. Belly light gray. Crissum rufous.

64. COCHABAMBA MOUNTAIN-FINCH H-S
Compsospiza garleppi 17

Gray. Forecrown, eyebrow, malar stripe and entire underparts rufous.

65. SHORT-TAILED FINCH H-O
Idiopsar brachyurus 17

Leaden gray, paler below, whitish on belly. Wings and tail black. Bill long and slender for a finch.

Poospizopsis *Spiza*
Diuca *Arremenops*
Saltatricula *Aimophila*

66. CHESTNUT-BREASTED MOUNTAIN-FINCH **H-S**
Poospizopsis caesar 17

Gray. Forecrown, lores and face black. Eyebrow, throat and belly white. Breast and crissum chestnut.

67. COMMON DIUCA-FINCH **LM-SO**
Diuca diuca 16

Ashy gray, partial eye-ring white. Throat and center of belly white. Crissum tinged chestnut. Tail black, ends of outers white.

68. WHITE-WINGED DIUCA-FINCH **H-O**
Diuca speculifera 16

Like 299-67 but spot below eye and broad patch on wing white. Rocky slopes.

69. MANY-COLORED CHACO-FINCH **L-S**
Saltatricula multicolor 16

Eyebrow white. Above light sandy brown, rump gray. Forehead, lores, cheeks and sides of neck black. Throat white. Sides cinnamon. Belly white.

1. DICKCISSEL **L-0**
*Spiza americana** 15

Nb male and female: Head pale gray, eyebrow yellow. Above brown, streaked black on back. Prominent chestnut area on shoulders. Throat white. Breast yellow to whitish on belly.

2. BLACK-STRIPED SPARROW **L-TS**
Arremonops conirostris 15

Head gray, striped black. Above olive green. Bend of wing yellow. Below whitish, sides darker.

3. TOCUYO SPARROW **L-SA**
Arremonops tocuyensis 13

Like 299-2 but brow whitish.

4. TUMBES SPARROW **L-SA**
Aimophila (Rhynchospiza) stolzmanni 14

Crown chestnut with broad gray center stripe and eyebrow. Above brown streaked dusky. Whisker black. Bend of wing yellow. Shoulder chestnut. Below whitish.

5. STRIPE-CAPPED SPARROW **L-O**
Aimophila strigiceps 15

Crown brown with gray stripes. Above streaked black. Eye stripe black. Throat white. Whisker dusky. Below gray to whitish.

Piezorhina
Arremon
Incaspiza
Poospiza

6. CINEREOUS FINCH **L-SA**
Piezorhina cinerea 15

Bill heavy, yellow. Lores and malar black. Above pale gray, sides of rump white. Below whitish tinged gray on breast.

7. SAFFRON-BILLED SPARROW **LM-TS**
Arremon flavirostris 15

Bill orange, ridge black. Head black. Crown stripe gray. Brows white. Back and wings olive. Mantle gray. Shoulders yellow.

8. BLACK-CAPPED SPARROW **L-TSA**
Arremon abeillei 14

Cap black, long eyebrow white. Above gray. No yellow on wing. Breast band black. F: Sides gray.

9. PECTORAL SPARROW **L-FT**
Arremon taciturnus 14

Head black, with three narrow, long whitish stripes. Above olive. Shoulders bright yellow. Below white, breast band black (f. lacking). Cf. 294-30

10. GOLDEN-WINGED SPARROW **L-S**
Arremon schlegeli 14

Bill yellow. Head black without stripes. Above olive, shoulders yellow. Underparts white. Patch at sides of breast black.

11. ORANGE-BILLED SPARROW **L-FT**
Arremon aurantiirostris 14

Bill bright orange. Head black. Crown stripe gray. Eyebrow white. Back olive green. Throat white. Breast band black. Underparts whitish.

12. GREAT INCA-FINCH **M-SA**
Incaspiza pulchra 15

Bill yellow. Back reddish brown. Eyebrow, face, neck and wings gray. Throat black. Below grayish. Tail black, edged white.

13. RUFOUS-BACKED INCA-FINCH **MH-SA**
Incaspiza personata 15

Bill and legs yellow. Above reddish brown, back bright chestnut. Wing coverts gray. Forehead, face and upper throat black. no eyebrow. Sides head, neck and breast gray. Belly whitish. Tail black, outer feathers white.

14. RUFOUS-SIDED WARBLING-FINCH **H-S**
Poospiza hypochondria 15

Eyebrow white. Throat buff. Whisker black. Breast band gray. Below white, flanks chestnut.

Xenospingus
Donacospiza
Poospiza
Melanodera
Dolospingus
Sicalis

15. SLENDER-BILLED FINCH L-SO
Xenospingus concolor 15

Uniform bluish gray. Slender bill and legs yellow. Forehead and lores black. Below pale bluish gray, whitish on center of belly.

16. LONG-TAILED REED-FINCH LM-SW
Donacospiza albifrons 15

female

Above brown becoming reddish on rump. Eyebrow white. Below buff,whiter in center. F: Crown and back streaked blackish.

17. RUFOUS-BREASTED WARBLING-FINCH H-TS
Poospiza rubecula 15

Above gray. Wings blackish edged gray. Cheeks and chin black (f. lacking). Eyebrow and underparts rufous.

18. BOLIVIAN WARBLING-FINCH H-TS
Poospiza boliviana 14

Above pale reddish brown, wings blackish. Long, broad eyebrow white. Below white. Breast band, sides and flanks cinnamon. Tail black, broadly tipped white.

19. PLAIN-TAILED WARBLING-FINCH H-S
Poospiza alticola 15

Above dark brown, wings blackish,edged white. Long, broad eyebrow white. Narrow whisker black. Below white, sides rufous. Tail black with no white.

20. YELLOW-BRIDLED FINCH LMH-SO
Melanodera xanthogramma 15

Above bluish gray. Eyebrow yellow. Lores and throat black bordered by yellow. Wing coverts bright yellow. Breast and belly olive yellow, sides gray. F: Grayish brown above streaked blackish.

21. WHITE-NAPED SEEDEATER L-O
Dolospingus fringilloides 14

female

Bill conical, pointed. Head all black, semi-collar white. Single broad wing-bar and small wing speculum white. Below white. F: Dark brown. Throat and center of belly paler.

22. GREATER YELLOW-FINCH MH-O
Sicalis auriventris 15

Head, neck and rump bright olive yellow. Back greenish gray. Below bright yellow, (f. in center only) sides pale gray. Wings and tail blackish, wing coverts edged gray.

23. CITRON-HEADED YELLOW-FINCH H-O
Sicalis luteocephala 14

Head bright olive yellow. Above grayish. Throat, breast and vent bright yellow, sides gray, belly white. F: Browner.

Sicalis
Phrygilus
Lysurus
Lophospingus
Zonotrichia

24. PATAGONIAN YELLOW-FINCH **LM-O**
Sicalis lebruni 13

Above yellowish olive broadly streaked grayish. Wings and tail dusky edged whitish. Below yellow, sides pale gray. Crissum white.

25. PLUMBEOUS SIERRA-FINCH **M-F**
Phrygilus unicolor 14

Uniform lead gray. Wings and tail darker. Legs pinkish F: Above brownish, below whitish, all heavily streaked dusky.

female

26. PATAGONIAN SIERRA-FINCH **H-T**
Phrygilus patagonicus 14

Head, neck, throat, wings and tail gray. Back cinnamon rufous, rump yellowish. Below greenish yellow, brightest on center of belly. F: Back dark olive green.

27. BAND-TAILED SIERRA-FINCH **MLH-SO**
Phrygilus alaudinus 14

Head, throat and breast gray. Above brown streaked black. Belly white. Bill and legs yellow. Tail black with conspicuous white band. F: Below whitish, streaked dusky except on belly.

28. OLIVE FINCH **LM-F**
Lysurus castaneiceps 14

Olive. Crown and nape chestnut. Face, throat and sides of neck gray. Wings and tail blackish.

29. GRAY-CRESTED FINCH **M-S**
Lophospingus griseocristatus 14

Gray, paler below. Long crest black. Center of belly white. Tail black, outer feathers broadly tipped white. F: Throat white.

30. RUFOUS-COLLARED SPARROW **LMH-SO**
Zonotrichia capensis 14

Head gray streaked black. Prominent semi-collar rufous. Above brown streaked black. Wing coverts tipped white. Below gray. Malar black.

Oryzoborus	*Incaspiza*
Sicalis	*Poospiza*
Melanodera	*Coryphosopingus*

31. GREAT-BILLED (GREATER LARGE-BILLED) SEED-FINCH **L-TSO**
Oryzoborus maximiliani 15

All black (with speculum in some races). Bill extremely thick, horn color. F: Above rufous brown, wings and tail darker. Below varies from reddish brown to bright cinnamon. Bill dark.

32. LARGE-BILLED SEED-FINCH **L-TS**
Oryzoborus crassirostris 11

Black. Bill thick, white. Prominent white wing speculum. F: Brown, wings darker. Underwing coverts white. No wing speculum. Bill dark.

female

33. PUNA YELLOW-FINCH **H-SO**
Sicalis lutea 13

Upperparts olive yellow. Face and underparts bright yellow. Wings and tail brown, feathers edged yellow. F: Face grayish.

34. BLACK-THROATED FINCH **LM-SO**
Melanodera melanodera 14

Upperparts gray. Wing coverts yellow. Face and throat black, surrounded by white line. Below yellow. F: Brown, mottled or streaked black.

35. BUFF-BRIDLED INCA-FINCH **MH-SA**
Incaspiza laeta 13

Forehead, face and throat black. Throat bordered white. Crown and nape gray. Back chestnut. Tail black, outer feathers white. Legs yellow.

36. BLACK-AND-RUFOUS WARBLING FINCH **LM-TSO**
Poospiza nigrorufa 14

Above dark gray. Long eyebrow white turning rufous behind eye. Face black. Below rufous.

37. RED-CRESTED FINCH **L-SO**
Coryphospingus cucullatus 14

Crest crimson bordered black not always visible. Eye-ring white. Above dark reddish brown, rump crimson. Underparts dark reddish. Wings and tail blackish. F: Above brownish, rump dull red. Eye-ring, lores and throat whitish. Underparts pinkish.

female

Catamblyrhynchus *Porphyrospiza* *Catamenia* *Sicalis* *Coryphaspiza* *Poospiza* *Phrygilus*

38. PLUSH-CAPPED FINCH MH-FT
Catamblyrhynchus diadema 13

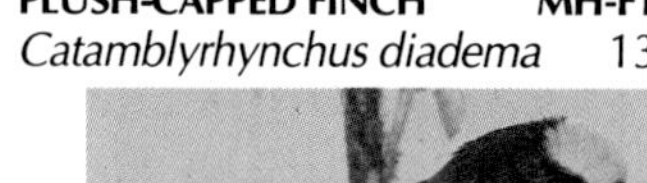

Forecrown yellow. Above dark gray. Face and underparts chestnut.

39. BLUE FINCH L-SO
Porphyrospiza caerulescens 13

Bright dark blue. Bill yellow. F: Rusty brown. Below whitish narrowly streaked blackish.

40. BAND-TAILED SEEDEATER H-SO
Catamenia analis 13

Slaty gray, forehead blackish. Bill yellow. Crissum chestnut. Tail centrals with white oval patch. F: Sparrow-like, brown, streaked dusky. Tail like m.

41. BRIGHT-RUMPED YELLOW-FINCH H-O
Sicalis uropygialis 13

Crown, nape and rump bright olive yellow. Cheeks and sides gray. Underparts yellow. Tail black, edged gray.

42. GREENISH YELLOW-FINCH MH-O
Sicalis olivascens 13

Crown and nape yellowish olive, back olive brown, all streaked gray. Rump and underparts olive yellow (no gray on sides), brightest on belly. Wings and tail blackish; feathers edged yellow.

43. BLACK-MASKED FINCH L-O
Coryphaspiza melanotis 13

Head black, long eyebrow white. Back olive brown broadly streaked black. Shoulders olive. Below white.

44. CINNAMON WARBLING-FINCH L-S
Poospiza ornata 12

Crown and rump dark gray. Back dark brown. Wings dusky, single bar white. Eyebrow cinnamon. Spot below eye white. Cheeks, throat, breast and sides rich chestnut. Belly rufous. Tail black, outer feathers broadly tipped white.

45. RED-RUMPED WARBLING-FINCH LM-TS
Poospiza lateralis 13

Above, face, throat and breast grayish. Rump rufous. Belly white, sides rufous. Tail black, outers white.

46. ASH-BREASTED SIERRA-FINCH H-SO
Phrygilus plebejus 13

Upperparts grayish streaked black. Rump gray. Below light gray, becoming white on belly and crissum. F: Above browner. Throat and breast streaked dusky.

Phrygilis
Catamenia
Sicalis
Poospiza
Oryzoborus

47. CARBONATED SIERRA-FINCH L-SO
Phrygilus carbonarius 14

Bill and legs yellow. Above gray, streaked black. Rump brown. Face and most of underparts black, sides gray. Tail black. Bill and feet yellow. F: Below whitish,narrowly streaked dusky on breast.

48. PARAMO SEEDEATER MH-T
Catamenia homochroa 13

Dark slaty gray, forehead and lores blacker. Bill yellow. Center of belly lighter gray. Crissum chestnut. F: Dark brown, streaked dusky above. Throat and breast grayish brown. Belly buffy.

49. SAFFRON YELLOW-FINCH (FINCH) LM-TSO
Sicalis flaveola 13

Crown orange or yellow. Back yelowish, more or less faintly streaked dusky. Below bright yellow (or dull yellow, tinged olive on breast). Wings and tail dusky edged olive. F: Like m. but duller. Imm: Sparrow-like.

50. CINEREOUS WARBLING-FINCH L-S
Poospiza cinerea 12

Above gray. Wings blackish, feathers edged gray. Area around eye black. Below white tinged yellowish on throat and breast. Tail black, outer feathers white.

51. RUSTY-BROWED WARBLING-FINCH MH-T
Poospiza erythrophrys 13

Head gray. Eyebrow, spot below eye, throat and breast deep rufous. Back gray. Belly white. Tail black, outers white.

52. LESSER SEED-FINCH L-TS
Oryzoborus angolensis 12

Black (underparts chestnut in e). Bill heavy, black. Usually small wing speculum white. F: Above dark brown. Below buff brown.

53. PLAIN-COLORED SEEDEATER H-SO
Catamenia inornata 12

Light gray, back streaked black. Bill light reddish brown. Crissum rufous. F: Above buffy streaked dusky. Below buff unstreaked.

female

Lophospingus
Poospiza
Passer

Spinus

54. BLACK-CRESTED FINCH L-SO
Lophospingus pusillus 12

female

Gray. Long crest and throat black. Broad eyebrow and belly white. Breast gray. F: Like m but throat white.

55. BLACK-CAPPED WARBLING-FINCH LM-S
Poospiza melanoleuca 12

Head black. Back gray. Wings black, feathers edged gray. Below white. Tail black, outer feathers broadly tipped white.

56. HOUSE SPARROW LM-TO
Passer domesticus 13

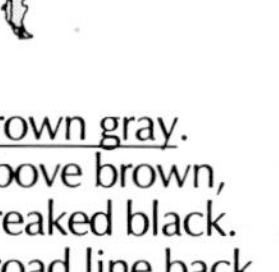

Crown gray. Above brown, streaked black. Broad line back of eye chestnut. Cheeks and sides of neck whitish. Throat and breast black. Belly gray. F: Grayish brown. Faint eyebrow whitish. No black. Usually near cities.

1. THICK-BILLED SISKIN H-S
Spinus crassirostris 13

Like 306-4 but larger and with much heavier bill. Wing patch and rump bright yellow. Belly white.

2. SAFFRON SISKIN LMH-TSO
Spinus siemiradzkii 12

Very like 306-4 but collar bright yellow.

3. OLIVACEOUS SISKIN MH-FT
Spinus olivaceus 12

Very like 306-4 but darker and generally more olivaceous.

4. HOODED SISKIN LMH-TSO
Spinus magellanicus 12

Hood black. Back yellowish olive. Narrow collar and rump bright yellow. Wings black with large yellow patch. White usually shows on inner wing feathers. Below bright yellow. Tail black. F: Like m but lacks black on head. Includes Santa Cruz Siskin in BSA.

5. BLACK-CHINNED SISKIN LM-TS
Spinus barbatus 11

Crown and center of throat black Back lightly spotted black. Center of belly white. Otherwise quite like 306-4.

Spinus
Haplospiza
Amaurospiza

6. BLACK SISKIN H-SO
Spinus atratus 11

Black. Yellow patch on wing. Center of belly and undertail coverts yellow. Tail black with much yellow at base.

7. YELLOW-RUMPED SISKIN H-SO
Spinus uropygialis 10

All deep black except wings with yellow patch. Breast, belly, base of tail and rump yellow.

8. YELLOW-BELLIED SISKIN MH-T
Spinus xanthogaster 10

All deep black except wings with yellow patch. Breast and belly yellow and base of tail yellow. F: Grayish olive in place of black.

9. ANDEAN SISKIN MH-TS
Spinus spinescens 11

Cap black (f. lacking). Above olive green. Wings with large yellow patch. White edges show on innermost wing feathers. Underparts olive yellow. Tail black.

10. YELLOW-FACED SISKIN L-SO
Spinus yarrellii 10

Like 307-9 but face, throat, breast and rump much brighter yellow. F: Lacks black cap.

11. RED SISKIN L-SO
Spinus cucullatus 9

Like 306-4 but red instead of yellow. F: Brownish above. Wings black with red markings. Whitish below. Red on sides.

12. UNIFORM FINCH LM-F
Haplospiza unicolor 12

Uniform bluish gray. Bill rather slender for a finch. Tail gray above and below. F: Above olive brown. Below streaked dusky.

female

13. SLATY FINCH MH-FT
Haplospiza rustica 12

Male and female very like 307-12. Separate by range.

14. BLACKISH-BLUE SEEDEATER LM-FT
Amaurospiza moesta 11

Dark bluish slate, blackish on lores and throat. Wings and tail black. F: Above reddish brown. Below light brown.

Gnathospiza
Coryphospingus
Ammodramus
Sporophila

15. SULPHUR-THROATED FINCH L-S
Gnathospiza (Sicalis) taczanowskii 11

Very heavy bill Upperparts light grayish brown, streaked brown on back. Wings edged pale yellow. Around eye white. Eyebrow and throat yellow. Below white

16. PILEATED FINCH L-S
Coryphospingus pileatus 12

Crest red, bordered black (f. lacking). Above light gray. Primaries brown, edged gray. Lores and eye-ring whitish. Below white tinged grayish on breast and sides. Tail black. F: Below like m but streaked pale gray.

17. GRASSLAND SPARROW LM-O
Ammodramus (Myospiza) humeralis 12

Very like 308-18 but only lores yellow and flight feathers chestnut.

18. YELLOW-BROWED SPARROW L-SO
Ammodramus (Myospiza) aurifrons 12

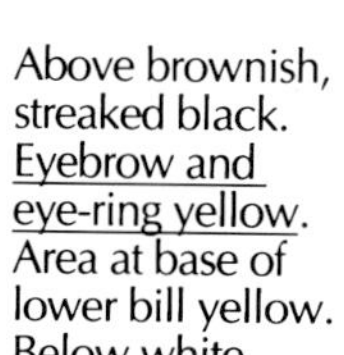

Above brownish, streaked black. Eyebrow and eye-ring yellow. Area at base of lower bill yellow. Below white, tinged grayish on breast. Tail dusky brown, the feathers edged paler.

19. GRASSHOPPER SPARROW LMH-0
Ammodramus savannarum 10

Above blackish brown streaked buffyish. Crown black, center stripe buff. Bend of wing yellow. Eye-ring and eyebrow buff. Throat and breast buff. Belly white.

20. BUFFY-FRONTED SEEDEATER LM-T
Sporophila frontalis 12

Dark brown. Narrow yellowish whisker and over eye. Below mostly brown.

21. WHITE-BELLIED SEEDEATER L-S
Sporophila leucoptera 12

Bill dull yellow. Above gray (or glossy black in Bolivia). White wing speculum prominent. Underparts white.

22. PARROT-BILLED SEEDEATER L-SO
Sporophila peruviana 12

female

Upperparts grayish brown. Bill very thick and curved. One wing-bar and speculum white. Throat and breast band black (f. lacking).

Sporophila

23. RUSTY-COLLARED SEEDEATER **L-SOW**
Sporophila collaris 11

female

Above black, spot at sides of forehead and below eye white.Collar whitish or rusty. Wing-bars buff.Rump whitish to cinnamon Throat white. Breast band black. Belly buff to cinnamon. F: Upperparts brownish. Below and rump lighter. Throat white. Wings black with two bars and speculum.

24. GRAY SEEDEATER **LM-SO**
Sporophila intermedia 11

Bill yellowish. Bluish gray. No white patch on side of neck or wing-bar. Speculum white (sometimes lacking). Cf. 309-26.

25. TEMMINCK'S SEEDEATER **L-FT**
Sporophia falcirostris 11

Like 309-24 but above lighter gray. Bill yellow. Center of belly white. Vent brownish (not white).

26. SLATE-COLORED SEEDEATER **L-T**
Sporophila schistacea 11

Bill bright yellow. Like 309-24 but darker gray. White on sides of neck or wing-bar (sometimes missing). White speculum usually present.

27. VARIABLE SEEDEATER **L-TS**
Sporophila americana 11

Variable. Bill black. Crown and back glossy black. Wings black, sometimes with double bar and or speculum. Rump gray or white. Throat and partial collar white. Band (sometimes incomplete) across breast black. Belly white.

28. YELLOW-BELLIED SEEDEATER **LM-SO**
Sporophila nigricollis 11

Crown, face, throat and breast black. Back, wings and tail olive. No speculum in most. Belly pale yellow.

29. DOUBLE-COLLARED SEEDEATER **LM-SO**
Sporophila caerulescens 11

Above dull gray to brownish gray, browner on wings and tail. Throat and band across breast black. Whisker and rest of underparts white. F: Like other f. seedeaters but lower bill yellow.

30. WHITE-THROATED SEEDEATER **L-S**
Sporophila albogularis 11

Like 309-29 but throat all white, wings and tail black edged gray.

Sporphila

31. BLACK-AND-WHITE SEEDEATER MH-SO
Sporophila luctuosa 11

Like 309-28 but has prominent white speculum and is blacker above and whiter below.

32. DUBOIS' SEEDEATER L-S
Sporophila ardesiaca 10

Like 309-28 but back gray not olive and belly white (not pale yellow).

33. DRAB SEEDEATER LM-S
Sporophila simplex 11

Grayish brown, rump and belly paler. Two wing-bars and speculum whitish. Throat white. Breast grayish F: Has conspicuous buffy double wing-bars.

34. PLUMBEOUS SEEDEATER L-O
Sporophila plumbea 10

Bill black. Body blue-gray, paler below. Distinct white spot below eye. Speculum white. Throat, whiskers and belly white.

35. LINED SEEDEATER L-SO
Sporophila lineola 10

Above black Crown stripe usually white. Broad malar stripe, speculum and rump white. Face and throat black.

36. BLACK-AND-TAWNY SEEDEATER L-O
Sporophila nigrorufa 10

Cap, hindneck and mantle black. Face and underparts cinnamon rufous. Speculum and edging on inner wing feathers white.

37. DULL-COLORED SEEDEATER LM-SO
Sporophila obscura 10

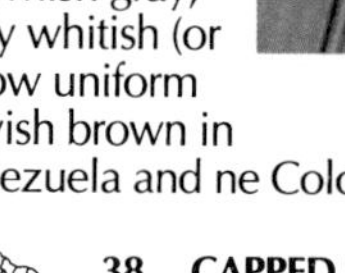

Above light reddish brown. Throat, breast and flanks brownish gray, belly whitish (or below uniform grayish brown in Venezuela and ne Colombia. F: Like m.

38. CAPPED SEEDEATER L-SO
Sporophila bouvreuil 10

Cap, wings and tail black, wing speculum white. Rest of plumage cinnamon rufous In s part of range, cinnamon buff below with pale grayish brown back.

39. BLACK-BELLIED SEEDEATER L-O
Sporophila melanogaster 10

Like 311-43 but paler gray above and on sides and belly. Throat and central underparts black instead of chestnut.

40. DARK-THROATED SEEDEATER L-O
Sporophila ruficollis 9

Like 311-42 but cheeks and breast black.

Sporophila
Poospiza
Incaspiza

41. MARSH SEEDEATER L-O
Sporophila palustris 9

Like 311-42 but cheeks and breast white.

42. RUDDY-BREASTED SEEDEATER LM-TSO
Sporophila minuta 9

Head, back, wings and tail ashy gray. Rump, sides and underparts rufous.

43. CHESTNUT-BELLIED SEEDEATER L-SO
Sporophila castaneiventris 9

Upperparts (including rump) bluish gray. Throat, breast, belly and crissum chestnut. Flanks gray. Tail black.

44. RUFOUS-RUMPED SEEDEATER L-O
Sporophila hypochroma 10

Like 311-42 but rump and entire underparts deeper chestnut.

45. CHESTNUT SEEDEATER L-O
Sporophila cinnamomea 10

Cap gray. Otherwise rufous chestnut. Wings and tail blackish with white on inner flight feathers. Speculum white.

46. CHESTNUT-THROATED SEEDEATER L-SO
Sporophila telasco 10

Above gray streaked blackish. White patch at base of black tail. Wings black, speculum white. Upper throat chestnut. Below white.

47. BAY-CHESTED WARBLING-FINCH LM-T
Poospiza thoracica 12

Above gray, wings with conspicuous white speculum. Cheeks gray, line below eye white. Below white. Band across breast chestnut. Flanks broadly chestnut.

48. COLLARED WARBLING-FINCH LM-SA
Poospiza hispaniolensis 12

Above gray. Face black, lower eyelid white. Below white , sides gray. Broad breast band black. Tail black, outers partly white.
F: Above brown, streaked dusky.

49. RINGED WARBLING-FINCH LM-S
Poospiza torquata 11

Like 311-48 but range different. Pectoral band all black, lacking gray on sides.

50. LITTLE INCA-FINCH L-SA
Incaspiza watkinsi 12

Crown and nape grayish brown. Back reddish. Bill and feet yellow. Below whitish. Eyebrow and face blue gray.

Amaurospiza
Charitospiza
Sicalis
Volantinia

51. BLUE SEEDEATER M-FT
Amaurospiza concolor 11

Uniform dark blue, slightly brighter on forehead and above eye. Lores and ear coverts black F: Bright cinnamon brown, paler below.

52. COAL-CRESTED FINCH L-SO
Charitospiza eucosma 11

Crest, face, throat and breast black. Cheeks white. Back gray. Belly chestnut. Tail black, white at base. F: Small crest but no black or white on head or breast

53. GRASSLAND YELLOW-FINCH LM-O
Sicalis luteola 11

Above yellowish olive, streaked black. Rump olive. Eye-ring, lores and underparts bright yellow (with gray breast band in s part of range). F: Like m. but browner.

54. RAIMONDI'S YELLOW-FINCH LM-OA
Sicalis raimondii 11

Like 312-53 but lacks yellow eye-ring; is grayer and less broadly streaked on back. Crown and nape yellowish on front and sides.

55. STRIPE-TAILED YELLOW-FINCH LMH-O
Sicalis citrina 10

Above olive green, back indistinctly streaked dusky. Forecrown and rump yellowish. Below yellow, tinged olive on breast. White patch on underside of tail. F: More brownish and all more or less streaked dusky.

56. ORANGE-FRONTED YELLOW-FINCH L-O
Sicalis columbiana 10

Upperparts yellowish olive with forehead reddish orange. F: Browner and paler (no streaks below).

57. BLUE-BLACK GRASSQUIT LM-TSO
Volatinia jacarina 9

Uniform glossy blue black. Note bill is more slender than a *Sporophila*.

imm male

female

Rhodospingus
Tiaris
Spinus

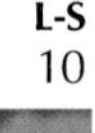

58. CRIMSON FINCH L-S
Rhodospingus cruentus 10

Bill quite narrow, pointed. Above blackish. Center of crown scarlet. Underparts scarlet. Underwing coverts white. F: Above brown, below buff to whitish.

female

59. SOOTY GRASSQUIT LM-O
Tiaris fuliginosa 10

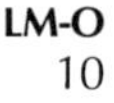

female

Uniform sooty black. Bill black. F: Above dull olive brown. Below olive brown, center of belly creamy whitish.

60. YELLOW-FACED GRASSQUIT LM-TSO
Tiaris olivacea 9

Forehead and face blackish. Eyebrow and throat yellow. Above olive. Breast black (extent of black variable). Belly olive, pale in center. F: Dull olive. Belly pale grayish olive. Eyebrow and throat dull yellow.

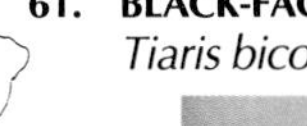

61. BLACK-FACED GRASSQUIT L-SO
Tiaris bicolor 9

Face, throat and breast dull black. Back, wings and belly dull olive. F: Pale olive gray. Belly whitish.

62. DARK-BACKED GOLDFINCH LM-TSO
Spinus psaltria 9

Above glossy black, wings with speculum. Underparts golden yellow. Tail black, outers white near base. F: Above olive. Wings dusky with white patches.

female

METHODS AND EQUIPMENT

Close-up photography of any moving object such as a bird involves two basic problems - getting enough light and sharp focus. Under tropical forest conditions it is extremely difficult, in many cases almost impossible, to solve these problems by the normal method: setting up camera and lights at some spot to which the bird will come. Many tropical forest birds spend most of their time in the treetops, up to 100 or more feet above the ground. At lower levels of the forest, reliable sunlight ("available light") is almost nonexistent. So we solve these problems by creating our own light with electronic stroboscopic flash and bringing the bird to the lights and camera, all set up in advance in an enclosure.

The bird is captured in a mist net, some 40 feet long and 10 feet high, constructed of very fine black nylon thread, which is practically invisible. After being carefully released , the bird is put in a cloth bag which gives sufficient air, yet is dark enough to keep the bird fairly quiet.

The next task is to mount the proper perch and fresh foliage in the enclosure. We try to use foliage similar to that which we have observed the bird using the wild. If the subject's natural food is known and available, it helps to put some in the enclosure.

If quiet is maintained after the bird is put in the enclosure, it usually soon calms down and rests on the perch, if it is a properly chosen one. Often within a half an hour the photography has been completed and the bird is released unharmed in it's own home area.

In the accompanying sketch, the enclosure is made of fairly heavy unbleached white muslin. This provides enough light inside for focusing but keeps the birds from seeing through it. Four collapsible poles (P) along each side, with two cross braces (CB) across the middle ones, holds the enclosure up, and it becomes quite firm and rigid when the four corners are tied to convenient trees or to stakes. There is a skirt, about 12 inches wide all around, to accommodate unevenness in the ground. It is weighted down with sticks or stones to prevent the bird's escape under the enclosure.

The eight poles are constructed of 7/16-inch (outside diameter) aluminum tubing, into which a 9/32-inch round aluminum bar slides. These poles, when collapsed to their shortest length, will just fit into a 26-inch suitcase for traveling. A thumbscrew (1/4-inch x 20 thread) on the tubing can be tightened to hold the inner rod at any position , thus making the poles the right length to suit ground conditions. This is made by putting a 1/4-inch x 20 aluminum nut on the thumbscrew and peening the end threads of the thumbscrew with a hammer, so that the nut cannot come off. A 9/32-inch hole is then drilled in the tubing approximately 3/4-inch from one end. The end of the thumbscrew is inserted in this hole and the aluminum nut on the thumbscrew is welded to the tubing. The bottom end of the tubing is welded tight to keep water and dirt from getting in.

The two cross braces are constructed of 7/16-inch aluminum tubing into which a 9/32-inch aluminum bar slides. A thumbscrew is welded to the tubing 3/4 inch from one end. The other end of the tubing is left open. A short piece of 7/16-inch aluminum tubing is welded on one end of the 9/32-inch aluminum bar. The two ends of the cross brace are slipped over the 1/8-inch pins on the poles. The cross brace is then extended until the top of the enclosure is firm and the thumbscrew is tightened

SKETCH OF ENCLOSURE
(not to scale)

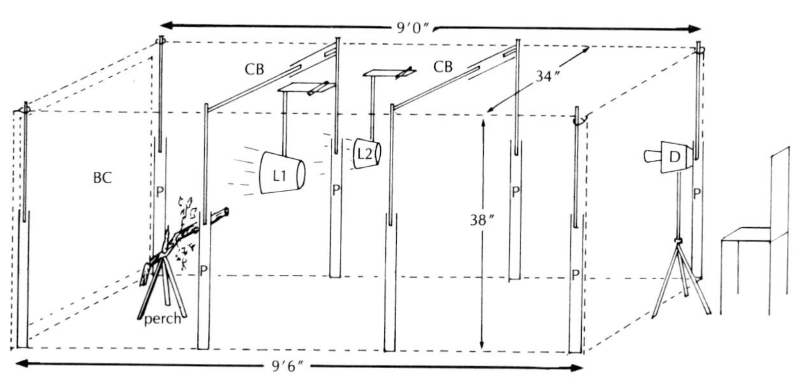

CROSS BRACE
2 needed

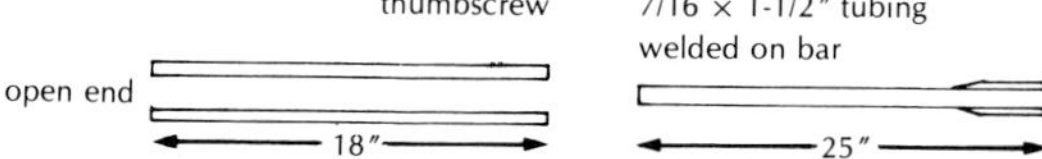

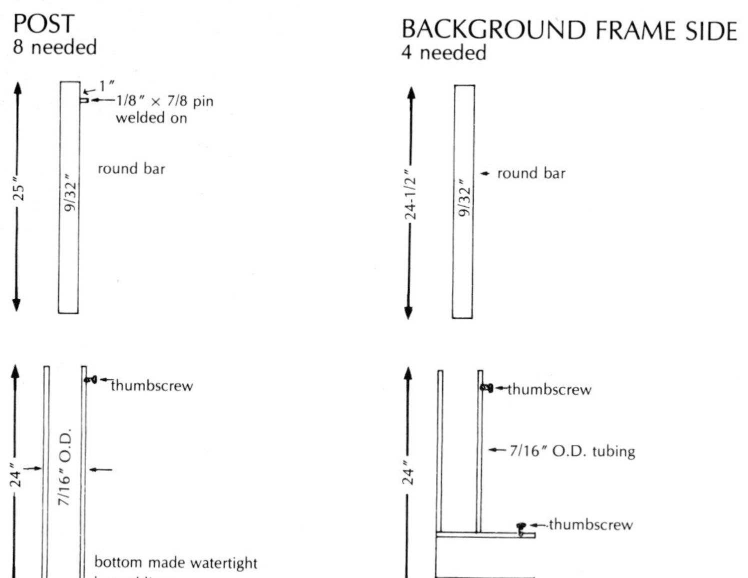

Eight loops-one at each corner of the enclosure and two on two opposite sides- slip over the tops of the eight poles to hold the enclosure up. To prevent each loop from slipping down the pole, a 1/8-inch pin is welded on the top section of the pole about 1 inch from the end.

There is a zippered opening at one end of the enclosure through which only the lens of the camera (D) is inserted, so that all operating parts of the camera are outside the enclosure. The camera is always mounted on a tripod. There are also zippers (not shown in the sketch) in the sides, for putting in the perches and background foliage, and in the top, for inserting the lights and the background cloth.

The strobe main light (L1) and the fill light (L2) are suspended from the canvas top of the enclosure through zippered openings. Flashbulbs could be used, but I have found strobes more useful. The light aluminum bars holding the lights are slipped through safety pins in the top of the enclosure to keep them positioned. The two lights must be kept far enough to the sides to avoid throwing a shadow on the background cloth, but within this limitation, the angle and distance of the lights can be varied to produce a variety of pleasing results.

Author shown here using enclosure to photograph birds in the tropics.
The canopy is used to keep off sun and rain.

The background cloth (BC) is stretched over a background frame formed of the same sizes of aluminum as the poles (see sketch). The four sides of the background frame fit together to make a rectangle over which the background cloth is stretched. The corners of the background cloth are sewn to form a pocket into which the frame fits. Then the background frame is expanded to make the background cloth tight, and the four thumbscrews are tightened to hold it there. The background cloth on the background frame is inserted inside the enclosure through a wide zipper (not shown in sketch) on the top of the enclosure at the back. It helps keep the cloth clean if it is tilted inward at the top about 6 inches. To allow for this, the enclosure is made 6 inches longer at the bottom than at the top.

The background cloths have been the subject of much experimenting. In general we think a light blue color gives pleasing results, but individual preference may govern that. Many of the newer synthetic fabrics look one color in daylight but photograph a different color. The background cloth is dampened thoroughly before being put on the frame to remove all wrinkles which would show in the picture. Of course spare cloths are needed, as they get soiled quickly.

Mounting the perch and background foliage inside the enclosure has to be worked out for each setup. Sometimes the perch is stuck into the ground, sometimes it is suspended from the top of the enclosure. I have found a low tripod with a Kodapod clamp invaluable. It is important to have the perch far enough away from the background cloth so that shadows do not show on the cloth.

Selecting the proper perch for the bird is a matter which often requires much trial and error. I have frequently had a bird refuse to land on a perch, then after I have changed the perch, pose almost immediately.

After the film has been exposed, I find it important to store it in a plastic bag with one or two containers of silica gel to keep it dry. Most film manufacturers advise development soon after exposure , but I have had no trouble keeping film up to six or eight weeks after exposure, provided it is kept dry and not over heated.

I have presented the details of my technique here solely as a guide. I am sure many variations could be used which would serve equally well – perhaps better . I hope many of my readers will work their own methods. I will be glad to help anyone in any way I can.

Aburria aburri, 3
pipile, 3
Accipiter bicolor, 35
collaris, 35
erythronemius, 35
poliogaster, 34
striatus, 35
superciliosus, 35
ventralis, 35
Acestrura berlepschi, 79
bombus, 79
heliodor, 93
mulsant, 92
Acrochordopus burmeisteri, 223
Acropternis orthonyx, 175
Actitis macularia, 20
Adelomyia melanogenys, 92
Aegolius harrisii, 58
Aeronautes andecolus, 62
montivagus, 62
Agamia agami, 11
Agelaius cyanops, 257
icterocephalus, 258
ruficapillus, 258
thilius, 258
xanthophthalmus, 258
Aglaeactis aliciae, 85
castelnaudii, 85
cupripennis, 85
pamela, 85
Aglaiocercus coelestis, 88
kingi, 88
Agriornis albicauda, 195
livida, 195
microptera, 195
montana, 195
Aimophila strigicaps, 299
stolzmanni, 299
Ajaia ajaja, 10
Alectrurus tricolor, 209
Allocotopterus deliciosus, 189,193
Alopochelidon fucata, 65
Amaurolimnas concolor, 19
Amaurospiza concolor, 312
moesta, 307
Amazilia amabilis, 76
amazilia, 77
castaneiventris, 85
chionogaster, 85
chionopectus,75
cyanifrons,76
distans, 76
fimbriata, 75
franciae, 86
lactea, 76
leucogaster, 76
rosenbergi, 76
saucerottei, 76
tobaci, 76
tzacatl, 77
versicolor, 75
viridicauda, 85
viridigaster, 76
Amazona aestiva, 49
amazonica, 50
autumnalis, 49
barbadensis, 50
brasiliensis, 49
farinosa, 49
festiva, 49
mercenaria, 50
ochrocephala, 49
pretrei, 50
tucumana, 50
vinacea, 49
xanthops, 50
Amazonetta brasiliensis, 25
Amblyramphus holosericeus, 258
Ammodramus aurifrons, 308
humeralis, 308
savannarum, 308
Ampelioides tschudii,182
Ampelion rubrocristatus,180
rufaxilla,179
Anabacerthia amaurotis, 138
striaticollis,138
variegaticeps,138
Anabazenops fuscus, 137
Anairetes alpinus, 219
flavirostris, 219
parulus, 219
reguloides, 219
Anas acuta, 23
americana, 23
bahamensis. 23
clypeata, 24
cyanoptera, 26
discors, 26
flavirostris, 25
georgica, 23
leucophrys , 26
platalea, 24
puna, 25
sibilatrix, 23
specularis, 24
versicolor, 25
Ancistrops strigilatus,139
Andigena cucullata, 107
hypoglauca, 107
laminirostris, 107
nigrirostris,107
Androdon aequatorialis, 69
Anhima cornuta, 11
Anhinga, 22
Anhinga anhinga, 22
Ani, Greater, 54
Groove-billed, 54
Smooth-billed, 54
Anisognathus flavinucha, 269
igniventris, 268
lacrymosus, 269
melanogenys, 268
notabilis, 268
Anodorhynchus hyacinthinus,42
Antbird, Ash-breasted, 162
Bananal, 159
Banded, 169
Band-tailed, 169
Bare-crowned,160
Bare-eyed, 161
Bicolored, 165
Black, 159
Black-and-white, 169
Black-chinned, 169
Black-faced, 162
Black-headed, 161
Blackish, 160
Black-tailed, 163
Black-throated, 164
Caura, 161
Chestnut-backed, 163
Chestnut-crested, 161
Chestnut-tailed, 164
Dot-backed, 168
Dull-mantled, 168
Dusky, 159
Dusky-tailed, 165
Esmeraldas, 168
Ferruginous, 165
Ferruginous-backed, 164
Goeldi's, 157
Gray, 159
Gray-bellied, 164
Gray-headed, 164
Hairy-crested, 160
Harlequin, 161
Immaculate, 157
Jet, 159
Long-tailed, 165
Lunulated, 160
Mato Grosso, 158
Ocellated, 157
Ochre-rumped, 166
Plumbeous, 158
Rio Branco, 159
Rio de Janeiro, 159
Rufous-tailed, 165
Rufous-throated, 165
Scale-backed, 167
Scaled, 165
Scalloped, 164
Serra, 167
Silvered, 162
Slate-colored, 162
Sooty, 157

Antbird, Spot-backed, 168
Spot-breasted, 164
Spotted, 168
Spot-winged, 162
Squamate, 163
Striated, 165
Stripe-backed, 161
Stub-tailed, 168
Warbling, 171
White-bellied, 163
White-bibbed, 163
White-breasted, 161
White-browed, 162
White-lined, 162
White-plumed, 168
White-shouldered, 157
White-throated, 160
Wing-banded, 161
Yapacana, 164
Yellow-browed, 171
Anthocephala floriceps, 92
Anthracothorax nigricollis, 71
prevostii, 71
viridigula, 71
Anthus bogotensis, 246
chacoensis, 246
correndera, 245
furcatus, 246
hellmayri, 246
lutescens, 245
nattereri, 246
Antilophia galeata, 186
Antpipit, Ringed, 217
Southern, 217
Antpitta, Amazonian, 156
Bay-backed, 155
Bicolored, 155
Black-crowned, 155
Brown-banded, 156
Brown-breasted, 156
Chestnut-crowned, 153
Chestnut-naped, 154
Crescent-faced, 156
Elusive, 155
Fulvous-bellied, 155
Giant, 153
Gray-naped, 155
Great, 153
Hooded, 157
Ochre-breasted, 156
Ochre-striped, 155
Peruvian, 157
Plain-backed, 154
Rufous, 156
Rufous-crowned, 155
Rufous-faced, 154
Rusty-breasted, 156
Santa Marta, 155
Scaled, 154
Scallop-breasted, 157
Slate-crowned, 157
Speckle-breasted, 156
Spotted, 155
Streak-chested, 156
Stripe-headed, 155
Tachira, 154
Tawny, 155
Thrush-like, 156
Undulated, 153
Variegated, 154
White-throated, 154
Antshrike, Amazonian, 150
Band-tailed, 148
Bar-crested, 149
Barred, 149
Black, 149
Black-backed, 148
Black-capped, 150
Black-crested, 148
Black-throated, 147
Blackish-gray, 149
Bluish-slate, 152
Castelnau's, 149
Cinereous, 152
Collared, 148
Dusky-throated, 152
Fasciated, 147
Giant, 147
Glossy, 148
Great, 147
Large-tailed, 147
Lined, 149
Mouse-colored, 151
Pearly, 151
Plumbeous, 152
Rufous-capped, 148
Rufous-winged, 151
Russet, 151
Saturnine, 152
Silvery-cheeked, 148
Slaty, 150
Speckled, 151
Spot-backed, 147
Spot-winged, 151
Streak-backed, 150
Tufted, 147
Undulated, 147
Uniform, 150
Upland, 151
Variable, 150
Western, 152
White-bearded, 148
White-shouldered, 149
Antthrush, Barred, 153
Black-faced, 153
Black-headed, 154
Rufous-breasted, 154
Rufous-capped, 154
Rufous-tailed, 153
Short-tailed, 153
Striated, 153
Antvireo, Plain, 169
Rufous-backed, 169
Spot-breasted, 168
Spot-crowned, 169
Antwren, Ash-winged, 170
Ashy,172
Band-tailed, 172
Black-bellied, 167
Black-capped, 166
Black-hooded, 170
Brown-bellied, 171
Checker-throated, 170
Cherrie's, 171
Chestnut-shouldered, 170
Dot-winged, 172
Gray, 172
Ihering's, 173
Klages', 173
Large-billed, 166
Leaden, 170
Long-winged, 172
Narrow-billed, 167
Ornate, 170
Pectoral, 166
Plain-throated, 173
Plain-winged, 170
Pygmy, 173
Rio Suno, 173
Roraiman, 166
Rufous-bellied, 173
Rufous-rumped, 170
Rufous-tailed, 170
Rufous-winged, 166
Rusty-backed, 167
Salvadori's, 173
Sclater's, 173
Serra, 167
Short-billed, 173
Slaty, 172
Spot-backed, 166
Spot-tailed, 166
Star-throated, 171
Stipple-throated, 172
Streak-capped, 171
Streaked, 171
Stripe-chested, 171
Todd's, 166
Unicolored, 172
White-eyed, 170
White-flanked, 171

White-fringed, 167
Yellow-breasted, 166
Yellow-rumped, 170
Yellow-throated, 173
Anumbius annumbi, 133
Anurolimnas castaneiceps, 19
Aphanotriccus audax, 219
Aphantochroa cirrhochloris, 74
Aphrastura spinicauda, 140
Ara ambigua, 42
ararauna, 43
auricollis, 43
chloroptera, 42
couloni, 44
macao, 43
manilata, 43
maracana, 43
militaris, 43
nobilis, 44
rubrogenys, 43
severa, 43
Aracari, Black-necked, 109
Chestnut-eared, 109
Collared, 109
Curl-crested, 109
Green, 109
Ivory-billed, 109
Lettered, 109
Many-banded, 109
Red-necked, 109
Aramides axillaris, 18
cajanea, 17
calopterus, 18
mangle, 18
saracura, 17
wolfi, 18
*ypecaha,*17
Aramus guarauna, 13
Aratinga acuticauda, 44
aurea, 45
auricapilla , 45
cactorum, 46
erythrogenys, 45
guarouba, 44
jandaya, 45
leucophthalmus, 45
mitrata, 45
pertinax, 45
solstitialis, 45
wagleri, 45
weddellii, 46
Ardea cocoi, 10
herodias, 10
Arremon abeillei, 300
aurantiirostris, 300
flavirostris, 300
schlegeli, 300
taciturnis. 300
Arremonops conirostris, 299
tocuyensis, 299
Arundinicola leucocephala, 231
Asio flammeus, 56
stygius, 56
Asthenes anthoides, 131
baeri, 131
berlepschi, 130
cactorum, 132
dorbignyi, 131
flammulata, 130
hudsoni, 130
humicola, 131
humilis, 131
maculicauda, 130
modesta, 132
ottonis, 131
patagonica, 131
pudibunda, 131
pyrrholeuca, 131
sclateri, 130
steinbachi, 131
urubambensis, 130
virgata, 130
wyatti, 131
Atalotriccus pilaris, 225
Atlapetes albiceps, 296
albofrenatus, 295
atricapillus, 294
brunneinucha, 294
citrinellus, 297
flaviceps, 296
fulviceps, 296
fusco-olivaceus, 296
gutturalis, 295
leucopis, 294
leucopterus, 296
melanocephalus, 295
nationi, 295
pallidiceps, 296
pallidinucha, 295
personatus, 295
rufigenis, 294
rufinucha, 295
schistaceus, 295
seebohmi, 296
semirufus, 296
torquatus, 294
tricolor, 294
Attagis gayi, 8
malouinus, 8
Atticora fasciata, 64
melanoleuca, 64
Attila bolivianus, 201
cinnamomeus, 202
citriniventris, 202
rufus, 201
spadiceus, 202
torridus, 202
Attila, Bright-rumped, 202
Cinnamon, 202
Citron-bellied, 202
Dull-capped, 201
Gray-hooded, 201
Ochraceous, 202
Rufous-tailed, 201
White-eyed, 201
Augastes lumachellus, 92
scutatus, 92
Aulacorhynchus,
coeruleicinctis, 107
derbianus, 108
haematopygus, 107
huallagae, 108
prasinus, 108
sulcatus, 108
Automolus dorsalis, 137
infuscatus, 135
leucophthalmus, 135
melanopezus, 137
ochrolaemus, 134
roraimae, 135
rubiginosus, 135
ruficollis, 137
rufipileatus, 135
Avocet, Andean, 14
Avocetbill, Mountain, 92
Avocettula recurvirostris, 74
Awlbill, Fiery-tailed, 74
Aythya affinis, 25

Baillonius bailloni, 108
Bamboo-wren, Spotted, 176
Bananaquit, 254
Bangsia aureocincta, 275
edwardsi, 275
melanochlamys, 274
rothschildi, 274
Barbet, Black-girdled, 105
Black-spotted, 104
Five-colored, 105
Lemon-throated, 105
Orange-fronted, 105
Red-headed, 105
Scarlet-crowned, 104
Scarlet-hooded, 105
Spot-crowned, 104
Toucan, 104
Versicolored, 105
White-mantled, 104
Barbtail, Roraiman, 136
Rusty-winged, 136

Barbtail, Spotted, 136
White-throated, 136
Barbthroat, Band-tailed, 68
Pale-tailed, 68
Sooty, 68
Bare-eye, Black-spotted, 158
Reddish-winged, 158
Bartramia longicauda, 16
Baryphthengus martii, 95
ruficapillus, 96
Basileuterus basilicus, 266
bivittatus, 266
chrysogaster, 267
cinereicollis, 267
coronatus, 265
culicivorus, 267
flaveolus, 266
fraseri, 266
griseiceps, 267
hypoleucus, 267
leucoblepharus, 266
leucophrys, 266
luteoviridis, 266
nigrocristatus, 266
rivularis, 267
rufifrons, 267
signatus, 266
trifasciatus, 267
tristriatus, 266
Batara cinerea, 147
Becard, Barred, 184
Black-and-white, 184
Black-capped, 184
Chestnut-crowned, 184
Cinereous, 184
Cinnamon, 184
Crested, 182
Glossy-backed, 183
Green-backed, 183
One-colored, 183
Pink-throated, 183
Slaty, 183
White-winged, 183
Bellbird, Bare-throated, 179
Bearded, 179
White, 179
Bentbill, Southern, 226
Berlepschia rikeri, 137
Berryeater, Black-headed, 181
Hooded, 181
Biatas nigropectus, 148
Bittern, Least, 14
Pinnated, 14
Stripe-backed, 14
Blackbird, Austral, 257
Bolivian, 257
Chestnut-capped, 258
Chopi, 257
Forbes', 257
Oriole, 257
Pale-eyed, 258
Red-breasted, 259
Saffron-cowled, 259
Scarlet-headed, 258
Scrub, 258
Unicolored, 257
White-browed, 258
Yellow-hooded, 258
Yellow-winged, 258
Blossomcrown, 92
Bobolink, 261
Bobwhite, Crested, 9
Boissonneaua flavescens, 89
jardini, 89
matthewsii, 89
Bolborhynchus aurifrons, 47
aymara, 47
ferrugineifrons. 47
lineola, 47
orbygnesius, 47
Botaurus pinnatus, 14
Brachygalba albogularis, 99
goeringi, 99
lugubris, 99
salmoni, 99
Brilliant, Black-throated, 70
Empress, 84
Fawn-breasted, 84
Green-crowned, 84
Pink-throated, 70
Rufous-webbed, 84
Velvet-browed, 84
Violet-fronted, 84
Bristlefront, Slaty, 175
Stresemann's, 175
Brotogeris, chrysopterus, 48
cyanoptera, 48
jugularis, 48
pyrrhopterus, 48
sanctithomae, 48
tirica, 48
versicolurus, 48
Brush-Finch, see Finch
Brush-runner, Lark-like, 130
Bubo virginianus, 56
Bubulcus ibis, 12
Bucco capensis. 102
macrodactylus, 103
noanamae, 102
tamatia, 102
Burhinus bistriatus, 4
superciliaris, 4
Busarellus nigricollis, 34
Bushbird, Black, 152
Recurve-billed, 151
Buteo albicaudatus, 31
albigula, 32
albonotatus, 32
brachyurus, 32
leucorrhous, 33
magnirostris, 32
nitidus, 32
platypterus, 32
poecilochrous, 31
polyosoma, 32
swainsoni, 32
ventralis, 31
Buteogallus anthracinus, 31
urubitinga, 31
Buthrapis eximia, 268
montana, 268
wetmorei, 268
Butorides striatus, 12
virescens, 12

Cacholote, Brown, 132
Rufous, 132
White-throated, 132
Cacicus cela, 256
chrysopterus, 257
haemorrhous, 256
holosericeus, 257
koepckeae, 257
leucorhamphus, 256
sclateri, 257
solitarius, 257
uropygialis, 256
Cacique,
Ecuadorian (Black), 257
Golden-winged, 257
Mountain, 256
Red-rumped, 256
Scarlet-rumped, 256
Selva, 257
Solitary (Black), 257
Yellow-billed, 257
Yellow-rumped, 256
Cairina moschata, 23
Calidris bairdii, 20
fuscicollis, 20
melanotus, 16
minutilla, 20
Calliphlox amethystina, 79
Calochaetes coccineus, 274
Calyptura cristata, 185
Calyptura, Kinglet, 185
Campephilus
gayaquilensis, 110
haematogaster, 110
leucopogon, 110

magellanicus, 110
melanoleucos, 110
pollens, 110
robustus, 110
rubricollis, 110
Camptostoma obsoletum, 223
Campylopterus duidae, 80
ensipennis, 80
falcatus, 80
hyperythrus, 80
largipennis, 69
phainopeplus, 80
villaviscensio, 80
Campylorhamphus
falcularius, 119
procurvoides, 119
pucheranii, 119
pusillus, 119
trochilirostris, 119
Campylorhynchus
albobrunneus, 240
fasciatus, 240
griseus, 240
nuchalis, 240
turdinus, 240
zonatus, 240
Canastero, Austral, 131
Berlepsch's, 130
Cactus, 132
Canyon, 131
Chestnut, 131
Cordilleran, 132
Cordoba, 130
Creamy-breasted, 131
Dusky-tailed, 131
Hudson's, 130
Junin, 130
Lesser, 131
Line-fronted, 130
Many-striped, 130
Patagonian, 131
Rusty-fronted, 131
Scribble-tailed, 130
Short-billed, 131
Streak-backed, 131
Streak-throated, 131
Capito aurovirens, 104
dayi, 105
hypoleucus, 104
maculicoronatus, 104
niger, 104
quinticolor, 105
squamatus, 105
Caprimulgus candicans, 60
carolinensis, 59
cayennensis, 60
hirundinaceus, 60
longirostris, 60
maculicaudus, 60
maculosus, 60
nigrescens, 60
parvulus, 60
rufus, 59
sericocaudatus, 60
whiteleyi, 60
Capsiempis flaveola, 223
Capuchinbird, 178
Caracara, Black, 36
Carunculated, 35
Chimango, 36
Crested, 35
Mountain, 35
Red-throated, 36
White-throated, 36
Yellow-headed, 36
Cardinal, Crimson-fronted, 297
Red-capped, 297
Red-cowled, 297
Red-crested, 297
Vermilion, 297
Yellow, 297
Yellow-billed, 297
Cardinalis phoeniceus, 297
Cariama cristata, 4
Carpodectes hopkei, 179
Carpornis cucullatus, 181
melanocephalus, 181
Caryothraustes canadensis, 293
humeralis, 293
Casiornis fusca, 206
rufa, 205
Casiornis, Ash-throated, 206
Rufous, 205
Casmerodius albus, 10
Cassidix mexicanus, 256
Catamblyrhynchus
diadema, 304
Catamenia analis, 304
homochroa, 305
inornata, 305
Cathartes aura, 28
burrovianus, 28
melambrotus, 28
Catharus aurantiirostris, 238
dryas, 238
fuscater, 238
fuscescens, 238
minimus, 238
ustulatus, 238
Catoptrophorus
semipalmatus, 14
Celeus elegans, 112
flavescens, 113
flavus, 112
grammicus, 113
loricatus, 112
lugubris, 113
spectabilis, 112
torquatus, 112
undatus, 113
Centropelma micropterum, 27
Cephalopterus ornatus, 177
penduliger, 177
Ceratotriccus furcatus, 228
Cercibis oxycerca, 13
Cercomacra brasiliana, 159
carbonaria, 159
cinerascens, 159
ferdinandi, 159
melanaria, 158
nigrescens, 160
nigricans, 159
serva, 159
tyrannina, 159
Certhiaxis cinnamomea, 141
mustelina, 141
Ceryle torquata, 96
Chachalaca, Chaco, 3
Chestnut-winged, 3
Little, 4
Rufous-headed, 3
Rufous-vented, 3
Variable, 4
Chaetocercus jourdanii, 93
Chaetura andrei, 62
brachyura, 63
chapmani, 63
cinereiventris, 63
egregia, 63
pelagica, 63
spinicauda, 63
vauxi, 63
Chalcostigma herrani, 90
heteropogon, 89
olivaceum, 89
ruficeps, 89
stanleyi, 89
Chalybura buffonii, 72
urochrysia, 72
Chamaepetes goudotii, 3
Chamaeza campanisona, 153
mollissima, 153
nobilis, 153
ruficauda, 153
Charadrius alticola, 21
collaris, 21
falklandicus, 21
semipalmatus, 21
vociferus, 17
Charitospiza eucosma, 312
Chat, Rose-breasted, 264

Chauna chavaria, 11
torquata, 11
Chelidoptera tenebrosa, 103
Chilia melanura, 127
Chilia, Crag, 127
Chirocylla uropygialis, 178
Chiroxiphia caudata, 186
lanceolata, 187
pareola, 187, 194
Chleophaga melanoptera, 22
picta, 22
poliocephala, 22
rubidiceps, 22
Chlorestes notatus, 74
Chloroceryle aenea, 97
amazona, 97
americana, 97
inda, 97
Chlorochrysa calliparaea, 286
nitidissima, 286
phoenicotis, 286
Chlorophanes spiza, 253
Chlorophonia cyanea, 288
flavirostris, 288
pyrrhophrys, 288
Chlorophonia, Blue-naped, 288
Chestnut-breasted, 288
Yellow-collared, 288
Chloropipo flavicapilla, 188
holochlora, 193
unicolor, 188
uniformis, 187
Chlorornis riefferii, 269
Chlorospingus canigularis, 279
flavigularis, 279
flavovirens, 279
ophthalmicus, 279
parvirostris, 279
semifuscus, 280
Chlorostilbon alice, 93
aureoventris, 93
gibsoni, 79
mellisugus, 93
poortmanni, 93
russatus, 93
stenura, 93
Chlorothraupis carmioli, 276
olivacea, 276
stolzmanni, 276
Chondrohierax uncinatus, 29
Chordeiles acutipennis, 61
minor, 61
pusillus, 61
rupestris, 61
Chrysolampis mosquitus, 79
Chrysoptilus atricollis, 111
melanochloros, 111
melanolaimus, 112
punctigula, 114
Chrysuronia oenone, 74
Chuck-Wills-Widow, 59
Chunga burmeisteri, 4
Ciccaba albitarsus, 57
huhula, 57
nigrolineata, 56
virgata, 57
Cichlocolaptes leucophrys, 132
Cinclodes antarcticus, 127
atacamensis, 127
excelsior, 127
fuscus, 127
nigrofumosus, 127
oustaleti, 127
palliatus, 127
patagonicus, 127
Cinclodes, Bar-winged, 127
Blackish, 127
Dark-bellied, 127
Gray-flanked, 127
Seaside, 127
Stout-billed, 127
White-bellied, 127
White-winged, 127
Cinclus leucocephalus, 21
schultzi, 21
Cinnycerthia peruana, 241
unirufa, 240
Circus buffoni, 34
cinereus, 34
Cissopis leveriana, 268
Cistothorus apolinari, 243
meridae, 243
platensis, 243
Claravis godefrida, 41
mondetoura, 41
pretiosa, 41
Clibanornis dendrocolaptoides, 127
Clypicterus oseryi, 255
Clytoctantes alixi, 151
Clytolaema rubricauda, 74
Cnemoscopus rubrirostris, 278
Cnemotriccus fuscatus, 213
Cnipodectes subbrunneus, 205
Coccyzus americanus, 55
cinereus, 55
erythropthalmus, 55
euleri, 55
lansbergi, 55
melacoryphus 56
minor, 55
pumilus, 56
Cochlearius cochlearius, 11
Cock-of-the-Rock, Andean, 179
Guianan, 178
Coeligena bonapartei, 81
coeligena, 80
helianthea, 82
iris, 81
lutetiae, 81
orina, 81
phalerata, 82
prunellei, 81
torquata, 81
violifer, 81
wilsoni. 81
Coereba flaveola, 254
Colaptes campestris, 111
campestroides, 111
pitius, 111
rupicola, 111
Colibri coruscans, 83
delphinae, 83
serrirostris, 83
thalassinus, 83
Colinus cristatus, 9
Colonia colonus, 214
Colopteryx galeatus, 231
Colorhamphus parvirostris, 217
Columba araucana, 38
cayennensis, 38
corensis, 38
fasciata, 38
goodsoni, 39
maculosa, 38
nigrirostris, 38
oenops, 38
picazuro, 38
plumbea, 38
speciosa, 38
subvinacea, 38
Columbina cruziana, 42
cyanopis, 42
minuta, 42
passerina, 42
picui, 42
talpacoti, 41
Comet, Bronze-tailed, 88
Gray-bellied, 83
Red-tailed, 88
Compsospiza baeri, 298
garleppi, 298
Condor, Andean, 28
Conebill, Bicolored, 250
Blue-backed, 250
Capped, 250
Chestnut-vented, 250
Cinereous, 250
Giant, 250
Pearly-breasted, 250
Rufous-crowned, 250

White-browed, 250
White-eared, 250
Conioptilon mcilhennyi, 180
Conirostrum albifrons, 250
bicolor, 250
cinereum, 250
ferrugineiventre, 250
leucogenys, 250
margaritae, 250
rufum, 250
sitticolor, 250
speciosum, 250
Conopias cinchoneti, 200
parva, 201
trivirgata, 201
Conopophaga ardesiaca, 174
aurita, 174
casteneiceps, 174
lineata, 174
melanogaster, 174
melanops, 174
peruviana, 174
roberti, 174
Conothraupis speculigera, 274
Contopus borealis, 205
cinereus, 212
fumigatus, 205
nigricens, 212
virens, 212
Coot, American, 26
Caribbean, 26
Giant, 26
Horned, 26
Red-fronted, 26
Red-gartered, 26
White-winged, 26
Coquette, Dot-eared, 78
Festive, 78
Frilled, 78
Peacock, 78
Racket-tailed, 78
Rufous-crested, 78
Spangled, 79
Tufted, 78
Coragyps atratus, 29
Corapipo gutturalis, 190, 194
leucorrhoa, 190,194
Cormorant, King, 22
Olivaceous, 22
Coronet, Buff-tailed, 89
Chestnut-breasted, 89
Velvet-purple, 89
Coryphaspiza melanotis, 304
Coryphistera alaudina, 130
Coryphospingus cucullatus, 303
pileatus, 308
Corythopis delalandi, 217
torquata, 217
Coscoroba coscoroba, 22
Cotinga cayana, 180
cotinga, 180
maculata, 180
*maynana,*180
nattererii, 180
Cotinga, Banded, 180
Bay-vented, 180
Black-and-gold, 179
Black-faced, 180
Black-necked Red-, 179
Blue, 180
Chestnut-crested, 179
Guianan Red-, 179
Plum-throated, 180
Pompadour, 180
Purple-breasted, 180
Purple-throated, 181
Red-crested, 180
Shrike-like, 181
Spangled, 180
Swallow-tailed, 179
White, 179
White-cheeked, 180
White-tailed, 180
White-winged, 180
Coturnicops notata, 20
Cowbird, Bay-winged, 261
Giant, 255
Shiny, 261
Screaming, 261
Crake, Ash-throated, 19
Black, 19
Black-banded, 19
Chestnut-headed, 19
Dot-winged, 19
Gray-breasted, 19
Ocellated, 20
Paint-billed, 19
Red-and-white, 19
Rufous, sided, 19
Russet-crowned, 19
Rusty-flanked, 19
Speckled, 20
Uniform, 19
Yellow-breasted, 20
Cranioleuca albicapilla, 144
albiceps, 144
antisiensis, 142
curtata, 142
demissa, 142
erythrops, 142
gutturata, 142
hellmayri, 142
marcapatae, 142
muelleri, 142
obsoleta, 145
pallida, 144
pyrrhophia, 144
semicinerea, 144
subcristata, 144
sulphurifera, 145
vulpina, 142
Crax alberti, 1
alector, 1
blumenbachii, 1
daubentoni, 1
fasciolata, 1
globulosa, 1
rubra, 1
Crescent-chest, Collared, 176
Elegant, 176
Maranon, 176
Olive-crowned, 176
Creurgops dentata, 275
verticalis, 275
Crotophaga ani, 54
major, 54
sulcirostris, 54
Crypturellus atrocapillus, 6
bartletti, 6
brevirostris, 6
boucardi, 6
casiquiare, 6
cinereus, 7
duidae, 6
erythropus, 6
kerriae, 6
noctivagus, 6
obsoletus, 7
parvirostris, 7
ptaritepui, 6
soui, 7
strigulosus, 6
tataupa, 7
transfaciatus, 6
undulatus, 6
variegatus, 6
Cuckoo, Ash-colored, 55
Banded Ground-, 54
Black-bellied, 55
Black-billed, 55
Dark-billed, 56
Dwarf, 56
Gray-capped, 55
Guira, 54
Little, 55
Mangrove, 55
Pavonine, 54
Pearly-breasted, 55
Pheasant, 54
Red-billed Ground-, 54
Rufous-vented Ground, 54

Cuckoo
Rufous-winged Ground, 54
Squirrel, 54
Striped, 55
Yellow-billed, 55
Culicivora caudacuta, 228
Curaeus curaeus, 257
forbesi, 257
Curassow, Bare-faced, 1
Black, 1
Blue-billed, 1
Crestless, 2
Great, 1
Helmeted, 1
Nocturnal, 2
Razor-billed, 1
Red-billed, 1
Salvin's, 1
Wattled, 1
Yellow-knobbed, 1
Cyanerpes caeruleus, 252
cyaneus, 252
lucidus, 253
nitidus, 253
Cyanicterus cyanicterus, 275
Cyanocompsa cyanea, 293
cyanoides, 293
Cyanocorax affinis, 233
caeruleus, 233
cayanus, 233
chrysops, 233
cristatellus, 234
cyanomelas, 233
cyanopogon, 233
heilprini, 233
mystacalis, 233
violaceus, 233
yncas, 234
Cyanoliseus patagonus, 44
Cyanoloxia glaucocaerulea, 293
Cyanolyca pulchra, 234
turcosa, 234
viridicyana, 234
Cyanopsitta spixii, 44
Cyclarhis gujanensis, 247
nigrirostris, 247
Cygnus melancoryphus, 21
Cymbilaimus lineatus, 147
Cyphorhinus arada, 243
phaeocephalus, 243
thoracicus, 243
Cypseloides cherriei, 62
cryptus, 62
fumigatus, 62
lemosi, 62
rutilus, 62
senex, 62
Cypsnagra hirundinacea, 283

Dacnis albiventris, 254
berlepschi, 254
cayana, 253
flaviventer, 254
lineata, 254
nigripes, 254
venusta, 253
viguieri, 253
Dacnis, Black-faced, 254
Black-legged, 254
Blue, 253
Scarlet-breasted, 254
Scarlet-thighed, 253
Tit-like, 254
Viridian, 253
White-bellied, 254
Yellow-bellied, 254
Damophila julie, 75
Daptrius americanus, 36
ater, 36
Deconychura longicauda, 123
stictolaema, 124
Dendrexetastes rufigula, 123
Dendrocincla fuliginosa, 123
homochroa, 123
merula, 123
tyrannina, 123
Dendrocolaptes certhia, 123
concolor, 122
hoffmannsi, 120
picumnus, 120
platyrostris, 120
Dendrocopos lignarius, 114
mixtus, 114
Dendrocygna autumnalis, 24
bicolor, 24
viduata, 24
Dendroica castanea, 263
cerulea, 262
fusca, 262
petechia, 264
striata, 262
Deroptyus accipitrinus, 50
Dichrozona cincta, 169
Dickcissel, 299
Diglossa albilatera, 252
baritula, 251
caerulescens, 252
carbonaria, 251
cyanea, 251
duidae, 251
glauca, 252
indigotica, 252
lafresnayii, 251
major, 251
sittoides, 251
venezuelensis, 252
Dipper, Rufous-throated, 21
White-capped, 21
Discosura longicauda, 78
Diuca diuca, 299
speculifera, 299
Diucon, Fire-eyed, 203
Dives warszewiczi, 258
Dolichonyx oryzivorus, 261
Doliornis sclateri, 180
Dolospingus fringilloides, 301
Donacobius atricapillus, 239
Donacospiza albifrons, 301
Doradito, Crested, 224
Dinelli's, 224
Subtropical, 223
Warbling, 223
Doryfera johannae, 82
ludoviciae, 82
Dotterel, Rufous-chested, 17
Tawny-throated, 17
Dove, Bare-eyed Ground-, 41
Bare-faced Ground-, 41
Black-winged Ground-, 41
Blue Ground-, 41
Blue-eyed Ground-, 42
Common Ground-, 42
Croaking Ground-, 42
Eared, 40
Golden-spotted Ground-, 41
Gray-chested, 40
Gray-fronted, 40
Gray-headed, 40
Large-tailed, 40
Lined Quail-, 39
Long-tailed Ground-, 41
Maroon-chested Ground-, 41
Ochre-bellied, 40
Olive-backed Quail-, 39
Pallid, 40
Picui Ground-, 42
Plain-breasted Ground-, 42
Purple-winged Ground-, 41
Ruddy Ground-, 41
Ruddy Quail-, 39
Russet-crowned Quail-, 39
Sapphire Quail-, 39
Scaled, 40
Scaly Ground-, 42
Tolima, 40

Violaceous Quail-, 39
White-throated Quail-, 39
White-tipped, 40
White-winged, 40
Dowitcher, Common, 15
Short-billed, 15
Dromococcyx pavoninus, 54
phasianellus, 54
Drymophila caudata, 165
devillei, 165
ferruginea, 165
genei, 165
malura, 165
ochropyga, 166
squamata, 165
Drymornis bridgesii, 122
Dryocopus galeatus, 111
lineatus, 110
schulzi, 111
Dubusia castaneoventris, 275
taeniata, 269
Duck, Black-
bellied Whistling-, 24
Black-headed, 25
Brazilian, 25
Comb, 23
Crested. 23
Flying Steamer-, 23
Fulvous Whistling-, 24
Lake, 25
Masked, 25
Muscovy, 23
Ruddy, 25
Spectacled, 24
Torrent, 25
White-
faced Whistling-, 25
Dysithamnus mentalis, 169
puncticeps, 169
stictothorax, 168
xanthopterus, 169

Eagle, Black-
and-chestnut, 30
Black-
and-white Hawk-, 31
Black-
chested Buzzard-, 31
Black Hawk-, 30
Crested, 30
Crowned, 31
Harpy, 30
Ornate Hawk-, 31
Solitary, 31
Earthcreeper, Band-
tailed, 127
Bolivian, 126
Buff-breasted, 126
Chaco, 126
Plain-breasted, 126
Rock, 126
Scale-throated, 126
Straight-billed, 126
Striated, 126
White-throated, 126
Egret, Cattle, 12
Great, 10
Snowy, 12
Egretta, caerulea, 12
thula, 12
tricolor, 12
Elaenia albiceps, 207
chiriquensis, 208
cristata, 208
dayi, 204
flavogaster, 207
frantzii, 208
gigas, 204
mesoleuca, 207
obscura, 204
pallatangae, 208
parvirostris, 207
pelzelni, 204
ruficeps, 208
spectabilis, 204
strepera, 207
Elaenia, Brownish, 204
Forest, 208
Gray, 209
Great, 204
Greenish, 208
Highland, 204
Large, 204
Lesser, 208
Mottle-backed, 204
Mountain, 208
Olivaceous, 207
Pacific, 208
Plain-crested, 208
Rufous-crowned, 208
Sierran, 208
Slaty, 207
Small-billed, 207
White-crested, 207
Yellow-bellied, 207
Yellow-crowned, 208
Elanoides forficatus, 29
Elanus leucurus, 29
Electron platyrhynchum, 96
Eleothreptus anomalus, 60
Emberizoides herbicola, 298
Embernagra longicauda, 294
platensis, 294
Emerald, Andean, 86
Amazilia, 77
Blue-chested, 76
Blue-tailed, 93
Chestnut-bellied, 85
Copper-rumped, 76
Coppery, 93
Glittering-bellied, 93
Glittering-throated, 75
Green-bellied, 76
Green-tailed, 93
Indigo-capped, 76
Narrow-tailed, 93
Plain-bellied, 76
Purple-chested, 76
Red-billed, 79
Rufous-tailed, 77
Sapphire-spangled, 76
Short-tailed, 93
Steely-vented, 76
Tachira, 76
Versicolored, 75
White-chested, 75
Empidonax euleri, 212
griseipectus, 212
traillii, 212
virescens, 212
Empidonomus
aurantioatrocristatus,
205
varius, 205
Enicognathus ferrugineus, 44
leptorhynchus, 44
Ensifera ensifera, 79
Entomodestes coracinus, 237
leucotis, 237
Entotriccus striaticeps, 224
Eremobius phoenicurus, 127
Eremophila alpestris, 245
Eriocnemis alinae, 87
cupreoventris, 87
derbyi, 86
glaucopoides, 87
godini, 87
luciani, 86
mirabilis, 87
mosquera, 86
nigrivestis, 87
vestitus, 87
Erythrothlypis salmoni, 287
Eubucco bourcierii, 105
richardsoni, 105
tucinkae, 105
versicolor, 105
Eucometis penicillata, 273
Eudocimus albus, 13
ruber, 13
Eudromia elegans, 5
formosa, 5
Eugralla paradoxa, 176
Eulidia yarrellii, 79
Eupetomena macroura, 83
Euphonia anneae, 288

Euphonia, cayannensis, 290
chalybea, 289
chlorotica, 289
chrysopasta, 290
concinna, 289
finschi, 289
fulvicrissa, 289
laniirostris, 288
mesochrysa, 289
minuta, 289
musica, 290
pectoralis, 290
plumbea, 290
rufiventris, 290
saturata, 289
trinitatis, 289
violacea, 289
xanthogaster, 288
Euphonia
Blue-hooded, 290
Bronze-green, 289
Chestnut-bellied, 290
Finsch's, 289
Fulvous-vented, 289
Golden-bellied, 290
Golden-sided, 290
Green-throated, 289
Orange-bellied, 288
Orange-crowned, 289
Plumbeous, 290
Purple-throated, 289
Rufous-bellied, 290
Tawny-capped, 289
Thick-billed, 288
Trinidad, 289
Velvet-fronted, 289
Violaceous, 289
White-lored, 290
White-vented, 289
Eurypyga helias, 14
Euscarthmus meloryphus, 228
rufomarginatus, 221
Eutoxeres aquila, 69
condamini, 69
Euxenura maguari, 10

Fairy, Black-eared, 78
Purple-crowned, 78
Falco columbarius, 37
deiroleucus, 37
femoralis, 37
kreyenborgi, 37
peregrinus, 37
rufigularis, 37
sparverius, 37
Falcon, Aplomado, 37
Barred Forest-, 37
Bat, 37
Buckley's Forest-, 36
Collared Forest-, 36
Laughing, 36
Orange-breasted, 37
Pallid, 37
Peregrine, 37
Plumbeous Forest-, 37
Slaty-backed Forest-, 36
Falconet, Spot-winged, 37
Finch, Ash-breasted Sierra-, 304
Band-tailed Sierra-, 302
Bay-chested Warbling-, 311
Bay-crowned Brush-, 296
Black-and-rufous Warbling-, 303
Black-capped Warbling-, 306
Black-crested, 306
Black-headed Brush-, 294
Black-hooded Sierra-, 298
Black-masked, 304
Black-throated, 303
Blue, 304
Bolivian Warbling-, 301
Bright-rumped Yellow-, 304
Buff-bridled Inca-, 303
Buff-throated Pampa-, 294
Carbonated Sierra-, 305
Chestnut-breasted Mountain-, 299
Chestnut-capped Brush-, 294
Cinereous, 300
Cinereous Warbling-, 305
Cinnamon Warbling-, 304
Citron-headed Yellow-, 301
Coal-crested, 312
Cochabamba Mountain-, 298
Collared Warbling-, 311
Common Diuca-, 299
Crimson, 313
Dusky-headed Brush-, 296
Fulvous-headed Brush-, 296
Grassland Yellow-, 312
Gray-crested, 302
Gray-hooded Sierra-, 298
Great Inca-, 300
Great Pampa-, 294
Great-billed Seed-, 303
Greater Large-billed Seed-, 303
Greater Yellow-, 301
Greenish Yellow-, 304
Large-billed Seed-, 303
Lesser Seed-, 305
Little Inca-, 311
Long-tailed Reed-, 301
Many-colored Chaco, 299
Mourning Sierra-, 298
Moustached Brush-, 295
Ochre-breasted Brush-, 296
Olive, 302
Olive-headed Brush-, 296
Orange-fronted Yellow-, 312
Pale-headed Brush-, 296
Pale-naped Brush-, 295
Pale-throated Pampa-, 294
Patagonian Sierra-, 302
Patagonian Yellow-, 302
Pileated, 308
Plain-tailed Warbling-, 301
Plumbeous Sierra-, 302
Plush-capped, 304
Puna Yellow-, 303
Raimondi's Yellow-, 312
Red-backed Sierra-, 297
Red-crested, 303
Red-rumped Warbling-, 304
Ringed Warbling-, 311
Rufous-backed Inca-, 300
Rufous-breasted Warbling-, 301
Rufous-eared Brush-, 294
Rufous-naped Brush-, 295
Rufous-sided Warbling-, 300
Rusty-bellied Brush-, 295
Rusty-browed Warbling-, 305
Saffron, 305
Saffron Yellow-, 305
Santa Marta Brush-, 295
Short-tailed, 298
Slaty, 307
Slaty Brush-, 295
Slender-billed, 301
Stripe-headed Brush-, 294

Stripe-tailed Yellow-, 312
Sulphur-throated, 308
Tanager-, 298
Tepui Brush-, 295
Tricolored Brush-, 294
Tucuman Mountain-, 298
Uniform, 307
Wedge-tailed Grass-, 298
White-headed Brush-, 296
White-rimmed Brush-, 294
White-throated Sierra-, 297
White-winged Brush-, 296
White-winged Diuca-, 299
Yellow-bridled, 301
Yellow-striped Brush-, 297
Yellow-throated Brush-, 295
Firecrown, Green-backed, 86
Fire-eye, White-backed, 158
White-shouldered, 158
Firewood-Gatherer, 133
Flamingo, American, 10
Andean, 10
Chilean, 9
Puna, 10
Flatbill, Dusky-tailed, 210
Eye-ringed, 210
Fulvous-breasted, 210
Large-headed, 210
Olivaceous, 210
Rufous-tailed, 210
Flicker, Andean, 111
Campo, 111
Chilean, 111
Field, 111
Florida caerulea, 12
Florisuga mellivora, 73
Flower-piercer, Bluish, 252
Carbonated, 251
Deep-blue, 252
Glossy, 251
Greater, 251
Indigo, 252
Masked, 251
Rusty, 251
Scaled, 251
Slaty, 251
Venezuelan, 252
White-sided, 252
Fluvicola albiventris, 197
nengeta, 215
pica, 197
Flycatcher, Acadian, 212
Apical, 203
Baird's, 201
Black-and-white Tody-, 232
Black-billed, 219
Black-headed Tody-, 226
Black-tailed, 216
Boat-billed, 200
Bran-colored, 218
Brown-crested, 203
Brownish, 205
Cliff, 197
Cinnamon, 227
Common Tody-, 232
Crowned Slaty- 205
Dusky-capped, 204
Dusky-chested, 199
Euler's, 212
Flavescent, 218
Fork-tailed, 209
Fuscous, 213
Golden-crowned, 201
Golden-winged Tody-, 226
Gray-breasted, 212
Gray-capped, 200
Gray-crowned, 213
Gray-headed Tody-, 226
Gray-hooded, 214
Great-crested, 203
Handsome, 219
Inca, 217
Lemon-browed, 200
McConnell's, 215
Ochraceous-breasted, 218
Ochre-bellied, 214
Ochre-faced Tody-, 226
Olive-chested, 218
Olive-sided, 205
Olive-striped, 214
Orange-banded, 218
Orange-crested, 218
Ornate, 231
Painted Tody-, 232
Pale-edged, 203
Piratic, 212
Roraiman, 219
Royal, 206
Ruddy Tody-, 226
Ruddy-tailed, 232
Rufous, 204
Rufous-breasted, 217
Rusty-fronted Tody-, 232
Rusty-margined, 200
Scrub, 209
Sepia-capped, 217
Short-crested, 203
Slate-headed Tody-, 225
Slaty-capped, 217
Smoky- fronted Tody-, 226
Social, 200
Sooty-crowned, 203
Spotted Tody-, 232
Streaked, 201
Streak-necked, 213
Suiriri, 209
Sulphur-bellied, 201
Sulphur-rumped, 216
Sulphury, 199
Swainson's, 203
Tawny-breasted, 216
Three-striped, 201
Traill's, 212
Tufted, 218
Unadorned, 227
Variegated, 205
Vermilion, 213
White-bearded, 200
White-ringed, 201
Yellow-breasted, 213
Yellow-lored Tody-, 226
Yellow-margined, 213
Yellow-olive, 213
Foliage-gleaner, Black-capped, 138
Brown-rumped, 137
Buff-browed, 135
Buff-fronted, 137
Buff-throated, 134
Chestnut-capped, 137
Chestnut-crowned, 135
Chestnut-winged, 138
Cinnamon-rumped, 136
Crested, 137
Guttulated, 137
Henna-hooded, 137
Lineated, 138
Montane, 138
Neblina, 138
Ochre-breasted, 135
Olive-backed, 135
Ruddy, 135
Rufous-necked, 137
Rufous-rumped, 138
Rufous-tailed, 135
Russet-mantled, 136
Scaly-throated, 138
Spectacled, 138
White-browed, 138
White-collared, 137
White-eyed, 135
White-throated, 135
Formicarius analis, 153
colma, 154
nigricapillus, 154
rufipectus, 154

Formicivora,
grisea, 167
iheringi, 167
melanogaster, 167
rufa, 167
serrana, 167
Forpus coelestis, 53
conspicillatus, 53
passerinus, 53
sclateri, 53
xanthops, 53
xanthropterygius, 53
Frederickena unduligera, 147
viridis, 147
Fruitcrow, Bare-necked, 177
Crimson, 177
Purple-throated, 177
Red-ruffed, 177
Fruiteater, Band-tailed, 182
Barred, 181
Black-chested, 182
Fiery-throated, 185
Golden-breasted, 182
Green-and-black, 181
Handsome, 182
Masked, 182
Orange-breasted, 182
Red-banded, 182
Scaled, 182
Scarlet-breasted, 182
Fulica americana, 26
armillata, 26
caribaea, 26
cornuta, 26
gigantea, 26
leucoptera, 26
rufifrons, 26
Furnarius cristatus, 128
figulus, 128
leucopus, 128
minor, 128
rufus, 128

Galbalcyrhynchus leucotis, 99
Galbula albirostris, 99
cyanescens, 98
dea, 98
galbula, 98
leucogastra, 98
pastazae, 98
ruficauda, 98
tombacea, 98
Gallinago andina, 16
gallinago, 16
nobilis, 15
stricklandii, 15
undulata, 15
Gallinula chloropus, 15
Gallinule, Azure, 15
Common, 15
Purple, 15
Spot-flanked, 15
Gallito, Crested, 175
Sandy, 175
Gampsonyx swainsonii, 30
Gelochelidon nilotica, 28
Geobates poecilopterus, 130
Geositta antarctica, 130
crassirostris, 129
cunicularia, 129
isabellina, 129
maritima, 130
peruviana, 130
punensis, 129
rufipennis, 129
saxicolina, 129
tenuirostris, 129
Geothalsia bella, 75
Geothlypis aequinoctialis, 264
agilis, 263
formosus, 263
philadelphia, 263
semiflava, 264
Geotrygon frenata, 39
goldmani, 39
linearis, 39
montana, 39
saphirina, 39
veraguensis, 39
violacea, 39
Geranoaetus melanoleucus, 31
Geranospiza caerulescens, 34
Glaucidium brasilianum, 58
jardinii, 58
minutissimum, 58
nanum, 58
Glaucis aenea, 68
hirsuta, 68
Glyphorhynchus spirurus, 124
Gnatcatcher, Cream-bellied, 247
Guianan, 247
Masked, 246
Slate-throated, 247
Tropical, 247
Gnateater, Ash-throated, 174
Black-bellied, 174
Black-cheeked, 174
Chestnut-belted, 174
Chestnut-crowned, 174
Hooded, 174
Rufous, 174
Slaty, 174
Gnathospiza taczanowskii, 308
Gnatwren, Collared, 246
Half-collared, 246
Long-billed, 246
Tawny-faced, 246
Gnorimopsar chopi, 257
Godwit, Hudsonian, 14
Goethalsia bella, 75
Goldenthroat, Green-tailed, 72
Tepui, 85
White-tailed, 71
Goldfinch, Dark-backed, 313
Goldmania violiceps, 86
Goose, Andean, 22
Ashy-headed, 22
Orinoco, 22
Ruddy-headed, 22
Upland, 22
Grackle, Carib, 256
Golden-tufted, 256
Great-tailed, 256
Mountain, 256
Red-bellied, 256
Velvet-fronted, 256
Grallaria albigula, 154
andicola, 155
bangsi, 155
chthonia, 154
dignissima, 155
eludens, 155
erythrotis, 154
excelsa, 153
gigantea, 153
griseonucha, 155
guatimalensis, 154
haplonota, 154
hypoleuca, 155
milleri, 156
nuchalis, 154
quitensis, 155
ruficapilla, 153
rufocinerea, 155
rufula, 156
squamigera, 153
varia, 154
Grallaricula cucullata, 157
ferrugineipectus, 156
flavirostris, 156
lineifrons, 156
loricata, 157
nana, 157
peruviana, 157
Granatellus pelzelni, 264
Grassquit, Black-faced, 313
Blue-black, 312
Sooty, 313
Yellow-faced, 313
Graydidascalus brachyurus, 51

Graytail, Double-banded, 136
Equatorial, 136
Grebe, Eared, 27
Great, 26
Least, 27
Pied-billed, 27
Puna, 26
Short-winged, 27
Silvery, 27
White-tufted, 27
Greenlet, Ashy-headed, 249
Brown-headed, 249
Buff-cheeked, 249
Buff-chested, 249
Dusky-capped, 249
Gray-chested, 249
Golden-fronted, 248
Lemon-chested, 249
Lesser, 249
Olivaceous, 249
Rufous-crowned, 248
Rufous-naped, 248
Scrub, 249
Tawny-crowned, 248
Tepui, 249
Grosbeak, Black-backed, 292
Black-throated, 292
Blue-black, 293
Indigo, 293
Red-and-black, 292
Rose-breasted, 293
Slate-colored, 292
Ultramarine, 293
Yellow, 293
Yellow-green. 293
Yellow-shouldered, 293
Ground-creeper, Canebrake, 127
Ground-Dove, see Dove
Ground-Tyrant, see Tyrant
Guan, Andean, 2
Band-tailed, 3
Baudo, 2
Black-fronted Piping-, 3
Blue-throated Piping-, 3
Chestnut-bellied, 2
Crested, 2
Dusky-legged, 2
Marail, 2
Red-faced, 2
Red-throated Piping-, 3
Rusty-margined, 2
Sickle-winged, 3
Spix's, 2
Wattled, 3
White-browed, 2
White-crested, 2
White-winged, 3
Gubernatrix cristata, 297
Gubernetes yetapa, 205
Guira guira, 54
Gull, Andean, 27
Brown-hooded, 27
Gray, 27
Gray-hooded, 27
Kelp, 27
Gyalophylax hellmayri, 145
Gymnocichla nudiceps, 160
Gymnoderus foetidus, 177
Gymnomystax mexicanus, 257
Gymnopithys leucaspis, 165
lunulata, 160
rufigula, 165
salvini, 160
Gymnostinops bifasciatus, 255
cassini, 255
guatimozinus, 254
yuracares, 254
Gypopsitta vulturina, 52

Habia cristata, 270
fuscicauda, 271
gutturalis, 270
rubica, 270
Haematoderus militaris, 177
Hapalopsittaca amazonina, 51
melanotis, 51
Hapaloptila castanea, 100
Haplophaedia aureliae, 86
lugens, 86
Haplospiza rustica, 307
unicolor, 307
Harpagus bidentatus, 30
diodon, 30
Harpia harpyja, 30
Harpiprion caerulescens, 13
Harpyhaliaetus coronatus, 31
solitarius, 31
Harrier, Cinereous, 34
Long-winged, 34
Hawk, Barred, 33
Bay-winged, 33
Bicolored, 35
Black-collared, 34
Black-faced, 33
Broad-winged, 32
Common Black-, 31
Crane, 34
Gray, 32
Gray-backed, 33
Gray-bellied, 34
Great Black-, 31
Mantled, 33
Plumbeous, 33
Plain-breasted, 35
Puna, 31
Red-backed, 32
Roadside, 32
Rufous-tailed, 31
Rufous-thighed, 35
Savannah, 34
Semicollared, 35
Semi-plumbeous 34
Sharp-shinned, 35
Short-tailed, 32
Slate-colored, 33
Swainson's, 32
Tiny, 35
Variable, 31
White, 33
White-browed, 33
White-necked, 33
White-rumped, 33
White-tailed, 31
White-throated, 32
Zone-tailed, 32
Heliactin cornuta, 78
Heliangelus amethysticollis, 90
exortis, 90
mavors, 90
spencei, 90
strophianus, 90
viola, 90
Helicolestes hamatus, 29
Heliobletus contaminatus, 140
Heliodoxa branickii, 84
gularis, 70
imperatrix, 84
jacula, 84
leadbeateri, 84
rubinoides, 84
schreibersii, 70
xanthogonys, 84
Heliomaster furcifer, 70
longirostris, 70
squamosus, 69
Heliornis fulica, 18
Heliothryx aurita, 78
barroti, 78
Hellmayrea gularis, 146
Helmetcrest, Bearded, 91
Hemispingus atropileus, 278
frontalis, 278
goeringi, 279
melanotis, 279
reyi, 278
superciliaris, 278
trifasciatus, 279
verticalis, 279
xanthopthalmus, 279
Hemispingus, Black-capped, 278

Hemispingus,
Black-eared, 279
Black-headed, 279
Drab, 279
Gray-capped, 278
Oleaginous, 278
Slaty-backed, 279
Superciliaried, 278
Three-striped, 279
Hemithraupis flavicollis, 286
guira, 286
ruficapilla, 286
Hemitriccus diops, 230
flammulatus, 230
obsoletus, 230
Henicorhina leucophrys, 244
leucosticta, 244
Hermit, Broad-tipped, 67
Bronzy, 68
Buff-bellied, 67
Cinnamon-throated, 67
Dusky-throated, 67
Gray-chinned, 68
Great-billed, 66
Green, 66
Hook-billed, 69
Little, 67
Long-tailed, 66
Minute, 68
Needle-billed, 67
Pale-bellied, 67
Planalto, 67
Reddish, 68
Rufous-breasted, 68
Saw-billed, 69
Scale-throated, 66
Sooty-capped, 67
Straight-billed, 67
Tawny-bellied, 66
White-bearded, 67
White-browed, 67
White-whiskered, 66
Heron, Bare-throated Tiger-, 11
Black-crowned Night-, 11
Boat-billed, 11
Capped, 12
Chestnut-bellied, 11
Fasciated Tiger-, 11
Great Blue, 10
Green, 12
Green-backed, 12
Little Blue, 12
Rufescent Tiger-, 11
Striated, 12
Tricolored, 12
Whistling, 12
White-necked, 10
Yellow-crowned Night-, 12
Zigzag, 14
Herpetotheres cachinnans, 36
Herpsilochmus axillaris, 166
dorsimaculatus, 166
longirostris, 166
pectoralis, 166
pileatus, 166
roraimae, 166
rufimarginatus, 166
stictocephalus, 166
sticturus, 166
Heterocercus aurantiivertex, 187
flaviverteax, 187
linteatus, 187
Heteronetta atricapilla, 25
Heterospingus xanthopygius, 275
Heterospizias meridionalis, 34
Hillstar, Andean, 84
Black-breasted, 84
Wedge-tailed, 83
White-sided, 84
White-tailed, 83
Himantopus himantopus, 14
Hirundinea ferruginea, 197
Hirundo rustica, 64
Hoatzin, 13
Honeycreeper,
Golden-collared, 253
Green, 253
Purple, 252
Red-legged, 252
Shining, 253
Short-billed, 253
Hookbill, Chestnut-winged, 139
Hoploxypterus cayanus, 17
Hornero, Crested, 128
Lesser, 128
Pale-legged, 128
Rufous, 128
Wing-banded, 128
Huet-huet, Black-throated, 175
Chestnut-throated, 175
Hummingbird, Amazilia, 77
Blue-chested, 76
Buffy, 72
Copper-rumped, 76
Giant, 79
Gilded Sapphire, 73
Green-and-white, 85
Green-bellied, 76
Indigo-capped, 76
Many-spotted, 70
Oasis, 69
Olive-spotted, 72
Pirre, 75
Ruby-topaz, 79
Rufous-tailed, 76
Sapphire-bellied, 75
Sapphire-throated, 75
Scaly-breasted, 73
Scissor-tailed, 83
Shining-green, 75
Sombre, 74
Speckled, 92
Spot-throated, 72
Steely-vented, 76
Swallow-tailed, 83
Sword-billed, 79
Tooth-billed, 69
Tumbes, 72
Violet-bellied, 75
Violet-capped, 86
Violet-chested, 81
Violet-headed, 92
Wedge-billed, 92
White-bellied, 85
White-chested, 75
White-throated, 74
Hydranassa tricolor, 12
Hydropsalis brasiliana, 59
climacocerca, 59
Hylexetastes perrotii, 122
stresemanni, 122
Hylocharis chrysura, 73
cyanus, 73
grayi, 73
sapphirina, 73
Hylocryptus erythrocephalus, 137
rectirostris, 137
Hyloctistes subulatus, 139
Hylomanes momotula, 96
Hylonympha macrocerca, 83
Hylopezus berlepschi, 156
fulviventris, 155
macularius, 155
ochroleucus, 156
perspicillatus, 156
Hylophilus aurantiifrons, 248
brunneiceps, 249
flavipes, 249
hypoxanthus, 249
minor, 249
muscicapinus, 249
ochraceiceps, 248
olivaceus, 249
pectoralis, 249
poicilotis, 248
sclateri, 249
semibrunneus, 248
semicinereus, 249
thoracius, 249
Hylophylax naevia, 168
naevioides, 168

poecilonota, 167
punctulata, 168
Hymenops perspicillata, 214
Hypnelus ruficollis, 101
Hypocnemis cantator, 171
hypoxantha, 171
Hypocnemoides
maculicauda, 169
melanopogon, 169
Hypoedaleus guttatus, 147
Hypopyrrhus pyrohypogaster, 256

Ibis, Bare-faced, 13
Buff-necked, 13
Green, 13
Plumbeous, 13
Puna, 13
Scarlet, 13
Sharp-tailed, 13
White, 13
White-faced, 13
Wood, 10
Icterus auricapillus, 260
cayanensis, 259
chrysater, 259
chrysocephalus, 260
galbula, 260
graceannae, 260
icterus, 259
mesomelas, 259
nigrogularis, 259
spurius, 260
Ictinia misisippiensis, 29
plumbea, 30
Idiopsar brachyurus, 298
Idioptilon aenigma, 224
granadense, 229
kaempferi, 224
margaritaceiventer, 224
mirandae, 229
nidipendulum, 230
orbitatum, 229
rufigulare, 229
spodiops, 224
striaticolle, 229
zosterops, 224
Ilicura militaris, 188
Inca, Black, 81
Bronzy, 80
Brown, 81
Collared, 81
Incaspiza laeta, 303
personata, 300
pulchra, 300
watkinsi, 311
Inezia inornata, 220
subflava, 221
tenuirostris, 221
Iodopleura fusca, 185
isabellae, 185
pipra, 185
Iridophanes pulcherrima, 253
Iridosornis analis, 276
jelskii, 276
porphyrocephala, 276
reinhardti, 276
rufivertex, 276
Ixobrychus exilis, 14
involucris, 14

Jabiru mycteria, 9
Jabiru, 9
Jacamar, Bluish-fronted, 98
Bronzy, 98
Brown, 99
Chestnut, 99
Coppery-chested, 98
Dusky-backed, 99
Great, 98
Green-tailed, 98
Pale-headed, 99
Paradise, 98
Rufous-tailed, 98
Three-toed, 99
White-chinned, 98
White-throated, 99
Yellow-billed, 99
Jacamaralcyon tridactyla, 99
Jacamerops aurea, 98
Jacana jacana, 15
Jacana, Wattled, 15
Jacobin, Black, 73
White-necked, 73
Jay, Azure, 233
Azure-naped, 233
Beautiful, 234
Black-chested, 233
Cayenne, 233
Collared, 234
Curl-crested, 234
Green, 234
Plush-crested, 233
Purplish, 233
Turquoise, 234
Violaceous, 233
White-naped, 233
White-tailed, 233
Jewelfront, Gould's, 70

Kestrel, American, 37
Killsdeer, 17
Kingbird, Eastern, 199
Gray, 199
Snowy-throated, 199
Tropical, 199
White-throated, 199
Kingfisher, Amazon, 97
Green, 97
Green-and-rufous, 97
Pygmy, 97
Ringed, 96
Kiskadee, Great, 200
Lesser, 200
Kite, Black-shouldered, 29
Double-toothed, 30
Everglade, 29
Gray-headed, 29
Hook-billed, 29
Mississippi, 29
Pearl, 30
Plumbeous, 30
Rufous-thighed, 30
Slender-billed, 29
Snail, 29
Swallow-tailed, 29
White-tailed, 29
Klais, guimeti, 92
Knipolegus, aterrimus, 207
cabanisi, 207
cyanirostris, 207
lophotes, 206
nigerrimus, 206
orenocensis, 206
poecilurus, 206

Lafresnaya lafresnayi, 82
Lampropsar tanagrinus, 256
Lamprospiza melanoleuca, 280
Lancebill, Blue-fronted, 82
Green-fronted, 82
Laniisoma elegans, 181
Lanio fulvus, 272
versicolor, 271
Laniocerca hypopyrrha, 202
rufescens, 202
Lapwing, Andean, 17
Southern, 16
Lark, Horned, 245
Larus, cirrocephalus, 27
dominicanus, 27
maculipennis, 27
modestus, 27
serranus, 27
Laterallus exilis, 19
fasciatus, 19
jamaicensis, 19
leucopyrrhus, 19

Laterallus
levraudi, 19
melanophaius, 19
spilopterus, 19
viridis, 19
Leafscraper, see Leaftosser
Leaftosser, Black-tailed, 128
Gray-throated, 128
Rufous-breasted, 128
Scaly-throated, 129
Short-billed, 128
Tawny-throated, 129
Legatus leucophaius, 212
Leistes militaris, 259
superciliaris, 258
Lepidocolaptes affinis, 122
albolineatus, 123
angustirostris, 121
fuscus, 122
souleyetii, 121
squamatus, 122
Lepidopyga coeruleogularis, 75
goudoti, 75
lilliae, 75
Leptasthenura aegithaloides, 125
andicola, 125
fuliginiceps, 125
pileata, 125
platensis, 125
setaria, 125
striata, 125
striolata, 125
xenothorax, 125
yanacensis, 125
Leptodon cayanensis, 29
Leptopogon amaurocephalus, 217
rufipectus, 217
superciliaris, 217
taczanowskii, 217
Leptosittaca branickii, 44
Leptotila cassinii, 40
conoveri, 40
megalura, 40
ochraceiventris, 40
pallida, 40
plumbeiceps, 40
rufaxilla, 40
verreauxi, 40
Leptotriccus sylviolus, 228
Lesbia nuna, 88
victoriae, 88
Lessonia rufa, 197
Leucippus baeri, 72
chlorocercus, 72
chionogaster, 85
chionopectus, 75
fallax, 72
taczanowskii, 72
viridicauda, 85
Leucochloris albicollis, 74
Leuconerpes candidus, 112
Leucopternis albicollis, 33
kuhli, 33
lacernulata, 33
melanops, 33
occidentalis, 33
plumbea, 33
polionota, 33
princeps, 33
schistacea, 33
semiplumbea, 34
Limnoctites rectirostris, 134
Limnodromus griseus, 15
Limnornis curvirostris, 134
Limosa haemastica, 14
Limpkin, 13
Liosceles thoracicus, 175
Lipaugus cryptolophus, 178
fuscocinereus, 178
lanioides, 178
streptophorus, 178
subalaris, 178
unirufous, 178
vociferans, 178
Lochmias nematura, 129
Loddigesia mirabilis, 89
Lophonetta specularioides, 23
Lophornis chalybea, 78
Lophornis delattrei, 78
gouldii, 78
magnifica, 78
ornata, 78
pavonina, 78
stictolopha, 79
Lopohospingus griseocristatus, 302
pusillus, 306
Lophostrix cristata, 56
Lophotriccus eulophotes, 230
pileatus, 225
vitiosus, 225
Lurocalis semitorquatus, 61
Lysurus castaneiceps, 302

Macaw, Blue-and-yellow, 43
Blue-headed, 44
Blue-winged, 43
Chestnut-fronted, 43
Golden-collared, 43
Great Green, 42
Hyacinth, 42
Little Blue, 44
Military, 43
Red-and-green, 42
Red-bellied, 43
Red-fronted, 43
Red-shouldered, 44
Scarlet, 43
Machaeropterus
pyrocephalus, 190, 192
regulus, 190, 193
Machetornis rixosus, 196
Mackenziaena leachii, 147
severa, 147
Macroagelaius imthurni, 256
subalaris, 256
Macropsalis creagra, 59
Malacoptila fulvogularis, 101
fusca, 102
mystacalis, 101
panamensis, 102
rufa, 102
semicincta, 102
striata, 102
Manacus manacus, 190, 192
vitellinus, 189
Manakin, Band-tailed, 191, 193
Black, 187, 194
Black-capped, 188
Blue, 186
Blue-backed, 187, 194
Blue-crowned, 192, 195
Blue-rumped, 192
Broad-billed, 186
Cerulean-capped, 192
Cinnamon, 190
Club-winged, 189, 193
Crimson-hooded, 191, 194
Dwarf Tyrant-, 193
Fiery-capped, 190, 192
Flame-crowned, 187
Golden-collared, 189
Golden-headed, 191, 192
Golden-winged, 189
Greater, 186
Green, 193
Greenish, 186
Helmeted, 186
Jet, 188
Lance-tailed, 187
Olive, 187
Opal-crowned, 192
Orange-crowned, 187
Pale-bellied Tyrant-, 188
Pin-tailed, 188
Red-capped, 191, 193
Red-headed, 191
Round-tailed, 191
Saffron-crested Tyrant- 188
Scarlet-horned, 189
Snow-capped, 191

Striped, 190,193
Sulphur-bellied Tyrant-, 188
Swallow-tailed, 186
Thrush-like, 186
Tiny Tyrant-, 193
White bearded, 190, 192
White-crowned, 191, 194
White-fronted, 192, 195
White-ruffed, 190, 194
White-throated, 190, 194
Wied's Tyrant-, 188
Wing-barred, 189
Wire-tailed, 189
Yellow-crowned, 187
Yellow-headed, 188
Mango, Black-throated, 71
Green-breasted, 63
Green-throated, 71
Margarornis, squamiger, 139
stellatus, 139
Marshbird,
Brown-and-yellow, 260
Yellow-rumped, 260
Martin, Brown-chested, 63
Gray-breasted, 63
Purple, 63
Southern, 63
Masius, chrysopterus, 189
Meadowlark, Eastern, 261
Lesser Red-breasted, 261
Long-tailed, 260
Pampas, 261
Peruvian, 261
Red-breasted, 261
Mecocerculus calopterus, 220
hellmayri, 220
leucophrys, 217
minor, 220
poecilocercus, 220
stictopterus, 220
Megarhynchus pitangua, 200
Megastictus margaritatus, 151
Megaxenops parnaguae, 139
Melanerpes cactorum, 115
chrysauchen, 114
cruentatus, 114
flavifrons, 114
formicivorus, 113
pucherani, 114
rubricapillus, 115
Melanodera melanodera, 303
xanthogramma, 301
Melanopareia elegans, 176
maranonica, 176
maximiliani, 176
torquata, 176
Melanotrochilus fuscus, 73
Merganetta armata, 25
Merganser, Brazilian, 23
Mergus octosetaceus, 23
Merlin, 37
Merulaxis ater, 175
stresemanni, 175
Mesembrinibis cayennensis, 13
Metallura aeneocauda, 91
baroni, 91
eupogon, 91
iracunda, 91
phoebe, 91
theresiae, 91
tyrianthina, 91
williami, 91
Metaltail, Black, 91
Coppery, 91
Fire-throated, 91
Perija, 91
Scaled, 91
Tyrian, 91
Violet-throated, 91
Viridian, 91
Metopothrix aurantiacus, 140
Metriopelia aymara, 41
ceciliae, 41
melanoptera, 41
morenoi, 41
Micrastur buckleyi, 36
mirandollei, 36
plumbeus, 37
ruficollis, 37
semitorquatus, 36
Microbates cinereiventris, 246
collaris, 246
Microcerculus bambla, 244
marginatus, 244
ustulatus, 244
Micromonacha lanceolata, 103
Micropalama himantopus, 16
Micropanyptila furcata, 63
Micropygia schomburgkii, 20
Microrhopias quixensis, 172
Microstilbon burmeisteri, 93
Milvago chimachima, 36
chimango, 36
Mimus dorsalis, 239
gilvus, 239
longicaudatus, 239
patagonicus, 239
saturninus, 239
thenca, 239
triuris, 239
Miner, Campo, 130
Coastal, 130
Common, 129
Creamy-rumped, 129
Dark-winged, 129
Grayish, 130
Puna, 129
Rufous-banded, 129
Short-billed, 130
Slender-billed, 129
Thick-billed, 129
Mionectes olivaceus, 214
striaticollis, 213
Mitrephanes phaeocercus, 218
Mitrospingus cassinii, 273
oleagineus, 273
Mitu mitu, 1
salvini, 1
tomentosa, 2
Mniotilta varia, 262
Mockingbird, Brown-backed, 239
Chalk-browed, 239
Chilean, 239
Long-tailed, 239
Patagonian, 239
Tropical, 239
White-banded, 239
Mocking-Thrush,
Black-capped, 239
Molothrus badius, 261
bonariensis, 261
rufoaxillaris, 261
Momotus momota, 96
Monasa atra, 100
flavirostris, 100
morphoeus, 100
nigrifrons, 100
Monjita, Black-and-white, 198
Black-crowned, 198
Gray, 198
Mouse-brown, 198
Rusty-backed, 198
White, 199
White-rumped, 198
Monklet, Lanceolated, 103
Morphnus guianensis, 30
Motmot, Blue-crowned, 96
Broad-billed, 96
Rufous, 95
Rufous-capped, 96
Tody, 96
Mountaineer, Bearded, 80
Mourner, Cinereous, 302
Grayish, 202
Pale-bellied, 202
Rufous, 203
Speckled, 202
Muscigralla brevicauda, 197
Muscipipra vetula, 198
Muscisaxicola albifrons, 195
albilora, 196

Muscisaxicola
alpina, 196
capistrata, 196
flavinucha, 195
fluviatilis, 196
frontalis, 196
juninensis, 196
macloviana, 196
maculirostris, 196
rufivertex, 196
Musivora tyrannus, 209
Myadestes leucogenys, 237
ralloides, 238
Mycteria americana, 10
Myiarchus apicalis, 203
cephalotes, 203
crinitus, 203
ferox, 203
phaeocephalus, 203
semirufous, 204
swainsoni, 203
tuberculifer, 204
tyrannulus, 203
Myiobius atricaudus, 216
barbatus, 216
villosus, 216
Myioborus albifacies, 265
albifrons, 265
brunniceps, 265
cardonai, 265
flavivertex, 265
melanocephalus, 265
miniatus, 264
ornatus, 265
pariae, 265
Myiodynastes bairdi, 201
chrysocephalus, 201
luteiventris, 201
maculatus, 201
Myiopagis caniceps, 209
flavivertex, 208
gaimardii, 208
subplacens, 208
viridicata, 208
Myiophobus cryptoxanthus, 218
fasciatus, 218
flavicans, 218
inornatus, 227
lintoni, 218
ochraceiventris, 218
phoenicomitra, 218
pulcher, 219
roraimae, 219
Myiopsitta monachus, 44
Myiornis auricularis, 227
ecaudatus, 232
Myiotheretes erythropygius, 198
fumigatus, 204
fuscorufus, 204
pernix, 204
signatus, 215
striaticollis, 198
Myiotriccus ornatus, 231
Myiozetetes cayanensis, 200
granadensis, 200
inornatus, 200
similis, 200
Myornis senilis, 176
Myospiza aurifrons, 308
humeralis, 308
Myrmeciza atrothorax, 164
disjuncta, 164
exsul, l63
ferruginea, 164
fortis, 157
goeldii, 157
griseiceps, 164
hemimelaena, 164
hyperythra 158
immaculata, 157
laemosticta, 164
longipes, 163
loricata, 163
melanoceps, 157
pelzelni, 164
ruficauda, 164
squamosa, 163
stictothorax, 164
Myrmia micrura, 79
Myrmoborus leucophrys, 162
lugubris, 162
melanurus, 163
myortherinus, 162
Myrmochanes hemileucus, 169
Myrmorchilus stirgilatus, 161
Myrmornis torquata, 161
Myrmothera campanisona, 156
simplex, 156
Myrmotherula ambigua, 173
assimillis, 170
axillaris, 171
behni, 170
brachyura, 173
cherriei, 171
erythronotos, 170
erythrura, 170
fulviventris, 170
grisea, 172
gularis, 171
guttata, 173
gutturalis, 171
haematonota, 172
hauxwelli, 173
iheringi, 173
klagesi, 173
leucophthalma, 170
longicauda, 171
longipennis, 172
menetriesii, 172
minor, 173
obscura, 173
ornata, 170
Myrmotherula
schisticolor, 172
sclateri, 173
sunensis, 173
surinamensis, 171
unicolor, 172
urosticta, 172
Myrtis fanny, 92

Nandayus nenday, 44
Nannopsittaca panychlora, 53
Nasica longirostris, 119
Negrito, Rufous-backed, 197
Nemosia pileata, 286
Neochelidon tibialis, 65
Neochen jubata, 22
Neocrex erythrops, 19
Neoctantes niger, 152
Neomorphus geoffroyi, 54
pucheranii, 54
radiolosus, 54
rufipennis, 54
Neopelma aurifrons, 188
chrysocephalum, 188
pallescens, 188
sulphureiventer, 188
Neopipo cinnamomea, 190
Neothraupis fasciata, 274
Neoxolmis rufiventris, 195
Netta erythrophthalma, 24
peposaca, 24
Nighthawk, Band-tailed, 61
Common, 61
Least, 61
Lesser, 61
Nacunda, 61
Sand-colored, 61
Semi-collared, 61
Short-tailed, 61
Nightjar, Band-winged, 60
Blackish, 60
Cayenne, 60
Ladder-tailed, 59
Little, 60
Long-trained, 59
Lyre-tailed, 59
Pygmy, 60
Roraiman, 60

Rufous, 59
Scissor-tailed, 59
Sickle-winged, 60
Silky-tailed, 60
Spot-tailed, 60
Swallow-tailed, 59
White-tailed, 60
White-winged, 60
Nonnula amaurocephala, 103
brunnea, 103
rubecula, 103
ruficapilla, 103
sclateri, 103
Notharchus macrorhynchus, 100
pectoralis, 100
ordii, 101
tectus, 103
Nothocercus bonapartei, 5
julius, 5
nigrocapillus, 5
Nothocrax urumutum, 2
Nothoprocta cinerascens, 7
curvirostris, 7
kalinowski, 7
ornata, 7
pentlandii, 7
perdicaria, 7
taczanowskii, 7
Nothura boraquira, 8
darwinii, 7
maculosa, 8
minor, 8
Nothura, Darwin's, 7
Lesser, 8
Spotted, 8
White-bellied, 8
Notiochelidon cyanoleuca, 65
flavipes, 65
murina, 65
Nunbird, Black, 100
Black-fronted, 100
White-faced, 100
White-fronted, 100
Yellow-billed, 100
Nunlet, Brown, 103
Chestnut-headed, 103
Fulvous-chinned, 103
Gray-cheeked, 103
Rusty-breasted, 103
Nuttallornis borealis, 205
Nyctanassa violacea, 12
Nyctibius aethereus, 59
bracteatus, 59
grandis, 58
griseus, 59
leucopterus, 59
Nycticorax nycticorax, 11
Nycticryphes semicollaris, 16
Nyctidromus albicollis, 61
Nyctiphrynus ocellatus, 61
Nyctiprogne leucopyga, 61
Nystalus chacuru, 101
maculatus, 101
radiatus, 101
striolatus, 101
Ochthoeca
cinnamomeiventris, 211
diadema, 211
frontalis, 211
fumicolor, 211
leucophrys, 211
oenanthoides, 211
piurae, 212
pulchella, 211
rufipectoralis, 211
Ochthornis littoralis, 215
Ocreatus underwoodii, 89
Ocyalus latirostris, 255
Odontophorus atrifrons, 8
balliviani, 9
capueira, 8
columbianus, 9
erythrops, 8
gujanensis, 8
hyperythrus, 9
melanonotus, 9
speciosus, 9
stellatus, 9
strophium, 9
Odontorchilus branickii, 243
cinereus, 243
Ognorhynchus icterotis, 44
Oilbird, 58
Oncostoma olivaceum, 226
Onychorhynchus coronatus, 206
Opisthocomus hoazin, 13
Opisthoprora euryptera, 92
Oporornis agilis, 263
formosus, 263
philadelphia, 263
Orchesticus abeillei, 273
Oreomanes fraseri, 250
Oreonympha nobilis, 80
Oreopholus ruficollis, 17
Oreophylax moreirae, 144
Oreopsar bolivianus, 257
Oreothraupis arremonops, 298
Oreotriccus griseocapillus, 222
plumbeiceps, 222
Oreotrochilus adela, 83
estella, 84
leucopleurus, 84
melanogaster, 84
Oriole, Baltimore, 260
Epaulet, 259
Moriche, 260
Northern, 260
Orange-crowned, 260
Orchard, 260
White-edged, 260
Yellow, 259
Yellow-backed, 259
Yellow-tailed, 259
Ornithion inerme, 226
semiflavum, 232
Oroaetus isidori, 30
Oropendola, Band-tailed, 255
Black, 254
Casqued, 255
Chestnut-headed, 255
Chestnut-mantled, 255
Crested, 255
Dusky-green, 255
Green, 255
Olive, 254
Para, 255
Russet-backed, 255
Ortalis canicollis, 3
erythroptera, 3
garrula, 3
motmot, 4
ruficauda, 3
Orthogonys chloricterus, 270
Oryzoborus angolensis, 305
crassirostris, 303
maximiliani, 303
Osprey, 34
Otus albogularis, 57
atricapillus, 57
choliba, 57
clarkii, 57
guatemalae, 58
ingens, 57
roboratus, 57
watsonii, 58
Ovenbird, 263
Owl, Andean Pygmy-, 58
Austral Pygny-, 58
Band-bellied, 56
Bare-shanked Screech-, 57
Barn, 56
Black-and-white, 56
Black-banded, 57
Buff-fronted, 58
Burrowing, 58
Crested, 56
Ferruginous Pygmy-, 58
Great Horned, 56
Least Pygmy-, 58
Long-tufted Screech-, 57
Mottled, 57

Owl,
Rufescent Screech-, 57
Rufous-banded, 57
Rufous-legged, 57
Rusty-barred, 57
Short-eared, 56
Spectacled, 56
Striped, 57
Stygian, 56
Tawny-bellied Screech-, 58
Tawny-browed, 56
Tropical Screech-, 57
Vermiculated Screech-, 58
West Peruvian Screech-, 57
White-throated Screech-, 57
Oxypogon guerinii, 91
Oxyruncus cristata, 245
Oxyura dominica, 25
jamaicensis, 25
vittata, 25

Pachyramphus albogriseus, 184
castaneus, 184
cinnamomeus, 184
marginatus, 184
polychopterus, 183
rufus, 184
spodiurus, 183
surinamus, 183
versicolor, 184
viridis, 183
Palmcreeper, Point-tailed, 137
Pandion haliaetus, 34
Panyptila cayennensis, 62
Parabuteo unicinctus, 33
Parakeet, Andean, 47
Austral, 44
Barred, 47
Black-capped, 46
Black-hooded, 44
Blaze-winged, 47
Blood-eared, 46
Blue-breasted, 46
Blue-crowned, 44
Brown-throated, 45
Cactus, 46
Canary-winged, 48
Cobalt-winged, 48
Crimson-bellied, 47
Dusky-headed, 46
Fiery-shouldered, 47
Flame-capped, 45
Flame-winged, 47
Golden, 44
Golden-winged, 48
Gray-cheeked, 48
Gray-hooded, 47
Green-cheeked, 46
Jandaya, 45
Maroon-faced, 47
Maroon-tailed, 46
Mitred, 45
Monk, 44
Mountain, 47
Ochre-marked, 46
Orange-chinned, 48
Painted, 47
Peach-fronted, 45
Pearly, 46
Plain, 48
Reddish-bellied, 46
Red-masked, 45
Rock, 46
Rose-crowned, 47
Rose-headed, 47
Rufous-fronted, 47
Santa Marta, 46
Scarlet-fronted, 45
Slender-billed, 44
Sun, 45
Tui, 48
White-breasted, 47
White-eyed, 45
White-necked, 47
Paroaria baeri, 297
capitata, 297
coronata, 297
dominicana, 297
gularis, 297
Parrot, Alder, 50
Black-eared, 51
Black-headed, 52
Blue-bellied, 52
Blue-cheeked, 49
Blue-headed, 50
Bronze-winged, 51
Brown-hooded, 52
Burrowing, 44
Caica, 52
Dusky, 51
Festive, 49
Golden-plumed, 44
Mealy, 49
Orange-cheeked, 51
Orange-winged, 50
Pileated, 52
Plum-crowned, 51
Red-billed, 51
Red-capped, 52
Red-fan, 50
Red-lored, 49
Red-shouldered, 50
Red-spectacled, 50
Rusty-faced, 51
Saffron-headed, 52
Scaly-headed, 51
Scaly-naped, 50
Short-tailed, 51
Speckled-faced, 51
Turquoise-fronted, 49
Vinaceous-breasted, 49
Vulturine, 52
White-bellied, 52
White-capped, 51
Yellow-eared, 44
Yellow-faced, 50
Yellow-crowned, 49
Yellow-headed, 49
Yellow-shouldered, 50
Parrotlet, Black-eared, 53
Blue-winged, 53
Brown-backed, 53
Dusky-billed, 53
Golden-tailed, 53
Green-rumped, 53
Lilac-tailed, 53
Pacific, 53
Red-winged, 52
Sapphire-rumped, 52
Scarlet-shouldered, 53
Spectacled, 53
Spot-winged, 52
Tepui, 53
Yellow-faced, 53
Parula pitiayumi, 267
Parula, Tropical, 267
Passer domesticus, 306
Patagona gigas, 79
Pauraque, 61
Pauxi pauxi, 1
Pelecanus occidentalis, 21
Pelican, Brown, 21
Penelope albipennis, 3
argyrotis, 3
dabbenei, 2
jacquacu, 2
jacucaca, 2
marail, 2
montagnii, 2
obscura, 2
ochrogaster, 2
ortoni, 2
pileata, 2
purpurascens, 2
superciliaris, 2
Peppershrike, Black-billed, 247
Rufous-browed, 247
Percnostola caurensis, 161
leucostigma, 162
lophotes, 162

rufifrons, 161
schistacea, 162
Periporphyrus erythromelas, 292
Perissocephalus tricolor, 178
Petrochelidon andecola, 64
fulva, 64
pyrrhonota, 64
Pewee, Blackish, 212
Greater, 205
Tropical, 212
Wood, 212
Phacellodomus dorsalis, 133
erythrophthalmus, 134
ruber, 133
rufifrons, 134
sibilatrix, 134
striaticeps, 134
striaticollis, 133
Phaenostictus mcleannani, 157
Phaeochroa cuvierii, 73
Phaeomyias leucospodia, 220
murina, 220
Phaeoprogne tapera, 63
Phaeotriccus hudsoni, 209
poecilocercus, 209
Phaethornis anthophilus, 67
augusti, 67
bourcieri, 67
eurynome, 66
gounellei, 67
griseogularis, 68
guy, 66
hispidus, 67
idaliae, 68
longuemareus, 67
malaris, 66
nattereri, 67
philippi, 67
pretrei, 67
ruber, 68
squalidus, 67
stuarti, 67
subochraceus, 67
superciliosus, 66
syrmatophorus, 66
yaruqui, 66
Phaetusa simplex, 28
Phalacrocorax albiventer, 22
olivaceus, 22
Phalarope, Wilson's, 17
Phalaropus tricolor, 17
Phalcoboenus algobularis, 36
carunculatus, 35
megalopterus, 35
Pharomachrus antisianus, 94
auriceps, 94
fulgidus, 94
pavoninus, 94
Phegnornis mitchellii, 21
Pheucticus aureoventris, 292
chrysopeplus, 293
ludovicianus, 293
Phibalura flavirostris, 179
Philodice mitchellii, 79
Philydor atricapillus, 138
dimidiatus, 136
erythrocercus, 138
erythropterus, 138
hylobius, 138
lichtensteini, 135
pyrrhodes, 136
ruficaudatus, 135
rufus, 137
Phimosus infuscatus, 13
Phlegopsis erythroptera, 158
nigromaculata, 158
Phleocryptes melanops, 136
Phloeoceastes gayaquilensis, 110
haematogaster, 110
leucopogon, 110
melanoleucos, 110
pollens, 110
robustus, 110
rubricollis, 110
Phlogophilus harterti, 77
hemileucurus, 77
Phoebe, Black, 197
Phoenicircus carnifex, 179
nigricollis, 179
Phoenicoparrus, andinus, 10
jamesi, 10
Phoenicopterus chilensis, 9
ruber, 10
Phrygilus alaudinus, 302
atriceps, 298
carbonarius, 305
dorsalis, 297
erythronotus, 297
fructiceti, 298
gayi, 298
patagonicus, 302
plebejus, 304
unicolor, 302
Phyllomyias fasciatus, 223
griseiceps, 228
Phylloscartes chapmani, 225
difficilis, 216
nigrifrons, 216
oustaleti, 231
paulistus, 231
superciliaris, 216
ventralis, 216
virescens, 216
Phytotoma raimondii, 245
rara, 245
rutila, 245
Piaya cayana, 54
melanogaster, 55
minuta, 55
Picoides lignarius, 114
mixtus, 114
Piculet, Arrowhead, 117
Bar-breasted, 118
Black-dotted, 117
Chestnut, 116
Ecuadorian, 118
Golden-spangled, 118
Gold-fronted, 118
Grayish, 117
Mottled, 117
Ocellated, 118
Ochraceous, 117
Ochre-collared, 118
Olivaceous, 117
Orinoco, 118
Plain-breasted, 117
Rufous-breasted, 116
Scaled, 117
Speckle-chested, 118
Spotted, 118
Varzea, 118
White-barred, 118
White-bellied, 116
Piculus aurulentus, 113
chrysochloros, 113
flavigula, 113
leucolaemus, 113
rivolii, 112
rubiginosus, 113
Picumnus aurifrons, 118
borbae, 118
castelnau, 117
cinnamomeus, 116
cirrhatus, 118
dorbygnianus, 118
exilis, 118
granadensis, 117
limae, 117
minutissimus, 117
nebulosus, 117
nigropunctatus, 117
olivaceus, 117
pumilus, 118
pygmaeus, 118
rufiventris, 116
sclateri. 118
spilogaster, 116
squamulatus, 117
steindachneri, 118
temminckii, 118
varzeae, 118

Piedtail, Ecuadorian, 77
Peruvian, 77
Piezorhina cinerea, 300
Pigeon, Band-tailed, 38
Bare-eyed, 38
Chilean, 38
Dusky, 39
Pale-vented, 38
Peruvian, 38
Picazuro, 38
Plumbeous, 38
Ruddy, 38
Scaled, 38
Short-billed, 38
Spot-winged, 38
Piha, Cinnamon-vented, 178
Dusky, 178
Gray-tailed, 178
Olivaceous, 178
Rose-collared, 178
Rufous, 178
Scimitar-winged, 178
Screaming, 178
Pilherodius pileatus, 12
Pintail, Common, 23
Northern, 23
White-cheeked, 23
Yellow-billed, 23
Pionites leucogaster, 52
melanocephala, 52
Pionopsitta barrabandi, 51
caica, 52
haematotis, 52
pileata, 52
pyrilia, 52
Pionus chalcopterus, 51
fuscus, 51
maximiliani, 51
menstruus, 50
seniloides, 51
sordidus, 51
tumultuosus, 51
Pipile cujubi, 3
jacutinga, 3
pipile, 3
Pipit, Chaco, 246
Correndera, 245
Hellmayr's, 246
Ochre-breasted, 246
Paramo, 246
Short-billed, 246
Yellowish, 245
Pipra aureola , 191, 194
coeruleocapilla, 192
chloromeros, 191
cornuta, 189
coronata, 192, 195
erythocephala, 191, 192
fasciicauda, 191,193
iris, 192
isidorei, 192
mentalis, 191, 193
nattereri, 191
pipra, 191, 194
rubrocapilla, 191
serena, 192, 195
Pipraeidea melanonota, 280
Pipreola arcuata, 181
aureopectus, 182
chlorolepidota, 185
formosa, 182
frontalis, 182
intermia, 182
jucunda, 182
lubomirskii, 182
pulchra, 182
riefferii, 181
whitelyi, 182
Piprites, chloris, 189
pileatus, 188
Pipromorpha macconnelli, 215
oleaginea, 214
rufiventris, 214
Piranga flava, 272
leucoptera, 285
olivacea, 272
rubra, 272
rubriceps, 272
Pitangus lictor, 200
sulphuratus, 200
Pithys albifrons, 168
Pittasoma michleri, 155
rufopileatum, 155
Pitylus fuliginosus, 292
grossus, 292
Plantcutter, Peruvian, 245
Rufous-tailed, 245
White-tipped, 245
Platycichla flavipes, 237
leucops, 237
Platypsaris homochrous, 183
minor, 183
rufus, 182
Platyrinchus coronatus, 229
flavigularis, 229
leucoryphus, 228
mystaceus, 229
platyrhynchos, 228
saturatus, 229
Plegadis chihi, 13
ridgwayi, 13
Plover, American Golden, 17
Collared, 21
Diademed Sandpiper-, 21
Lesser Golden, 17
Pied, 17
Puna, 21,
Semipalmated, 21
Two-banded, 21
Plovercrest, Black-breasted, 92
Plumeleteer, Bronze-tailed, 72
White-vented, 72
Plushcrown, Orange-fronted, 140
Pluvialis dominica, 17
Pochard, Rosy-billed, 24
Southern, 24
Podager nacunda, 61
Podiceps dominicus, 27
major, 26
nigricollis, 27
occipitalis, 27
rolland, 27
taczanowskii, 26
Podilymbus podiceps, 27
Poecilotriccus ruficeps, 225
Poecilurus candei, 145
kollari, 145
scutatus, 146
Pogonotriccus eximius, 228
flaviventris, 221
gualaquizae, 221
ophthalmicus, 221
orbitalis, 221
poecilotis, 221
venezuelanus, 221
Polioptila dumicola, 246
guianensis, 247
lactea, 247
plumbea, 247
schistaceigula, 247
Polyborus plancus, 35
Polyonymus caroli, 88
Polyplancta aurescens, 70
Polystictus pectoralis, 225
superciliaris, 225
Polytmus guainumbi, 71
milleri, 85
theresiae, 72
Poorwill, Ocellated, 61
Poospiza alticola, 301
boliviana, 301
cinerea, 305
erythrophrys, 305
hispaniolensis, 311
hypochondria, 300
lateralis, 304
melanoleuca, 306
nigrorufa, 303
ornata, 304
rubecula, 301
thoracica, 311

torquata, 311
Poospizopsis caesar, 299
Popelairia conversii, 77
langsdorffi, 77
popelairii, 77
Porphyriops melanops, 15
Porphyrolaema porphyrolaema, 181
Porphyrospiza caerulescens, 304
Porphyrula flavirostris, 15
martinica, 15
Porzana albicollis, 19
carolina, 18
flaviventer, 20
Potoo, Common, 59
Great, 58
Lomg-tailed, 59
Rufous, 59
White-winged, 59
Premnoplex adusta, 136
brunnescens, 136
tatei, 136
Premnornis guttuligera, 136
Prickletail, Spectacled, 136
Procnias alba, 179
averano, 179
nudicollis, 179
Progne chalybea, 63
modesta, 63
subis, 63
tapera, 63
Protonotaria citrea, 262
Psarocolius angustifrons, 255
atrovirens, 255
decumanus, 255
viridis, 255
Pseudattila phoenicurus, 202
Pseudocolaptes boissonneautii, 137
lawrencii (see boissonneautii)-
Pseudocolopteryx
acutipennis, 223
dinellianus, 224
flaviventris, 223
sclateri, 224
Pseudodacnis hartlaubi, 288
Pseudoleistes guirahuro, 260
virescens, 260
Pseudoseisura cristata, 132
gutturalis, 132
lophotes, 132
Pseudotriccus pelzelni, 230
ruficeps, 230
simplex, 230
Psilorhamphus guttatus, 176
Psophia crepitans, 4
leucoptera, 4
viridis, 4
Pterocnemia pennata, 1
Pteroglossus aracari, 109
beauharnaesii, 109
bitorquatus, 109
castanotis, 109
flavirostris, 109
inscriptus, 109
pluricinctus, 109
torquatus, 109
viridis, 109
Pterophanes cyanopterus, 80
Pteroptochos castaneus, 175
megapodius, 175
tarnii, 175
Puffbird, Barred, 101
Black-breasted, 100
Black-streaked, 101
Brown-banded, 101
Chestnut-capped, 103
Collared, 102
Crescent-chested, 102
Moustached, 101
Pied, 103
Rufous-necked, 102
Russet-throated, 101
Semicollared, 102
Sooty-capped, 102
Spot-backed, 101
Spotted, 102
Striolated, 101
White-eared, 101
White-chested, 102
White-necked, 100
White-whiskered, 102
Puffleg, Black-breasted, 87
Black-thighed, 86
Blue-capped, 87
Colorful, 87
Coppery-bellied, 87
Emerald-bellied, 87
Glowing, 87
Golden-breasted, 86
Greenish, 86
Hoary, 86
Long-tailed, 86
Sapphire-vented, 86
Turquoise-throated, 87
Pulsatrix koeniswaldiana, 56
melanota, 56
perspicillata, 56
Purpletuft, Buff-throated, 185
Dusky, 185
White-browed, 185
Pygarrhichas albogularis, 140
Pygiptila stellaris, 151
Pyriglena leuconata, 158
leucoptera, 158
Pyrocephalus rubinus, 213
Pyroderus scutatus, 177
Pyrope pyrope, 203
Pyrrhocoma ruficeps, 288
Pyrrhomyias cinnamomea, 227
Pyrrhura albipectus, 47
calliptera, 47
cruentata, 46
devillei, 47
egregia, 47
frontalis, 46
hoematotis, 46
leucotis, 47
melanura, 46
molinae, 46
perlata, 46
picta, 47
rhodocephala, 47
rhodogaster, 47
rupicola, 46
viridicata, 46

Quail, Black-frontead Wood-, 8
Chestnut Wood-, 9
Dark-backed Wood-, 9
Gorgeted Wood-, 9
Marbled Wood-, 8
Rufous-breasted Wood-, 9
Rufous-fronted Wood-, 8
Spot-winged Wood-, 8
Starred Wood-, 9
Stripe-faced Wood-, 9
Tawny-faced, 9
Venezuelan Wood-, 9
Quail-Dove, see Dove
Querula purpurata, 177
Quetzal, Crested, 94
Golden-headed, 94
Pavonine, 94
White-tipped, 94
Quiscalus lugubris, 256

Racket-tail, Booted, 89
Rail, Austral, 18
Blackish, 18
Bogota, 18
Brown Wood-, 18
Giant Wood-, 17
Gray-necked Wood-, 17
Little Wood-, 18
Plumbeous, 18
Red-winged Wood-, 18
Rufous-necked Wood-,18
Sora, 18

Rail,
Slaty-breasted Wood-, 17
Spotted, 18
Virginia, 18
Rallus antarcticus, 18
limicola, 18
maculatus, 18
nigricans, 18
sanguinolentus, 18
semiplumbeus, 18
Ramphastos ambiguus, 106
brevis, 106
citreolaemus, 106
culminatus, 106
dicolorus, 107
sulfuratus, 106
swainsonii, 106
toco, 106
tucanus, 106
vitellinus, 106
Ramphocaenus melanurus, 246
Ramphocelus bresilius, 271
carbo, 271
dimidiatus, 271
flammigerus, 269
icteronotus, 270
melanogaster, 271
nigrogularis, 271
Ramphodon dohrnii, 69
naevius, 69
Ramphomicron dorsale, 91
microrhynchum, 90
Ramphotrigon fuscicauda, 210
megacephala, 210
ruficauda, 210
Rayadito, Thorn-tailed, 140
Recurvebill, Bolivian, 133
Peruvian, 133
Recurvirostra andina, 14
Redstart, American, 264
Brown-capped, 265
Golden-fronted, 265
Saffron-breasted, 265
Slate-throated, 264
Spectacled, 265
White-faced, 265
White-fronted, 265
Yellow-crowned, 265
Yellow-faced, 265
Reed-haunter, Curve-billed, 134
Straight-billed, 134
Reinarda squamata, 62
Rhea americana, 1
Rhea, Greater, 1
Lesser, 1
Reinarda squamata, 62
Rhegmatorhina berlepschi, 161
cristata, 161
gymnops, 161
hoffmannsi, 161
melanosticta, 160
Rhinocrypta lanceolata, 175
Rhinoptynx clamator, 57
Rhodinocichla rosea, 270
Rhodopis vesper, 69
Rhodospingus cruentus, 313
Rhynchocyclus brevirostris, 210
fulvipectus, 210
olivaceus, 210
Rhynchortyx cinctus, 9
Rhynchospiza stolzmanni, 299
Rhynchotus rufescens, 5
Rhytipterna holerythra, 203
immunda, 202
simplex, 202
Riparia riparia, 64
Roraimia adusta, 136
Rostrhamus sociabilis, 29
Ruby, Brazilian, 74
Rupicola peruviana, 179
rupicola, 178
Rushbird, Wren-like, 136
Rynchops niger, 28
nigra, 28

Sabrewing, Buff-breasted, 80
Gray-breasted, 69
Lazuline, 80
Napo, 80
Rufous-breasted, 80
Santa Marta, 80,
White-tailed, 80
Sakesphorus bernardi, 148
canadensis, 148
cristatus, 148
luctuosus, 148
melanonotus, 148
melanothorax, 148
Saltator albicollis, 292
atricollis, 291
atripennis, 291
aurantiirostris, 291
cinctus, 291
coerulescens, 291
maxillosus, 292
maximus, 291
nigriceps, 291
orenocensis, 292
rufiventris, 291
similis, 291
Saltator, Black-cowled, 291
Black-throated, 291
Black-winged, 291
Buff-throated, 291
Golden-billed, 291
Grayish, 291
Green-winged, 291
Masked, 291
Orinocan, 292
Rufous-bellied, 291
Streaked, 292
Thick-billed, 292
Saltatricula multicolor, 299
Sandpiper, Baird's, 20
Buff-breasted, 20
Least, 20
Pectoral, 16
Solitary, 20
Spotted, 20
Stilt, 16
Upland, 16
White-rumped, 20
Sapayoa aenigma, 186
Sapphire, Blue-chinned, 74
Blue-headed, 73
Gilded, 73
Golden-tailed, 74
Rufous-throated, 73
White-chinned, 73
Sapphirewing, Great, 80
Sappho sparganura, 88
Sarcoramphus papa, 28
Sarkidiornis melanotos, 23
Satrapa icterophrys, 210
Sayornis nigricans, 197
Scaphidura oryzivora, 255
Scardafella squammata, 40
Scaup, Lesser, 25
Scelorchilus albicollis, 175
rubecula, 175
Schiffornis major, 186
turdinus, 186
virescens, 186
Schistes, geoffroyi, 92
Schistochlamys melanopis, 274
ruficapillus, 274
Schizoeaca coryi, 124
fuliginosa, 124
griseomurina, 124
harterti, 124
helleri, 125
palpebralis, 124
Schoeniophylax
phryganophila, 124
Sclateria naevia, 162
Sclerurus albigularis, 128
caudacutus, 128
guatemalensis, 129
mexicanus, 129
rufigularis, 128

scansor, 128
Screamer, Horned, 11
Northern, 11
Southern, 11
Screeh-owl, see Owl
Scytalopus femoralis, 176
indigoticus, 177
latebricola, 177
macropus, 176
magellanicus, 177
novacapitalis, 177
panamensis, 176
speluncae, 177
superciliaris, 177
unicolor, 176
Scythebill, Black-billed, 119
Brown-billed, 119
Curve-billed, 119
Greater, 119
Red-billed, 119
Seedeater, Band-tailed, 304
Black-and-tawny, 310
Black-and-white, 310
Black-bellied, 310
Blackish-blue, 307
Blue, 312
Buffy-fronted, 308
Capped, 310
Chestnut, 311
Chestnut-bellied, 311
Chestnut-throated, 311
Dark-throated, 310
Double-collared, 309
Drab, 310
Dubois' 310
Dull-colored, 310
Gray, 309
Lined, 310
Marsh, 311
Paramo, 305
Parrot-billed, 308
Plain-colored, 305
Plumbeous, 310
Ruddy-breasted, 311
Rufous-rumped, 311
Rusty-collared, 309
Slate-colored, 309
Temminck's, 310
Variable, 309
White-bellied, 308
White-naped, 301
White-throated, 309
Yellow-bellied, 309
Seedsnipe, Gray-breasted, 8
Least, 8
Rufous-bellied, 8
White-bellied, 8
Seiurua aurocapillus, 263
motacilla, 263
noveboracensis, 263
Selenidera culik, 108
maculirostris, 108
nattereri, 108
reinwardtii, 108
spcetabilis, 108
Semnornis ramphastinus, 104
Sephanoides sephanoides, 86
Sericossypha albocristata, 268
loricata, 268
Seriema, Black-legged. 4
Red-legged, 4
Serpophaga araguayae. 219
cinerea, 197
hypoleuca, 227
nigricans, 219
subcristata, 220
Setophaga ruticilla, 264
Sharpbill, 245
Sheartail, Peruvian, 77
Shoveler, Northern, 24
Red, 24
Shrike-Vireo, Green, 248
Slaty-capped, 247
Sicalis auriventris, 301
citrina, 312
columbiana, 312
flaveola, 305
lebruni, 302
lutea, 303
luteocephala, 301
luteola, 312
olivacens, 304
raimondii, 312
taczanowskii, 308
uropygialis, 304
Sicklebill, Buff-tailed, 69
White-tipped, 69
Sierra-Finch, see Finch
Simoxenops striatus, 133
ucayalae, 133
Sipia berlepschi, 168
rosenbergi, 168
Siptornis striaticollis, 136
Siptornopsis
hypochondriacus, 144
Sirystes sibilator, 205
Sirystes, 205
Siskin, Andean, 307
Black, 307
Black-chinned, 306
Hooded, 306
Olivaceous, 306
Red, 307
Siskin, Saffron, 306
Thick-billed, 306
Yellow-bellied, 307
Yellow-faced, 307
Yellow-rumped, 307
Sittasomus griseicapillus, 124
Skimmer, Black, 28
Smaragdolanius leucotis, 247
pulchellus, 248
Snethlagea minor, 225
Snipe, Common, 16
Cordilleran, 15
Giant, 15
Noble, 15
Puna, 16
South American Painted, 16
Softtail, Orinoco, 139
Plain, 139
Russet-mantled, 139
Striated, 139
Solitaire, Andean, 238
Black, 237
Rufous-brown, 237
White-eared, 237
Spadebill, Cinnamon-crested, 229
Golden-crowned, 229
Russet-winged, 228
White-crested, 228
White-throated, 229
Yellow-throated, 229
Sparrow, Black-capped, 300
Black-striped, 299
Golden-winged, 300
Grasshopper, 308
Grassland, 308
House, 306
Orange-billed, 300
Pectoral, 300
Rufous-collared, 302
Saffron-billed, 300
Stripe-capped, 299
Tocuyo, 299
Tumbes, 299
Yellow-browed, 308
Spartanoica maluroides, 126
Spatuletail, Marvelous, 89
Speotyto cunicularia, 58
Spinetail, Ash-browed, 142
Azara's, 143
Black-faced, 146
Blackish-headed, 146
Buff-browed, 143
Cabanis', 141
Chestnut-throated, 144
Chicli, 141
Chotoy, 124
Cinereous-breasted, 143
Creamy-crested, 144

Spinetail,
Crested, 144
Dark-breasted, 143
Dusky, 143
Gray-bellied, 146
Gray-browed, 143
Gray-headed, 144
Great, 144
Hoary-throated, 145
Itatiaia, 144
Light-crowned, 144
Line-cheeked, 142
Marcapata, 142
Necklaced, 146
Ochre-cheeked, 146
Olive, 145
Pale-breasted, 143
Pallid, 144
Plain-crowned, 145
Red-and-white, 141
Red-faced, 142
Red-shouldered, 145
Ruddy, 143
Rufous, 141
Rufous-capped, 141
Russet-bellied, 145
Rusty-backed, 142
Rusty-headed, 141
Scaled, 142
Silvery-throated, 143
Slaty, 143
Sooty-fronted, 143
Speckled, 142
Streak-capped, 142
Stripe-breasted, 146
Stripe-crowned, 144
Sulphur-bearded, 145
Tepui, 142
White-bellied, 145
White-browed, 146
White-whiskered, 145
Yellow-chinned, 141
Yellow-throated, 141
Spinus atratus, 307
barbatus, 306
crassirostris, 306
cucullatus, 307
magellanicus, 306
olivaceus, 306
psaltria, 313
siemiradzkii, 306
spinescens, 307
uropygialis, 307
xanthogaster, 307
yarrellii, 307
Spiza americana, 299
Spizaetus ornatus, 31
tyrannus, 30
Spizastur melanoleucus, 31
Spiziapteryx circumcinctus, 37
Spoonbill, Roseate, 10
Sporophila albogularis, 309
americana, 309
ardesiaca, 310
bouvreuil, 310
caerulescens, 309
castaneiventris, 311
cinnamomea, 311
collaris, 309
falcirostris, 309
frontalis, 308
hypochroma, 311
intermedia, 309
leucoptera, 308
lineola, 310
luctuosa, 310
melanogaster, 310
minuta, 311
nigricollis, 309
nigrorufa, 310
obscura, 310
palustris, 311
peruviana, 308
plumbea, 310
ruficollis, 310
schistacea, 309
simplex, 310
telasco, 311
Starfrontlet, Blue-throated, 82
Buff-winged, 81
Dusky, 81
Golden-bellied, 81
Rainbow, 81
Violet-throated, 81
White-tailed, 82
Starthroat, Blue-tufted, 70
Long-billed, 70
Stripe-breasted, 69
Steatornis caripensis, 58
Steganopus tricolor, 17
Stelgidopteryx ruficollis, 64
Stephanophorus diadematus, 270
Stephanoxis lalandi, 92
Sterna superciliaris, 28
trudeaui, 28
Sternoclyta cyanopectus, 81
Stigmatura budytoides, 214
napensis, 214
Stilt, Common, 14
Stork, Maguari, 10
Wood, 10
Streamcreeper, Sharp-tailed, 129
Streptoprocne biscutata, 62
zonaris, 62
Strix hylophila, 57
rufipes, 57
Sturnella bellicosa, 261
defilippi, 261
loyca, 260
magna, 261
Sublegatus modestus, 209
Suiriri suiriri, 209
Sunangel, Amethyst-throated, 90
Gorgeted, 90
Merida, 90
Orange-throated, 90
Purple-throated, 90
Tourmaline, 90
Sunbeam, Black-hooded, 85
Purple-backed, 85
Shining, 85
White-tufted, 85
Sunbittern, 14
Sungem, Horned, 78
Sungrebe, 18
Swallow, Andean, 64
Bank, 64
Barn, 64
Black-collared, 64
Blue-and-white, 65
Brown-bellied, 65
Cave, 64
Chilean, 65
Cliff, 64
Pale-footed, 65
Rough-winged, 64
Tawny-headed, 65
White-banded, 64
White-rumped, 65
White-thighed, 65
White-winged, 65
Swallow-Tanager, 276
Swallow-Wing, 103
Swan, Black-necked, 21
Coscoroba, 22
Swift, Andean, 62
Ashy-tailed, 62
Band-rumped, 63
Biscutate, 62
Chapman's, 62
Chestnut-collared, 62
Chimney, 63
Fork-tailed Palm-, 62
Gray-rumped, 63
Great Dusky, 62
Lesser Swallow-tailed, 62
Pale-rumped, 63
Pygmy, 63
Short-tailed, 63
Sooty, 62
Spot-fronted, 62

Vaux's, 63
White-chested, 62
White-chinned, 62
White-collared, 62
White-tipped, 62
Sylph, Long-tailed, 88
Violet-tailed, 88
Sylviorthorhynchus desmursii, 126
Synallaxis albescens, 143
albigularis, 143
azarae , 143
brachyura, 143
cabanisi, 141
cherriei, 144
cinerascens, 146
cinnamomea, 146
frontalis, 143
fuscorufa, 141
gujanensis, 145
gularis, 146
hypospodia, 143
moesta, 143
poliophrys, 143
propinqua, 145
ruficapilla, 141
rutilans, 143
spixi, 141
stictothorax, 146
subpudica, 143
superciliosa, 143
tithys, 146
unirufa, 141
zimmeri, 145
Syndactyla guttulata, 137
rufosuperciliata, 135
subalaris, 138
Syrigma sibilatrix, 12

Tachuri, Bearded, 225
Gray-backed, 225
Tachuris rubrigastra, 231
Tachybaptus dominicus, 27
Tachycineta albiventer, 65
leucopyga, 65
leucorrhoa, 65
Tachyeres patachonicus, 23
Tachyphonus coronatus, 277
cristatus, 277
delatrii, 278
luctuosus, 283
phoenicius, 277
rufiventer, 277
rufus, 277
surinamus, 278
Taeniotriccus andrei, 231
Tanager, Ash-throated Bush-, 279
Azure-shouldered, 272
Bay-headed, 285
Beryl-spangled, 285
Black-and-gold, 274
Black-and-white, 274
Black-backed, 283
Black-backed Bush-, 274
Black-bellied, 271
Black-capped, 285
Black-cheeked Mountain-, 268
Black-chested Mountain-, 268
Black-chinned Mountain-, 268
Black-faced, 274
Black-goggled, 275
Black-headed, 287
Blue-and-black, 283
Blue-and-yellow, 273
Blue-backed, 275
Blue-browed, 287
Blue-capped, 273
Blue-gray, 272
Blue-necked, 284
Blue-whiskered, 281
Blue-winged Mountain-, 269
Brassy-breasted, 281
Brazilian, 271
Brown, 273
Brown-flanked, 280
Buff-bellied, 280
Buff-breasted Mountain-, 269
Burnished-buff, 283
Carmiol's, 276
Chestnut-backed, 283
Chestnut-bellied
Mountain-, 275
Chestnut-headed, 288
Cinnamon, 274
Common Bush-, 279
Crested Ant-, 270
Crimson-backed, 271
Diademed, 270
Dotted, 287
Dusky-bellied Bush-, 280
Dusky-faced, 273
Emerald, 282
Fawn-breasted, 280
Flame-crested, 277
Flame-faced, 282
Flame-rumped, 269
Fulvous-crested, 278
Fulvous-headed, 280
Fulvous Shrike-, 272
Gilt-edged, 281
Glistening-green, 286
Golden, 282
Golden-chested, 274
Golden-chevroned, 273
Golden-collared, 276
Golden-crowned, 276
Golden-eared, 282
Golden-hooded, 284
Golden-naped, 284
Gold-ringed, 275
Grass-green, 269
Gray-and-gold, 280
Gray-headed, 273
Gray-hooded Bush-, 278
Green-and-gold, 282
Green-headed, 281
Green-throated, 287
Guira, 286
Hepatic, 272
Hooded, 286
Hooded Mountain-, 268
Lacrimose Mountain-, 269
Lemon-browed, 276
Lemon-spectacled, 276
Magpie, 268
Masked, 284
Masked Crimson, 271
Masked Mountain-, 268
Metallic-green, 285
Moss-backed, 275
Multicolored, 286
Ochre-breasted, 276
Olive-backed, 273
Olive-green, 270
Opal-crowned, 281
Opal-rumped, 281
Orange-eared, 286
Orange-headed, 280
Orange-throated, 270
Palm, 272
Paradise, 281
Plain-colored. 287
Purplish-mantled, 276
Red-billed Pied, 280
Red-crowned Ant-, 270
Red-hooded, 272
Red-necked, 286
Red-shouldered, 277
Red-throated Ant-, 271
Rose-breasted Thrush-, 270
Rosy Thrush-, 270
Ruby-crowned, 277
Rufous-cheeked, 282
Rufous-chested, 280
Rufous-crested, 275
Rufous-headed, 286
Rufous-throated, 285
Rufous-winged, 285
Rust-and-yellow, 280
Saffron-crowned, 284
Sayaca, 272

Tanager,
Santa Marta Mountain-, 268
Scarlet, 272
Scarlet-and-white, 287
Scarlet-bellied Mountain-, 268
Scarlet-browed, 275
Scarlet-throated, 268
Scrub, 282
Seven-colored, 281
Short-billed Bush-, 279
Silver-beaked, 271
Silver-throated, 284
Silvery, 284
Slaty, 275
Sooty Ant-, 270
Speckled, 284
Spotted, 287
Summer, 272
Swallow-, 276
Tawny-crested, 278
Turquoise, 285
Turquoise Dacnis-, 288
Vermilion, 274
White-banded, 274
White-capped, 268
White-lined, 277
White-rumped, 283
White-shouldered, 283
White-winged, 285
White-winged Shrike-, 271
Yellow-backed, 286
Yellow-bellied, 287
Yellow-crested, 277
Yellow-green Bush-, 279
Yellow-rumped, 270
Yellow-scarfed, 276
Yellow-throated, 276
Yellow-throated Bush-, 279
Yellow-whiskered, 279
Tangara argyrofenges, 287
arthus, 282
callophrys, 281
cayana, 283
chilensis, 281
chrysotis, 282
cyanicollis, 284
cyanocephala, 286
cyanoptera, 287
cyanotis, 287
cyanoventris, 281
desmaresti, 281
fastuosa, 281
florida, 282
guttata, 284
gyrola, 285
heinei, 285
icterocephala, 284
inornata, 287
johannae, 281
labradorides, 285
larvata, 284
lavinia, 285
mexicana, 285
nigrocincta, 284
nigroviridis, 285
palmeri, 280
parzudakii, 282
peruviana, 283
preciosa, 283
punctata, 287
ruficervix, 284
rufigenis, 282
rufigula, 285
schrankii, 282
seledon, 281
varia, 287
vassorii, 283
velia, 281
viridicollis, 284
vitriolina, 282
xanthocephala, 284
xanthogastra, 287
Taoniscus nanus, 8
Tapaculo, Andean, 177
Ash-colored, 176
Brasilia, 177
Brown-rumped, 177
Chucao, 175
Large-footed, 176
Mouse-colored, 177
Ocellated, 175
Ochre-flanked, 176
Pale-throated, 176
Rufous-vented, 176
Rusty-belted, 175
Unicolored, 176
White-breasted, 177
White-browed, 177
White-throated, 175
Tapera naevia, 55
Taphrospilus hypostictus, 70
Taraba major, 147
Teal, Blue-winged, 26
Cinnamon, 26
Puna, 25
Ringed, 26
Silver, 25
Speckled, 25
Teledromas fuscus, 175
Teleonema filicauda, 189
Tephrolesbia griseiventris, 83
Terenotriccus erythrurus, 232
Terenura callinota, 170
humeralis, 170
maculata, 171
sharpei, 170
spodioptila, 170
Tern, Gull-billed, 28
Large-billed, 28
Snowy-crowned, 28
Yellow-billed, 28
Tersina viridis, 276
Thalurania furcata, 71
glaucopis, 71
watertonii, 71
Thamnistes anabatinus, 151
Thamnomanes ardesiacus, 152
caesius, 152
occidentalis, 152
plumbeus, 152
saturninus, 152
schistogynus, 152
Thamnophilus aethiops, 149
amazonicus, 150
aroyae, 151
caerulescens, 150
cryptoleucus, 149
doliatus, 149
insignis, 150
multistriatus, 149
murinus, 151
nigriceps, 149
nigrocinereus, 149
palliatus, 149
punctatus, 150
ruficapillus, 148
schistaceus, 150
torquatus, 151
unicolor, 150
Thaumastura cora, 77
Theristicus caudatus, 13
Thick-knee, Double-striped, 4
Peruvian, 4
Thinocorus orbignyianus, 8
rumicivorus, 8
Thistletail, Black-throated, 124
Eye-ringed, 124
Mouse-colored, 124
Ochre-browed, 124
Puna, 125
White-chinned, 124
Thlypopsis fulviceps, 280
inornata, 280
ornata, 280
pectoralis, 280
ruficeps, 280
sordida, 280
Thornbill, Black-backed, 91
Blue-mantled, 89
Bronze-tailed, 89
Olivaceous, 89

Purple-backed, 90
Rainbow-bearded, 90
Rufous-capped, 89
Thornbird, Chestnut-backed, 133
Freckle-breasted, 133
Greater, 133
Little, 134
Plain, 134
Red-eyed, 134
Rufous-fronted, 134
Streak-fronted, 134
Yellow-eyed, 133
Thorntail, Black-bellied, 77
Green, 77
Wire-crested, 77
Thraupis bonariensis, 273
cyanocephala, 273
cyanoptera, 272
episcopus, 272
ornata. 273
palmarum, 272
sayaca, 272
Threnetes leucurus, 68
niger, 68
ruckeri, 68
Thripadectes flammulatus, 132
holostictus, 133
ignobilis, 133
melanorhynchus, 133
scrutator, 132
virgaticeps, 132
Thripophaga berlepschi, 139
cherriei, 139
fusciceps, 139
macroura, 139
Thrush, Austral, 235
Bare-eyed, 236
Black-billed, 235
Black-capped Mocking-, 239
Black-hooded, 236
Chestnut-bellied, 235
Chiguanco, 234
Clay-colored, 235
Cocoa, 237
Creamy-bellied, 235
Glossy-black, 234
Gray-cheeked, 238
Great, 234
Lawrence's, 236
Maranon, 237
Orange-billed Nightingale-, 238
Pale-breasted, 235
Pale-eyed, 237
Pale-vented, 236
Plumbeous-backed, 235
Rufous-bellied, 234
Slaty, 236
Slaty-backed Nightingale-, 238
Spotted Nightingale-, 238
Swainson's, 238
Unicolored, 236
White-necked, 236
Yellow-legged, 237
Thryothorus coraya, 241
euophrys, 241
fasciatoventris, 242
genibarbis, 241
griseus, 242
guarayanus, 242
leucopogon, 242
leucotis, 241
longirostris, 242
maculipectus, 242
nicefori, 241
nigricapillus, 242
rufalbus, 241
rutilus, 242
spadix, 242
superciliaris, 241
thoracicus, 242
Tiaris bicolor, 313
fuliginosa, 313
olivacea, 313
Tigrisoma fasciatum, 11
lineatum, 11
mexicanum, 11
Tijuca atra, 179
Tinamotis ingoufi, 5
pentlandii, 5
Tinamou, Andean, 7
Barred, 6
Bartlett's, 6
Black, 5
Brazilian, 6
Brown, 7
Brushland, 7
Chilean, 7
Choco, 6
Cinereous, 7
Curve-billed, 7
Dwarf, 8
Elegant Crested-, 5
Gray, 5
Gray-legged, 6
Great, 4
Highland, 5
Hooded, 5
Kalinowski's, 7
Little, 7
Ornate, 7
Pale-browed, 6
Patagonian, 5
Puna, 5
Quebracho Crested-, 5
Red-legged, 6
Red-winged, 5
Rusty, 6
Slaty-breasted, 6
Small-billed, 7
Solitary, 5
Taczanowski's, 7
Tataupa, 7
Tawny-breasted, 5
Tepui, 6
Undulated, 6
Variegated, 6
White-throated, 5
Yellow-legged, 6
Tinamus guttatus, 5
major, 4
osgoodi, 5
solitarius, 5
tao, 5
Tit-Spinetail, Andean, 125
Araucaria, 125
Brown-capped, 125
Plain-mantled, 125
Rusty-crowned, 125
Streaked, 125
Striolated, 125
Tawny, 125
Tufted, 125
White-browed, 125
Tityra cayana, 181
inquisitor, 181
semifasciata, 181
Tityra, Black-crowned, 181
Black-tailed, 181
Masked, 181
Todirostrum calopterum, 226
capitale, 232
chrysocrotaphum, 232
cinereum, 232
fumifrons, 226
latirostre, 232
maculatum, 232
nigriceps, 226
plumbeiceps, 226
poliocephalum, 226
russatum, 226
sylvia, 225
Tody-Flycatcher, see Flycatcher
Tody-Tyrant, see Tyrant
Tolmomyias assimilis, 213
flaviventris, 213
poliocephalus, 213
sulphurescens, 213
Topaz, Crimson, 70
Fiery, 70
Topaza pella, 70

Topaza
pyra, 70
Toucan,
Black-billed Mountain-, 107
Black-mandibled, 106
Channel-billed, 106
Chestnut-mandibled, 106
Choco, 106
Citron-throated, 106
Gray-breasted Mountain-, 107
Hooded Mountain-, 107
Keel-billed, 106
Plate-billed Mountain-, 107
Red-billed, 106
Red-breasted, 107
Toco, 106
Yellow-ridged, 106
Toucanet, Blue-banded, 107
Chestnut-tipped, 108
Crimson-rumped, 107
Emerald, 108
Golden-collared, 108
Groove-billed, 108
Guianan, 108
Saffron, 108
Spot-billed, 108
Tawny-tufted, 108
Yellow-browed, 108
Yellow-eared, 108
Touit batavica, 53
dilectissima, 52
huetii, 53
melanonota, 53
purpurata, 52
stictoptera, 52
surda, 53
Trainbearer, Black-tailed, 88
Green-tailed, 88
Treehunter, Black-billed, 133
Buff-throated, 132
Flammulated, 132
Pale-browed, 132
Sharp-billed, 140
Streak-capped, 132
Striped, 133
Uniform, 133
Treerunner, Fulvous-dotted, 139
Pearled, 139
White-throated, 140
Trichopicus cactorum, 115
Trichothraupis melanopus, 275
Triclaria malachitacea, 52
Tringa flavipes, 16
melanoleuca, 16
solitaria, 20
Troglodytes aedon, 243
rufulus, 244
solstitialis, 244
Trogon collaris, 94
comptus, 94
curucui, 95
massena, 94
melanurus, 94
personatus, 94
rufus, 95
surrucura, 95
violaceus, 95
viridis, 95
Trogon, Black-tailed, 94
Black-throated, 95
Blue-crowned, 95
Blue-tailed, 94
Collared, 94
Masked, 94
Slaty-tailed, 94
Surucua, 95
Violaceous, 95
White-tailed, 95
Troupial, 259
Trumpeter, Dark-winged, 4
Gray-winged, 4
Pale-winged, 4
Tryngites subruficollis, 20
Tuftedcheek, Buffy, 137
Streaked, 137
Tumbezia salvini, 215
Turca, Moustached, 175
Turdus albicollis, 236
amaurochalinus, 235
chiguanco, 234
falcklandii, 235
fulviventris, 235
fumigatus, 237
fuscater, 234
grayi, 235
haplochrous, 236
ignobilis, 235
lawrencii, 236
leucomelas, 235
maranonicus, 237
nigriceps, 236
nudigenis, 236
obsoletus, 236
olivater, 236
reevei, 235
rufiventris, 234
serranus, 234
Tyranneutes stolzmanni, 193
virescens, 193
Tyranniscus bolivianus, 227
cinereicapillus, 227
cinereiceps, 222
gracilipes, 222
nigrocapillus, 222
uropygialis, 222
villissimus, 227
viridiflavus, 228
Tyrannopsis luteiventris, 199
sulphurea, 199
Tyrannulet, Ashy-headed, 222
Bananal, 219
Bay-ringed, 228
Black-capped, 222
Black-fronted, 216
Bolivian, 227
Buff-banded, 220
Chapman's, 225
Golden-faced, 228
Gray-and-white, 220
Gray-capped, 222
Greenish, 215
Mottle-cheeked, 216
Mouse-colored, 220
Olive-green, 216
Oustalet's, 231
Pale-tipped, 221
Paltry, 227
Plain, 220
Planalto, 223
Plumbeous-crowned, 222
Red-billed, 227
Reiser's, 215
River, 227
Rough-legged, 223
Rufous-browed, 216
Rufous-winged, 220
Sao Paulo, 231
Sclater's, 215
Serra do Mar, 216
Slender-billed, 221
Slender-footed, 222
Sooty, 219
Sooty-headed, 228
Southern Beardless, 223
Sulphur-bellied, 220
Tawny-rumped, 222
Torrent, 197
White-banded, 220
White-crested, 220
White-lored, 226
White-tailed, 220
White-throated, 217
Yellow, 223
Yellow-bellied, 232
Yellow-crowned, 223
Tyrannulus elatus, 223
Tyrannus albogularis, 199
dominicensis, 199
melancholicus, 199
niveigularis, 199
tyrannus, 199

Tyrant, Agile Tit-, 227
Amazonian, 209
Amazonian Black-, 209
Ash-breasted Tit-, 219
Black-billed Shrike-, 195
Black-chested, 231
Black-fronted Ground-, 196
Black-throated Tody-, 229
Blue-billed, 207
Blue-billed Black-, 207
Bronze-olive Pygmy-, 230
Brown-backed Chat-, 211
Brown-breasted Pygmy-, 230
Buff-breasted Tody-, 229
Buff-throated, Tody-, 229
Cattle, 196
Chocolate-vented, 195
Cinereous, 224
Cinnamon-bellied Ground-, 196
Cock-tailed, 209
Crested, 206
Crested Black-, 206
Crowned Chat-, 211
Dark-faced Ground-, 196
D'Orbigny's Chat-, 211
Double-banded Pygmy-, 225
Drab-breasted Pygmy-, 230
Drab Water-, 215
Eared Pygmy-, 227
Ecuadorian Bristle-, 221
Eye-ringed Tody-, 229
Flammulated Pygmy-, 230
Fork-tailed Pygmy-, 228
Golden-browed Chat-, 211
Gray-bellied Shrike-, 195
Great Shrike-, 195
Greater Wagtail-, 214
Hangnest Tody-, 230
Hazel-fronted Pygmy-, 230
Helmeted Pygmy-, 231
Hudson's, 209
Hudson's Black-, 209
Jelski's Bush-, 215
Kaempfer's Tody-, 224
Lesser Wagtail-, 214
Long-crested Pygmy-, 230
Long-tailed, 214
Little Ground-, 196
Many-colored Rush-, 231
Marble-faced Bristle-, 221
Masked Water-, 215
Ochre-naped Ground-, 195
Pale-eyed Pygmy-, 225
Patagonian, 217
Pearly-vented Tody-, 224
Pied-crested Tit-, 219
Pied Water-, 197
Piura Chat-, 212
Plain-capped Ground-, 196
Plumbeous, 207
Puna Ground-, 196
Red-rumped Bush-, 198
Riverside, 206
Rufous-bellied Bush-, 204
Rufous-breasted Chat-, 211
Rufous-crowned Tody-, 225
Rufous-headed Pygmy-, 230
Rufous-naped Ground-, 196
Rufous-sided Pygmy-, 221
Rufous-tailed, 206
Rufous-webbed, 198
Santa Marta Bush-, 204
Scale-crested Pygmy-, 225
Sharp-tailed, 228
Shear-tailed Gray-, 198
Short-tailed Field-, 197
Short-tailed Pygmy-, 232
Slaty-backed Chat-, 211
Smoky Bush-, 204
Snethlage's Tody-, 225
Southern Bristle-, 228
Spectacled., 214
Spectacled Bristle-, 221
Spot-billed Ground-, 196
Strange-tailed, 209
Streak-throated Bush-, 198
Streamer-tailed, 205
Stripe-necked Tody-, 229
Tawny-crowned Pygmy-, 228
Tufted Tit-, 219
Tumbes, 215
Variegated Bristle-, 221
Velvety, 206
Velvety Black-, 206
Venezuelan Bristle-, 221
White-browed Chat-, 211
White-browed Ground-, 196
White-eyed Tody-, 224
White-fronted Ground-, 195
White-headed Marsh-, 231
White-tailed Shrike-, 195
White-winged, 207
White-winged Black-, 207
Wing-barred Water-, 197
Yellow-bellied Bristle-, 221
Yellow-bellied Chat-, 211
Yellow-billed Tit-, 219
Yellow-browed, 210
Yungas Tody-, 224
Zimmer's Tody-, 224
Tyto alba, 56
Umbrellabird, Amazonian, 177
Long-wattled, 177
Upucerthia albigula, 126
andaecola, 126
certhioides, 126
dumetaria, 126
harterti, 126
jelskii, 126
ruficauda, 126
serrana, 126
validirostris, 126
Urochroa bougueri, 83
Uromyias agilis, 227
Uropelia campestris, 41
Uropsalis lyra, 59
segmentata, 59
Urosticte benjamini, 85
Urothraupis stolzmanni, 274

Vanellus chilensis, 16
resplendens, 17
Veery, 238
Velvetbreast, Mountain, 82
Veniliornis affinis, 115
callonotus, 116
cassini, 115
dignus, 115
frontalis, 115
fumigatus, 115
kirkii, 115
maculifrons, 116
nigriceps, 114
passerinus, 116
sanguineus, 116
spilogaster, 115
Vermivora chrysoptera, 262
peregrina, 262
Violet-ear, Brown, 83
Green, 83
Sparkling, 83
White-vented, 83
Vireo altiloquus, 248
flavifrons, 248
gilvus, 248
leucophrys, 248
olivaceus, 248
Vireo, Black-whiskered, 248
Brown-capped, 248
Red-eyed, 248
Yellow-throated, 248
Visorbearer, Hooded, 92
Hyancinth, 92
Volatinia jacarina, 312
Vultur gryphus, 28
Vulture, Black, 29
Greater Yellow-headed, 28

Vulture,
King, 28
Lesser Yellow-headed, 28
Turkey, 29

Warbler, Bay-breasted, 263
Black-and-white, 262
Blackburnian, 262
Black-crested, 266
Blackpoll, 262
Canada, 264
Cerulean, 262
Citrine, 266
Connecticut, 263
Flavescent, 266
Golden-bellied, 267
Golden-crowned, 267
Golden-winged, 262
Gray-and-gold, 266
Gray-headed, 267
Gray-throated, 267
Kentucky, 263
Mourning, 263
Pale-legged, 266
Prothonotary, 262
River, 267
Rufous-capped, 267
Russet-crowned, 265
Santa Marta, 266
Tennessee, 262
Three-banded, 267
Three-striped, 266
Two-banded, 266
White-bellied, 267
White-browed, 266
White-striped, 266
Yellow, 264
Warbling-Finch, see Finch
Waterthrush, Louisiana, 263
Northern, 263
Wetmorethraupis sterrhopteron, 270
Whitestart, Brown-capped, 265
Golden-fronted, 265
Saffron-breasted, 265
Slate-throated, 264
Spectacled, 265
White-faced, 265
White-fronted, 265
Yellow-crowned, 265
Yellow-faced, 265
Whitetip, 85
Wigeon, American, 23
Southern, 23
Willet, 14
Wilsonia canadensis, 264
Wiretail, Des Murs', 126
Woodcreeper, Bar-bellied, 122
Barred, 123
Black-banded, 120
Black-striped, 120
Buff-throated, 120
Chestnut-rumped, 120
Cinnamon-throated, 123
Concolor, 122
Dusky-billed, 120
Elegant, 120
Great Rufous, 122
Hoffmanns', 120
Lesser, 122
Lineated, 123
Long-billed, 119
Long-tailed, 123
Moustached, 119
Narrow-billed, 121
Ocellated, 120
Olivaceous, 124
Olive-backed, 121
Plain-brown, 123
Planalto, 120
Red-billed, 122
Ruddy, 123
Scaled, 122
Scimitar-billed, 122
Spix's, 121
Spot-crowned, 122
Spotted, 121
Spot-throated, 124
Straight-billed, 121
Streak-headed, 121
Striped, 121
Strong-billed, 119
Tyrannine, 123
Wedge-billed, 124
White-chinned, 123
White-throated, 119
Zimmer's, 121
Woodhaunter, Striped, 139
Woodnymph, Fork-tailed, 71
Long-tailed, 71
Violet-capped, 71
Woodpecker, Acorn, 113
Bar-bellied, 114
Black-bodied, 111
Black-cheeked, 114
Black-necked, 111
Blond-crested, 113
Blood-colored, 116
Checkered, 114
Chestnut, 112
Cinnamon, 112
Cream-backed, 110
Cream-colored, 112
Crimson-bellied, 110
Crimson-crested, 110
Crimson-mantled, 112
Dot-fronted, 115
Golden-breasted, 112
Golden-collared, 115
Golden-green, 113
Golden-naped, 114
Golden-olive, 113
Green-barred, 111
Guayaquil, 110
Helmeted, 111
Lineated, 110
Little, 116
Magellanic, 110
Pale-crested, 113
Powerful, 110
Red-crowned, 115
Red-necked, 110
Red-rumped, 115
Red-stained, 115
Ringed, 112
Robust, 110
Rufous-headed, 112
Scale-breasted, 113
Scarlet-backed, 116
Smoky-brown, 115
Spot-breasted, 114
Striped, 114
Waved, 113
White, 112
White-browed, 113
White-fronted, 115
White-spotted, 115
White-throated, 113
Yellow-eared, 116
Yellow-fronted, 114
Yellow-throated, 113
Yellow-tufted, 114
Yellow-vented, 115
Wood-Quail, see Quail
Woodstar, Amethyst, 79
Chilean, 79
Esmeraldas, 79
Gorgeted, 93
Little, 79
Purple-collared, 92
Purple-throated, 79
Rufous-shafted, 93
Short-tailed, 79
Slender-tailed, 93
White-bellied, 92
Wren, Apolinar's Marsh-, 243
Band-backed, 240
Bay, 242
Bicolored, 240
Black-bellied, 242

Buff-breasted, 241
Chestnut-breasted, 243
Coraya, 241
Fasciated, 240
Fawn-breasted, 242
Flutist, 244
Grass, 243
Gray, 242
Gray-breasted Wood-, 244
Gray-mantled, 243
House, 243
Long-billed, 242
Mountain, 244
Moustached, 241
Musician, 243
Niceforo's, 241
Nightingale, 244
Paramo, 243
Plain-tailed, 241
Rufous, 240
Rufous-and-white, 241
Rufous-breasted, 242
Sepia-brown, 241
Song, 243
Sooty-headed, 242
Spot-breasted, 242
Stripe-backed, 240
Stripe-throated, 242
Superciliated, 241
Tepui, 244
Thrush-like, 240
Tooth-billed, 243
White-breasted Wood-, 244
White-headed, 240
Wing-banded, 244
Wren-Spinetail, Bay-capped, 126

Xanthomyias reiseri, 215
sclateri, 215
virescens, 215
Xanthopsar flavus, 259
Xenerpestes minlosi, 136
singularis, 136
Xenodacnis parina, 254
Xenopipo atronitens, 187, 194
Xenops milleri, 140
minutus, 140
rutilans, 140
tenuirostris, 140
Xenops, Great, 139
Plain, 140
Rufous-tailed, 140
Sharp-billed, 140
Slender-billed, 140
Streaked, 140
Xenopsaris albinucha, 185
Xenopsaris, White-naped, 185
Xenornis setifrons, 151
Xenospingus concolor, 301
Xiphocolaptes albicollis, 119
falcirostris, 119
major, 122
promeropirhynchus, 119
Xipholena atropurpurea, 180
lamellipennis, 180
punicea, 180
Xiphorhynchus elegans, 120
erythropgius, 121
eytoni, 120
guttatus, 120
lachrymosus, 120
necopinus, 121
obsoletus, 121
ocellatus, 120
pardalotus, 120
picus, 121
spixii, 121
triangularis, 121
Xolmis cinerea, 198
coronata, 198
dominicana, 198
irupero, 199
murina, 198
rubetra, 198
rufipennis, 198
velata, 198

Yellow-Finch, see Finch
Yellowlegs, Greater, 16
Lesser, 16
Yellowthroat, Masked, 264
Olive-crowned, 264
Yetapa risora, 209

Zaratornis stresemanni, 180
Zarhynchus wagleri, 255
Zebrilus undulatus, 14
Zenaida asiatica, 40
auriculata, 40
Zonibyx modestus, 17
Zonotrichia capensis, 302